EUROPE (IN THEORY)

Roberto M. Dainotto

EUROPE (IN THEORY)

DUKE UNIVERSITY PRESS

DURHAM AND LONDON

2007

© 2007 Duke University Press

All rights reserved

Printed in the United States of America

on acid-free paper ∞

Designed by C. H. Westmoreland

Typeset in Minion with Univers display

by Keystone Typesetting, Inc.

Library of Congress Cataloging-in-

Publication Data appear on the last

printed page of this book.

There is a damaging and self-defeating assumption

that theory is necessarily the elite language of the socially

and culturally privileged. It is said that the place of the

academic critic is inevitably within the Eurocentric archives

of an imperialist or neo-colonial West.

—HOMI K. BHABHA, *The Location of Culture*

Contents

Acknowledgments

I want to thank for their suggestions, time, and support all the people who have heard, read, and commented on parts of this book: Albert Ascoli, David Bell, Joe Buttigieg, miriam cooke, Sergio Ferrarese, Roberto Ferrera, Mia Fuller, Edna Goldstaub, Margaret Greer, Michele Longino, Walter Mignolo, Marc Schachter, Helen Solterer, Barbara Spackman, Philip Stewart, Carlotta Surini, Eric Zakim, and Robert Zimmerman. Also invaluable has been the help offered by the Ethical Cosmopolitanism group and the Franklin Humanities Seminar at Duke University; by the Program in Comparative Literature at Notre Dame; by the Khan Institute Colloquium at Smith College; by the Mediterranean Studies groups of both Duke and New York University; and by European studies and the Italian studies program at the University of North Carolina at Chapel Hill. I am very grateful to the editors of Duke University Press for their precious help and suggestions. A final thank-you goes to the National Endowment for the Humanities, which sponsored my research for this book in the summer of 2003.

Some material has already appeared, in a different form, in the journals *Nepantla: Views from South*; *Nineteenth-Century Contexts*; and *European History Quarterly*. One final note regards translations: with the exception of English translations consulted and referenced in the works cited, all other translations are mine.

Introduction

A PIGS EYE VIEW OF EUROPE

You know, Europe is a hell of a long way from here.
—JOSÉ SARAMAGO, *The Stone Raft*

And from now on, who knows who "I" really is!
—GESUALDO BUFALINO, *L'uomo invaso*

I had been suspecting it for a while. But it was on the morning of March 26, 1995, that seemingly overwhelming evidence almost convinced me the metamorphosis was on its way: I, Roberto M. Dainotto, no longer was an Italian; slowly but surely, I was becoming European!

Hints of an imminent transformation had been around for a while: with the Treaty of Rome of 1957, as its preamble stated, Italians had "determined to lay the foundations of an ever closer union among the peoples of Europe"; and in 1992, the Maastricht Treaty, according to article A, had pushed us toward "an ever closer union among the peoples of Europe." Neither Rome nor Maastricht, however, could possibly compare with the news of March 26. On that day, the European Union (EU) had taken, or so I believed then, the most decisive step ever toward the final accomplishment of my personal fate—my ultimate transubstantiation into "the people of Europe": "Bonn, March 26—In a move that showed the limits as much as the extent of their common purpose, 7 of the 15 European Union members formally dismantled border controls between their countries today—meaning that travelers will be able to journey between them without passports . . . Italy . . . [has] also signed the convention setting up the passport-free zone" (Cowell A6).

If "feeling European" was really a matter of "travel[ling] constantly across [Europe] on cheap interrail tickets" (Byatt 50), it meant that only then could I, *finally*, feel part of the imagined community of other faraway creatures holding, like me, a European passport. I say "finally" because the citizens of France, Germany, Belgium, Luxembourg, and the Netherlands had already been circulating freely across their borders since 1985, when the Schengen treaty was signed. In fact, even some non-EU members—Norway and Iceland—were let into the passport-free zone, which looked rather like a Nordic alliance. The Italians, on this side of the Alps—which no lesser spirit than Johann Wolfgang von Goethe justly called "the dividing line between north and south" (31)—had not been invited to join at that time.

The anxiety we felt at that initial exclusion is hard to describe. As Giuseppe Turani used to write on the pages of the daily *La Repubblica*, we badly wanted "to become like all others . . . to become a European country, not so Mediterranean, not so pizza-and-mandolin, not so defective" (36). And how could we possibly overcome our parochial—let alone "defective"—identities if we were denied the "promised disappearance of physical borders" that alone granted "an enhanced meaning of Europe" as a cultural identity (Bamyeh 35)?

So, when in 1995 Italy—along with the other southern countries of Portugal, Greece, and Spain—finally made it to the borderless Europe, signs of elation were palpable: "Champagne was on offer at Milan and Rome airports to mark the country's full membership of Schengen," the *Economist* reported ("Europe: Those Fuzzy Frontiers"). The euphoria, however, did not last long. European clerks in Brussels soon started referring to the Giovanninos-come-lately with an unflattering acronym: Portugal, Italy, Greece, and Spain—the PIGS, no less, as Lindsay Waters reported. We *could* cross borders now; but "a southern accent . . . does not help who carries it around" (De Luca 22). The usual, unmistakable glimmer of suspicion still met us in the eyes of our northern cousins, hardly waiting for us with open arms on the other side of the border. In fact, land borders, after a brief token opening of a few days, were soon shut closed again on our face. We were Europeans—only in theory, though!

No matter how hard we Italians had managed "all the way to erase our identity" (Goffredo 58); no matter how we tried to forget the pizza and mandolin; no matter how much we worked to "northernize our habits and customs" (Cassano, *Modernizzare* 123); no matter all the sacrificing of piece after piece of the welfare state and the relentless privatization of all for the sake of "modernizing" and "Europeanizing" (Morlino 237)— we were no longer Italians, but we were not Europeans either. The international press did not take long to register the fact that despite the opening of borders, Italy, along with the other PIGS, remained nothing more than a southern country in the eyes of Europe. It was, so to speak, different:

> Northerners have tended to stress differences between the political cultures of cold and warmer climes. Up north, the primmer attitudes of Protestantism, stricter laws against influence-peddling, older and stronger individual rights before the state, judges less in hock to the executive, and a more independent press were all thought to have ensured higher standards of public and political conduct. In the south, where democracy was generally a more fragile plant, family and clan loyalties held more sway than any sense of obligation to the state. ("Is Europe Corrupt?" 49)

Articles such as this (written, incidentally, on the occasion of the scandals of party finance corruption not in the south but in Germany and France) were reminders of how the old theses of Edward Banfield's southern backwardness and amoral familism—of ones older, in fact, going back to Montesquieu's climatology—had trickled down and cemented into commonplaces of both popular and political imaginations. Newspapers' titles kept beating the same news from Europe: "Northerners Sniff at 'Club Med'" (Kamm); "Sober North Vies with Siesta South" (Boyes); or, more ominously, "Europe's Southern Shadow." In the meantime, Brussels' parliamentarians still talked of a "two-speed Europe"; the Franco-German axis still saw a "southern problem," a pathological "Mediterranean syndrome" threatening to infect the whole of Europe (see Borzel 141); and the indefatigable Turani kept reminding us that even in the Europe of open borders, and despite all talks of common identity, Italy remained "some kind of Disney nation . . . a Latin American country from the old times . . . transplanted in the heart of wise, austere and virtuous Europe" (Turani 32). The hopes of 1995, in short, were soon to turn into indignation: to hell with virtuous Europe!

Ressentiment, admittedly, is not a very noble human instinct—nor is it conducive to serene scholarly research. In order to write this book on Europe from the notoriously vindictive perspective of the clan of PIGS, I have tried, then, to ennoble that most bathetic of emotions with the philosophical mantle of Nietzschean genealogy. (It was Nietzsche, after all, who presaged the age of the Euro: "Only money can force Europe to unite" [qtd. in Iiritano 32].) Could a genealogy of the concept of Europe help me explain the peculiar place of the south in that very concept? Where did the idea of the south as PIGS of Europe come from? Did

Montesquieu's climatology survive even the advent of air-conditioning? How could the south, at the same time, be Europe and non-Europe?

What follows is therefore an attempt to single out, in eighteenth- and nineteenth-century theorizations of Europe, the surfacing of structures and paradigms that have since informed ideas of the continent and of its cultural identity. On the one hand, what I am to propose is a genealogy of Eurocentrism—the emergence of modern theories of Europe that assume one can explain Europe "without making recourse to anything outside of Europe" (Dussel, "*Europe*" 469–70). On the other, I want to argue that those modern theories cannot be explained according to the usual paradigm of European identity-formation, that "the concept of Europe must have first been formed as an antithesis to that which is not Europe: . . . the first opposition between Europe and something that is not Europe . . . is . . . Asia" (Chabod 23). It would be against the logic of Eurocentrism, in fact, to form a sense of European identity by making recourse to Asia or anything outside of Europe. As I will imply in the next few chapters, Eurocentrism properly begins when a modern theory of identity—identity as dialectics of the same—takes its first tentative shape in the pages of Montesquieu, and from the latter finds its final systematization in Hegel's understanding of Europe as the "end of history." A modern European identity, in other words, begins when the non-Europe is internalized—when the south, indeed, becomes the sufficient and indispensable *internal* Other: Europe, but also the negative part of it.

Indebted to the subaltern historiography of Ranajit Guha, Homi Bhabha, and Dipesh Chakrabarty, as well as to the subaltern epistemology of Enrique Dussel and Walter Mignolo, *Europe (in Theory)* questions Eurocentrism not from the outside but from the marginal inside of Europe itself. One objective is to trouble the tranquil waters of European studies, often driven—either by spontaneous enthusiasms or by EU grants and sponsorships—to advertise a lofty Europe of "inventiveness and creativity, democracy, liberty, critical sense and tolerance, and respect of other cultures" (Kapuscinski 64). Another objective is to state the facts of the dialectical nature of Eurocentrism: the way in which "the parochiality of its universalism" ends up "reducing, rather than expanding, the possibility of . . . inclusiveness, of genuinely cosmopolitan or internationalist perspective, of intellectual curiosity" (Said, *Humanism* 53). Eurocentrism, in short, is one category through which I am trying to explain the dialectical inclusion and exclusion of the south—its historical necessity for the formation of a parochial universalism and its liminality in any modern theory of European identity.

This is as far, however, as the concept of Eurocentrism—or, for that matter, the paradigms of subaltern studies—can carry *Europe (in Theory)*. The homogenizing assumptions of the term, in fact, run the perpetual risk of obliterating the interior borders and fractures of European hegemony; they hide from view Europe's own subaltern areas—the south—of knowledge production. Along with the "damaging assumption" that theory is limited to some "Eurocentric archive" (H. K. Bhabha 19)—an assumption that still dominates what is being called European studies—there is a similarly damaging assumption that the archive of European theory is located somewhere between Franco-Scottish Enlightenment and Anglo-German Romantic nationalism. It is not enough to say, en passant, that even Europe had and has its margins. In subaltern historiography's usual reliance on what is assumed to be European theory—Said's French and British archives for the definition of Orientalism; Marx and Heidegger in Chakrabarty's denunciation of the "artifice of history"—the blatantly Eurocentric gesture marginalizing what Franco Cassano has called "southern thinking" (*Pensiero*) is mirrored perhaps too closely. Was there no other Orientalism than that of Silvestre de Sacy and William Jones? No philosophy of history but Hegel's?

Coeval with the emergence of a theory of Europe as a self-sufficient system, there was, on the contrary, the development of other theories that, from the margins of the so-called southern question, were trying to imagine a different Europe. It is the task of *Europe (in Theory)* to bear witness to the mere fact of the historical existence of such theories, whose traces seem otherwise to have been lost both to European and subaltern studies. After an outline of ancient theories of Europe in chapter 1—from Aristotle's classical antithesis of European freedom and Asiatic despotism to the so-called crisis of classical thought in the seventeenth century (Hazard, *European Mind*)—my story begins, in chapter 2, with Montesquieu's rhetorical *inventio* of Europe's north-south divide. Montesquieu, I maintain, inaugurates the Eurocentric archive understood as a theory of Europe in which a supposedly ancient understanding of European identity—"The nations . . . in Europe, are . . . comparatively free," while those "in Asia . . . [are] ruled and enslaved" (Aristotle 7.7)—is reoriented to find the figure of antithesis no longer in external Asia, but in an internal south "moved away from morality itself" (Montesquieu, *Oeuvres* 2.477).

After this exploration of the Eurocentric archive opened by Montesquieu, and after discussing the identification of Europe with a seventeenth-century so-called Republic of Letters, chapter 3 looks then at the work of the Spanish Jesuit Juan Andrés, the first noncanonical figure that this book tries to reevaluate. Expelled from Spain in 1779, Andrés moved to Parma, Italy, and published a seven-volume history of nothing less than the literatures of the whole world. A first attempt at what would be called comparative literature, Andrés's work challenged the dominant thesis of a French origin of modern literature and proposed what is known today as the Arabist theory. If Montesquieu had claimed that as colonies of the Oriental world of Islam, the civilizations of Spain and Italy did not constitute an integral part of Europe but were its negative south, Andrés was then ready to declare Al-Andalus and Sicily as the very origin of Europe's modernity—and such origin of Europe, interestingly enough, was to be located in the Orient.

I return to hegemonic theories in chapter 4, devoted to the apparent paradox of nationalism as the distinguishing feature of European identity. Madame de Staël, differentiating between "two very distinct literatures: the one that comes from the south, and the one which descends from the north" (*Littérature* 203), laid the basis for later theories of southern backwardness and defective nationalism. Such a dialectics of north and south, which Staël had borrowed from Montesquieu, reappears by the end of the chapter in Hegel's idea of Europe as the "synthesis of Universal History," and in his full-fledged theory of dialectical identity. Chapter 5 then concludes the book by giving space to another southern answer to the Europe of Montesquieu, Hegel, and the newly formed nation-states. Michele Amari, an Italian Orientalist of the 1840s, represents a peculiar case of southern Orientalism. Not only does he attempt a reevaluation of the south as the cradle of an "original social democracy" (Amari *Storia* 1.171) brought into Europe by Islam; moreover, he strives for a plurilingual, pluriconfessional, and pluriethnic Europe—Caucasian, Jewish, and Islamic at the same time—that may still be worthy of some consideration as an antidote to any clash of civilizations. Far from being any antithesis to the Orient, Amari claims, Europe's history and civilization find their roots in the East.

The contamination of what would otherwise remain a pantheon of European classics—Montesquieu, Voltaire, Staël, Hegel—with the peripheral figures of Andrés and Amari intends to introduce an element of historical contestation to that idea of modern Europe taking shape between the eighteenth and the nineteenth centuries. What was at stake in such controversies was not only the question of borders and identity—who was European and who was not (or who was European in theory only). The core of the quarrel was who, and from which geopolitical position, was entitled to define those borders and identities. In other words, who had the right to produce knowledge and theory of and for Europe?

In outlining my story, I have thus been reading some historical attempts to theorize Europe, both from the center and from the southern margin—other margins could be thought, such as the Balkans (Todorova), Eastern Europe (Wolff), or the extreme North (Davidson)—not so much for their scientific as for their *rhetorical* contribution to the discourse of Europe. Their historical importance lies for me not in their ability to represent adequately any European reality—the European genius, after all, may consist exactly in this refusal to see reality (says María Zambrano)—but in shaping it. Theories of Europe, in other words, have perhaps *described* little, but have *prepared* lots of the commonplaces—correct or false arguments that equally "seem to be true since all, as it were, acknowledge them as such" (Aristotle 2.21.11)—that still shape what we think, say, legislate, and, in the end, make, of Europe. The idea of the defective Europeanness of the south that has shaped the policies of the two-tier Europe; the belief in the centrality of a European culture guiding the work of the European Task Force on Culture; the mission of Europe's human rights and civilizing role that has led the Italian premier Silvio Berlusconi to declare "the superiority of our civilization" and his involvement in the war in Iraq against "the heritage of Islamic culture" (Commission on Human Rights 13); the idea that "France and Germany, above all others [are central] . . . to Europe's future" (Charlemagne 13); Pope Ratzinger's claim of Turkey's "extraneity" to Europe, along with Pierre Manent's editorial in *Le Figaro* recommending the expulsion of all Muslims from Europe's "Christian soil" (Introvigne 25)—words, feelings, and actions of today's politics and journalism still rely, consciously or not, on the conceptual and verbal forms, on the thesaurus of images, on the rhetoric of figures that have historically defined Europe in theory.

Europe, to rephrase the same concept in the words of the anthropologist Eric Wolf, is not only "the reality of the natural world [geography] and its human transformations by techniques [science and economy] and organization [politics]" but also "the reality of schemata of organized knowledge and symbolic operations learned and communicated among human beings" (xiv). The legal scholar Miriam Aziz has also hinted at the relevance of the symbolic when, in discussing contemporary European law, has shown how legislative activity is determined not only by present interests (national or otherwise) but also, and conspicuously, by the legislators' historical memory of "visions and versions of Europe" that have been theorized across the centuries (1–22). The way in which Europe has been theorized and imagined, in other words, still determines the praxis of legislative and political activity. Instead of *visions*, I have used here and there the term *rhetorical unconscious*: it hints at the way in which contemporary discussions—on Europe's Christianity, on the "clash" of East and West, or the fracture of north and south— are still informed by old commonplaces, expectations of what we take Europe to mean. To take my words from Peter Carravetta: "It will be interesting, and highly problematic, to see how some interpretations [and theories of Europe], that at some moments in history were considered factual truths, keep influencing [even when they are discredited as factual truths] both the rhetoric and the action of different peoples in different epochs," including the present one (25).

Europe (in Theory) therefore implies the idea that social realities and institutions—say, Europe with its undergoing unification—are not the mere by-product of journalism and policy papers, which in turn would create social consciousness or consensus around some ideas and thus determine practical decisions. Social consciousness about what Europe is, and a consensus around its meaning, are, rather, at least in good part, the product of what I have called a rhetorical unconscious. It is what has been said and written for around three centuries about and around Europe that *still* determines what we think and do about it; what our dailies report; and what our policy makers decide.

The sociological literature about Europe seems in fact to confirm my hypothesis, while failing to draw its immediate consequences. In recent statistical studies of popular support for European integration (Lindberg and Scheingold; Ammendola and Isernia) we find a differentiation between "specific support" (a utilitaristic rationale of benefits and costs) and "affective support" (a prelogical desire to be part of Europe). What we learn is that even in the absence of real economic or political advantages, and sometimes despite economic sacrifices paid to the fiscal policies of Maastricht, "a substantially affective support" for integration has remained strong in many countries since the 1950s (Ammendola and Isernia 140). What eludes the logic of statistics, however, is exactly the nature—and logic!—of that affective support. It is the task of what Edward Said has called "humanism as democratic criticism," therefore, to go beyond the limit of statistics and start investigating not only the attachment of historical societies to "words [such as Europe] as bearers of reality" but also to make such words "disclose what may be hidden or incomplete or masked or distorted. . . . In this view of language, then, words are not passive markers or signifiers standing in unassumingly for a higher reality; they are, instead, an integral formative part of that reality" (*Humanism* 58).

The problem, in this context, is no longer whether the humanities with their tools—rhetoric, philology, historicism—will be adequate or relevant to the technologized, quantified, and statistic-oriented sciences, but whether the latter are still capable of responding to the humanities (in the way in which Aristotle's *Politics* and *Logics* were responding to the *Topica*; and the way in which Plato's *Republic* anxiously had to respond to the arts).

Rhetoric, philology, and historicism provide the critical theory guiding this book. They restitute Europe to the history of its construction (which is not a Montesquieu-like history of progress, nor a chronology of progressive realizations of ideas). They make today's Europe less of a given, less of a "real" that can only be managed by economics, politics, and its pundits, and more of a historical accident still open to the possibility of change and to what used to be called praxis. In this practical sense, this is a book about Europe (in theory).

But theory, as Homi Bhabha warns us in the epigraph to this book, is located "inevitably within the Eurocentric archives" (19). In order to become praxis, a history of theories of Europe needs to start questioning the very presuppositions of those theories—the ways in which theory itself is enmeshed in the construction of a Eurocentric universe. In "Eurocentrism and Its Avatars," Immanuel Wallerstein argues that "science emerged in response to European problems at a point in history when Europe dominated the whole world-system," and that it is therefore "virtually inevitable that its choice of subject matter, its theorizing, its methodology, and its epistemology all reflected the constraints of the crucible within which it was born" (93–94). What both Bhabha and Wallerstein suggest is that "Eurocentrism is not a matter of attitudes in the sense of values and prejudices, but rather . . . a matter of science, and scholarship, and informed and expert opinion" (Blaut 9); Eurocentrism, in other words, is embedded in the same theories that, between the eighteenth and the nineteenth centuries, have shaped, and continue to shape, our own teaching and academic curricula. As Eric Wolf has suggested, Eurocentrism is inseparable from either pedagogy or disciplinary formations: it is what "we have been taught" (5), if not explicitly, through what and how we study.

In this book, Bhabha's epigraph therefore stands to signify that theorizations of Europe have coincided with, or at least have not been extraneous from, theorizations of, well, theories of the various disciplines of knowledge. Montesquieu's intention to theorize a modern Europe, for instance, ends up theorizing modern historiography. Juan Andrés theorizes comparative literature and literary historiography in order to re-theorize Europe after Montesquieu. The Romantics' theories of the nation as a model of bureaucratic and state organization superior to, and more modern than, all other kinds of state organization run parallel to their theorizations of a Europe of nations. Finally, Michele Amari felt the need to theorize both Orientalism and national history (*storia patria*) anew in order to theorize a different Europe of nations founded not on the myth of the French Revolution but on that of Muslim Sicily. *Europe (in Theory)*, in sum, looks at some of the ways in which theorizations of Europe have produced Bhabha's Eurocentric archive. Needless to say, this Eurocentric archive is European in theory only: it is to my reader to imagine the various ways in which such an archive has extended, like Tocqueville's "gradual and continuous progress of the European race," to the entire West with "the solemnity of a providential event" (*Democracy* 398).

1 The Discovery of Europe

> From a work of criticism, we expect today concrete results, or, at least, demonstrable theses and viable hypotheses. Yet when the word appears in the dictionary of European philosophy, "criticism" means rather an investigation concerning the limits of knowledge— concerning that which, precisely, is not possible to hypothesize or maintain.—GIORGIO AGAMBEN, *Stanze*

In his relentless (and relentlessly cited) *Clash of Civilizations*, the very man Henry Kissinger once commended as "one of the West's most eminent political scientists" (qtd. in J. Bhabha 597n17) confidently argued that "Europe ends where Western Christianity ends and Islam and Orthodoxy begin" (Huntington 158). For us in the humanities—still afflicted perhaps by some "realism of uncertainty" (Newman)—the absolute *certainty* with which Huntington could draw such a neat map of Europe was, to say the least, enviable. Putting an end to the hairsplitting sophistries of Brussels bureaucrats and academic theorists who kept chewing over the "old problems of boundaries" (Slack and Innes 3) and "what is meant by the term 'Europe'" (Brugmans 11), Huntington almost gave us the specific coordinates to trace the boundaries of Christian and Western Europe: it was as if Santiago de Campostela in the northwest and the Virgin Mary's House of Ephesus in the southeast could provide a definite and unquestionable geographical body to Europe.[1]

Such a clerical map was at once the confirmation of Martin Lewis and Kären Wigen's notion that continents were but cultural constructs and the outdoing of "metageography" itself. Is not a continent, the skeptical metageographers would have asked, "one of the main continuous bodies of land on the earth's surface" (the definition, after all, is as authoritative as the *Oxford English Dictionary*)? But, if so, rather than a continent,

Europe would only be "a small heading of the Asiatic continent, . . . a western appendix of Asia" (Valéry 24 and 38; see also Rougemont 33; and Derrida, *Other Heading* 11–17). It looks as if the term *continent*, as applied to Europe despite the land continuum of Eurasia, embodies only some European fantasies, and no more: the fantasy of a Europe that *wants* to imagine itself different, that wants to separate itself from Asia; the fantasy, moreover, of a Europe that *wants* to think itself as a geographical, natural, and factual unity. But then again, where does Europe end? On the Adriatic? In Yugoslavia? Turkey? Or perhaps even Russia? One can see why Lewis and Wigen, writing only one year before the *Clash*, thought that "there are many reasons to believe that the . . . continental scheme . . . obscures more than it reveals" (2–3). But where Lewis and Wigen saw difficulties, Huntington only saw the certainties of (political) science.[2] Ipse dixit! Centuries of beating about the bush of Europe and its borders had been ended with the straightforward ways that have always marked the "practical science" of the "Geheimrat" (Hardt and Negri 33–34)—what Immanuel Kant called the "political moralist, i.e., one who forges a morality . . . to influence the current ruling power . . . even at the expense of the people, and, where possible, of the entire world" ("*Perpetual Peace*" 128–29). Too bad that such practical science did not believe its business to be overly concerned with the limits of that morality. Too bad it had to do away with all complexities of a definition of Europe. Too bad it aimed instead at producing readily usable, if fundamentalist, civilizational hypotheses that the current power could immediately translate into "momentary commands" (Kant, "*Perpetual Peace*" 129).

What does the fortune of the clash theory tell us about cultural production today? If what we expect of theory is a set of readily usable hypotheses that can be promptly translated into political action, Huntington's book has proven a sign of the times: "We have become all too practical. Fear of the impotence of theory supplies a pretext for bowing to the almighty production process" (Adorno 44). Between one cavalier theory of Europe and another of the West, the *Clash* has crowned an age in which all that has been asked from an increasingly scientific, practical, and Sokalized academia was not criticism and complications, but usable theses by the pound.[3] The humanities have quickly succumbed; criticism—"questioning, upsetting and reformulating so much of what is presented to us as commodified, packaged" (Said, *Humanism* 28)—

disbanded as an unnecessary complication, while the practical sciences have become hegemonic in all cultural discussions.

In all fairness (and to avoid some unnecessary clash of the disciplines here), quite a good number of social scientists have seen little science and lots of cultural prejudice in Huntington's confessional view of world geography in which alternatives are homogenous and civilizational borders as unmovable as the mountain that never went to Muhammad. The civilizational thesis has accordingly been castigated as a "one-sided conjecture" (Wilson 255), and one, moreover, that "does not survive historical scrutiny" (Amartya 16). To which one must add, still, that Huntington did not really discover the civilizational boundaries of Europe, but adopted them ready-made, like Marcel Duchamp's famous urinal, from an age-long cultural tradition of European thought in the process of discovering itself as European. The chapter that begins here would like to trace a brief and critical history of such a "discovery of Europe."[4]

Before the incipit of this story brings us back to another conflict of civilizations (in the beginning were the Persian Wars), let me offer an apology and a preface first. The apology concerns the telegraphic brevity, undoubtedly fraught with many simplifications, with which this opening chapter attempts to outline the story—after all, "no history could be written" (Pagden, introduction 1)—of the discovery of Europe from 500 BC to the early 1700s. Although the real concern of this book is with the emergence of an idea of dialectical and self-sufficient Europe in the late eighteenth century, I find that a brief outline of what precedes such surfacing is altogether necessary to my later argument. Not because I believe a history of the idea of Europe should or could be offered here: such history is impossible not in Anthony Pagden's sense—too much has been written already (the same argument in Lützeler)—but in the sense that history, as Dipesh Chakrabarty suggests in *Provincializing Europe*, is the very thought that *produces* Europe as its own "sovereign, theoretical subject" (27). Writing a history of Europe, or of the idea of Europe, means, then, tautologically, to write a history of the European idea of history.

I will try to enter the logic of this tautology later in this book. Before doing that, however, what I would like to accomplish here is to reconstruct the repertoire of ideas and commonplaces, and analyze some critical points, that the eighteenth-century theorists of Europe will find available to them, ready to use and argue in their definitions of either

Europe or, mutatis mutandis, "Universal History." As a preface, I would like to justify the title of this chapter by saying that Europe, too, had to be discovered. Not only in the sense that at different times in their histories, also Africa (Northrup), Islam (B. Lewis; Abu-Lughod), Japan (Keene), and the by now ubiquitous American tourist (Rahv) had to discover firsthand the "old continent" they only knew from literature or legend. More important than that, Europe had to discover itself *as* Europe—that is, to find unity in the plurality of all its imperial, national, local, cultural, and civilizational differences. When did Europe begin to see itself as one?

E Pluribus Unum: Theories of Beginnings

> Sometimes it can seem hopeless. How do you mould a single European people out of the lumpen masses scattered across the continent? European citizens . . . still insist on speaking different languages, they read different papers, worship at the shrines of different celebrities, chortle at different television programmes. But there is one exception. . . .
> —CHARLEMAGNE, "The Players Do Better Than the Politicians in Making Europe Loved"

In a chapter of his *The Civilization of Europe in the Renaissance*, programmatically titled "The Discovery of Europe," John Hale begins: "When in 1623 Francis Bacon threw off the phrase 'we Europeans,' he was assuming that his readers knew where 'Europeans' were, who they were, and what, in spite of national differences, they shared. This was a phrase, and an assumption, that could not have been used with such confidence a century and a half before" (3). For Hale, therefore, it was between 1450 and 1620 "that the word Europe first became part of common linguistic usage and the continent itself was given a securely map-based frame of reference, a set of images that established its identity in pictorial terms, and a triumphal ideology that overrode its internal contradictions" (3).

Robert Bartlett's *The Making of Europe*, instead, follows Marc Bloch's idea of the Middle Ages as the "childhood of Europe" (Bloch, *Feudal* 442) and sees Europe becoming one already in the eleventh and twelfth centuries, when a militarily hegemonic Frankish center (Germany, France, North Italy) begins conquering, colonizing, and "Europeanizing" the rest of the "continent" (Britain, Flanders, the Low Countries, Iberia, Southern Italy). Such colonization changed a previously "highly compartmentalized world" into one where religion, economy, and systems of education were shared by all, so that, eventually, a "cultural homogenization of Europe" was achieved under Frankish rule: "By 1300 Europe existed as an identifiable cultural entity. It could be described in more than one way, but some common features of its cultural face are the saints, names, coins, charters, and educational practices . . . . By the late medieval period Europe's names and cults were more uniform than they had ever been; Europe's rulers everywhere minted coins and depended upon chanceries; Europe's bureaucrats shared a common experience of higher education. This is the Europeanization of Europe" (Bartlett 291).

Adopting a similar line of reasoning, but implicitly refuting the Frankish beginnings of Europe, Norman Davies's *Europe: A History* dates a "birth of Europe" back to the period of "barbarian" migrations, invasions, and conquests that penetrated the Roman Empire from around 330 (date of the founding of Constantinople) to 800 AD. For Davies, Europe was (and still ought to be) an ethnic melting pot, the product of centuries-long racial dispersals and mixings—a cosmopolitan project, that is, forgotten by a later age of nationalism:

> By the eighth century, therefore, the ethnic settlement of the Peninsula [Celts, Slovenes, Huns, Goths, Jewish, Afro- and Indo-European "Romans"] was beginning to achieve a lasting pattern. The eighth century, indeed, was the point when important social crystallizations occurred. Yet five more major migrations [Vikings, Magyars, Mongols, Moors, and Turks] had to happen before all the basic population of the future Europe was complete. Europe was conceived from the most diverse elements, and her birth was painfully protracted. (238)

Enrique Dussel, who has other continents in mind, goes forward to 1492, "date of the 'birth' of modernity," to trace back an origin of Europe "as a unified ego exploring, conquering, colonizing an alterity" ("Eurocentrism" 66). Only through a confrontation with its colonial Other, not through Bartlett's internal forms of colonialism or Davies's migrations, can Dussel's Europe emerge as an identity. And while Helmut Reinicke (iii) maintains the same colonial beginning of Europe in the year 1492, Bernard Lewis, in *The Muslim Discovery of Europe*, goes back to another confrontation (and another Other) to find Europe born on the day

Charles Martel faced the Muslim armies in Poitiers. The year was 732: "It was indeed on this occasion that the very notion of Europe as an entity which could be threatened or saved appeared for the first time" (18).

M. E. Yapp, on the other hand, convinced that Poitiers is ideologically still a Christian, rather than a European, coming together, does not agree with Lewis in the least: "The emergence of the concept of Europe required . . . the waning of the power of the idea of Christendom. For that process we must look at a much later period" (138). Europe emerges then for Yapp with a much (much!) later "secular shift" (142)—when the religious threat of Islam wanes and, in 1714, the treaty of Utrecht remains the last testament to Europe as a "Christian Republic." After 1714, in other words, with the secular "emergence of Britain as the leading naval and military power in Europe" (O'Brien 65), Yapp's true and secular Europe began.

While some venture as far back as the *homo abilis* (Cunliffe; Phillips) to find the beginnings of Europe, others see the latter as a yet unfinished project, a still "hopeless goal" best left to Beckham to bend into conceptual and cultural unity under the auspices of the European Football Federation: "Over the past decade [in the 1990s] European football teams have turned into [the only] living, breathing embodiment of European integration" (Charlemagne, "Players" 55).

Rather than attempting the impossible task of determining which one is the true beginning of a self-consciousness of Europe, we would better ask ourselves, simply: Why so much ado about beginnings in the first place? The fact is that beginnings, as Edward Said once wrote, are always disingenuous: one begins from A not because there is some irrefutable reason to do so, but only because "the beginning A leads to B" (*Beginnings* 6). It is quite likely, in this sense, that Hale begins in 1450 (A) only to argue, as the undoubtedly Eurocentric reviewer does not miss a chance to remark, the universal value (B) of the Renaissance's "stunning achievements that shaped (for better and for worse, but mainly for better) the future not only of Europe but of the whole world" (Nauert 1087). Bartlett and Davies (like Geary) begin with medieval conquest (A) only to dispel the myth (B) of *all* ethnonationalisms, whose "idea of exclusive national homelands is a modern fantasy" (Davies 217). And Bernard Lewis suggests the battle of Poitiers as a beginning of Europe (A) with the clear intent to theorize (B) the original and fundamental importance of Muslim-Christian rivalries—the clash of civilizations—in the shaping of Europe and the West.[5]

To paraphrase Denis Donoghue's "America in Theory" (4), you *think* you are reading about the beginning of Europe—in the Renaissance, at Poitiers, in 1450 or 1492—and you suddenly find yourself within a systematic theory hinging on the word *Europe* and all its supposed meanings. It is in this first sense that, as the title of the present book maintains, Europe is *in theory*: speaking of Europe means—implicitly or explicitly, consciously or not—creating a theory not only of Europe itself but of a whole series of other things, such as culture (Hale), modernity (Dussel), nationalism (Bartlett), secularization (Yapp), and so on.

Assuming the game of beginnings is then not entirely naive, let me begin my story from the Persian Wars (500–449 BC), when the Greek states first reunited as "Europe" in order to confront the threat of Darius's Persian Empire. It is a good date, after all, to start understanding the very secular and military origin of the east/west antithesis that still informs, as a rhetorical unconscious, more recent civilizational clash theories. It brings us back to an old Europe, no doubt, but one that may still bear on the ways a new one is imagined.

Old Europe

> Today, the center of gravity is shifting.
> —DONALD RUMSFELD, press briefing, January 23, 2003

> I'm looking for a permanent center of gravity.
> —FRANCO BATTIATO, "Centro di gravitè permeneate"

In a transcription of the notes he took for a course held at the University of Milan in 1943 (while yet another clash of civilizations was haunting Europe), Federico Chabod wrote:

> European consciousness means differentiation of Europe, as a political and moral entity, from other entities . . . the concept of Europe must have first been formed as an antithesis to that which is not Europe. . . . Now, the first opposition between Europe and something that is not Europe . . . is the fruit of Greek thought. Between the age of the Persian Wars and the age of Alexander the Great emerges, for the first time, the sense of an Europe opposed to Asia—opposed in habits and culture, but, mainly, in political organization: Europe represents the spirit of "freedom," against Oriental despotism. (23)

Before the Persian Wars, as we know from Denys Hay, "the word Europe was associated in the first place with myth" (1)—the myth, later popularized by Ovid, of Europa, daughter of Agenor, king of Tyre, who lived in what we now call Lebanon. From there, she was kidnapped by Zeus disguised as a white bull, and brought to, well, Europe: "The god little by little edges away from the dry land, and sets his borrowed hoofs in the shallow water; then he goes further out and soon is in full flight with his prize on the open ocean. She now trembles with fear and looks back at the receding shore, holding fast a horn with one hand and resting the other on the creature's back" (Ovid 1.121).[6] Europa's flight *may* have meant "to record the westward flight of Canaanite tribes early in the second millennium BC"; and her rape *may* have represented the historical facts of "an early Hellenic occupation of Crete" (Graves 1:196–97). All that is certain, however, is that an explicitly political, cultural, and moral distinction of Europe, beyond the reach of mythology, was achieved only when Darius's armies started threatening with insistence the Greek cities. Isocrates (436–339 BC), urging a pan-Hellenic unity against the Persian threat, leaves us the first written record, in his *Panegyricus*, of a political understanding of Europe (see Momigliano; de Romilly): the latter is a strategic alliance to make common front against the Eastern menace. If strategy requires uniting the cities' forces into one Europe, war propaganda necessitates a demonizing of the enemy, which is accordingly depicted as ideologically and culturally opposed to "us." Europe, though geographically united with Asia, begins then to emerge as a commonplace ideologically separated from, and rhetorically opposed to, a negative place "of lavish splendour, of vulgarity, of arbitrary authority, of all that was antithetical to Greece and Greek values" (Hay 3). To summarize with the unforgiving words of Neal Ascherson, "In this particular encounter [with Asia] began the idea of 'Europe' with all its arrogance, all its implications of superiority" (49).[7]

What is intriguing about Arnaldo Momigliano's theory is that it makes Europe originate quite instrumentally from a simple rhetorical antithesis concocted for specific military ends: for Isocrates, Europe is the land of freedom and good government; Asia is the threat and commonplace of slavery and despotism. Fighting together against Persia means, then, nothing less than to protect civilization against evil. As Aeschylus puts it in *The Persians*, those "Europeans" will *never* be vanquished—freedom, if not God, is on their side: "They are slaves to none, neither are they subject" (qtd. in Davies 102). A theory of Europe, from its very outset, is a theory of Orientalism, which is this book's intention to follow throughout.[8]

All this is nice. But it is also quite puzzling: Whatever happens to Africa—third continent in the Greeks' tripartite *oecumene*—in this rhetorical construction of free Europe against the despotic Orient? Well, it looks like Africa is a continent de trop in the fable of early European identity. It is as if, in Denys Hay's poignant words, "two continents suited the Greeks better than three" (2).

Jacques Derrida could not have put it better: it is a binary logic of identity and otherness, a binary way of thinking, that begins "Europe." Put differently, Europe arises as a structure "of dichotomies or polarities: good vs. evil . . . identity vs. difference . . . . The second term in each pair [being] considered the negative, corrupt, undesirable version of the first" (*Of Grammatology* viii). In this second sense, Europe is *in theory*, and born inseparably from it: at the same moment in which a place that starts calling itself Europe develops its peculiar logic—its binary way of thinking, its structure of language, its deep grammar, its logos, its "grammatology"—it also institutes the cultural and epistemological limits that make it possible for that place to identify itself as Europe: "The reflection on identity as open question and as relation to alterity, begins from the 'philosophy' and the way of thinking of Europeans . . . it may be that European peoples recognize in the question of identity their own different and common identity, the game of alterity as identity" (Gnisci 86).

In the theory of Greek beginnings—a theory of the origin of European identity in a Greek thinking characterized by an "attitude of continuous comparison and confrontation with the other" (Gnisci 20)—Europe thus emerges with (or as) a new way of binary thinking and dialectical antitheses: "All derives from this original ambivalence that has always been the foundation of European identity" (Iiritano 41); "the originality [of Europe] is exactly in its having developed a thought of oppositions that is absent, instead, in any other culture" (Perniola 117); "the antithesis East-West is a mythical-symbolic asset that is proper of Europe only" (Marramao 59); "in Europe, one thinks one is identical with oneself in as far as one is different from the other—identity is built on difference" (*Le Monde*, qtd. in Pisano 289). Europe is the coming together of "Iranian oracles and Athenian rationalists" (Cassano, *Pensiero* 25–30), of Dyonisian and Apollinean (Nietzsche), of "the world of nature (*physis*) and that of men (*nomos*)" (Pagden, "Europe" 37).

While the ideological limits are set, the geographical boundaries, however, remain (until Huntington, that is) vague and mobile, as the most recent discussions on the European Union's inclusions and exclusions still attest. Isocrates' Europe, for instance, coincided with Greece, southern Spain, Southern Italy, Sicily, and lower France; Herodotus did not even take the idea of Europe as a continent very seriously at all, since, geographically speaking, Europe and Asia were not even separated by any sea (Herodotus 2.16). At any rate, wherever it was or ended, Europe was for the Greeks a heaven blessed by perfect weather (Herodotus 2.26), an "extremely beautiful land," one "of highest excellence" (Herodotus 7.5). We will follow the unfolding of climatology—the idea, namely, that gentle and temperate climates engender gentle and temperate peoples living in gentle and temperate political systems—in the following chapter on Montesquieu. The first step of such unfolding, however, can already be found in Hippocrates (460–370 BC), for whom Europe and Asia form not only ideological but also climatic and moral antitheses:

> A variable climate produces a nature which is coupled with a fierce, hotheaded and discordant temperature, for frequent fears cause a fierce attitude of mind whereas quietness and calm dull the wits. Indeed, this is the reason why the inhabitants of Europe are more courageous than those of Asia. Conditions which change little lead to easy-going ways; variations to distress of body and mind. Calm distress and pain increase courage. That is one reason for the more warlike nature of Europeans. But another cause lies in their customs. They are not subjects of a monarchy as the Asiatics are and, as I have said before, men who are ruled by princes are the most cowardly. (Qtd. in Mikkeli 8–9)

To which Aristotle added the following in the seventh book of the *Politics*: "The nations in cold regions, particularly in Europe, are full of [courage] . . . which is why they continue to be comparatively free . . . . By contrast, those in Asia . . . lack [courage]; which is why they continue to be ruled and enslaved" (7.7). Strabo (63 BC–21 AD), the link between Greek and Roman culture, followed by declaring Europe's climate best "suited to the development of excellence in men and in governments" (Strabo 2.5.26).[9] Both political and natural considerations, in sum, identified Europe against Asia and claimed the superiority of the former over the latter. Arguably, nature and geography were being transformed into symbols and commonplaces, into systems of meaning: cold was given a moral and political significance (courage), and heat another (cowardice).

The Romans, by and large, inherited much of the Greek definition of Europe, including the idea of Europe's perfect weather. Pliny (23–79 AD), who called Europe "by far the fairest of lands," was certain that its gentle climate had produced "gentle [people], clear reason, fertile intellects . . . and they also have governments, which the outer races never have possessed" (1.2.80). Yet the East had started to lose much of its immediate political signification for Rome: the Persian threat was on the wane, and, more significantly, Constantine had moved the capital from western Rome to eastern Byzantium (renamed Constantinople for the occasion) in 331. This does not mean that the memory—what I am calling the "rhetorical unconscious"—of a fundamental antithesis was lost. Traces of it were preserved in fact in the very science that had invented it—rhetoric—where the term *Asiatic*, for instance, started meaning a deviation from normative *humanitas*, and "tended to become pejorative . . . in a literary sense—bombastic and over elaborate composition could be thus described" (Hay 4).

At any rate, it is agreed that the term *Europe* was of little interest for the Romans, for whom Europe existed, at most, as a relatively superfluous geographical concept: "Caesar never used the word. Virgil referred to it now and then, but merely in passing; and the same is true of Cicero, Horace, Statius, Sallust, Tacitus, Appianus, and St. Augustine" (Duroselle 65). The Mediterranean, not Europe, was the organizing principle for a Roman rhetoric of self-definition, of politics, and even of mapmaking (Hay 6). The vague borders set by the Roman Empire, though "not always precise lines on a map or judicially defined" (Kormoss 84), configured, then, an identity pushing southward and comprehending the northern coasts of Tunisia, Libya, and Algeria.[10] At the same time, a northern barrier, set between the Rhine river and the Hadrian Wall (begun in 122 AD), would separate a sedentary civilization from the nomadic barbarians of Tacitus's *Germania* and Caesar's Gauls. In a way, traditional east/west divisions were supplemented, if not replaced, by new north/south ones—with the south as the locus of a desirable *humanitas*, and the north as the site of barbarism (see Fournier 97): "On one side of the frontier the reunited Roman Empire held firm; on the other a restless mass of peoples, largely in the tribal stage of development, tilled the forest clearings or roamed the plain. Understandably enough, most Romans saw this division in terms of black and white. For them, the Empire was 'civilized'—that is, subject to ordered government; the barbarians were, by definition, 'uncivilized' " (Davies 213–14).

Despite its scarce interest in Europe, the Roman Empire will play a very important role in the genesis of modern Europe that I will follow in the next chapters: the Romans had been the first "Europeans" to conceive of the city-state (Pliny's "governments") as a legal person, a res publica that belonged not to the emperor (who could die and be replaced), but to its inhabitants. The Twelve Tables (450 BC), and the later *Codex* of Theodosianus (438 AD), along with the Justinian Laws (529 AD), had been the first attempts to legislate the limits of political power and individual rights ("individual" being understood as a nonslave, propertied male) within the republic. The Italian humanists of the fifteenth century were instrumental in making of Rome the symbol of whatever is good about, and culturally proper to, Europe: their work was meant as a preservation and recovery of Roman culture after the destruction caused by the barbarians from the north.

It was only with the growth, initially within the Roman Empire itself, of two oriental religions—Judaism first, and Christianity following— that *Europe* regained importance and began to acquire a new sacred connotation underpinned by the authority of the scriptures. While Arab-controlled Jerusalem replaced Rome and Byzantium as the center of the *orbis christianus* exemplified in the so-called T-O (or *terrarum orbis*) maps, the three continents of the Greek *oecumene* were tied to precise theological meanings through the myth of the diaspora of Noah's progeny.[11] According to Christian exegesis, the great human diaspora mentioned in the sacred texts of Christianity prepared what Maurice Olender has called "a geography of malediction":

> [Ham commits the sin] to expose publicly his Father's [Noah's] obscenity by laughing and making fun of his nudity. Ham therefore sees his cursed descendants become "servant of servants . . . unto his brethren" (Gen.9.25). The Church Fathers, who had read Josephus, attribute the peopling of Africa to him. To his two brothers who "went backward, and covered the nakedness of their father; and their faces were backward, and they saw not their father's nakedness" (Gen.9.23), tradition grants two other continents. Shem, marked in Genesis by his privileged link to the eternal Elohim, receives Asia. Japheth, whose Hebraic name evokes "beauty" as well as "openness," the "wide space" of a legacy capable of "dilation" and "expansion," will be the father of Europe. For the readers of the Septuagint, the Greek translation of the Old Testament, the etymological fiction of a "Euru-opa," meaning "wide vision," could serve to

confirm the providential ambition of this continent which "sees far" (eurus, ops). Since Hecataeus of Miletus in the sixth century B.C. the Greeks had divided the world into three parts: Africa, Asia, and Europe. From this point on, this ancient geography was christianized thanks to the new biblical ancestors of humanity. (10; see also Ricceri 4–5)

Japheth's descendants were then said to have occupied Europe, Ham's Africa, and Shem's Asia. In this "ethnic rationalization of space" (Mignolo, *Renaissance* 219), the subaltern position of Africa, and the hegemonic one of Europe, were sanctioned for the second time. Moreover, west and east, Europe and Asia, Japheth and Shem were once again bound together in a series of rhetorical antitheses of European and, as Edward Said calls it after Freud, "non-European" (*Freud*): uncircumcised/circumcised, New/Old Testament, future/past of monotheism, Hellenic/Semitic. The Jew would then occupy, to the days of Auschwitz and beyond, the formal place that was once assigned to the Persian as the very antithesis to Europe.[12] To the Jew, a new child of Shem would soon be added as the figural antithesis to Europe's race.

When Muhammad had his vision in a cave of Mount Hira, north of Mecca, it was the year 610 of the Christian calendar. The privileged place of Christianity as the latest prophesy that amended an older one was immediately shattered by the newer parvenu from the east that arrogated onto itself the privilege of all emendations. It was the beginning of a long warfare between Christianity and Islam, which eased only, and temporarily, with the breakup of the caliphate in the ninth and tenth centuries. Islam's armies had soon started pushing at the doors of Europe, and the speed and extent of their conquests had been unseen since the times of Julius Caesar: by 643, they had reached Tripoli; by around 652, they started attacking Sicily (discussed in chapter 5 of this book); between 660 and the 670s, Arab navies kept besieging an apparently impregnable Constantinople; and by 711 Córdoba, Toledo, and most of Spain were in the hands of Muslim armies, now advancing toward the Pyrenees. The threat of Islam made different peoples—Romano, Gallic, and "barbarians" or Arian Christians—enter into a coalition, in 732, which the chronicler Isidor Pacensis called "Europeenses" (B. Lewis 18). This was a Europe, as Denis de Rougemont notices, quite limited in extension to "the people who live north of the Pyrenees and the Alps" (47). The Mediterranean was being replaced by the Alps as the center of a new Europe.

What the advent of Islam accomplished was to halt the spread of a self-declared universalistic and ecumenical religion on the Asian and African borders, thereby making Christianity coincide with a geography tentatively called Europe. It is at this point that Europe began, in a way, to lose some of its political meaning and reduced itself to a mere religious and geographical denotation: "The moral . . . almost ideological content of this Europe is the Roman Church" (Chabod 29–30). As an example of the loss of moral connotations, "it is instructive to witness the efforts of Bede, writing as late as the early decades of the eighth century. . . . He describes Gregory the Great as being pope 'over the whole world,' and being set over 'all the churches which obey the true faith.' Faced with exactly the same linguistic problem a century earlier, St. Columba had . . . addressed the pope as 'Head of all the churches of the whole Europe'" (Hay 28). As Novalis would reminisce with longing in 1799, Europe *is* Christianity in those happy years known as Europe's Middle Ages: "What a beautiful and happy time when Europe was a Christian land, and *one* Christianity humanly lived in this part of the world; *one* great common interest reunited all provinces of this spiritual kingdom" (10–11).[13]

The symbol of such a Christian Europe is undoubtedly Charlemagne, king of the Franks (768–814), "inventor" of Europe for some (Curcio; Jordan), and, for others, the one who made Europe disappear behind the hegemonic concept of Christianity (Perroy): "His title was none other than that of the true monarch of the West, of the monarch ruling over that entity which was called *Europa* by some, and the *imperium Christianum* by others, and also *imperium Romanum* by still others" (Ullmann 105). Between 800 and 814 AD, Charlemagne was at work trying to reconstruct the waning Roman Empire into his new Holy *and* Roman Empire. Yet whether this domain was imagined as Europe or Christianity is not a matter of mere nominalism. A Christian world *is* one: it is the *orbis christianus* of T-O maps, made of the sons of Noah, brothers everywhere—some already enlightened by the glow of Providence, some others, like the children of Shem, still ignorant of Truth but convertible nonetheless. This wholesome world stood in intimate contrast with that of Europe, which coincided instead with a gens (Japheth's), one "ethnic" (Lyser 37) people united under a *secular* authority. The distance between the terms, rather than suggesting synonymy, may have marked a perceived tension, instead, between a *factual* geographical Europe—a limit of Charlemagne's expansion—and an *ideal*, speculative one—a "destiny," as it will later be called by Hegel—still in the process of becoming, and toward which Charlemagne imperially strived. As K. J. Lyser puts it, "Europe is here the geographical . . . setting of that world order that alone counted, the Christian one" (34).

If Christendom was then the bearer of all moral and political meanings, Europe remained the limit of its geographical realization. As a limit, Charlemagne's Christian Europe, unable until the end to reconstitute the old empire, "only succeeded to half of the Roman dominations, and grew up on the north-western provinces" (Woodruff 1). As the Venerable Bede saw it, Europe was composed of Gallia, Germania, and Spain (Rougemont 48). Whereas the Romans, focused as they were on the Mediterranean, had comprehended the African coast as part of the empire's identity, Charlemagne's Holy Roman Empire clearly marked a southern frontier: the Mediterranean was periphery and extreme limit of Europe. In fact, in his study of the linguistic usage of the terms *Oriens*, *Occidens*, and *Europa* between the sixth and the tenth centuries, the philologist Jürgen Fischer follows Marian Henryk Serejski and counts at least thirty mentions of *Europe* in the years of Charlemagne. Such zealous accounting is meant to suggest that *European* was, around the Carolingian court, a token of Frankish identity signifying an opposition to, and independence from, anything southern, Mediterranean, and Roman. Although the lands immediately above the Mediterranean were then technically part of the empire, the term *Europe*, if we follow Fischer's suggestion, was already alluding to a northern *difference* from a south that was European in theory only: a negative Europe increasingly abhorred as the site of corruption, decadence, and decay.

It is for this reason that theories about Charlemagne as the "origin" of Europe will usually be enmeshed in some kind of north/south polemics—from Montesquieu's theory of a Carolingian rebirth of Europe, through Madame de Staël's romantic Middle Ages, to the historiographies of François Pierre Guillame Guizot, Jules Michelet, and Henry Pirenne. Around Charlemagne hinges in fact the vexed question of whether the origin of European freedoms had been Roman or, rather, Frankish. Were the Romans those who gave freedom and the law to Europe? Or where they despots, whose chains were broken by the proud Germans with their customary laws?[14] The polemic, in fact, had begun as early as 1573, when François Hotman wrote his *Franco-Gallia* against the dismissal of the "barbaric" Middle Ages theorized by Italian (and therefore Romano-centric) humanists.

Hotman's text "narrates the German conquest of Gaul in order to show that the conquerers possessed among them freedom and equality" (Carravetta 46). The theory was based on some vague allusions taken from Tacitus's *Germania*, but, no matter if "the improbability of . . . these assumptions is obvious to all" (Sergi 34), it acquired authority first with Montesquieu's theorization of feudalism (discussed in the following chapter), and then with the German Romantics' theories of the *Markgenossenschaft* (a communal village putatively typical of early German tribes). Tacitus's allusions, in a way, were the rhetorical unconscious that started informing theories—let alone the historiography of Armand Maurer or the political science of Friedrich Engels—which served indifferently both the nationalist Right and the internationalist Left to theorize an "original" Europe beginning not with Rome but with the northern Germans (see Sergi 33–36).

In terms of chronology, the polemics between Roman and German origin of Europe meant an endless controversy over the issue of the Middle Ages: were they the ages of darkness, or the rebirth of (Carolingian) Europe? On the one side, southern humanists (we will follow Juan Andrés in chapter 3) claimed that the Middle Ages were a period of decay from the glorious epoch of Rome; on the other, the northern *philosophes* were unwilling to share humanism's "pejorative concept of mediaevalism, whose purpose had been to undermine the legitimating doctrine of *translatio imperii*" (Pumfrey, Rossi, and Slawinski 60)—the shift of hegemony from southern Rome to Charlemagne's Frankish Holy Roman Empire.

Along with the north/south divide, at any rate, remained the east/west one. Charlemagne and the Christian-Frankish Empire, first of all, identified and defined themselves in opposition to, once again, the Orient: "The Frankish Empire would probably never have existed without Islam, and Charlemagne without Mahomet would be inconceivable" (Pirenne 27). Moreover, the Byzantine Empire, with its wealth and ostentation, with its display of a new kind of "Oriental" luxury in daily life and liturgy, created a new longitudinal division between Latin or Roman Christianity, on the one hand, and Greek and Slav orthodoxy on the other. The iconoclastic wars between an eastern church accused of worshipping images and a purer western one replacing crucifixes with crosses and Virgin Marys with whiteouts had begun already in the eighth century. Charlemagne, paying homage to Rome, and breaking away from Byzantine orthodoxy, had increased a sense of western Christian distinctiveness that had come close to establishing, in Robert Bartlett's words, "a quasi-ethnic" identity.[15] The schism was finally formalized in 1054, with the Papal Bull excommunicating the Patriarch Cerularius, and with the latter's Synodal Edict formalizing the breach. "This was no mere quarrel between rival sects. . . . It involved real hatred" (Duroselle 127). The Greeks, once central in the formation of the idea of Europe, became one "of the 'borders of Europe' . . . , one of the 'peripheral' countries of Europe" (Balibar 1). Dante's casting of Ulysses and Diomedes in hell is a chapter in this marginalization of Greece. For its re-Europeanization, we need to wait until the 1820s, when the Greek wars of national liberation against the Ottoman Empire will fuel the Romantic generation of Lord Byron.

Back to the Middle Ages: it is in the name of Christianity, and not of European expansion, that the crusades began to protect the loathed Byzantines from the continuing pressures of the eastern "Saracens."[16] In 1095, just as Europe was starting to grow toward Bohemia, Poland, and Hungary (Lyser 136–37), pope Urban II called on Christendom to take arms against Seljuk's advance: "Dios lo volt" (God wishes it). The call, which would result in the forty-day siege and mass massacres of Jerusalem in 1099, had an effect similar to Poitiers: French, German, Provençal, and North Italian armies united and mobilized against the common enemy from the east. Once again, however, the unifying principle was not Europe—understood as a territorial or political concept—but Christendom, with its symbolic cross painted in red as the badge of a union authorized by the divine.[17]

The Christian God of love had wanted a holy war. Under Him, Christendom constituted not only a moral and political concept but a race:

> In 1098, for example . . . after the crusaders had taken Antioch, Jesus appeared in a vision to a priest in the army, [and] asked: "Man, what race is this (*quaenam est hec gens*) that has entered the city?" and received the answer: "Christians." . . . French *chansons* and rhymed chronicles talk of *la gent cristiane*, and in one of them, *La chanson d'Antioche*, Jesus is pictured hanging on the cross, explaining to the good thief alongside him that "from across the sea a new people (*novele gent*) will come, who will take revenge for the death of their father." (Bartlett 251–52)

As a race, Christianity had the imperative to defend itself from Shem's Muslim progeny and take revenge on the Jew, time allowing, "for the death of their father." The world had become, in the Christian mentality of the Middle Ages, a clash of civilizations, a "territorial dichotomy that shaped mental geography in the eleventh, twelfth, and thirteenth centuries. The abstract 'Christendom' also summoned into being its mirror image: 'heathendom' . . . The world was seen as the arena of the clash of great religio-territorial spheres" (Bartlett 253–54).

Despite the monomaniacal obsession to conquer Jerusalem, which lasted for around two hundred years and climaxed in horrors—eight thousand Jews killed in Rhineland, seventy thousand Arab civilians in Jerusalem—that even the most pious Saint Bernard could not but denounce, the Christians never managed to "free" the Holy Land. As Jacques Le Goff summed up the results of the seven Crusades from 1096 to 1291, "their only fruit . . . was the apricot" that the Christians had brought from Armenia (95). Some indirect effect of the Crusades, however, can still be observed. First, they confirmed the Franks as the leading European power and as the paladins of its Christianity. Second, they exacerbated the implicit theory of the essential Christianity of Europe. Third, and just as important, the Crusades established a pan-European set of knights' orders, and a landed aristocracy diffused over the territory. Like Charles Martel after Poitiers (Trevor-Roper 96) and Charlemagne in his undertaking to defend the territories of Christendom, the Crusader kings had to reward obedience and service in battle with landed property—the *foeudum*—and therefore divide the land of the empire among a class of landlords (Bloch, *Feudal*). For Montesquieu (see next chapter), feudalism was that uniquely European institution that created the social conditions for freedom to mature there and not elsewhere.

The rise of a popular literature in vulgar tongues, sometimes religious and didactic (the Italian "rhythms" of *Lawrence* and *Saint Alexis*), more often celebrating and codifying the oppositions of "courteous paladin[s]" and "heathen Arabs" (*Chanson de Roland* verses 576 and 2810), constitutes another contribution of the age of the Crusades to the culture of Europe. For the first time, imperial Latin was abandoned in favor of popular languages singing the "pride of France, renowned land, you see" (*Chanson de Roland* verse 3315); for the first time, rhetorical argumentation was leaving room to a catechistic acceptance of revealed facts that Erich Auerbach saw hinging on the rhetorical figure of parataxis;[18] and for the first time, the kings and queens of tragedy, along with the serves of comedy, were being replaced by the intermediate baronial classes. The result was a new literary code, as well as a new ethical one, both resulting in the codification of a Christian worldview in the chanson de geste:

> The knightly will to fight, the concept of honor, the mutual loyalty of brothers in arms, the community of the clan, the Christian dogma, the allocation of right and wrong to Christians and infidels, are probably the most important of these views. . . . They are posited without argument as pure theses: these are the facts. No argument, no explanatory discussion whatever is called for when, for example, the statement is made: *paien unt tort et chrestiens unt dreit* (heathens are wrong and Christians are right). (Auerbach, *Mimesis* 101)

Supplementing the chanson de geste, which celebrated the exploits of Frankish and Arthurian chivalry, the chanson d'amor entertained the courts of Europe with songs of courting and love. The troubadours would bring these songs from one court to another, thus assuring the formation of a common European canon based, roughly, on a predilection for accent-based prosody, rhyme, decasyllabic verse, and the topos of courtly love.

Both the *philosophes* and, again, the Romantics saw the chanson d'amor as intimately tied to the development of one European culture: courtly love was for them a peculiarly European phenomenon, necessitating, as I will discuss in chapter 4, of a non-Oriental understanding of love, of women's role, and of heterosexual, monogamous marriage (see Passerini). Despite this retroactive eighteenth- and nineteenth-century theorization of love and epic poetry as European, the chansons were still written under the hegemony of the concept of *Chrestientet* (Christianity). Christian knights, not European warriors, people the *laisses* (strophes) of the *Song of Roland*, from which the very word *Europe* remains conspicuously absent:

> D'altre part est li arcevesque Turpin.
> Sun cheval broche e muntet un lariz;
> Franceis apelet, un sermun lur ad dit:
> "Seignurs baruns, Caries nus laissat ci;
> Pur nostre rei devum nus ben murir.
> Chrestientet aidez a sustenir!
> Bataille avrez, vos en estes tuz fiz,
> Kar a voz oijz veez Jes Sarrazins."

[On the other side is the Archbishop Turpin.
He spurs his horse and mounts upon a hill;
he calls the Franks, and tells them:
"My lords, barons, Charles brought us here;
He is our King, and we would die for our king,
and to help him defend Christendom.
You will fight, you all are bound to it,
for you'll see with your own eyes the Saracens"]
(*Chanson de Roland* verses 1124–31)

It is only with the institution of universities in the thirteenth century that a more secular culture of Europe begins to disengage itself from Christianity. Built on the remains of Alcuin and Charlemagne's system of schools and monasteries, shaped after merchants' guilds and corporations, and characterized by the extraordinary mobility—"from one end of the former Carolingian empire to the other" (Wieruszowski 21)—of its teachers and students, the university or *studium generale* soon became the main instrument for the hypostatization of *a* European culture as Culture, and for its dissemination in the Christian territories of the West.[19] In Robert Bartlett's words, the medieval universities, imposing "a common experience of higher education" through both curricular standardization and teachers' mobility, were the true engine for "the Europeanization of Europe" (288–91). The university centers of Bologna, Paris, and Oxford, while establishing "a kind of metropolitan cultural dominance" (Bartlett 288), also theorized what culture was and divided it into the two complementary parts of *trivium* (grammar, rhetoric, and dialectic) and *quadrivium* (arithmetic, geometry, astronomy, and music).

Central in this curriculum, despite ecclesiastical resistance, was the figure of Aristotle.[20] He soon began to represent "a veritable encyclopedia of knowledge" (Daly 79) for the medieval student to work on and study; "the entire encyclopedic and pedagogic project of the West was being founded" (Sini 63) on his concept of logics. Through Aristotle, indeed, the need for logic and demonstrable hypotheses was upheld in the new universities against the catechistic predilection for parataxis that had distinguished the previous age. What was canonized *through* the *Analytica*, the *Metaphysics*, *Topica*, and *Politics* was a veritable way of thinking, a theory of knowledge that competed with the authority of the scriptures and posited "empiricism as the basis of all knowledge, the role of reason in the treatment of empirical matter and the eventual presentation of knowledge in logico-deductive systems of definitions, hypotheses (axioms), postulates, and theorems or propositions" (Pedersen 274). Abelard's *Sic et non*, "set[ting] side by side judgments which seemed at first view contradictory" (Daly 11) only to solve them later through the mediation of reason, was but one example of the necessity to submit even revealed truth to the scrutiny of reason. Through Aristotle, the academic centrality of dialectics as the proper method of critical thinking and cultural transmission in Europe was, in short, instituted. Growing from the initial antithesis of east and west, Europe was now developing into a veritable dialectical and secularized thinking, into a binary logic recognized, undoubtedly with some Eurocentric presumption, as the only valid epistemology.

Already in the medieval university a theory of knowledge came close to fully theorizing Europe itself. It did not do that, however, because the kind of knowledge on which such a university depended was still in large measure reliant on an element that later theories of Europe would have to obliterate and repress in order to claim a purer Europeanness: the Arab (see Menocal, *Arabic Role*). While the Carolingian schools had confined themselves within the strictures of religious education, the enlightened Abassid caliphs of Persia (750–1258) had equipped the so-called House of Wisdom of Baghdad (762), the observatories of Cairo (1005), and the schools of Córdoba (1010) with all the Greek manuscripts they could import from Byzantium. Aristotle, forgotten, if not abhorred, in the lands of Christianity, had been "discovered" in the European universities of the thirteenth century only through the translations and commentaries of Ibn Sina (Avicenna) and Ibn Rashid (Avverroës), who had preserved his texts. The study of geometry, arithmetic, mathematics, and astronomy, having fallen into oblivion in Charlemagne's Europe, had also been brought from Córdoba and Toledo via Islam. Secular poetry, finally, marginalized by Christian diction, had entered Europe through the Sicilian court of Fredrick II, an "eighteenth-century man born in the thirteenth" (Amari, *Musulmani* 4:730), who had managed to create a center of cultural exchange among Greek, Arab, and Jewish cultures between 1196 and 1250.[21]

What came to be known as "Graeco-Arab philosophy" (Campanini 5) was the metaphysical and cosmological imaginary of medieval Europe— an imaginary famously depicted by Dante in the *Comedy*. But whether Arab philosophers could, in the end, be foundations to anything European at all—this was to be the core of endless controversies: was the Arabs' role that of passive preservationists of an originally European culture (O'Leary)? Had the Arabs merely translated, as in a famous title by Richard Walzer, "Greek into Arabic"? Had they even "alienated" their Islamic faith in order to embrace Plato and Aristotle (Netton)? Or were the Arabs creating and planting the very roots of Europe's modern science (Saliba)? Despite their differences, all these positions inherently deny a fundamental (and fundamentalist) opposition between Europe and Islam. In order to claim such fundamental opposition again, Arabs and Jews—the progeny of Shem—had to be transformed, in the European imaginary, from producers to objects of knowledge. The transformation, which will culminate in the academic institutionalization of Oriental studies (Said, *Orientalism*) that I discuss in chapter 5, begins perhaps in 1311, when the Council of Vienna first instituted the teaching of Hebrew and Arab in the major European universities. The new discipline of "oriental philology" (Pedersen 298; Dvornik 65) was a science largely understood within the logic of the church's ecumenical mission of speaking to the unbeliever: knowledge of the unbeliever was useful for conversion; or, plainly, for the self-defense of Christianity. The most serious consequence of this creation and institutionalization of a new discipline was that the "Oriental" element, now symbolically relegated within the field of "oriental philology," left the disciplines of philosophy and logic uncontaminated by any spurious, non-European element.

Bracketing away Ibn Rashid, Aristotle became, then, the foundation of *European* knowledge—and such knowledge could study, but not be studied by, the "Oriental." At any rate, the canonization of Aristotle despite Christian reservations clearly hints at the emergence of a secular Europe somewhat independent from Christendom. The hegemony of the Roman Church was slowly breaking down. Among the causes of its enfeeblement is, in 1378, the establishment of the residence of the French antipope in Avignon, France. The French attempt to take away the papacy from Rome started a rather unbecoming dispute:

> No one conducted a more vigorous campaign against the residence of the popes at Avignon than the Florentine exile, Petrarch. In 1366 he published a letter claiming that only the crudest motives retained pope and cardinals in the Rhone valley. From this point a lively controversy developed between Petrarch and a series of French apologists for Avignon. The exchanges were scarcely edifying and much turned on Petrarch's accusa-

tion that the French were barbarians, like all other trans-Alpine peoples, and counter charges of corruption and incivility in Italy: all a curious anticipation of the later battle of the books which developed between the two countries in the sixteenth century. (Hay 73–74)

This was the seed that would later produce the schisms of the national churches (Gallican, Anglican) from Rome. The weakening of Christian unity, however, was its most immediate effect. By 1396, when the Crusaders were defeated in Nicopolis, the idea of a common Christianity seemed unable to maintain a unitary front against the emboldened enemy. The Crusades were over. Christendom immediately saw its confines shriveling under the attacks from the east: in 1427, the Turks occupied Serbia; in 1446, Mourad III invaded Greece; in 1448, after the victory of Kosovo, the Turks held total control of the Balkans; in 1453, Constantinople fell—scandal and wake-up call for Christianity—and the victorious Mohammed II started moving toward Bosnia, which fell in 1465.

Another Europe—an eastern one with Poland as frontier, "periphery and shield" (Mikkeli 38)—was being shaped by the advance of Turkish and Muslim armies: to the rest of the continent, this other Europe appeared dark, threatening, and quite Oriental; its sinister symbol, concocted between 1462 and 1465 by Florentine writers at the service of the Christian court of Hungary, was Dracula, the demon from the east haunting the dreams of Christianity (Berenger). What was clearly a living dead, however, was the unifying force of Christendom. Another imagined community, so to speak, was needed to defend "us" from the scurrying Turks: a linguistic shift from Christianity to Europe had to occur once Christianity had lost any cementing power. It is not that, to be sure, Christianity disappeared altogether; simply, some of its moral and political signification was being transferred, relocated, and translated into the idea of Europe.[22] Traces of this translation are clearly visible as late as in Sebastian Münster's *Universal Cosmography of the Whole World* (1575), or in Abraham Ortelius's *Theater of the Universe* (1587)—one insisting that "Europe comprehends today Christendom," the other that "Europe is name of the part of the world since ancient times comprising Christendom" (qtd. in Céard 58).[23]

Translation was, slowly but surely, effacing its original, and incorporating it. Eager to submit Christendom to the concept of Europe was the Vicar of Christ himself, Silvio Enea Piccolomini, elected pope Pius II in 1458. At the congress of Mantua (1459), he already seemed less interested to recapture the holy places to Christendom than "to drive the Turk out of Europe." And in the letter to Mohammed II, the conqueror of Constantinople, the pope did not ask the victorious Saracen to convert for the gain of paradise, but to surrender, rather, for the sake of "admiration from the whole of Europe" (qtd. in Hay 85). The importance of this pope in the promotion of the concept of Europe, which had been previously eclipsed by the linguistic hegemony of his own faith, should not be underestimated. For one, to quote Denys Hay, Pious II

> turned the word [*Europe*] into an adjective. There was little classical encouragement for a use of "European": *Europaeus* and *Europensis* are found, but not commonly or in the most admired authors . . . . Dante, for instance, goes out of his way to avoid the word in a passage where he writes of "Asians and Africans" but styles the natives of the third continent as "inhabitants of Europe." . . . In Pius II, however, the word has come to stay. Its usefulness made it have real significance. (86–87)

So *Europe* became a quality, an attribute that could determine or qualify the object to which it was attributed. Just as heat makes the iron warm, or blueness makes the sky blue, so did Europe now make its inhabitants Europeans.[24] It was a spirit of the place, shaping its people in its own image. This may imply, incidentally, that a relative cultural consensus had already been achieved regarding what, exactly, Europeanness was supposed to qualify: in the cultural horizon within which Europe emerged as an adjective, *European* meant a cultural, humanistic value based on the tradition of the so-called classics, on the cult of ancient Rome, and on the study of ancient thought. It was Jacob Wimpfeling's *Europa colta*—the place of culture (Chabod 45–47)—that would become the core of Europe as the Republic of Letters I discuss in chapter 3.

Europe was back—as a unifying, moral, and political concept. Yet this was not necessarily the same Europe of Isocrates, but one decidedly moving northward: "Enea Silvio [Piccolomini]," suggests Philippe Braunstein, "gave [Europe] a German body" (35). The true spirit of classical Europe, for Piccolomini, was no longer to be found in the "heretic" (read orthodox) Greeks, nor in the corrupted Romans, but in the Frankish and German north, raised up from barbarity by Charlemagne, the new center and heart of modern Europe. Nor was the pope the only one to push the center of Europe up north: as the decline of Christendom had been in good measure determined by frictions between the Roman papacy and the nascent Gallican church of Avignon, it is unsurprising to see the new Europe bearing the signs of this tension. The anonymous writer of a pamphlet advocating a move of the papal see from Rome to Avignon insisted that France (more precisely, Marseille), not Rome, was the geometric center of Europe (qtd. in Hay 74–75).

In 1407, Richard Young, from England, would rehearse similar arguments: "The French are at the very heart of Europe" (qtd. in Martene and Durand 749). In sum, a growing interest in the word *Europe*, increasingly privileged over *Christianity*, seems historically to coincide with "a transfer of the center of gravity away from the Mediterranean . . . to the triangle Germany-France-England" (Elton 97). Long gone are the days when Francesco Petrarca (in *Italia mia*) could boast the self-confident superiority of Mediterranean Europe separated by the providential Alps from a ranting and raving north: "Ben provide Natura al nostro stato, / quando de l'Alpi schermo / pose fra noi et la tedesca rabbia" (Nature well sought after our well-being / when She posed the Alps / as a shield between us and the German rage) (611). In the age of Pope Piccolomini, a Mediterranean hegemony is no more. From now on, a Mediterranean dignity will need to be defended, more or less hysterically, through the usual and desperate claims to origins—that modern European poetry begun in Spain (Andrés's claim, discussed in chapter 3); or that philosophy, the "thinking of Europe," must have begun midway between the Greek archipelago and Southern Italy (for a history of such a claim, see Casini 35–67).[25]

Continuing with our story of the unfolding of dialectical Europe, we should stop, at this point, to single out two "discoveries" that seem quite important for the Renaissance self-understanding of Europe: the printing press and America.[26] By embedding language in the manufacturing process of mass-produced books, the printing press transformed words and ideas into commodities (Ong, *Orality* 118) that could be sold and exchanged in markets much wider—continental—than the ones the amanuenses could have ever dreamed of covering. Printing, then, made local phenomena (the Italian Renaissance, German Protestantism) pan-European ones; it made old classics and new authors widely (and cheaply) reproducible, thereby promoting the canonization of (European) culture; it made maps of the world easily accessible, thereby articulating a new consciousness of space, and of Europe's place in it; it moved Europe toward a new stage of the Aristotelian cult for logics and precision by imposing unprecedented standards (dictionaries, grammars) to linguistic expression; it also made the exchange logic of early capitalism an integral part of the cultural production, embedded already in the printing, circulation, and sale of the book commodity (Eisenstein).

In 1469, Giovanni di Spira introduced printing in Venice, and the next year presses would be found in Milan, Verona, Foligno, and Florence. Niccolò Machiavelli would publish one of the very first European best sellers—*The Prince*—in the brand-new Blado Press of Rome on January 4, 1532. Starting to imagine politics as a science, Machiavelli's text, like the *Art of War* that was to follow, theorized not only an entirely secular Europe—Christendom being reduced to the all-too-secular papal state— but also, and most important, a certain self-sufficiency of Europe.[27] Apart from very few examples taken from Asia—I count Moses, Cirus, and Darius—*all* possible forms of government, and an entire repertoire of princely conducts, could be theorized by looking at Europe, and at Europe only: "My reasoning in matters of war needs not go beyond Europe. Hence, I need not recount what the Asian habits were" (566). To legitimate such closure of Europe, and bracket away the world entire, Machiavelli had to theorize a plurality of the European world that both Montesquieu (chapter 2) and Hegel (chapter 5) would put at the basis of their dialectical Europe (on Europe's plurality and multiplicity, also see Morin 27): "Europe has had many excellent men of war; Africa a few; and Asia even less. This has happened because in these last two parts of the world, there have always been one or two empires at most, and only a few republics; only Europe has had a few empires, and an infinite number of republics" (585).

A fragmentation of power among different states, for Machiavelli, made Europe the place where courage and military genius had to grow: if no single authority existed and controlled all others, each prince then needed to acquire political skills (which political science would impart), military cleverness (which war could form), and personal fortitude (which republican freedom nourished). Not only did Machiavelli's Europe have many republics; moreover, each of its republics had multiple centers of power that balanced authority among each other, thereby preventing a single authority from becoming despotic: "The examples of the two kinds of governments can be observed today in Turkey and France. The Turkish monarchy is governed by one lord, and all others are servants. But the king of France is placed amidst a multitude of long-established lords" (127). Machiavelli's theory (or its rhetorical unconscious) will return for instance in Houdar de la Motte's ballet *L'Europe galante* (1697), where Europe is represented as a set of different national characteristics (see Hazard, *European Mind* 54). It will also reappear in Montesquieu's distinction of Europe from an Asia "where [instead] the rules of politics are everywhere the same" (1.252). On the other hand, Machiavelli is already echoing here the memory—or rhetorical unconscious—of Isocrates' initial definition of political Europe as the locus of freedom. Curiously enough for a book published after 1492, also Isocrates' binary *oecumene* returns to inform Machiavelli's political science: not only Africa but also, and most strikingly, America, is now absent from Machiavelli's antithesis of Europe versus Asia. Has America not registered yet in the symbolic order and rhetorical unconscious of the Europeans? The new geographical fact means nothing yet? Machiavelli, in fact, is not an exception: "It has . . . been shown that during the sixteenth century books . . . on the New World were relatively few in comparison with those on Asia Minor and the Orient" (Hay 99).

Despite Machiavelli's silence, Columbus's return from the Americas would, in the end, spur a novel interest in the self-theorization of Europe. Reshaping the whole European notion of space, the existence of America "shattered at a blow traditional geography and especially the traditional geography of religion" (Hay 99) that so far had divided the world into three continents; it "forced a redefinition of Europe and its place on the globe" (Mignolo, *Renaissance* 264). Paul Hazard adds:

> Of all the lessons derived from the idea of space, perhaps the latest had to do with relativity. Perspectives changed. Concepts which had occupied the lofty sphere of the transcendental were brought down to the level of things governed by circumstance . . . . Practices deemed to be based on reason were found to be mere matters of custom, and, inversely, certain habits which, at a distance, had appeared preposterous and absurd, took on an apparently logical aspect once they were examined in the light of their origin and local circumstances. (Hazard, *European Mind* 11; see also Dupront)

A process of Occidentalization—which had begun, if not with the Persian Wars, then at least when "Christendom" had separated from eastern orthodoxy—reached the final stage when "Europe began to look West to build an extension of [its] own destiny" (Mignolo, *Renaissance* 325). Europe was moving further from the Mediterranean; now, Europe *was* the West, and western was its future. The new allegorical world maps, such as Nicholas Visscher's 1658 "Orbis terrarum," personified the four continents in the corners of the map and earnestly attested this Occidentalization of Europe: "In a culture with alphabetic writing, where conventions have established that reading proceeds from left to right and from top to bottom, a hierarchy for a meaningful distribution of objects on the space of the page has also been established. The places where the four continents were located are highly significant, reinforcing the meaning already expressed by clothing and sitting positions. Europe, of course, is at the upper left corner" (Mignolo, *Renaissance* 279).

While becoming the West, Europe, which in the т-о map had usually (but not necessarily) occupied the *lower* left corner, was also moving up north. And, as if this were not enough, it was becoming *center* too: in 1569, the Flemish cartographer Gerhard Mercator produced what would soon become the most widely used cartographic projection of the world (now spherical again) on a plane surface. In the attempt to represent compass directions (useful for commercial navigation) as straight lines, Mercator's projection had to distort proportions: and it may not be mere chance that, centering between Paris and London, such distortion "shows . . . Europe . . . as relatively large with respect to most of the colonized nations" (Turnbull 7).

This frenetic activity of mapmaking, which both the cheaper printing process and the "discovery" of America had ushered in, must have had some considerable effect on European minds: first, it canonized, once and for all, a *definite* position of Europe in the world—west, center, and north—all at the same time.[28] Moreover, Columbus's deed (like Vespucci's, Magellan's, Drachs's, and even Cortez's) could be easily read as a sign of Europe's superiority—the "smallest continent" on earth, yet capable of conquering, "with its skills and courage," all others (Louis Moreri, qtd. in Céard 63).[29] Mapmaking, in this sense was only asked to represent such superiority in visual ways, and to compensate for relative smallness with the centering on Europe in Mercator's projection.

Mapmaking was also instrumental in personifying Europe again, long after the myth of Europa had downed, as a type, a character, and a genius loci. Represented as a woman-queen, Europe graciously accepts, in a condescending version of colonial exploitation, the gifts of the other continents. Here is Walter Mignolo describing Visscher's personifications of the four continents on the edges of a 1636 "Orbis geographica":

> Europe and Asia are represented by well-dressed ladies, while Africa and
> America are represented by seminaked women. Comparing the represen-

tation to that of Asia, a difference emerges in position. Europe is sitting on the ground, while Asia is sitting on a camel. Thus, while Asia is similar to Europe in that both are well-dressed ladies, they differ in the surface on which they are sitting. However, Asia is similar to America, since both these seminaked women are sitting on an armadillo and the crocodile, respectively. Asia, because she is well dressed, resembles Europe, while she also resembles Africa and America because she is sitting on an animal. (*Renaissance* 273)

And here, as a supplement, is Denys Hay describing, in more general terms, the typical European iconology of the four continents between 1577 (the anonymous *Habitus praecipuorum populorum*) and 1611 (Cesare Ripa's *Iconologia*): "Europa—crowned, cuirassed, holding a scepter and an orb, with weapons, scientific instruments, a palette, books and Christian symbols; Asia—garlanded and richly dressed, holding an incense-burner, and supported by camels and monkeys; Africa—naked, with elephants and lions, snakes and palms, and often with the sun's rays like a halo on the head; America—naked, with a feathered head-dress, holding a bow and arrow" (104). Personifying Europe was an immensely powerful rhetorical procedure of definition and selection: at the most explicit level, such personification founded the identity/sameness of Europe and its peoples against that of other continents. It did so by fashioning an identity that was highly appealing to the Europeans of the time: Europe was not the pillager of tribal communities or the continent torn by wars of religion and dynastic succession, but, rather, represented elegance, science, culture, Christian ethos, and, in a word, civility. Sure, it wore the insignia of the warrior, but how else could it face the animal threat of Asia or the plain savagery of Africa and America? The confrontation of civilization and savagery, as often remarked, generated two apparently contrasting paradigms of the "European man's discovery of himself as . . . a moral being" (Elliott 159). On the one hand, the prevailing European position was the one taken by François Ranchin in his *History of the World* (1637). For Ranchin, savagery ought to be civilized by Europe—and Europe, accomplishing this most pious mission that admittedly brought back some gold, was not pilfering America's wealth, since robbery was said to presuppose property, and property civilization (qtd. in Céard 58). A "Europeanization of the world" (Cocks 16) was a moral mission that meant, among other things, an education of the savage into the bourgeois ethics of property. The other position was

Montaigne's critique of European civilization (the thirtieth of the *Essais* titled "Cannibals," 1588), or Bartolomé de Las Casas's accusation of Cortez's (*Brevísima relación de la destrucción de las Indias*, 1552), in the name of a purer "good savage." Despite obvious differences, both positions do assume a European superiority in relation to the savage: European superiority is argued explicitly in the case of Ranchin's civilizing mission—some kind of "white man's burden" that Europe (and later the West) ought to carry in order to bring social, cultural, and moral development to all corners of the world; and the same superiority is assumed implicitly in the case of Montaigne and Las Casas, as "denunciation of one's faults becomes intellectual gymnastics [for strengthening and bettering the image of Europe], not recognition of the superiority of the other" (Dupront 51).

Ranchin's thesis of a fundamental coincidence of civilization and property, and of both with Europe, will be put (see chapter 2) in the service of the theorization of Europe as the place of true wealth—that is, private property—different from the apparent or "unrealized" wealth typical of the "vacant places of America" (Locke 5:120). Its most immediate effect, however, was to open for Europe one of the major sources of its primitive accumulation (and, therefore, of its capitalistic modernization): colonial plunder.[30]

Personifications of Europe, finally, gave an immediate, conceptual image of unity symbolized by the harmony of the body in all its parts. We can find such symbol neatly represented in Sebastian Münster's famous *Cosmographia universalis* (1544), which represents Europe as a woman with Spain as its head (France and England have not yet displaced her from hegemonic position). Unity, in turn, meant the implicit institution of some standards of Europeanness: if Europe was a person, then it had, like a person, one character, one way of life, one "genius," and one mode of conduct.[31] This was the duck stage of the theorizations of Europe: a place had to walk like Europe, look like Europe, and quack like Europe in order to *be* Europe. What Europe had to look like, in turn, was sufficiently summarized in the iconology of Europe—"a scepter and an orb, with weapons, scientific instruments, a palette, books and Christian symbols." Any deviation from this standard, abroad but also within Europe itself, was to be considered as nothing less than a defect of Europeanness: could the ugly-duckling Turks without Christian symbols ever be Europeans for Montesquieu (chapter 2)? Could eighteenth-century Spain (chapter 3), alleged to be behind by now in both scientific instruments and books, be considered fully European? And would Sicily, eternal colony without a scepter (chapter 5), ever claim to be a part of Europe? 1492, the year of the "discovery," is, then, also the year of Europe's first planned ethnic cleansing, of her cohering into *one* character: the fall of Grenada, with the ensuing conversion or expulsion of Jews and Moors ordered by bishop Francisco Jiménez de Cisneros in that year, points already to the disturbing fantasies of one "'pure' European identity" (Ali 37).

From this process of differentiation, personification, and identification, a sclerotic and one-way consciousness of Europe—both in its geographic and in its moral and political sense—was cementing between the sixteenth and the seventeenth centuries. England, in the meantime, was rising as a major player in European affairs. The Portuguese state (which had begun European expansion overseas in 1415 with the seizure of the Muslim port of Ceuta, followed by Madeira in 1420, Mauritania in 1448, and the Congo River in 1482), and the Spanish crown (which had financed Columbus in 1492) were quickly declining, suffocated by debts contracted with foreign merchants to cover the military and commercial costs of their colonies overseas. A more entrepreneurial class of merchants, instead, had begun British expansion overseas: its exploitation of the colonies profited the state enough cash in taxation to grant, in turn, sufficient military power to consolidate possession, protect the routes from pirates, and monopolize commerce with the Orient. Once British expansion was in motion, the system kept reproducing and amplifying itself: exploitation of the colonies' riches and labor power kept generating new wealth; exploitation of the colonies' preexisting ethnic, caste, or tribal divisions kept providing the low-cost bureaucratic and military apparatuses for the control of the territories. Marginal to Europe in terms of both geography and demography, England soon became not only a visible part of Europe but its antonomasia. For the explorer of Francis Bacon's *New Atlantis*, therefore, it was only natural to compare Atlantis's food not simply to England's but to "any collegiate diet that I have known in Europe" (107); to desire to "see Europe" in the moment of despair (108); or to speak comfortably of "we in Europe" (113). Also, William Shakespeare's Sebastian, in *The Tempest*, could confidently talk of "our Europe" (act 2, scene 1, verse 103). Europe was England, and the other way around.

Even outside of England, Europe was in everyone's mind—first of all, after the obsession with space that the "discovery" had entailed as a precise geographic place on the map. Rabelais's *Gargantua* (1534), comforting cuckolded Panurge with a little lesson in geography, goes to show what sharp interest in cartographic matters the man of the Renaissance, cuckold or not, must have had: "Thy beard, with its hues of grey, white, yellowish, and black, hath to my thinking the resemblance of a world-map. Look, look here. Here's Asia. There are Tigris and Euphrates. Africa's at this juncture. And here is the mountain of the Moon. See the fenny march of Nile? On this side lies Europe" (438). *Don Quixote* (1605–15) echoes such interest in geography while advancing the author's classicist criticism of the kind of modern "comedies that would start one day in Europe, continue with a second day in Asia, and a third in Africa; and if there were a fourth day, it would be in America, so all four parts of the world would be covered" (Cervantes Saavedra 1.358). Ironies apart, Don Quixote had an assured vision of a wholeness of Europe (*toda la Europa*) (Cervantes Saavedra 1.156)—an idea of wholesomeness and unity that would be taken up, in turn, by the "whole Europe" (*Europa toda*) of the Portuguese poet Luís Vaz de Camões, enthused to see Lusitania at the head of this unity:[32]

> Eis aqui, quase cume da cabeça
> De Europa toda, o Reino Lusitano,
> Onde a terra se acaba e o mar começa,
> E onde Febo repousa no Oceano.
> [Lusitania is here,
> almost like the head of the whole Europe,
> where the earth ends and the sea begins,
> and where Phoebus rests in the Ocean.] (54)

While echoes of the "false kidnapper of Europe" (Góngora y Argote 63) would return in the mythologizing of Góngorismo and baroque theater alike, it was images of Europe's unity that prevailed since the sixteenth century. John Donne, most dramatically, wrote in the *Devotions* (1631): "No man is an island, entire of itself; every man is a piece of the continent, a part of the main. If a clod be washed away by the sea, Europe is the less" (126). Even the inhabitants of the Low Countries, who since the technical introduction of windmills with rotating turrets, circa 1550, had managed to drain their lands to new levels of security and prosperity, had combined ideals of independence (from the Hapsburg family) with ideas of European wholesomeness. Erasmus of Rotterdam, in the *Consultatio de bello Turcis inferendo* (1643), reestablished the need for European military unity vis-à-vis the despotic Turk—and added, with a wink to the nascent economy of capital (what Blom calls "commercial republicanism"), that another difference between "us" and the east had now to be noticed: "European wealth" (qtd. in Hay 106). In fact, if by European wealth one understands the nascent economy of capital, the emergence (quite literally!) of the Low Countries defined Europe as an ethic of capitalism opposed not only to the east but also to the south, and to Spain in particular.[33]

Perhaps more exemplary of the rehabilitation of the notion of Europe around the Renaissance was Ludovico Ariosto, whose *Orlando furioso* (1516–32) secularized and Europeanized those very women, knights, armies, and loves that the chanson de geste had kept instead under the banner of Christianity. A geographic consciousness of Europe animates the travels and adventurous moves of Ariosto's characters. In canto 4, stanza 45, Atlas sends a hippogriff to Roger to help him flee Europe ("perché d'Europa con questa arte il toglia"). Roger flies on his winged horse, and eventually "lasciato avea di gran spazio distante / tutta l'Europa" (he left all Europe far behind) (Ariosto 6.17). What constituted "all Europe" seemed, in spite of an ironic tone, a certainty for Ariosto: Russia was the border, the threshold separating the "continents" of Europe and Asia.[34] A bird's eye view of Europe's border could then be precisely mapped out when Roger "giunse alle parti di Sarmazia: e quando / fu dove Asia da Europa si divide, / Russi e Pruteni e la Pomeria vide" (he made it to Sarmatia [between the Vistula river and the Caspian Sea]; / and once he got where Asia and Europe separate, / he saw Russia, Pruteni, and Pomeria [the Baltic region]) (10.71).

More than a geographic designation, however, Ariosto's Europe was a prosopopoeia: "Europe is in arms [against the Moor], and looks forward for the battle" (Ariosto 5.99). As a persona, her alter ego is the "cruel Saracen" (*Saracin crudele*, 14.47 and 18.10); the "uncanny Saracen" (*Saracin bizzarro*, 18.36); the "haughty Saracen" (*Saracin superbo*, 24.68 and 35.41); and, last but not least, the "rascal Saracen" (*Saracin ribaldo*, 26.59). Nothing new, one might say, under the skies of Europe: Ariosto's was the old antithesis of east and west, of Christianity and Islam. The Christian age of the *Chanson de Roland*, however, was clearly over, and secular Europe had become the limit and interpellation of a *cultural* community.

So much insistence on European unity, in truth, only veiled the reality of profound conflicts that traversed and fragmented the region. The Hundred Years War (1337–1453)—which had nothing to do with any eastern menace but rather with inter-European religious, dynastic, territorial, and commercial conflicts—was still fresh in Europe's memory. A new nationalist spirit seemed to have possessed the continent, to the point that *Christian* Europe, too, was now divided: the Gallican church in France, the Anglican one in England, the Teutonic churches in Germany, all of which followed different flavors from place to place according to one "Germanic liberty" or another. More important still, Protestantism—Lutherans in Germany and Scandinavia, Episcopalians in England, Zwingli's Reformers in Switzerland, and Calvinists between Geneva and Edinburgh—had divided Europe once more after the break of Byzantium. As the Orthodox Church had split Europe between east and west, Protestantism was now parting Europe between the reformed churches of the north and the Roman Catholic ones of the south. The Catholic south took, in Protestant eschatology, the place of antithesis once assigned to the Muslim of the east:

> Eschatology had been used in anti-Islamic polemic since the Middle Ages, but during the Reformation, it became widely prominent among both theologians and preachers. With its emphasis on the imminent return of Jesus, eschatology enabled communities within the Reformation movement to affirm their unique role in the fulfillment of God's design in history—when God would raise His elect to glory and destroy their enemies. Particularly in the exegesis of Martin Luther, the figure of the Turk became associated with the Papal enemy of God—both of whom were identified with the "Little horn" in the Book of Daniel and the "Beast" in Revelation. For Luther, the eschatological kingdom of Christ was to prevail after the destruction of the Catholic and the "Mahometan" adversaries. (Matar 153)

With the Reformation, a latitudinal crisis "between an increasingly wealthy protestant North and an increasingly impoverished Catholic South" (Pagden, introduction 13) completed the latitudinal fracture of Europe, shifting its center of influence away from the Mediterranean. From this crisis, according to some, would be born "the Spirit of modern Europe" (Ritter 15).[35]

That spirit, however, was a restless one. Neither the foundation of the Jesuit Order in 1540 (see chapter 3), nor the spread of this "spiritual militia" in the service of the Roman Church in the four corners of the continent (and the known world) served to pacify such religious zeal. France was the very eye of its storm: from 1559 to 1598, Paris was bloodied by incessant wars of religion. The edict of Nantes, signed by the French king Henry IV in 1598 to grant freedom of religion within his territory, only partially diminished the tensions between Protestant Huguenot and Roman Catholics, which flared up again in 1685 when Louis XIV revoked the edict of tolerance. Also Northern Italy, Central Europe, and Germany were troubled, since 1618, by the Thirty Years' War fueled by the religious controversies between Catholics and Protestants. It was enough to make the likes of Gottfried Wilhelm von Leibniz nostalgic of the lost Carolingian unity, and eager to protect the spoils of the Holy Roman Empire—the German Reich coinciding with the novel notion of "Mitteleuropa"—not only from the Turks of the Orient but also from the Catholics of the South (Baruzi 28; Le Rider 10). England, for its part, had finished a civil war (1642—49) with the spectacular execution of its king. And if religious controversies and regicides were not enough, other imperial and dynastic wars were flaring up all over: the Franco-Spanish wars (1515–1713); the Anglo-Dutch wars (1641–74); the eight Franco-British wars (1689–1815); the Swedish expansionist movements for a Scandinavian empire. This was the background in which Thomas Hobbes, perhaps unsurprisingly, started looking "in the nature of man, [to] find three principall causes of quarrel" (185).

Apart from some vague reference in *Leviathan* (Hobbes 684 and 685), however, Thomas Hobbes's concern hardly centered around Europe: what really mattered was the legitimacy of sovereignty—divine right, original consent, or popular representation—in "these parts of Europe" (392), in England, that is. Less than ten years after the *Leviathan*, Europe mattered quite a lot, instead, to Maximilien de Béthune, the Duke of Sully and a high minister of the just assassinated King Henry IV of France. In the generalized European state of warfare he saw around, Sully managed to bring discussions about Europe to an entirely new level when, in the thirtieth book of his *Oeconomies royales* (1662), he tried to revive the assassinated king's "grand design." The idea was that of bringing all warring factions together by creating nothing less than a united Europe—or, in Sully's words, "of bringing the whole of Europe together as a family" (De Béthune 77). Such a family, which Sully unsurprisingly believed ought to be paternalistically fathered by France, was to create nothing less than a "union" (87), a "general counsel of Europe" (88), and a "confederation" (90).[36] What else could anyone want in a Europe that was, slowly but surely, becoming *caput mundi*, the leader of the world, and expanding its empires in the whole known world? "No, the French have nothing else to desire, if not that the heavens give them pious, good, and wise kings; and that those kings will use all their power to keep Europe in peace" (74). After Sully, the themes of Europe's more or less utopist union for the sake of perpetual peace—which, beyond utopia, answered well to the mercantilist need of breaking down local barriers to trade (Cocks 17)—was taken up by William Penn ("Essay towards the Present and Future Peace of Europe," 1693), the Abbé de Saint Pierre ("Projet de paix perpétuelle en Europe," 1712), Gottfried Wilhelm von Leibniz ("Observations sur le projet de paix perpétuelle en Europe," 1714), Jean-Jacques Rousseau ("Jugement sur la paix perpétuelle," 1756), and Immanuel Kant ("Zum ewigen Frieden," 1795), among others.[37]

Just as instrumental for a self-consciousness of Europe were all the real and fictional encounters with often exoticized other cultures that now included, along with the usual Arabs, also Persians, Americans, Indians, and, increasingly, the Chinese.[38] The growth of an exotic literature from the late seventeenth century is certainly a sign of the times, but it is also a sign of the kind of ideal *place* that Europe was starting to mean. *Les six voyages* of J. B. Tavernier (1676) in Persia, the *New Voyage* (1697) of the buccaneer William Dampier, the *History of Japan* (1727) by Engelbert Kaempfer, the *Travels in Arabia* of J. L. Burckhardt; and then Daniel Defoe's *Robinson Crusoe* (1719) and Jonathan Swift's *Gulliver's Travels* (1726)—as critical of Europe as these texts could sometimes be, they all proceeded from some shared assumption of what Europe, despite its local differences, actually meant: culture versus nature, society versus kinship, dressed versus naked, cooked versus raw, civilization versus naivety. In sum, Mr. Lemuel Gulliver "was an Englishman" (Swift 180), and, as such, "the scourge of France" (127). But he was also, despite such contrasts, profoundly European in culture: "I spoke," he says, "High and Low Dutch, Latin, French, Spanish, Italian, and Lingua Franca" (19). He was European in "infernal habits" too: "Yahoo as I am, it is well known through all Houyhnhnmland, that, by the instructions and example of my illustrious master, I was able in the compass of two years (although I confess with the utmost difficulty) to remove that infernal habit of lying, shuffling, deceiving, and equivocating, so deeply rooted in the very souls of all my species; especially the Europeans" (vi).

In the literature of perpetual peace, as well as in the exotic one, a concept of Europe, infernal or heavenly, starts crystallizing to the point of becoming prescriptive and didactic: Europe is in need of unity, and, after all, differences apart, it *is* one if compared to any exoticized place. No need to beat this dead horse since a few authoritative quotes may indeed suffice: "In this literature, the concept of Europe is ultimately defined" (Chabod 85); through this literature, "Europe looked as if it had taken permanent shape" (Hazard, *European Mind* 53); and so, "in the course of the seventeenth century the processes which had led to this result were finally brought to a conclusion. By the beginning of the eighteenth century it is in terms of Europe that Europeans view the world" (Hay 117). Which is to say: by the early eighteenth century, Europe is already "made" (Treasure), "discovered" (Hale), "invented" (Pagden, "Europe" 70), "germinated" (Mikkeli 61), and one.

Toward a Modern Europe

> To recognize the importance of European unity hardly
> means that someone has to suffer passively the ways and
> methods through which such unity is constructed.
> —FRANCO CASSANO, *Modernizzare stanca*

> Expanded from North to South. . . .
> —WILLIAM BLAKE, *Europe: A Prophecy*

It is then at this point that canonical histories of the idea of Europe stop, short of an *interruptus*, their otherwise turgid narratives: for Denys Hay, by the beginning of the eighteenth century Europe has "emerged," is well formed, and *rien ne va plus*; for Heikki Mikkeli, who sees postwar theories of European unities and European federations as a completion of an otherwise unfinished project of the Enlightenment, it is "towards the beginning of the eighteenth century [that] a feeling of belonging together prevailing among the European intellectuals . . . had been growing stronger and stronger" (60); and for Federico Chabod, what happens next is but a *disappearing* of Europe, its retreat "in the second half of the eighteenth century . . . with the affirmation of the idea of nation" (122)— an affirmation, namely, which culminates in National Socialism and against which Chabod tries to resurrect the idea of Europe.

But it is exactly from this point that I need to start my real story. Because, first of all, it would be wrong to assume that this Europe, which has formed by the eighteenth century through confrontations with exotic Others and fantasies of perpetual peace, was in fact an amiable affair. The sort of perpetual peace that Europe could insure for Sully, we should not forget, was predicated on the hegemony of France. A *True-Born Englishman*, for one, would hardly agree to being subaltern to a country "where mankind lives in haste, and thrives by chance. A dancing nation, fickle and untrue" (Defoe). (Nor did the Englishman love Spain, "President of Hell"; or Italy, "where Blood ferments in Rapes and Sodomy").

The idea that a sense of nationalism would begin only in the late eighteenth century, and immediately ruin a sense of beautiful and peaceable Europeanness, sounds, frankly, a little disingenuous. A modicum of ephemeral peace in Europe was obtained, whenever it was, through the never-theorized but ordinarily practiced doctrine of the balance of power. According to it, any change in one nation's power constituted a potential threat to all others: not only colonial expansions but also domestic territorial partitions and distributions had to be regulated by internationally negotiated treaties—Utrecht in 1713, Vienna in 1738, Aix-la-Chapelle in 1748, and Paris in 1763—that prevented one power from becoming preponderant. Such a balance of power obviously mirrored preexisting conditions of supremacy: risen and rising empires—France, England, the Dutch—divided territories overseas and within Europe between themselves. Weaker territories—like the Italian ones discussed in chapter 5—were treated as bargaining chips exchanged by the big nations in a debonair "spirit of cheerful cynicism" (Davies 582). Moreover, the context in which this eighteenth-century Europe "emerges" is one in which the previous religious divide between a (Protestant) north and a (Catholic) south is doubling into more fundamental contrasts—economic, cultural, political—between north and south.

With such a state of affairs, it would be quite surprising if the concept of Europe that emerged in the eighteenth century did not also mirror, and legitimate, the same division of power. Since the fulcrum of the seventeenth-century balance of power, the center of "the intellectual hegemony of Europe" (Hazard, *European Mind* 55), and "far and away Europe's greatest power" (Davies 579) was certainly France, it would be quite surprising if the "Europe" that Mikkeli, Hay, and Chabod accept as Europe were not, in fact, what Rougemont with less scruples claims as "a French Europe" (143). Moreover, it would be equally surprising if the same eighteenth-century Europe, which the scholarly *doxa* insists to see as fundamental for any new one, would not carry within itself the germ of a north-south divide: after all, as Heikkii Mikkeli concedes, "by 1700 the term 'Europe' was, *especially in the political thinking of the Protestants, in regular use*" (60; emphasis mine). Eighteenth-century Europe, in short, is a French theory of Europe, and one expanding from north to south—privileging the former and marginalizing the latter.

French and northbound Europe begins to be theorized through a French theoretical quarrel between the ancients and the moderns: "The Past abandoned; the Present enthroned in its place!" (Hazard, *European Mind* 30).

> In France, several ideological conflicts conjoined to produce a climate in which attitudes to the past became highly politicized and dangerous indicators. France was evolving rapidly into a centralized state, for which French apologists sought a cultural history which revolved neither around Rome nor the Roman conquest. Secular pressure to invent a Gallican culture was compounded by pressures for a Gallican Catholicism with greater autonomy from Rome. And these conflicts were minor compared with the tensions building in France between sympathizers and opponents of the German Reformers. Finally, the Wars of Religion were incited by a feuding nobility, whose arguments over monarchical succession and the balance of power between king and nobility were naturally backed up by competing histories of the "true" French constitution. . . . The concern of some of the French noblesse de robe with a proper, critical practice of history reflects their attempts to find new, sure and useful ways to legitimate French institutions. (Pumfrey, Rossi, and Slawinski 62)

To be precise, French Europe begins not with a *dismissal* of history—Cartesian submission of history to transhistorical reason; Jansenist submission of history to morality; and the *philosophes'* submission of history to the superior relevance of the present. It begins, rather, with a *retheorization* of history that, following Paul Hazard, we can date to the year 1668, when Charles de Saint-Évremond *Réflexions sur le divers génie du peuple romaine* first appeared in print. From its very outset, Saint-Évremond's celebration of modernity relies on a clear philosophy of history: humankind is endlessly perfectible, and history is the story of its endless progress. Antiquity, accordingly, is now assigned the unflattering task of representing nothing more than backwardness. All this has at least one consequence: the place of authority once assigned to Rome and Greece as the perfect models of Europe is now questioned in the name of more recent perfections that Saint-Évremond can hardly find in the Greco-Roman Mediterranean. If Europe has any model at all, it is not the foundation of Rome but that of the French Academy: "It would appear, in short, that the powers who have the moulding of our destinies had then no other concern than the founding of the city of Rome. . . . I hate admiring references which repose on mere fables" (qtd. in Hazard, *European Mind* 38).

What about the Greeks? Were *they* not viable models in the formation of a modern European culture? Not so for another Frenchman, Bernard Le Bovier de Fontenelle, who, in the *Digression sur les anciens et les modernes* (1688), dismissed the Greeks as childish pranksters, good only at spreading bogus fables from which modern Europe should promptly be disabused:

> As children, we are taught so much about Greek myths, and get so accustomed to them that when we grow up we do not recognise how extravagant they really are; but if we could disabuse our minds of our ingrained idea of them, if we could see them with fresh eyes, we should realize with amazement that what is called a nation's early history is in reality nothing but a phantasmagoria, a string of childish tales. Can it really be, we ask ourselves, that such things were ever given out as truth? If those who passed them on did not believe them, what was their motive for deceiving us? (qtd. in Hazard, *European Mind* 38)

For Fontanelle, a European "quality of mind or genius" is the achievement of a more recent age. Not only is Europe better than Asia, Africa, and America. *Modern* Europe is, also, better than the ancient one. Modern Europe, moreover, begins exactly in those Middle Ages that southern humanists had condemned as periods of barbarity and decay, and which the new French historians now praised by "inventing complex Frankish and Gallic societies" (Pumfrey, Rossi, and Slawinski 61) that resisted Roman conquest, gloriously defeated Rome, and, in so doing—as we will see very clearly with Montesquieu—laid the foundations for modern Europe to grow. If *modern* history should be rewritten and retheorized, then, it is because the "mere fables" of the Romans and the "childish tales" of the Greeks can hardly account for the luminous present in which France first, and, second, the whole northern world of Europe, stand today. To understand that present, a new history should now be devised (see Pisano).[39]

What we have, then, codified already in Jacques-Bénigne Bossuet's

Discours sur l'histoire universelle (1681), is a new theory of history understood not as a recovery of the past, but as metaphysics—a *universal*
history, that is, shaped as a chronology and a teleology of great epochs
carrying a precise meaning in the great scheme of things. At the heart of
their meaning, and at the end of these histories, lay a new, modern
theory of Europe: its end was nothing else than the formation of a theory
not of the universe, but of "what Europe is in the universe" (Bossuet 4).[40]
And, within this Eurocentric theory, there was a supplementary one, one
concerned not with the centrality of Rome or Greece in any theory of
Europe, but with "what Paris and the Ile de France mean within Europe"
(4).

Much of what passes today as modern Europe begins—this is the
contention of the present book—from this theorization of history. From
it begins, for instance, a theory of Europe as the end of history claimed,
before Hegel (chapter 4), already by Montesquieu (chapter 2) and John
Locke, who saw America arrested in history, representing, as it were,
"still a pattern of the first ages of . . . Europe" (5:151). *Progress, teleology,*
and *manifest destinies*—these are the key terms of the history of univer-
salized Europe that only begins in the eighteenth century. Yet in this
history, it is no longer the confrontation with the exotic Other (the
Persian, the Muslim, the American savage, and so on) that interests the
theorists of Europe, but rather a dialectical confrontation of Europe with
itself, with its own internal Other. History, so to speak, unfolds as a
geography pitting a past of Europe—the Greek and Roman south—
against its most luminous and giddy present—what Paul Hazard calls
"the light from the North" (*European Mind* 53–59).

Europe (in Theory) starts from this crisis of north and south, from
where theories of Europe have typically ended. Its objective, as my epigraph suggests, is not to create a demonstrable theory of Europe and
patch the crisis with viable hypotheses, but rather to study the limits (its
south?) of a theory of Europe that becomes hegemonic with the names
of Charles Louis de Secondat, Baron of La Brède, and of Montesquieu,
around the year 1740. This is not a theory of Europe, but an analysis of
that which, precisely, a theory of Europe has found recurrently impossible "to hypothesize or maintain" (Agamben, *Stanze* xi).

2 Montesquieu's North and South

HISTORY AS A THEORY OF EUROPE

> Is Europe but a category effectuated by Montesquieu's reflection?
> —JEAN GOLDZINK, "Montesquieu et l'Europe"

"The concept of Europe must have first been formed as an antithesis to that which is not Europe" and "the first opposition between Europe and something that is not Europe . . . is . . . Asia"—Federico Chabod's pronouncement, reported in the previous chapter along with Samuel Huntington's and Bernard Lewis's insistence that Europe's cultural identity is fundamentally opposed to Islam and historically formed against its threat, still forms an integral part of today's theories of Europe. According to such theories (summarized by Bugge), Europe is the antithesis of what Jean-Marc Moura calls "the Orient"—a "vague" and "imaginary place" that refers indifferently to *any one* of "three areas of an undefined geography that subsume the notion of the Orient: Asia; the Mediterranean and Islamic territories; and the space of Byzantine Christianity" (14).

Arguably such theories of European identity as the antithesis to the Orient proceed from philosophical theories of identity based on "the opposition of the I and the 'other' by which the I knows itself" (Habermas 145). In other words, since identity is always difficult to establish in isolation, everybody and everything, "including Europe," as Peter Rietbergen writes in *Europe: A Cultural History*, "exists only by virtue of its contrast or its opposite" (xxi). Accordingly, Roger Ballard's "Islam and the Construction of Europe," starting from the assumption that European identity is not "a self-evident fact of nature" and thus impossible to maintain per se, concludes that only "the disjunction between Christianity and Islam" (20) and the opposition between the two can give Europe the possibility to know itself as "I" (against "them"). Similarly, François Hartog locates the Greek foundations of the idea of Europe in the Persian Wars: "The Persian Wars gave a meaning [to Europe], by providing it with an antithetical figure: that of the Persian" (20). Of the same opinion is Michel Foucault: "In the universality of Western *ratio* there is one dividing line, which is the Orient" (*Histoire de la folie* iv). Massimo Cacciari reaches the same conclusion: "[Europe] emerges, first of all, from the contrast between the irreducible archipelago of the [Greek] *póleis* . . . and the powerful kingdom of the [Persians]" (*Geo-filosofia* 15). If one adds to all this Silvio Berlusconi's distinction between free Europe and enslaved Islam, Oriana Fallaci's discrimination between Western culture and Eastern barbarity, and the endless EU discussions about the Europeanness or non-Europeanness of "Asiatic" Turkey—well, you get the point.

Before I hear *Eurocentric*, let me notice that even scholars from a less Europeanist school than the ones just cited seem to take the figural antithesis Europe-Asia for granted. Once again, the starting assumption (stated this time by Edward Said in *Orientalism*) is that "the construction of identity . . . involves establishing opposites and 'others'" (45); ergo, Europe, in order to imagine and theorize its own identity, has "to polarize the distinction" (46) between Western and Oriental, European and Arab, or us and them: in sum, "European culture gained in strength and identity by setting itself off against the Orient" (3). Ditto for Abdel Malek, who accuses Europe of constituting itself as a subject by constructing the Orient as its own demonic object. or negative Other (107).

Disjunction, contrast, contraposition, opposition, antithesis, polarization: these are the figures that crop up, since Chabod, in reflections on Europe. The consensus is such that one can hardly resist the temptation of being a bit skeptical about all of this. The problem is that this rhetorical paradigm's canonical status seems to prevent us from seeing the question of Europe's self-formation in any other thinkable way. The present chapter intends, then, to test one hypothesis, namely, that the Europe-versus-Orient paradigm may be overlooking a supplementary and modern genesis of Europe. In the same eighteenth century in which the idea of Europe seems to solidify, and in which Orientalism, as Said has discussed, is established as an academic discipline, Europe starts conceiving a *new* logic for self-definition that renders the Other superfluous. This new logic, which grows under the eighteenth-century economic imperative of Europe's self-reliance (Bassand), and which culminates in Hegel's "dialectic of the same" (Descombes), forms an integral part of the much discussed European "dream of a full . . . clos[ure] of history: the suppression of contradiction and difference" (Derrida,

Grammatology 115): it coincides with Eurocentrism, in other words, understood as the assumption "that one can explain Europe without looking at [the rest of the world]" (Jubran 233). Around the eighteenth century there seems to arise a new desire, within European theory, to concoct an idea of Europe as "complete knowledge of itself" (Berthold-Bond 15). No Other is needed in such a novel fable of identity: exotic difference is, instead, "occluded" (Dussel, "Eurocentrism" 65), translated, and replaced by one contained within Europe itself.

In order for European theory to dispense of the absolute Other, a different rhetoric of antithesis between what Europe is (identity) and what it is not (difference) must, nonetheless, be organized. Difference has to be translated from the radical Other onto a negative part, or moment, of the European self. In *Orientalism*, Edward Said already alluded to such a translation when he mentioned European theory's "domestication" (4) and "encompassing" (65) of the Oriental other. Said's interpreters have usually taken this to mean that Orientalism as an academic discipline domesticated the otherwise untamable Orient to European knowledge and colonial designs. It seems to me, however, that Said was hinting at a *supplementary* kind of domestication when he suggested, for example—admittedly en passant—that "the Oriental was linked [by European anthropology] to elements in Western society (delinquents, the insane, women, the poor)" (207). If such "elements of Western society" were made to represent the same characteristics as the Orient, it can then be argued that one was the translation of the other: Europe, in the context described by Said, could fathom its identity not only by opposing itself to the Orient but by matching itself against those *internal* elements of Western society.

What needs to be added to Said's hint is that these deviant elements of Western society are not only molded in the image of the Oriental but, also, geographically determined: the deviant, the internal Other of Europe, *is* a southerner (see Petraccone). As Italy had been consistently represented in the European thought of the eighteenth and nineteenth centuries as Europe's backward south (Moe 13–36), it is not surprising to see that Italy soon became the hotbed for more or less scientific discussions trying to distinguish, at least, a good and European Italy—a northern one—from a bad and barbaric one—the south. If Orientalism had canonized the Oriental as "lethargic" (Said, *Orientalism* 39) and led by a "need for vengeance that overrides everything" (49), Cesare Lombroso, the patriotic anthropologist from the northern Italian city of Verona, observed southern Calabria in 1862 as a "barbaric" place where "sloth was hypostatized as merit, vengefulness as system" (89). Just as Orientalism had canonized the Orient as a place of backwardness representing "a distant European past" (Said, *Orientalism* 85) and the Oriental as an epiphany of "primitiveness . . . [that] had not been subject to the ordinary processes of history" (230), so Lombroso's southerner served as the example of an "atavist primitiveness . . . the effect of a hindered development, in the collective moral sense, resulting in the permanence of a barbaric stage" (514).

Lombroso had made the discovery of southern "atavism" in 1870, when he had examined the cranium of Giuseppe Vilella, a Calabrese peasant and brigand by race—no matter that the authorities had always missed the chance to suspect him of anything.[1]

Alfredo Niceforo, a Sicilian member of the Roman Anthropological Society and of the Italian Society of Geography, could not but internalize the theory and confirm: the south "has been atrophied on the path to civilization and has conserved moral ideas of primitive societies; men thus present an individual psychic atavism, and the entire region shows forms of social atavism" (*Delinquenza* 41). Niceforo could then distinguish within Italy itself between a properly "European" and a "Mediterranean" race. The south was a deficiency of Europeanness; put differently, it was its past. Niceforo's reviewer for the daily *Il Secolo* asked, then, rhetorically: "Isn't it like in a nightmare? Isn't it shocking to read that habits typical of Arab tribes before Mohammed are still alive today in some regions of Italy? Isn't it shocking to find that such behavior is enacted not by Tuaregs and Bedouins, but by Italian citizens?" (qtd. in Petraccone 164).[2]

The atavism of the south—a latitude blocked "within ideas and sentiments that belong to the European civilization of the past" (Niceforo, *Italia* 38)—was thus largely translated by the anthropology of Lombroso and his descendants from the original texts of Orientalism: in both scientific and popular literature (see Dickie 100–119), the Orient *was* the south, and Europe's Other was to be found, as in a nightmare, within Europe's own borders, The editorial introduction to the first issue of the *Revue de l'Orient*, 1843, had already prepared the context for such translation: "Our Orient comprehends the European countries of the Mediterranean" (Hugo 8). What Italian anthropology could contribute to the *Revue*'s translation was a positivist explanation of such southern difference: "the influence of climate," had determined Lombroso (42);

"northern and southern climate," had agreed the gymnast of criminology Enrico Ferri,[3] because "in the northern climate man's stubborn confrontation with an ungenerous nature forces individuals and generations to an endless intellectual and physical exercise. Hence the development of a robust character, which will make this man less artistic than the pleasure-seeking southerner, but stronger because made of iron" (*Delitti* 48).

Yet neither Orientalism nor anthropology lay at the origin of such a domestication of the antithesis of Europe into Europe's own south. The cultural climate for this reorientation of Europe's identity had already been set in 1737, in a dark laboratory of the rue Margaux, in Bordeaux, France, where the carcass of a sheep was being sacrificed at the altar of Europe's resurgent science of climatology.

The Silence of the Sheep: Climate (in Theory)

> Let your lips, proposing a hypothesis
> Not know about the hand faking the experiment.
> —CZESLAW MILOSZ, "Child of Europe"

It all began when Monsieur le President of the Academy of Bordeaux, Charles Louis de Secondat, the baron of Montesquieu and member of the up-and-coming *noblesse de robe* (nobility attained by office) with something always to prove to an older feudal nobility, "undertook experiments, described in *De l'Esprit des Lois*, on a sheep's tongue under the microscope with the aim of discovering its reactions to changes in temperature" (Shackleton, *Montesquieu* 305–6):

> I have observed the outermost part of a sheep's tongue, where, to the naked eye, it seems covered with papillae . . . I froze the half of this tongue, and, observing it with the naked eye, I found the papillae considerably diminished: even some rows of them were sunk into their sheath. I examined the outermost part with the microscope, and perceived no pyramids. As I defrosted the half of the tongue, the papillae seemed to rise, and under the microscope I could see the glands beginning to reappear. (Montesquieu, *Oeuvres* 2:476)

The episode is considered by Montesquieu's biographer, who does not seem to stomach well the gothic odors of the dissecting room, as an example of the somewhat naive but marginal scientific observations that Montesquieu was undertaking while preparing *De l'esprit des lois*. For Shackleton, Montesquieu's analytic interest in the effects of heat and cold on physical bodies was secondary in his research, and by no means meant to suggest "the paramountcy of climate" (Shackleton, *Montesquieu* 317) as a determining factor of his science of the body politic. No doubt, Shackleton is right. Yet the kind of scientific experiment that Montesquieu was concocting in the rue Margaux went clearly beyond a naive approach to the physical sciences and was to prepare, in fact, the greatest and most disingenuous rhetorical *demonstratio* for the hypothesis of Europe that Montesquieu was at that point working to articulate.

Montesquieu's critical experiment was moved, more than by science, by a singular sociological mysticism: the conviction, in other words, that the tongue of the sheep could speak, through the president's shamanic powers of observation, the whole complexity of social relations in the world. In that tongue, Montesquieu had found the grail, the philosopher's stone—the key to it all. In it was hidden the secret principle that, once revealed, could tell humankind "what gives a specific character to a nation or a certain spirit to one particular individual; what modifies a whole sex and what affects a single man; what forms the genius of societies and the genius of a single person at the same time" (Montesquieu, *Oeuvres* 2:39). The sheep's tongue was a little *système du monde*, a microcosm that contained, in itself, the secret essence of all—a particular case, in other words, that represented a more general and universal law: "I have posed the principles," Montesquieu had announced in the preface to the *Spirit*, "and I have seen the particular case tied with another law, or depending on another, more general law" (*Oeuvres* 2:229).

A law was, in Montesquieu's understanding of the word, a relation (*un rapport*) between things. These relations were humanly perceived, rather than mere facts of nature: "The law, in general, is human reason, insofar as reason governs all the people on earth" (*Oeuvres* 2:237). Social relations, which constitute the positive laws that relate individual bodies to the general political body of a nation, were in turn predetermined by *natural* relations and natural laws: "They [positive laws] must be relative to the *physics* of the country: to the frigid, or hot, or temperate climate" (*Oeuvres* 2:238; original emphasis). In this metatheory of the law, in other words, the relation between physical/climatological realities and political formations was not a casual but a necessary one ("They *must* be relative"). An analysis of social relations had then to begin, necessarily, from an analysis of physical rapports, that is to say, from an analysis of the relationship "between a body in motion and another body" (Montesquieu, *Oeuvres* 2:233). The problem, since at least Galileo Galilei, had been how to make those bodies—"man as a physical being" (Montesquieu, *Oeuvres* 2:234)—communicate their laws, so as to decipher the book of nature, the secret, perhaps divine, language of mute things. What the experiment of the tongue, then, signified for Montesquieu was the possibility of finally giving a tongue to these silent bodies: to have them speak, through the medium of his presidential observations, their otherwise unuttered natural laws that lay at the very basis of any positive ones.

What the tongue spoke to Montesquieu was one of those "beautiful, grand, and simple ideas, quite worthy of the majesty of nature" that the president had always assumed distinguished the findings of "us, the moderns" from the forgettable ones of the ancients (Montesquieu, *Oeuvres* 1:33). Assuming those papillae were the organs of taste through which the sheep (a gourmand one at that) enjoyed her food, Montesquieu could therefore deduce that *all* pleasures, like the particular one of taste, had to be correlated to climate. The colder the temperature, the smaller becomes the papilla—and the lesser is the capacity to taste. The warmer the environment gets, the larger grows the papilla—and so the pleasure of taste reaches its heights: "This observation [of the sheep's tongue] confirms what I have been saying, that in cold countries . . . one has little sensibility to pleasure; in temperate countries, one has more; in warm countries, their sensibility is exquisite. As climates are distinguished by degrees of latitude, we might distinguish them also in some measure by those of sensibility" (Montesquieu, *Oeuvres* 2:476).

What this natural law meant for the establishment of human, positive, and social laws was that "in warm climates," where a sensibility for pleasures is extreme, "despotic power generally prevails" (Montesquieu, *Oeuvres* 2:297). An extreme drive toward pleasure engenders an extreme drive to satisfy it: "More lively passions multiply crimes that will satisfy those same passions" (2:477). Cold climates are climates of cooperation between men: their union is their strength, and the consciousness of their strength makes them courageous. Warm climates, instead, are climates of fear: they engender either abuses or cowardice. In warm climates, therefore, only despotism, the law of the strongest capable of instilling fear in all others, can rule: "One should therefore not be surprised if the cowardice of the peoples of warm climates has almost always made them slaves, whereas the courage of the peoples of cold climates has kept them free. It is an effect that derives from its natural cause" (2:523).

At this point, *pour ainsi dire*, it does not matter if the adequate understanding of societies can be found in the examination of men or in the observation of a sheep's tongue; the conclusion is one and the same: "One can conclude that climate contributes infinitely to modify the spirit" (2:44). Humankind, like the tongue, is one and the same everywhere and under every climate on earth; but heat and cold have different effects on otherwise equal bodies. Cold tightens the pores. All the vigor that remains inside the body produces a "more vigorous" and courageous race of men. Heat, on the contrary, dilates the pores, so that vigor escapes. We have, then, the feeble, cowardly, vengeful, lazy, and passive character unable to fight for his or her freedom that Montesquieu swears to have found in the hot climates: "The heat of the climate may be so excessive as to deprive the body of all vigor and strength. The faintness is therefore communicated to the mind; there is no curiosity, no noble enterprise, no generosity of sentiment; the inclinations are all passive; indolence constitutes the utmost happiness; scarcely any punishment is so severe as mental employment; and slavery is more tolerable than the force and vigor of mind that would be necessary for human conduct" (2:477).

Climatology was certainly not a new theory for Montesquieu (see Shackleton, *Montesquieu* 302–19). Jean Bodin's *La méthode de l'histoire* (1566) and *La république* (1576), which had set forth a theory of the effect of climate on society and government, were among Montesquieu's regularly consulted books. In the "Réflexions sur la monarchie universelle" (1734), climatology had already been mentioned as a providential engine of human history that had saved many times Germans and Gauls from the Roman hordes: "It is very difficult for nations of the South to conquer those of the North, and all Histories prove that. Southern Nations find in the North an unconquerable enemy: climate" (Montesquieu, *Oeuvres* 2:28). The only enemy of the otherwise proud nations of the north remains climate itself: "The Roman historians have constantly observed that the people of the North, almost unconquerable in their countries, were no longer such when they were in warmer countries" (1:1354). Also, in the "Considérations sur les causes de la grandeur des romains et de leur décadence," written in the same year, climate had explained such disparate social "facts" as the Macedonians' military prowess in war (2:94) or the fecundity of Oriental women (2:187).

By the time he had jotted down the preparatory notes for *De l'esprit des lois*, Montesquieu was quite certain that a "temperate climate," as the Aristotelian good middle between extreme heat and excessive cold, was conducive to progress and civilization (Montesquieu, *Oeuvres* 2:1075). Aristotle himself, for his part, had never talked of a *temperate* climate, when, revisiting Hippocrates' climatology in the seventh book of the *Politics*, he had opened the road for Montesquieu's theory of the social implications of temperature: "The nations in cold regions, particularly in Europe, are full of [courage] . . . which is why they continue to be comparatively free . . . . By contrast, those in Asia . . . lack [courage]; which is why they continue to be ruled and enslaved (Aristotle, *Politics* 7.7).

After Aristotle and before Montesquieu, however, the science of climatology had managed to move the commonplace of the courageous nation from an unqualified "cold" region to a more "temperate" zone. Ibn Khaldun, writing around 1377, had presented not the cold, but the temperate zones of the Mediterranean (today's Maghreb, Middle East, and southern Europe) as the most perfect for the constitution of societies. *Europe (in Theory)* discusses the nineteenth-century recuperation of Ibn Khaldun's climatology (and of the Mediterranean as a locus of perfection) in chapter 5. In eighteenth-century France, however, Montesquieu does not want the Mediterranean, but rather a putatively *northern* France, to be identified with the perfection of what is temperate and therefore not excessive but just. It is then very likely, and it has been suggested (for instance by Gates) that Montesquieu knew of Ibn Khaldun's climatology, which had become popular in France since the publication of Jean-Baptiste Chardin's *Voyages en Perse et autres lieux de l'Orient* in 1680. The fact that Montesquieu never mentions Ibn Khaldun is then highly significant: Montesquieu's temperate (climatologically and therefore politically) zone is not Ibn Khaldun's Mediterranean, but a European north comprising England, Holland, Germany, Belgium, and France. North of this temperate north was for Montesquieu the *excessive* cold of Siberia and Lapland, which reduced people to a state of savagery. South of it was exactly Ibn Khaldun's Mediterranean, demoted to a hot, dry place. In a way, both the extremely cold north of Lapland and Siberia and the excessively hot south of Spain and Italy produced a similar breed of humans: savage, non-European, and with a brown skin (see Duchet 254–65).

Rather than from Ibn Khaldun, Montesquieu therefore inherits the notion of a temperate climate directly from Jean Bodin, who, in the *République*, had divided the world into a colder north inhabited by rude and "dirty" peoples, a hotter south inhabited by cunning and malicious ones, and a temperate "Europe" with France at its center (Carravetta 42). Montesquieu, at first glance, *seemed* then to translate Aristotle's seventh book of *Politics* almost word by word: "It is not surprising that the cowardice of the people of hot climates has almost constantly rendered them slaves, and that the courage of the people of cold climates has kept them free" (*Oeuvres* 2:523). But his move of the zone of perfection from Aristotle's (and Ibn Khaldun's) Mediterranean to a temperate north was full of strategic significance: "You will find, in the climates of the north, peoples who have few vices, many virtues, and much sincerity and candor. As you move toward the countries of the south, you will believe you have moved away from morality itself" (2:477).

Plenty has been written, since, about Montesquieu's climatological politics and about his spatial logic of difference. While some scholars have insisted on Montesquieu's "environmental determinism" (Sprout and Sprout 50) and on the way "physical environment, especially climate, impinges upon human character and political institutions" (Shklar 12), others have minimized the importance of climate in Montesquieu's politics by stressing instead the primacy of social factors and moral causes (e.g., Shackleton, *Montesquieu* 317) or by restricting the influence of geographical factors to the limits of a "qualified determinism" (Richter 134). Although climate is certainly not the one and only cause that Montesquieu singles out, it seems problematic, on the other hand, to dismiss or minimize it excessively after Montesquieu himself wrote, for instance, that "it is the different needs depending on different climates that have formed different ways of living; and these different ways of living have formed the different kinds of laws" (*Oeuvres* 2:483–84); or that "it is climate that decides [the relations between the sexes]" (2:517). It may be that in order to save the "father" of political science from a determinism that is less credible to us, a complete "emancipation [of political theory] from the environment, has been accomplished by [some] critics with too much ease" (Kriesel 566).

At any rate, despite differing interpretations regarding the importance of climate in Montesquieu, critics seem to agree that the goal of *De l'esprit des lois* was to theorize European freedom against Asiatic despotism (see, for example, Chabod 106). Franco Venturi, minimizing the importance of climate in his old but still pertinent essay entitled "Oriental Despotism," takes *De l'esprit des lois* as the pivotal text that canonized the antithesis Europe-Orient in a modern context: "Synthesizing the political wisdom of past ages," says Venturi, Montesquieu moved away from a narrowly political definition of despotism which claimed that "it is only governments which are despotic" toward a modern one that assumed that "society may be so too" (134). Differently put, despotism is not the product of political systems, but of general social conditions, or "culture" (Abrahamian 4). For Venturi, Oriental despotism and European freedom were, then, not the conditions of specific forms of authority, but political drives embedded in the structure itself—culture, morality, systems of belief—of Oriental and European societies. Perry Anderson gives instead significant importance to climate and geography. Yet he comes to the same conclusion as Venturi: "Montesquieu's declared principle of explanation for the differential character of European and Asian States was, of course, geographical: climate and topography determined their separate destinies" (465).

In truth, the antithesis Europe-Orient was a well-established commonplace in Montesquieu's times (see, for example, Longino). Since at least 1704, when Antoine Galland had translated *The Thousand and One Nights* into French, the Orient—a concept that hardly differentiated between India, Persia, and Arabia (Mariani Zini 20n3)—had cohered into popular imagination as the "Other" place to everyday France. For good and for bad, the Orient was, once again, the antithesis of modern Europe, which had, in turn, Paris at its center: this was the sure lesson drawn from reading the endless number of Galland's imitators—from François Pétis de la Croix's *Mille et un jour* (1710–1812), to Charles de Fieux, Chevalier de Mouhy, who rewrote Marguerite de Navarre's *Heptaméron* in 1740 as *Les milles et une faveurs*. The more the French genius prided itself for being utterly and Cartesianly reasonable, the more it needed, it seems, to imagine an Orient of magic, flying carpets, and genies in the bottle. Even Voltaire (*Vision de Babouc*, 1746; *Bababek et les fakirs*, 1750) and Diderot (*L'oiseaux blanc*, 1748; *Les bijoux indiscrets*, 1748), or Montesquieu himself with the *Lettres persanes* (1721), would put aside reason for a while and indulge instead in the pleasures of the "Other" life in the east.

The Orient as the unreasonable antithesis to the (French) West was the horizon of expectations against which *De l'esprit des lois* was, and still largely is, interpreted. Nicolas Antoine Boulanger, in the *Recherches sur les origines du despotisme orientale* of 1761, had soon noticed in Montesquieu a paradigmatic distinction between Europe and the east. Also, Abraham Hyacinte Anquetil-Duperron, in a spirited defense of his beloved Asia printed as *Législation orientale* (1778), had accused Montesquieu of creating stereotypes of Asia that could only serve the colonial interests of Europe. The *philosophes* themselves, led by Voltaire, had come to the same conclusion, while accepting that Montesquieu's text was in fact the theorization of the Europe-Asia difference.

What seems to be lost in this kind of interpretation, however, is nothing less than the *modernity* of Montesquieu's science of politics—the way in which climatology is slowly but surely abandoning Aristotle's longitudinal difference and preparing instead the modern and romantic latitudinal distinctions that Madame de Staël would set, in the year 1800, between *two* European cultures: one "that come from the south," and one "that descend from the north" (*Littérature* 203). To begin with, Montesquieu could not care less about Aristotle—or, for that matter, about the authority of the ancients in general. They did not know better, and, at best, they wrote "without knowing what they said" (Montesquieu, *Oeuvres* 2:43).[4] So while *De l'esprit des lois* could *appear* to be following Aristotle and the ancients in its identification of climate as the natural cause that divides free and progressive nations from despotic and backward ones, the conclusion of book 17, chapter 2, announced an unarguably modern thesis: it is not in the west, but "in the climates of the north" that peoples have "few vices, many virtues"; and it is not in the east, but in "the countries of the south" that one finds oneself "away from morality itself."

What is immediately apparent here is that the old discussion between freedom (Europe) and despotism (Asia) has been translated into a modern, latitudinal rhetoric of north and south. Heat and cold, rather than physical geographies fixed in the reality of Aristotle's Greece and Persia, have become for Montesquieu two rhetorical commonplaces that can be translated at will in order to articulate and unfold a new idea of Europe.

"Europe," writes Montesquieu, "has come to such a high degree of power, that history cannot compare it to anything else" (*Oeuvres* 2:644). The Oriental—once the Persian, later the Muslim and the Turk—has ceased to represent any menace at all. By 1782, in fact, his fundamentally comic role in the unfolding of modern European history will be canonized by young Wolfgang Amadeus Mozart's *Die Entführung aus dem Serail*. It is consequently useless to judge Europe against Asia and the East in 1748: ideally, if not geographically (see the discussion on Eurasia in chapter 1), "Europe is separated from the rest of the world" (Montesquieu, *Oeuvres* 2:710). This does not mean that Europe can now define itself without a confrontation with a negative Other: it means, rather, that since "one finds the same difference within Europe" (2:481), a modern theory of Europe can now dispense with any comparison "to anything else" and focus instead on this internal difference within Europe. It is not only in Asia, after all, "but in the south of Europe that laws do exactly the contrary" of what European laws ought to do (2:481). And it is not only in Asia that freedom, constitutive of Europe according to Aristotle, is negated; freedom, alas, is "never to be seen in the *southern* climates" of Europe itself (2:526; emphasis mine).

Interlude: A Theory of Postcolonialism

> The ordinary effect of colonies is to weaken the colonizing
> country, without increasing the population of the colonized one.
> —CHARLES DE SECONDAT MONTESQUIEU, *Lettres Persanes*

If Montesquieu's "modernity" was, in G. Bonno's words, the attempt to theorize "a moment in which European hegemony was being extended all over the world" (289), it must be noticed that such theorization followed one very firm assumption: that such an extension of Europe all over the world had now to be balanced by a new centrifugal movement— by a return to Europe. Montesquieu's eagerness to declare colonialism a closed chapter in the history of Europe—especially after the failures of Colbertism[5]—bears directly on his attempt to make of Europe a self-contained system in which difference (north and south) is represented as an internal dialectic of the same. The logic of colonial expansion, from its very outset, runs counter to the logic of *De l'esprit des lois*: if laws are proper to one specific locale (climate and geography) and to one people's sense of morality (culture), colonialism then poses the problem, discussed for instance in book 19, of how to establish an alien colonial rule in a place that is naturally disinclined to it (Montesquieu, *Oeuvres* 2:574–83).[6] The *Lettres persanes* had already warned Europe that such a colonial effort was in fact to weaken the conquering country; the same point had been advanced, a propos the decline of Spain, in the "Considérations sur les richesses de l'Espagne" (ca. 1728); and the "Considérations sur les causes de la grandeur des romains" had condemned "the folly of conquering new territories in a movement of extension that brings the conqueror nothing but the illusion of power and the reality of weakness" (Volpilhac-Auger 51). It was now *De l'esprit des lois* that dramatized the need for an abandonment of colonialism—by producing, for one, a theory of Europe as complete knowledge of itself, and which no longer wishes to find its Other in any faraway colony or land.

Montesquieu's rationale for declaring the age of global conquest and expansion over was modern in the most businesslike sense of the word: *De l'esprit des lois*, as David Carrithers suggests, "considered the prioritization of commerce [as] the chief distinguishing feature of modernity" ("Introduction" 18). Not only was colonialism hindering the free circulation of goods and capitals by imposing such "unnatural" regulations as the colonial power's exclusive right of negotiation with the colonies (Montesquieu, *Oeuvres* 2:643). Worse, colonialism was prone to confuse the end (commerce) with the means (war of conquest). A criticism of colonial expansionism began, then, in the name of business, with a consideration of the commercial failure of the most illustrious of colonial conquests—the Spanish one of the Americas. The Spaniards—a backward southern nation—certainly did not know better the principles of modern commerce: "The Spaniards considered these newly discovered lands as the subject of conquest; while others, more refined in their views, found them to be the proper subjects of commerce" (Montesquieu, *Oeuvres* 2:643).

Yet the problem was not simply military conquest; what was truly problematic about colonialism was that its conquests of faraway lands were quite difficult to turn into productive commercial enterprises—even for more modern and refined countries than Spain. It is not surprising that for a thinker so interested in geography as Montesquieu was, the problem could be described in spatial terms: simply put, for commerce to be fruitful to European countries, distance had to be taken into account. What worth, then, was the immense gold of the distant Americas? Montesquieu answered with an accountant's precision:

> To extract the gold from the mines, to give it the requisite preparations, and to import it into Europe, must be attended with some certain expense. I will suppose this to be as 1 to 64. When the specie was once

doubled, and consequently became by one-half less precious, the expense was as 2 to 64. Thus the fleets that brought to Spain the same quantity of gold, brought a thing which really was of less value by one-half, though the expenses attending it had been twice as high. If we proceed doubling and doubling, we shall find in this progression the cause of the impotency of the wealth of Spain. (2:646–47)

Compared to the squandering of faraway colonialism, even German and Hungarian mines, though relatively poorer than the American ones, revealed themselves as more useful—"extremely useful," as it were—than the ones overseas: "Those mines of Germany and Hungary, which produce little more than the expense of working them, are extremely useful. They are found in the principal state; they employ many thousands of men, who there consume their superfluous commodities, and they are properly a manufacture of the country. The mines of Germany and Hungary promote the culture of land; the working of those of Mexico and Peru destroys it" (2:648).

Distrust for the commercial viability of colonialism was only one of the reasons that had led Montesquieu to close Europe's doors in the face of the entire world. Hygiene was a second one, since at least the days when syphilis had landed in Europe with Columbus's caravels (2:485). A third was the maximization of productivity that, as the discussion of slavery concluded (2:496–97), was achieved more easily by giving incentives to local salaried laborers (who could in turn buy produced goods and thus increase the wealth of the nation) than by importing slaves from other lands. And a final reason was the troubles of Europe themselves. Too much energy, believed Montesquieu, had been spent thinking about colonialism, and too little trying to solve the most immediate problems of Europe. Such immediate problems were not transcontinental but internal: Europe had certainly come to "such a high degree of power"; but it was also, at the height of its hegemony, profoundly sick at its core: "A new sickness has spread over Europe: has taken our princes, and has made them organize a disproportionate number of soldiers" (2:470). After the endless wars of religion discussed in chapter 1, the war of the Spanish succession was now pitting "one half of Europe against the other half" (1:1356).[7] Sully's "chimerical" project of perpetual peace, which was to answer, as we have seen in chapter 1, the disunities of the wars of religion, had miserably failed (*Pensées* number 1482). A new project was now needed, and Montesquieu, unaccustomed to despair, identified such a project with the modern ethics of the market: "The effect of commerce is to tend toward peace" (Montesquieu, *Oeuvres* 2:585; also see Rosso). In a modern world, in which successful commerce was not between metropolis and colony but "done mainly between north and south" (Montesquieu, *Oeuvres* 2:603), a focus on inter-European commerce could suffice to guarantee a perpetual peace between all European nations.

What such a modern project of perpetual peace entailed was the shift from "a model of brutal and ephemeral conquest, [to] a model of organization of an empire [where . . .] commerce reigned" (Volpilhac-Auger 49). This passage from an old colonial model to a modern and commercial one was for Montesquieu not only an epochal or historical but a geographical one. To move from colonialism to commerce meant, in other words, to move the center of European hegemony from the south to the north. Colonialism had been for Montesquieu the soul of the Roman Empire—of an empire centered on the Mediterranean, that is, that no longer constituted the center ("L'Italie n'est plus au centre") but only a "corner of the world" (Montesquieu, *Oeuvres* 1:1380). And colonialism had been the drive of another southern empire—the Spanish one—that had eventually collapsed and was now to be put under the supervision of Europe ("en tutelle dans l'Europe"; see Montesquieu *Oeuvres* 1:1380, 1382). Commerce, instead, was the new ethics of a protestant north, and of France in particular, the "most powerful nation" (2:375), "heart or even head" of the new Europe ("au milieu d'Europe [France] en étoit le coeur si elle n'en étoit pas la tête" (2:30). If northern nations had engaged in the adventures of colonialism, and even started quarrelling over colonies, Montesquieu now warned them: colonial interests were against their nature, against their modern, protestant, commercial European spirit. Colonialism, in short, would only bring them to disaster.

As climatology had divided Europe into north and south, so did the advent of modern commerce split Europe into two perfectly balanced, antithetical parts:

> In Europe there is a kind of balance between the southern and the northern nations. The first have every riches of life, and few wants: the second have many wants, and few riches. To one Nature has given much, and demands little; to the other she has given but little, and demands a lot. The equilibrium is maintained by the laziness of the southern nations,

and by the industry and activity which Nature has given to those in the north. The latter have to work a lot, or else they would lack everything, and degenerate into barbarianism. This has naturalized slavery for the people of the south: as they can easily dispense with riches, they can even more easily dispense with liberty. (Montesquieu, *Oeuvres* 2:603)

What is crucial here is not so much that southern Europeans *could* be militarily conquered and enslaved (servitude is, after all, natural in the south), but that north and south formed for Montesquieu a perfect economic system: the south was an immense reservoir of natural riches that existed there in excess; and the north was the center for the industrious manufacture of finished goods. It was the nearby European south, to which "Nature has given much," which had now to be controlled and exploited by the laborious and progressive northern nations—not the distant Americas, which only yield a return of "2 to 64."

The logic of excess and industriousness was in fact quite reminiscent of the second of the *Two Treatises on Civil Government* (1690) in which John Locke had tried to justify the "private dominion" of things against a natural law commanding that "all the fruits [Mother Nature] naturally produces . . . belong to mankind in common" (5:115–16). Locke, intent to justify private property as the very institution that distinguished the progressive and "civilized part of mankind" (5:117) from another that was still in "a pattern of the first ages" of Europe (5:151), had claimed that "labour put a distinction between [private] and common" (5:116) and "removed . . . [the object] from the state of Nature wherein she was common" to make it "mine" (5:117). Labor, in other words, legitimated property: "Cultivating the earth and having dominion, we see, are joined together" (5:119). Excess was, then, available to appropriation through labor: "As much as any one can make use of to any advantage of life before it spoils, so much he may by his labour fix a property in. Whatever is beyond this is more than his share, and belongs to others" (5:117).

Locke's theory of property, however, aimed at founding an ethics of colonialism and of legitimating the exploitation of the putatively "vacant places of America" (5:120) by industrious Europe.[8] What Montesquieu now needed was a translation of Locke's theory of property from a colonial context into one in which "European commerce is done mainly between north and south."[9] Commerce, in a way, had already realized such a translation. It was a theory of Europe, now, that needed to be conceived to represent adequately the way in which Europe had *already* become a system, a complete whole in which its two complementary parts worked in perfect—can we say dialectical?—synergy.

To theorize such a balance of one Europe divided in two, a new theory of identity was needed, and what Elena Russo calls Montesquieu's "modern psychology" could have certainly been a first step in this direction. Montesquieu's modern individual, different from the unselfconsciously wholesome one of the ancients, appeared split by an internal contradiction "that tear[s] the modern man apart": he "conflates the two functions of man and citizen into a single identity" (Russo 115). As a man, this individual was led by nature to satisfy his immediate needs; as a citizen, he was limited by culture to reconcile his satisfaction with the social good. A similar split between nature and culture, in fact, formed the identity and character of Montesquieu's nations: "There exists, in every nation, a general character. It is produced in two ways: by physical causes which depend upon the climate . . . and by moral causes which are a combination of the laws, religion, habits and manners" (Montesquieu, *Oeuvres* 2:58).

It might not have taken much imagination to the undoubtedly quite imaginative president to translate this paradigm of dialectical identity onto Europe itself. So while he had begun book 5 by listing as an antithesis to Europe all the usual suspects of Orientalism—the Turks, Persia, and the Mongols (2:296)—by the time he got to book 14, Montesquieu had already split Europe into two "functions" of a single identity: a south determined by nature ("away from morality itself"); and a north led instead by a culture of cooperation with the state ("few vices, enough virtues, and much sincerity and frankness"). The antithesis of European freedom, too, had been relocated within Europe's own south. Europe was *in itself* "torn apart" by two conflated drives—one to liberty, the other to slavery: "It is the peoples of the north who have and always will have a spirit of independence and liberty that is lacking in the peoples of the south" (2:718). The other political climate that Aristotle had imagined in Persia had been now brought within the borders of Europe.

Back to the Tongue

The whole idea of climatology, after all, had come to Montesquieu neither from reading about Asia in the *Politics* nor from thinking of the vanquished and vanished Persian Empire. It had been a more modern preoccupation—the southbound Grand Tour—that had led Montesquieu to Italy, where the idea of climatology had hit him like a revelation. The rising industry of guide-books and travel memoirs had already warned him about the noxiousness of Italian air:

> Returned travelers had often given evil reports of the air of Rome, and guide-books seldom failed to comment on the noxious and even lethal effects of the atmosphere either of the city itself or of the Roman *campagna*. Rogissart's *Les Délices de l'Italie*, Misson's *Nouveau Voyage d'Italie*, and Addison's *Remarks on several parts of Italy*, all of them known to Montesquieu, cited by him, and possessed by him at La Brede, allude to the unhealthy qualities of the Roman air. Shortly before departing for Italy, he had made the acquaintance of the *Reflex ions critiques sur la poésie et sur la peinture*, by the Abbé Dubos. The learned Abbé asserts the influence of climate on national character. Giving a fairly detailed analysis of its mode of operation. (Shackleton, *Montesquieu* 303)

In 1729, when Montesquieu entered Rome, he was confronted by a scene even more desolate than his readings had prepared him for: the place was "without commerce or industry," and all was totally opposed to the economic and social logic of what Montesquieu called "the system of Europe" (*Oeuvres* 1:661). In this wasteland, internal but also alien to a European system, Montesquieu was promptly informed by his compatriot Cardinal de Polignac—the same who had explained to the Holy Father the "difference" between France and Italy ("Saint Père, vous ne savez la différence de la France à l'Italie"; 1:667)—of Rome's distinctly bad weather ("l'intempérie de Rome"; 1:663). Naples's weather was quite bad too ("l'air n'y est pas des plus sains"; 1:717), and Pozzuoli's was even worse ("l'air y est très mauvais"), especially after the heat of summer had made it absolutely and unredeemably pestilential ("lorsque le chaleur de l'été . . . l'air doit être empesté"; 1:725).

The voyage south of the European system soon became for Montesquieu a descent into an inferno whose heat was the most proximate secular metonymy reminiscent of the theological flames of hell: at the baths of Pozzuoli, the heat was suffocating ("la chaleur m'ayant presque suffoqué") and waters were boiling ("une eau bouillante"; 1:725). From the ground, sulfuric smoke exhaled ("une fumée de soufre sort de plusieurs endroits"; 1:726). Not even a miracle could redeem such a place!

Speaking of miracles, the Neapolitans regularly celebrated the one of

San Gennaro, whose blood, preserved in two glass bowls from the time of his martyrdom (he was beheaded in 305), was said to liquefy three times every year—on the first Sunday of May (the anniversary of the translation of his body to Naples from nearby Pozzuoli); on September 19 (the date of the martyrdom); and on December 16 (the date of the eruption of the Vesuvius in 1631). On September 19, 1729, Montesquieu stood among a crowd of ecstatic Neapolitans to witness the liquefaction of the saint's blood, which the priest had brought from the crypt of the homonymous church to the open square. "Miracle!" howled the crowd. Not so quick, annotated instead Montesquieu, with ethnographic scruple and empirical skepticism, in his diaries. Far from being a miracle, the liquefaction could in fact be easily explained according to the principles of climatology, whose hermeneutic virtues Montesquieu was clearly contemplating already: "I am convinced that all this is the result of temperature change" (*Oeuvres* 1:728). By bringing the coagulated blood from the cold crypt to the sunny square, the priest, helped only by a providential change in temperature, had caused the "miracle" to happen.

Marginal as this little episode may be in the production of Montesquieu's oeuvre, it should, at the very least, give us anecdotal proof of how many things, really, climate could explain. Just as it explained the miracle of San Gennaro, it explained the social reality of the south: the unbearable heat of Naples had formed human beings that were "the most miserable in the world," a people that was "more vulgar and popular than any other" ("bien plus peuple qu'un autre") (1:729). They were people, in other words, in the sense of a "corrupt people that rarely does great things." Sure enough, they celebrated, along with their saint, their hero too—Masaniello. But Masaniello wanted to change the government into a republic, start a revolution, and talked of freedom too. Did the people of Naples join him in his fight for liberty? Of course not (1:729): as *De l'esprit des lois* would later explain, revolution "can seldom be effected without infinite pains and labor, and hardly ever by idle and debauched persons" (2:281). And infinite pains and labor, as we know, can hardly arise in the debauchery of heat.

The palimpsest of Aristotle's political climatology, which had established the antithesis between a hot and despotic east on the one hand, and a cold and free Europe on the other, was then totally rewritten according to the climatological findings of the *Voyages*. Already there, Europe had appeared as a continent fractured by a deep latitudinal divide: "It looks to me that the more northward one moves, the more easily one finds people who are resilient to travails; the further one moves towards the hot countries of the south, one finds flaccid bodies and a looser spirit" (Montesquieu, *Oeuvres* 2:701–2).

The task of *De l'esprit des lois* was, then, to theorize, after the empirical observations of the Italian *Voyages*, a political science of the north-south difference. The climatic hell of the *Voyages* was to become, in *De l'esprit des lois*, the very natural cause for the positive institution of cultural, political, moral, and even religious commonplaces of the south's negativity:

> When the Christian religion, two centuries ago, became unhappily divided into Catholic and Protestant, the people of the north embraced the Protestant, and those of the south adhered still to the Catholic. The reason is plain: the people of the north have, and will forever have, a spirit of liberty and independence, which the people of the south have not; and therefore a religion that has no visible head is more agreeable to the independence of the climate than that which has one. (2:718)[10]

After the revocation of the Edict of Nantes, Montesquieu's suggestion that "the people of the north embraced the Protestant [religion]" and that Catholicism constituted the renunciation of "the spirit of liberty and independence" obviously had clear political significance. In 1598, King Henry iv had promulgated a decree at Nantes to restore internal peace in France after the wars of religion. The edict defined the rights of the French Protestants and granted them liberty of worship, full civil rights, and even subsidies for Protestant schools and city governments. Cardinal Richelieu during the reign of Louis xiii, and then Cardinal Mazarin under Louis xiv, had slowly stripped the French Protestants of all political rights, until the final revocation of the edict in 1665. For Montesquieu, Richelieu's and Mazarin's catholicization of France equaled a southernization of the country—a progressive loss of liberty and a move toward a southern religion "away from morality itself": "In Rome there is nothing as convenient as a church to pray to God and to assassinate your neighbor. People are not restrained here as in other countries, and, if you don't like the looks of an other man, you only need to order your valet to stab him two or three times, and then take refuge in a church" (1:677). France, for Montesquieu, was a northern country— and thus it opened to Protestantism and religious freedoms. The imaginary dividing line between north and south could be singled out for him, with great geographic precision, in the Apennine Mountains:

There is, in Italy, a southern wind, called Sirocco, which passes through the sands of Africa before reaching Italy. It rules that country; it exerts its power over all spirits; it produces a universal weightiness and slowness; Sirocco is the intelligence that presides over all Italian heads, and I am tempted to believe that the difference one notices between the inhabitants of northern Lombardy, and those of the rest of Italy, derives from the fact that Lombardy is protected by the Apennines, which defend her from the havoc of the Sirocco. (2:45)[11]

Europe, to be sure, *is* one, like the sheep's tongue: but heat and cold have different effects on this one tongue. "I froze the half of this tongue," and, as the drive to pleasure cooled down, "a spirit of independence and liberty" condensed; the other half, under relentless heat and African winds, compelled only by pleasure, made the very idea of freedom evaporate. This was, in the last analysis, the lesson to be learned from the fall of Rome. Sure, the causes of Rome's fall lay in its warlike and colonial nature. Yet Roman decadence had arrived, first and foremost, with a general covetousness for pleasure: "Their desires became immense" (2:353). All sorts of "Oriental" excesses, indolence, and lust (2:122), drowned Rome in the path to decadence. In the "Reflections on the Inhabitants of Rome," at the conclusion of the *Voyages*, Montesquieu recalled those excesses, and, above all, decadent Rome's "prodigious appetite," the "debauchery of the table," the "art of eating in excess" that involved the "use of emetics to eat more" (1:910–11). Now we know the reason of it all: the Romans' papillae, like the sheep's, had enlarged in an excessive search for taste.

From a sheep's tongue, an entire theoretical system was thus born: it encompassed all and explained the universe. It theorized, at least, Europe as the climate antithetical to all such debauchery. The antithesis to such Europe, however, was no longer east, but was to be found in the history of Europe itself—in its past, that is, which was its south. In the beginning, there was the tongue.

The Geography of History

Since the human mind has the experience of time but does not have a representation for it, it represents time through spatial images.
—GIORGIO AGAMBEN, *Infanzia e storia*

Climate, Robert Shackleton insists, was not the only cause *De l'esprit des lois* had singled out for the formation of the general spirit of a nation. Montesquieu would have certainly agreed, but with an important qualification: "Mankind is influenced by various causes: by the climate, by religion, by the laws, by the maxims of government, by precedents, morals, and customs; whence is formed a general spirit of nations. In each country, as any one of these causes acts with more force, the others weaken in proportion. Nature and climate rule almost alone over the savages" (*Oeuvres* 2:558).[12] Certainly, a whole series of cultural factors—religions, laws, governments, precedents, morals, and customs—balanced for Montesquieu the effects of nature, and hence of climate, in human societies. Savagery, however, as the borderline circumstance of a complete subjection to a state of nature, prevented culture from modifying or taming the effects of nature. These, as we already know, were felt mainly through pores and papillae contracting and dilating under the action of temperature.

Perfect sociability, on the one hand, and a state of nature, on the other, were the two extremes of the human condition—extremes that represented, in fact, the dual or dialectical nature of humankind discussed above: "Man, as a physical being, is governed like all the other bodies by invariable laws. As an intelligent being, he tirelessly transgresses the laws that God has established, and changes the ones he himself has established" (Montesquieu, *Oeuvres* 2:234). Like man (the particular), like nations (the general law): "The life of nations is like the life of men" (2:377). In an absolute state of nature, the law of climate was absolute. In an absolute state of civilization, the law of nature was nothing, and the law of man, politics, was all.

In this sense, neither the state of nature, nor perfect sociability, were possible conditions for humankind: being "man," for Montesquieu, meant to partake of a dual nature. The hypothesis of a state of nature— that is, of "man before the establishment of society" (2:235)—was, then, just a hypothesis, useful only insofar as it helped theorize the differences in social realities as tensions toward one of the two hypothetical extremes. For Montesquieu, there were, in other words, societies that *tended* toward the "state of nature, and in which [men are] unrestrained either by a political or civil law" (2:913); and there were societies that *tended* toward perfect sociability: they could be republics ("moins il y a de luxe dans une république, plus elle est parfaite"; 2:334); aristocracies ("plus une aristocratie approchera de la démocratie, plus elle sera par-faite"; 2:247); or monarchies ("[quand] chacun va au bien commun, croyant aller à ses intérêts particuliers"; 2:257).

For Montesquieu, who concurred with Hobbes on at least this point (Lowenthal 494), the state of nature was the hypothetical beginning of human history; the end of that history was to be the utopic realization of politics as the final transgression of the natural laws that God has estab-lished. It was not Hobbes's fantasy of a state of nature, but the reality of the different kinds of societies that stood between beginning and end, that interested Montesquieu: his question, if any was central to *De l'esprit des lois*, was how to escape an undesirable proximity to the state of nature and establish, as close as humanly possible, the reign of the law. The perfecting of the law was the slow progress of politics, "a smooth file, which cuts gradually, and attains its end by a slow progression" (*Oeuvres* 2:487). If the utopic end of politics was the fulfillment of per-fection, its most attainable and practical one was the understanding and preservation of the circumstances that had allowed "our admirable law of today" (2:317) to flourish from previous conditions of savagery and barbarity.

A progress from savagery to the law, however, was not for Montes-quieu a merely historical telos. A distrust for history was certainly in the air of Montesquieu's France: "The reformation of knowledge which Des-cartes [had] envisaged, and actually did bring about, was designed to contribute nothing to historical thought, because he did not believe history to be, strictly speaking, a branch of knowledge at all" (Colling-wood 59). Especially the kind of universal histories à la Bossuet, in-formed by an ecumenical ethos too much in odor of biblical orthodoxy, were consistently perceived as "incompatible with the new spirit of sci-entific enquiry stirring in the late seventeenth century" (Barraclough 84). Despite such epochal skepticism, Montesquieu had expressed in his *Pensées* the "intention to write a historical work" (Shackleton, *Montes-quieu* 227). That he eventually discarded such a project to write instead *De l'esprit des lois* does not mean that Montesquieu had abandoned his historicist ambitions altogether (see Hulliung 3–5, 140–72): on the con-trary, already in the preface we are informed that *De l'esprit des lois* intends to trace, from a set of "principles," nothing less than "the histo-ries of all nations" (Montesquieu, *Oeuvres* 2:229); and by book 3, we are reminded that Montesquieu's was not a refutation of previous histories, but, rather, its ultimate synthesis and "confirmation of the entire body of historiography" (2:251).

De l'esprit des lois presented, then, not a local history of France or Europe, but a universal history with Europe and France as the last stage— modernity—of a linear chronology of infinite betterment. This was universal history as philosophy of history: written from France, it recapitulated and comprehended in a retrospective gaze the entire body of historiography and transcended the various "chronicle[s] of miscellaneous facts" into a unitary perspective giving meaning to and "affirming the superiority of the present age" (Carrithers, "Philosophy of History" 61). Undoubtedly, Montesquieu's philosophy of history was not Bossuet's universal history. It was not guided, for example, by the assumption of a theological design. A *teleological* design, however, was certainly present in Montesquieu; only, it had to be derived not deductively from a putative will of God, but inductively, from the empirical order of physical realities (on Montesquieu's historical empiricism, see Oake 48–49). This was Montesquieu's "dialectics of history" (Althusser 37–58): it began from empirical observations and finished by arranging them into a telos pointing to "the manifestation of an intemporal truth" (Gearhart 180).

And while the creation of the Lord Almighty no longer appeared perfect in all its parts, humankind's secularized progress from imperfect savagery, through barbarism, to "the laws of today" was then imagined as an empirically observable telos. Progress was observable in the sense that it was not simply something that could be grasped by history—the science of a past that no one can see any longer—but the subject matter of geography. Progress, in other words, was understood by Montesquieu as a series of contiguous, observable places. "Savage" could no longer be for Montesquieu the myth of a prehistoric past impossible for the scientist to observe, but an ethnographic space open still to the gaze of the analyst: "savage" was the "new world" of Louisiana (Montesquieu, *Oeuvres* 2:292) and of America in general (2:536), which had not yet entered the West; savage was Siberia (2:537), as was part of North Africa (2:602). In these *places* resided the observable origin of historical progress that the reportages of merchants, travelers, local historians, and missionaries had but begun, ethnographically, to reconstruct.

Geography was, then, becoming the new organizing principle of Montesquieu's theory of progress. History was, like a branch of the *ars memorandi*, a progress best represented as a movement from one place to another. Barbarity was its second stage, observable in the farming tribes of North Africa (2:602), in the despotic regimes of the Near East (2:537), in the customs of India (2:478), and, "no matter what others say," in those of China (1:1358). Barbarous was a *place* of history, where nomadic hunting had been successfully replaced by a farming culture rooted in the communal territory (2:537). Barbarous, more important, was a place where "histories always feel servitude" (2:537).

History was thus spatialized, and time converted into place: Asia, Africa, and America represented old, prehistoric moments in the geography of universal history. They "were assigned a place 'elsewhere'" of the present, marginalized as the not-yet of the European "structure of time" (Chakrabarty 8). It was in Europe, and in Europe only, that the historical passage from barbarity to "the laws of today" could finally be observed.

Europe, indeed, was the present—or, in fact, it was the synthesis of human history, the place of the final fulfillment of modernity overcoming a past of barbarity.[13] In the *Pensées* that Montesquieu was collecting for his eventually aborted attempt at writing a universal history, we read that Greece had opened nothing less than a "new time": "In those new times, the fervor for liberty gave them [Greeks] love for the country, heroic courage, and hatred of kings—and this drove them to do great things" (*Oeuvres* 1:1364). Love of freedom was the "proof of the novelty of the Greeks" in the telos of universal history. If savagery and barbarism were, then, prehistorical stages, true history seemed to open, for Montesquieu, with the "new times" of freedom. This new history was the story of freedom's unfolding: "History is thus converted into a tale about the furtherance of virtue" or a "moral success story" (Wolf 5). Moreover, this was a story that coincided with a place—Europe, whose "circumstances," comments a reader of Montesquieu, "are always contained within the story of liberty" (Courtois 321).[14]

Rome—after Greece, and for only a short while—represented the second stage of the European progress to freedom, at least "until this democracy [Rome] became corrupted" (Montesquieu, *Oeuvres* 1:1369). With the fall of Rome, it was then "our German fathers" (2:329)—"The people of the North of Europe, source of freedom" (1:1354)—who came to answer the historical task of realizing liberty in Europe once and for all.

German, like its counterpart *Roman*, was a term loaded with political overtones in Montesquieu's France: Romanists imagined the French monarchy as the ideal heir of the absolute powers of the Roman emperor; Germanists, instead, argued for a Germanic origin of France, in which the monarch's powers were subject to a check by the intermediate feudal nobility—intermediate because this nobility would mediate politically between the interests of the monarch and those of amorphous servant masses with no rights which the eighteenth century called, with no hint of Romantic and nationalist connotations, "the people" ("people as a social, rather than a national entity," writes Hof 74). Hardly any argument about Rome and Germania, in fact, was free from political overtones in this context. Attempts to sever France from southern and specifically Roman origins had noticeably begun at the time of the Gallican schism of the fifteenth century, and a politico-religious question had soon turned into a wider cultural one concerning the relation of France with Rome. Put simply: was France the heir of Rome, or was its ancestry to be located somewhere else, as in the German forests? For François Hotman, author of *Franco-Gallia* (1573), the German conquest of French Gaul had brought to the country a love for freedom and equality (brotherhood had to wait for two more centuries!) and had dispelled the despotism with which Hotman identified the Romans. Politically, this meant—for Hotman before Montesquieu—that "the monarch's absolute power in France was therefore an usurpation of that primitive [German] freedom, and needed some correction" (Carravetta 46).

Translating such question in philological terms, Guillame de Postel's *De originibus* of 1538 (echoed in 1580 by Joachim Périon's *Linguae gallicae origine*) had steadfastly refuted, for instance, a Latin origin of the French language. Still in the *Encyclopédie*, and until the emergence of German Romantic philology,[15] an independence of the French language from Latin was in fact de rigueur in antiabsolutist circles—and an argument to the contrary was a clear avocation of monarchic unlimited power.

Following Martin Thom, I should observe that this dispute had very important bearing on theories and historical chronologies of Europe. The question was whether *modern* Europe had originated in the Mediterranean, during classical times; or whether it had begun in the Middle Ages, with the Northern Franks' destruction of the Roman Empire. Romanists were ready to "condemn rather than celebrate the medieval order" (Thom 26), whereas the Germanists, anticipating a Romantic cult of the Middle Ages that I will discuss in chapter 4, made modern Europe originate from a northern overcoming of ancient and Mediterranean Europe. In other words, the antithesis was not simply a political one pitting against each other the Romanist defenders of absolute monarchy and the Germanist proponents of an aristocratic middle class between monarch and third estate. The antithesis was also, in the full sense of the word, geopolitical: whereas Germanism "celebrated the contribution of the Aryan nomadic tribes to European culture," Romanism, instead, "argued that it was the urban traditions of Egypt, Phoenicia and Asia Minor that had created a basis for civilization in the Mediterranean" that had peaked with Rome (Thom 27).

Far from "de-mythologizing" (as claimed by Hulliung 60) the myth of either a Roman or a German origin of Europe (ergo France), Montesquieu was ready to take from the diatribes of Romanists and Germanists a twofold conclusion: Roman laws (in political terms, monarchical absolutism) belonged to an ancient cycle of history that had by now ended with the fall of Rome; German laws (i.e., monarchical power mediated by the nobility) had opened yet a new historical cycle—modernity—that had now climaxed in France. The admonition addressed to the French monarchy was clear: in Louis Althusser's words, absolute power was an "ancient" form of government, and a reintroduction of absolutism in France "today" would have meant a regress into history's past; "modern times belong to feudal monarchy, and feudal monarchy belongs to modern times" (64–65).

I will get in a moment to Montesquieu's understanding of feudal monarchy as a separation of powers between king and nobility and the foundation of modern freedoms. What I should notice first is the idiosyncratic way in which Montesquieu translated the political split between Germanists and Romanists in his own geohistorical terms. Germans and Romans, in other words, became for him concepts dividing Europe into two complementary antitheses, and its history into an ancient and a modern time. Book 4 had already established, in some Manichaean way, the "Differences of the Effects of Education in the Ancients and the Moderns," as the title goes. Also a part of book 21 had been devoted to "the principal difference between the commerce of the ancients and the moderns." In truth, De l'esprit des lois in its entirety was committed to contrasting the "tyrannical and arbitrary principles" that were "guided by ancient histories" to "our modern reason" (2:379). Germania and Rome were now the places and times of all these differences.

Rome, southern and Mediterranean Rome, stood as the synecdoche of an ancient past that no longer was. It was not only Rome as a historical empire that was ancient, premodern, and precommercial: "their [the Romans'] genius, their glory, their military education, and the form of their government kept them from commerce" (2:632). But also contemporary Rome, the one Montesquieu had seen in the present of 1729, was a premodern, precommercial space where "every one is at his ease except those who labor, those who cultivate the arts, those who are industrious, those who have land, those who are engaged in trade" (2:713). Not Rome as a historical empire but Rome as a *place* emerges as "ancient." What *is* Rome, then? Rome, simply, *is* the past—the time of Europe's yore that archeology and tourism are already reclaiming for the northern gaze: "We can never leave the Romans; so it is that still today, in their capital, we overlook the new palaces and go look for the ruins of the past" (2:414).

Against this backward and southern place, "our German fathers" open instead the way to modernity. "In northern regions a machine robust and well built but heavy finds pleasure in whatever is apt to throw the spirits into motion" (2:477). What this meant was that, if "mankind are influenced by various causes," and if "in each country, as any one of these causes acts with more force, the others weaken in proportion," one could then conclude that climate was the strongest cause in the south (Rome), history in the north (Germania). The historical progress from ancientness to modernity remained the prerogative of a northern spirit "in motion": "According to Montesquieu, climate in the north and in the temperate zones is such that in the end it has little visible effect on political institutions. It is in the zones close to the equator, according to Montesquieu, that climate has a determining role in a direct sense . . . it is in the 'south' where the particular circumstances of climate have a directly determining effect" (Gearhart 187).

Only Europe, compared to the savagery and barbarity of other continents, has a history. In a way, history is Europe, whereas other continents are only fragments of its past stages. Yet history is also a progress that goes from an ancient south—"a bad country" (*un mauvais pays*) governed by climate—to the modern north—"a better one" (*un [pays] meilleur*) (Montesquieu, *Oeuvres* 2:532–33). It was in this better north that one had to look, then, to discover the traces of Europe's modernity: its constitutional freedoms; its forms of government (2:409); and, above all, its most modern institution of all—private property.

Gallic Feudalism

These Romans are fools!

—RENÉ GOSCINNY AND ALBERT UDERZO, *Asterix le Gaulois*

What François Bernier had gained after his thirteen years of travels in the Mogul Empire (first published in 1663 as *Mémoires sur quelques affaires de l'Empire Mogol*) was the undisturbed certainty—reinforced rather than weakened by the very fact "that he failed to grasp the basic tenets of Brahamanism" (Mukherjee 11)—that freedom was a uniquely European good, and that such uniqueness had something to do with another uniquely European good—private property. The Other of Europe —Oriental India in this case—was despotic not so much because of Aristotle's climatic conditions, but simply because lacking of a concept of private property: "The King is proprietor of all the lands in the empire, there can exist neither dukedoms nor marquisates, nor can any family be found possessed of wealth arising from a domain and living upon its own patrimony" (Bernier 227). Differently than Francis Bacon, who believed that knowledge is power, Bernier rather believed that property is power, and that on its fair division resides a fair division of political authority. What had made Europe free, for Bernier, was the rise of a propertied class: ownership had entailed all subsequent divisions of power, and led, as a necessary consequence, to constitutionalism, freedom, justice, and wealth. As Bernier concluded his address to Colbert, the minister of finances for Louis xiv, he wrote: "Yes, my dear Lord, to conclude briefly I must repeat it; take away the right of private property in land and you introduce as a sure and necessary consequence tyranny, slavery, injustice, beggary and barbarism" (Bernier 238).

With the *Travels in the Mogul Empire* Bernier had thus introduced a new commonplace, complementary to the climatological one, in the rhetorical distinctions of free Europe from the despotic Orient. Henri de Boulainvilliers, in the *Histoire de l'ancien gouvernement de France* (1727), had brought the question of the relationship between property and freedom to the fore when he had maintained that despotism resulted from "the barbaric law of the Orient [which] annihilated private property" (qtd. in Venturi, "Oriental Despotism" 139). Montesquieu had little patience for Boulainvilliers (Montesquieu, *Oeuvres* 2:891); but the idea of private property as the foundation for European freedoms certainly proved an attractive one, at least to the extent that private property meant for him an overcoming of the state of nature and a historical progress toward civil liberty: "As men renounced their natural independence to live under political laws, they also renounced the natural community of goods to live under civil laws. Those first laws established freedom; the second, property" (2:767).

Freedom and private property were, then, the two sides of the same coin—of the difference, that is, between Europe and the rest of the world. The problem, for Montesquieu, was that both Bernier and Boulainvilliers had seen private property as something short of miraculous, which "suddenly appeared over all Europe without being connected with any of the former institutions" (2:883). Once again, Montesquieu's scientific ambitions could not allow for miracles to go unexplained: "I should think my work imperfect if I did not speak about these laws" that established freedom and private property at the same time (2:883). Book 30 of *De l'esprit des lois*, announced as a "Theory of Feudal Laws," served as Montesquieu's explanation of Europe's miracle. Feudalism was, with an allusion to Virgil's *Georgics*, the metaphoric "root" from which Europe had grown tall: "The feudal laws form a very beautiful prospect. A venerable old oak raises its lofty head to the skies, the eye sees from afar its spreading leaves; upon drawing nearer, it perceives the trunk but does not discern the root; one must look under the ground to discover it" (Montesquieu 2:883–84).

Digging around the tree of European freedoms, Montesquieu found the roots of feudalism. That such roots were firmly implanted in northern soil should not, at this point, come as a surprise. Briefly, this was the argument of book 30: the "dark labyrinth" of the history of feudalism brings us back to the German laws (2:884). When the German princes were fighting the Romans, they instituted laws, which rewarded the most valorous soldiers by elevating them to the rank of "companions," and by compensating them with the fruits of the booty. These nomadic princes had no lands to give away; the companions were, then, not proper feudatories, but early antecedents of them (2:885–86). Companions were subsequently transformed into so-called *antrustiones* when the German tribes of the Franks founded a monarchy in what had been Roman Gaul; the princes now had lands to give away as revocable rewards. The "unique property" of the prince was, for the first time in human history, divided (2:887). Vassalage grew from the institution of the *antrustiones* when growingly powerful landlords started opposing the king during the Merovingian and Carolingian periods: they obtained that land property be made hereditary and irrevocable for their descendants; and they started attracting to their sphere of authority all the freemen that had been, until then, under the tutelage of the monarch. As fiefs became patrimonial, the vassals grew into an aristocracy by birth: its titles and power were now perpetual and no longer depending on the discretion of the king (2:890–92). Finally, the authority of the king was counterbalanced by the growing authority of the aristocracy: privatization of property had then created the presuppositions for a political division of power, and for the political liberties of the Franks (2:892). This first division of power, in turn, engenders other ones, and becomes the founding stone of European freedom: "There is no freedom if judicial power is not separated from legislative and executive powers" (2:397).

Feudalism thus confirmed Bernier's theory: private property *was* the cause for the growing influence of the European aristocracy, which served to balance the otherwise absolute power of the king-despot found in the east. Such confirmation, however, also produced two corollaries: that the barbarous and prehistoric east dispensed altogether with any concept of private property (in chapter 5 of this book I will discuss some dissenting opinions); and that ancient Roman property was not real or modern property. In the early Roman republic, Montesquieu explained, possessions were not patrimonial but personal. Instead of being inherited from father to son, property was "disposed through a popular assembly" (2:780). In the times of Justinian, on the other hand, private property was patrimonial, but fragmented, at the death of the owner, between all sons and daughters. The effect of these laws of transmission was to render impossible any accumulation of power alternative to the emperor's (2:789): without patrilineal inheritance of private property, the republic was doomed to end with the dissolution of Caesarism. It was only with the Franks that the supposedly ancient history of property took a new and modern turn toward the feudal establishment of patrimonial assets, and the consequent creation of an alternative source of power concentrated in the nobility. Modern Europe, as the overcoming of barbarity and the foundation of a new mediated sovereignty, then came into being with Charlemagne, who remains Montesquieu's very personification of the spirit of modern Europe: "Charlemagne's continuous victories, the sweetness and justice of his government, seemed to found a new monarchy . . . Arts and Sciences seemed to reappear. One can say that the people of France was destroying Barbarity" (1:1095).

If Europe was, since Aristotle, the land of freedom, Frankish patrimonial law was for Montesquieu the only conceivable origin of Europe. It was also the origin of a new end of history, which was neither despotism (Asia) nor colonialism (the South), but rather the progress of man to freedom and commercial wealth. In theorizing such origin, old classical distinctions acquired a new and modern flavor: the freedom that Europe could boast vis-à-vis Oriental despotism was now reframed to embody the needs of a rising capitalist Europe concerned less with climate and abstract ideals than with "the preservation of every man's right and property" (Locke 5:62).[16] More important, the east-west antithesis was supplemented by a new one that divided Europe into a before and an after of the institution of private property—between an ancient precapitalist south and a modern and capitalist north. The combination of climate (nature) and private property (culture), then, served Montesquieu "to establish the intrinsic superiority of Europe over the rest of the world, Asia in particular. At the same time, it provide[d] the basis for Montesquieu's assertions of the superiority of one part of Europe over another" (Moe 26–27).

Put differently, after 1748 Europe coincided with a theory of history in which the south figured already as the negative term—nature, the past—posited by the spirit of a progressive north on the path toward its self-definition and self-realization. History, understood metaphysically as universal history, was a progress in space—from an ancient south to a modern north. At the basis of this theory was climatology, along with some bizarre experiment on a sheep's tongue. Not much, one would think, to make the theory credible. But the ways of the rhetorical unconscious are many.

Coda

> Who does not know how much the question of the influence of climate has been studied, along with the importance that Montesquieu gave to climate! If one considers the direct influence of climate on man, that influence may well be less powerful than it has been supposed. But the indirect influence of climate.
>
> —FRANÇOIS PIERRE GUILLAUME GUIZOT,
> *Histoire de la civilisation en Europe depuis la chute de l'Empire romain jusqu'à la rèvolution française*

In 1769, William Robertson, a firm proponent of the theory of northern feudalism as the origin of European modernity, trustingly echoed Montesquieu's climatology of northern pride:

> The same circumstances that prevented the barbarous nations from becoming populous, contributed to inspire, or to strengthen, the martial spirit by which they were distinguished. Inured by the rigour of their climate, or the poverty of their soil, to hardships which rendered their bodies firm and their minds vigorous; accustomed to a course of life which was a continual preparation for action; and disdaining every occupation but that of war or of hunting, they undertook and prosecuted their military enterprises with an ardour and impetuosity, of which men softened by the refinements of more polished times can scarcely form any idea. (5)

Around ten years later, however, Edward Gibbon had to entertain the possibility that climatology, questioned as a science, could interfere with, and weaken, his theory put forth in *The Decline and Fall of the Roman Empire*. Did this mean that, along with climatology, one had to throw away anything built with it? Certainly not! Even after the fall, he wrote, "the name of Rome must yet command our involuntary respect: the climate (whatsoever may be its influence) was no longer the same" (3:978). Whatsoever may be its influence . . . . Luckily, climatology was no longer necessary for Gibbon to claim that the Germans, not the Romans, were "the rude ancestors of the most polished nations of modern Europe" (1:1); or that "the northern countries of Europe . . . were filled with a hardy race of barbarians, who despised life when it was separated from freedom" (1:32). What had replaced climatology to give scientific authority to these claims? Empirical historiography had: rather than dissecting goats, Gibbon consulted archives, annotated pages, compared documents, evaluated circumstances—and, above all, he read so carefully "the comprehensive genius of the president de Montesquieu" (472n). Not Montesquieu the climatologist, mind you, but Montesquieu the legal historian of Gallic feudalism, the one who had claimed that constitutional freedoms were first "found in the northern woods" (Montesquieu, *Oeuvres* 2:407): "The Franks, after they mingled with their Gallic subjects, might have imparted the most valuable of human gifts, a spirit and system of constitutional liberty . . . which had been sketched in the woods of Germany" (Gibbon 2:489). The northern woods of Montesquieu thus returned in Gibbon's woods of Germany.

Montesquieu, who had to find in the empirical science of climatology the legitimacy for his theory, was transformed into a legitimating authority himself. The process—*from* climatology *to* German freedoms—had been bracketed away, when not even denounced as faulty. Its end result, however, began to return as the rhetorical unconscious: it had become archival truth.

From Scottish historians to Italian physiologists, physiognomists, biologists, and anthropologists—the gap was not an unbridgeable one for the rhetorical unconscious. Montesquieu's Europe became ethnography for Cesare Lombroso; climatology turned into fieldwork and biology: social maturity, instead, remained a progress from the prehistory of a *homo meridionalis* under the yoke of climate and natural factors to the full realization of the *homo europaeus* (see Teti 154). Perfectly sociable, perfectly cultured, "an intelligent being" ready to "transgress the laws that God has established," the *homo europaeus* was the distinguished member of this new and modern Europe in formation—a refined Republic of Letters that the *homo meridionalis* awkwardly entered with that constant fear of being mistaken for the delivery boy of the Café Orientale downstairs.

3   Republics of Letters

WHAT IS EUROPEAN LITERATURE?

Which literature, whose world?
—DAVID DAMROSCH, *What Is World Literature?*

The concept of a republic of letters—ideal of "an intellectual community transcending space and time" (Dibon 26)—had been circulating widely in Europe for quite some time. Never before or after the publication of the monthly *Nouvelles de la République des Lettres*, however, had the republic seemed such a reality: from 1684 to 1687, Pierre Bayle had run and edited the journal with the purpose of transcending national boundaries and of creating an atmosphere of cooperation and mutual toleration among cosmopolitan and learned readers. The son of a French Protestant family, Bayle knew well how constricting national boundaries and laws could be for intellectual research and curiosity: with the revocation of the Edict of Nantes and the reimposition of state religion in 1685, Bayle had to renounce his faith in order to continue his studies at the Jesuit school of Toulouse. When, after the completion of his courses, he reconverted to Protestantism, he became the victim of utter discrimination and intolerance. His works were attacked and censored, and his brother was even jailed because of Bayle's "heretic" publications. When he managed to flee to Holland to join the Protestant Academy of Sedan, Bayle soon started to look for ways of overcoming state censorship and intellectual silencing. His ultimate aim was the creation of a class of scholars whose reflection would be free and unhindered by any state: truly cosmopolitan scholars, in short. His main instrument to reach such goal was the *Nouvelles*.

In 1751, only three years after the publication of *De l'esprit des lois*, Voltaire reminisced (in *Le siècle de Louis* XIV) "that happy century" crowned by the *Nouvelles* as the beginning of a new era of intellectual cooperation that the journals, salons, and—last but not the least—the *Encyclopédie* were now to bring back to life:

A Republic of Letters was established imperceptibly in Europe, despite wars and despite religious differences. All sciences, all arts thus received mutual help. Academies have formed this Republic. Italy and Russia have been united by literature [*unies par les lettres*]. English, Germans, and French went to study in Leyde. The famous physician Boerhaave was consulted at the same time by the pope and the czar. His greatest students have attracted foreigners in the same way, and have become in a way the doctors of all nations. Those who really know, in any branch of knowledge, have tightened their bond with this great society of learning, scattered everywhere, and everywhere independent. (*Oeuvres historiques* 1027)

As utopia, the Republic of Letters represented the possibility of a free flow and exchange of ideas unhindered by religious, political, or territorial divisions: As Annie Barnes has remarked, academies, universities, journals, symposia, public debates, and even epistolary exchanges promised the formation of a cosmopolitan "ideal state" based on "international intellectual cooperation" (qtd. in Goodman 15). What politics and religions divided, *lettres*, said Voltaire, united.

A Theory of Literature

> Literature: this word is one of those vague terms that are so
> frequent in all languages . . . . Literature . . . designates, in all of
> Europe, knowledge of works of beauty, an acquaintance with
> history, poetry, eloquence, and criticism.
> —VOLTAIRE, *Dictionnaire philosophique*

What Voltaire meant by *lettres* is probably best understood by making reference to the homonymous entry signed by Louis, the chevalier de Jaucourt for the *Encyclopédie, ou dictionnaire raisonné des sciences, des arts et des métiers, par une société de gens de lettres*:

> Letters. This word designates in general the enlightenment [*lumières*] produced by study, in particular the study of belles lettres or literature. In this last sense, one distinguishes literate people [*gens de lettres*], who only cultivate the erudition of varied and amusing amenities, from those who devote themselves to abstract sciences, and to sciences of a more sensible utility. Yet one cannot acquire them [abstract and practical sciences] to

an eminent degree without knowledge of *lettres*. Derives that *lettres* and proper sciences have, among them, the tightest bonds, liaisons, and relations. It is the task of the *Encyclopédie* to demonstrate that . . . *lettres* are the key to sciences; that sciences, on their part, contribute to the perfection of *lettres* . . . . Grammar, Eloquence, Poetry, History, Criticism—in one word, all the parts of Literature (*Littérature*)—will be seriously defective, if the sciences do not reform and perfect them . . . one must be a philosopher and a literate man [*homme de lettres*] at the same time. (Diderot 9.409)[1]

For *lettres* one must then not only understand literature (grammar, eloquence, poetry, history, and criticism), which limits itself to "knowledge." *Lettres* also includes the capability to translate such knowledge into practice and into things "of a more sensible utility." Letters are the synthesis of the arts, the "amusing" literature, and sciences, which are eminently useful. Such a synthesis is possible only through philosophy— the abstract science—that draws from the otherwise useless knowledge of literature a method for its usability. What is important, however, is first of all the difference between literature and letters. Hence the question of erudition: literature, in and by itself, is only a sterile, unproductive amenity. Its pleasure, as Jaucourt seems to notice with some degree of matter-of-fact skepticism, is the pleasure of talking well and namedropping: to what possible use?

Sure enough, literature is necessary—the key, as it were—to produce anything of some utility. We know the logic from more recent discussions: the workforce—Jaucourt's "trades"—needs "literature" (I guess today we call it "literacy") to read manuals, be flexible, on top of a world that changes rapidly, and happy. Literature, in other words, *is* necessary —as a means, however, not as an end. Jaucourt writes: "Literature (*Littérature*), s.f. (Sciences, Belles Lettres, Antiq.). General term that indicates erudition, the knowledge of Belles Lettres and of the subjects related to it. Look under *Lettres*, where they are praised, and where has been demonstrated their intimate unity with proper Sciences" (Diderot 9.594). As a matter of fact, literature's "intimate unity" with the sciences had been hardly "demonstrated" under *Lettres*, which had in fact taken such unity apodictically, while leaving to the whole *Encyclopédie* the arduous task to prove anything. (Brilliant method, in fact, if you think about it: it is not that I cannot demonstrate anything—I have already done it elsewhere!) At any rate, Jaucourt's point is that literature *should* be (whether or not this can be demonstrated) intimately tied to the practical sciences: left by itself, literature is vacuous knowledge, "erudition" and, in one word, "pedantry." How unfortunate, then, that many men of letters, "today," have become such pedantic bores. The very expression *man of letters* has turned—vox populi!—into a "most offensive insult" ("injure plus offensante") (Diderot 9:594). All this has happened not because of literature's own faults, but because its pedantic clerks have betrayed literature's true mission. And what is, exactly, such mission? To offer a key to praxis, no doubt; but also, and more important, to create, maintain, and improve the perfectly polite and urbane society of the Republic of Letters:

> Despite the bitter criticism of ignorant buffoons, we dare to assure our readers that only the letters (*lettres*) can polish the spirit, perfect taste, and lend grace to the Sciences. However, to be profound in Literature (*Littérature*), we must abandon those authors who do nothing but embellish things, and rest on the sources of antiquity: on the knowledge of religion, of politics, of government, of customs, of habits, of ceremonies, of games, of celebrations, of sacrifices e spectacles that was proper to ancient Greece and Rome. (Diderot 9.595)

Apart from a continuous (and not always convincing) attempt at separating *lettres* from *littérature*, what is clear is that a modern notion of literature, overcoming a stale cult of Greek and Roman antiquities, is prescribed here for the reader of the *Encyclopédie*: not literature as erudition, then, but literature as key to practical knowledge; not literature as a cult of the past, but as praxis on the present and creation of a progressive future; not literature as knowledge for knowledge's sake, in the end, but literature as the formation of citizens—of a society of polished spirits, perfect taste, and graceful sciences. This is literature, in sum, understood as the basis of the transnational Republic of Letters of poets, doctors, and mathematicians already praised in *Le siècle de Louis* xiv.

In the entry on *Lettres*, Jaucourt had in fact advised his reader to "look under Literate People." Here we find, penned by Voltaire, a very clear statement regarding the cosmopolitan nature of *littérature* and *lettres* at the time of the *Encyclopédie*:

> Literate People. This word corresponds to that of *grammarians*. For the Greeks and the Romans, *grammarian* was a man versed not only in grammar properly speaking, but in all branches of knowledge . . . . The

meaning of this word is today more extended than it was for the Greeks and the Romans. The Greeks only knew their language. The Romans studied only Greek. Today, the man of letters adds to the study of Greek and Latin also the study of Italian, Spanish, and, above all, English. (Diderot 7.599)

More sympathetic than Jaucourt to Greeks and Romans, Voltaire, too, is eager to stress the difference between literature—or, more precisely, the man of letters—of today and the one of the olden days. Once monolingual, this man has become today a true cosmopolite: he speaks in tongues! The knowledge he needs to possess is not simply that of his home country but that of the universe. Literature, in sum, is not national, but universal.

No matter if this man of letters was not a woman; and no matter if a hierarchy—"above all, English"—is already becoming apparent here: cosmopolitan in spirit, multilingual in language, Voltaire really saw the Republic of Letters as the true realization of a benign universalism—a multiculturalism of sorts already pitted against the yet unborn Nicolas Chauvin of Rochefort and against the already dead Jacques Bénigne Bossuet. Let me insist on this point: Voltaire believed in his own universalism. For its sake, he had (pitilessly) demoted Bossuet's *Discours sur l'histoire universelle* to a "Discourse *on a part* of universal History" (Voltaire, *Oeuvres complètes* 11:158; emphasis mine). What was the problem with Bossuet? Voltaire did not have a word for it, but it was, undoubtedly, his Eurocentrism. How could Bossuet—Voltaire would complain at the opening of the *Essai sur les moeurs et l'esprit des nations* (1756)— dismiss the "powerful empire" of the Arabs as *un déluge de barbares*, an "overflow of barbarians" (*Oeuvres complètes* 11:158)? How could he fail to mention China—where, after all, silk, paper, glass, porcelain, gunpowder, and even the printing press had originated (11:171–72)? What kind of *universal* history was his, when it did not even refer to India—as if the most beautiful, intelligent, and human game, chess, had not been invented there, along with the idea of the popular state and many other things still (11:185–89)?

All this truly irritated Voltaire. A universal history, like an accurately cosmopolitan knowledge, *had to* extend beyond Europe. Even more so, since in comparison to such antique civilizations as the Chinese, the Indian, and the Arab, Europe was just a mere parvenu on the scene of universal history: "From any point we look at it, we must acknowledge that we were only born yesterday" (11:215). The Chinese, the Indians, and the Arabs—those same Arabs that Montesquieu had condemned to a destiny of climatological barbarism—were civilized when the Europeans were still living in caves. They had literature when we had yowls! So spoke the voice of cosmopolitan conscience to Voltaire. After that, feeling certainly good about his enlightened refusal of Bossuet's Eurocentrism, Voltaire could earnestly go on: yes, those people were civilized before we were, and developed their literatures before we did—but then they no longer progressed, as we did instead. All those civilizations, which came to history before Europe, have not managed to progress beyond a certain stage; whereas the Europeans, who came later, have continued, and continue still, to progress on the path of history:

> We ask ourselves why the Chinese, having gone so far in older times, have always remained at the same stage; why their astronomy is so old and so dim-witted; why their music still ignores semitones. It looks as if nature has given that kind of men, so different than ours, organs made to find all at once what is strictly necessary, and incapable to go beyond that. We, on the contrary, developed our knowledge much later, and have since perfected it very rapidly. (11:173)

Bossuet has certainly been left behind by Voltaire's more enlightened cosmopolitanism. A comparison with Montesquieu, however, still seems necessary. Rather than being "barbarians," Arabs, Indians, and Chinese did possess for Voltaire beautiful and refined civilizations. This is not as blunt as Montesquieu's Europeanism, then. Voltaire's cosmopolitanism, however, comes to very similar conclusions to those of *De l'esprit des lois*: history is a teleology of progress that moves, "like the sun" ("en suivant le cours apparent du soleil"; Voltaire, *Oeuvres complètes* 11:184), from east to west. Whereas the east is the beginning of universal history, Europe is its modernity. If not history tout court, at least progress is the peculiar endowment of Europe—the only continent, in fact, where knowledge does not come "all at once," but through stages of continuous evolution. As proof of Europe's advancements and eastern stagnation, it is enough to look at literature; and since "one of the infallible proofs of the superiority of a nation in the spiritual arts is the culture perfected by poetry" (11:215), Voltaire starts looking at, and comparing, Arab and Chinese poetry, on the one hand, and European poetry, on the other. Conclusion: both Arabs and Chinese had poetry before Europeans did; but it was only in the Europe of Augustus and of Louis xiv that poetry truly improved. If, from poetry, one then goes on to belles lettres, and from them—the key—to the practical sciences, one single truth seems to emerge from Voltaire's cosmopolitan investigation: "they" came before "we" did; but they have remained "like we were two hundred years ago" (11:217). Two hundred years: counting backward from Voltaire, we can now understand the reason for the superiority of European literature— Francis Bacon and the scientific revolution. One understands now why, of all modern language, the man of letters needs to learn "above all, English." What Europe had two hundred years ago, and the other continents did not, was the kind of literature prescribed by the *Encyclopédie*. The Arabs had their literary amenities, and the Chinese their erudites. But only Europe had the true wisdom of *gens de lettres* like Francis Bacon, who put knowledge and belles lettres to the service of Jaucourt's "more sensible utility."

In the meantime, the cosmopolitan overture to the universe predicated by the unwritten constitution of the putative Republic of Letters brought Voltaire back precisely to Montesquieu's more frank (pun intended) Europeanism. If literature was *now* climaxing in Europe, this did not mean that the Republic of Letters could forgo the study of the Orient, which, pace Bossuet, was an origin of sorts (Orient, from Latin *origo*, or origin, as in the origin of the sun) and had had, as such, its own literary glories. But this did not mean, either, that Orientals could be part of the Republic of Letters: they could be *objects*, but never *subjects*, of study. In the words of Hans Bots and Françoise Waquet, the Republic of Letters "limited itself to territories identified with the values of [arts and sciences]—in fact to Europe only" (71). As the opening issue of the *Journal des savantes* (1665) assumed, authorship itself—the possibility of being the subject of writing, theorizing, historicizing, or philosophizing —seemed to be a peculiarly European characteristic: "The design of this journal being to inform of what happens in the Republic of Letters, it will mainly be composed of a precise catalogue of the major books published *in Europe*" (Bots and Waquet 71; emphasis mine).

The fact is that the universalism of the Republic of Letters, as well as its cosmopolitanism, remained, in Im Hof's expression, "a purely academic and theoretical question" (104). In practice, the republic was a rather limited affair. It included not Europe tout court, but merely its courtly and mobile nobility, which recognized "the same rules of class everywhere: the military code of honor for the officers; duty and faithfulness; the matrimony with persons of equal standing only" (Hof 103). In this restricted sense, the Republic of Letters had become the figure of identity for Voltaire's Europe: through publications such as the *Gazette littéraire de l'Europe* (1764), the republic managed to establish a "good taste" common in the courts all over Europe; it gave Europe *one* common literary canon shared "from Paris to Saint Petersburg" (Marino 13), and it provided courtly Europe with an imaginary "single body, a cultural and spiritual unity distinguished from the rest of the world" (Chabod 117).

Following Montesquieu's hint about the fundamentally "Oriental" nature of the European south, Voltaire's *Essai* had observed that "the Oriental climate, nearer to the South, obtains everything from nature; while we, in our northern West [*Occident septentrional*], we owe everything to time, to commerce, and to a belated industry" (*Oeuvres complètes* 11:158–59). The east, like the south, owes everything to a nature that, in Montesquieu's words, gives "all the riches of life, and few wants." Europe, western Europe, is produced instead by "time." It is, as *De l'esprit des lois* had remarked, the transgression of "the laws that God has established." Nature versus culture: history coincides, then, for Voltaire as for Montesquieu, with Europe itself. Consider for instance Voltaire's entry for "History" in the *Encyclopédie*, where Europe, with France at its center, would be the degree zero of history, the one and only perspective of history into which any other needs to be translated:

> If you make a history of France, you are not compelled to describe the course of the Seine and the Loire rivers; but if you give to the public the conquests of the Portuguese in Asia, it is necessary a topography of the discovered countries. One needs that you take your reader by the hand along Africa, the coasts of Persia and India. One expects from you some instructions about the customs, the laws, and the habits of these nations, which are new for Europe. (Diderot 8.221)

If Europe's development is belated vis-à-vis the Orient, this is because the time of Europe is modernity—the only possible perspective from which history, the past, can be conceived qua past. Europe only can retroactively *look at* the past. The Orient, instead, *is* the past. Only Europe, therefore, can be the subject of history. What also emerges from Voltaire's discussion of the "Oriental climate, nearer to the South," is that Europe is divided into a western Europe—the antithesis of the Orient—

and a southern one—the dialectical negation and internal Other of the *Occident septentrional*. The south of Europe, very much like the exotic Orient, is a place of nature. It owes nothing to progress, history, or the arts and sciences. Like the Orient, southern Europe too developed early—but did not continue to do so.

Also in this marginalization of the south of Europe, Voltaire's north-centric cosmopolitanism was confirmation of, rather than deviation from, the practice of the Republic of Letters. Bots and Wacquet, again, remind us that "Italy seemed [to the self-declared citizens of the republic] to be in an inexorable process of decline, which Spain sadly shared. Portugal did not deserve a mention. . . . The Loire river was a dividing line; it is in the north that one found the centers of importance: Rouen, Troyes, Lyon, and, above all, Paris" (74). In Voltaire's words, neither the Italians nor the Spaniards—the south, that is—but, rather, the French were the "legislators" of this modern Europe of culture ("les Français furent les législateurs de l'Europe"; *Oeuvres historiques* 1002). Besides France, only the north—England, "above all"—could participate in the creation of Europe's modern literature.

We have followed the theorization of French Europe in the previous chapter on Montesquieu. In fact, it was already by the middle of the eighteenth century, in the heyday of Bayle's *Nouvelles*, that "French men of letters saw themselves as the leaders of a project of Enlightenment that was both cultural and moral, if not political. By representing French culture as the leading edge of civilization, they identified the cause of humanity [and certainly of Europe] with their own national causes and saw themselves as at the same time French patriots and upstanding citizens of a cosmopolitan Republic of Letters" (Goodman 4). "Far and away Europe's greatest power" (Davies 579), France was certainly the seventeenth-century leading cultural force: its châteaux and gardens had become the object of imitation all over Europe, its cogito the method, its modernity the standard, its classicism the aesthetics, and its language the lingua franca of the European cultivated classes from Palermo to Amsterdam. As Timothy Reiss maintains in *The Meaning of Literature*, it was since the constitution of the Académie Française by Cardinal Richelieu in 1635 that France had taken his task to legitimate its own values—"increasing social tranquility, the growth of commerce, the settlement of military discipline, and the reform of finance and luxury expenditure" (70)—as the very logos of a modern Europe moving already, as Jean

Baptiste Le Ron D'Alembert would soon record, to a capitalist epistemology "greedy of utilizable knowledge" ("avides de connoissances utiles"; Diderot iv).

Accordingly, France had finished to consolidate, through the work of a centrally controlled academy, the status of French as "the 'most perfect of modern' languages" (Reiss 71)—one whose "genius" was to utter and incarnate the culture of modern Europe. Voltaire, in the preface to *Oedipe* (1729), was among those who believed that "each language has its own genius, determined by the nature of the construction of its sentences, by the frequency of its vowels or its consonants, its inversions, and its auxiliary verbs" (qtd. in Folkierski 227). Beginning already with Cartesian linguistics, the supposed genius of the French language was seen as an immediate propensity for rational discourse. As an index of its natural rationality, its logical construction—subject, verb, object—was most often mentioned (see Rosiello; Puppo 42–56; Mercier Faivre 176–79). Such theses had been abundantly theorized by Dominique Bouhours in 1673. The *philosophes*—the most authoritative of which would be Antoine Rivarol in 1785—had then further theorized the necessity for "French as the language of the Republic of Letters" (Goodman 21): "Since our language has spread throughout Europe, we thought that the time had come to substitute it for Latin, which since the renaissance of learning had been the language of scholarship. I must say that there is more excuse for a philosopher to write in French than for a Frenchman to compose verses in Latin. I would even agree that the use of French has helped to make the Enlightenment a more universal phenomenon" (Diderot xxx). As a corollary, even literary good taste, in the words of J. E. Spingarn, had to be judged against the standard of French: taste was "the result of the application of [Cartesian] reason to aesthetic pleasure" (18). Since French, as the naturally rational language, was also the most Cartesian, it had then to be the most beautiful as well. French, along with the literature written in it, had to be elevated to a model of good literary taste. As Paul Hazard wrote, "Beauty is reason; and reason is France" (*Révolution* 121).

French literature is the legislating literature; French history the perspective on universal history; and French language—which since the Treaty of Rastadt, 1714, was also the language of European diplomacy (Duroselle 234)—the language of the French Enlightenment as "a more universal phenomenon." In the words of Louis Réau, eighteenth-century Europe was, fundamentally, a "French Europe"; and, as Louis-Antoine

Caraccioli's 1776 treatise (obviously written in French) offered as an echo, this was the time best described as *Paris, le modèle des nations étrangères ou l'Europe française.* The *Encyclopédie,* in this context, was nothing more than a monument erected to this hegemony of France.

Montesquieu himself, who was not new to the collaborative ideals of the republic (Deuvres 1:21), contributed to the *Encyclopédie* with an essay entitled "Essai sur le goût dans les choses de la nature et de l'art." In 1753, D'Alembert had asked the president to contribute an essay on despotism and one on democracy. What D'Alembert in all likelihood expected was a recapitulation of the very arguments of *De l'esprit des lois*: Asia is despotic, Europe is democratic, and the head and heart of this Europe is France. Montesquieu, instead, wrote about taste, and the essay was published in 1757, two years after the author's death (Shackleton, *Essays* 103– 7). Sure enough, Montesquieu's testament was not a masterpiece of originality: taste is the arbiter of beauty; beauty is that which gives pleasure; and what gives pleasure is unity in variety. Groundbreaking or not, however, Montesquieu's essay intended, rather than repeating the argument of *De l'esprit des lois*, to now extend French hegemony from political to aesthetic issues. In this sense, the "Essai sur le goût" was symptomatic of an epochal shift in the understanding of Europe: Europe was to be defined not only in political and climatic terms but also in cultural ones.[2] Prescriptive in tone—refrain from enjoying the voice of the Italian castrati; despise the "insufferable" arias of Italian opera (Montesquieu, *Oeuvres* 2:1261)—the "Essai sur le goût" educated the aspiring man of letters to develop good taste: and good taste was not only defined in a French book—the *Encyclopédie*—but dictated from France speaking on behalf of humankind. "In *our* present way of being"; "the pleasures of *our* soul" (2:1240–41; emphases mine): was that "our" the generalization of French taste over all humankind?

The presence of Montesquieu's Europe in the *Encyclopédie*, in fact, went well beyond his actual contribution. At the entry "Europe," Jaucourt, for instance, wrote that: "No matter what, Europe remains the smallest part of the world; yet, as remarks the author of *De l'esprit des lois*, Europe has come to such a high degree of power, that history has hardly anything to compare it to" (Diderot 6.211). Montesquieu had already sanctioned the wonderful uniqueness of modern Europe. And Montesquieu had prepared the promotion of France, recapitulated in Jaucourt's entry about it, as the marvel of the modern Republic of Letters: "Around the last century, the Arts, the Sciences, Commerce, Navigation, and the Navy appeared under Colbert, with such an admirable speed as to astonish Europe" (Diderot 6.211, 7.282). Jaucourt's logic derives from Montesquieu, and the mention of *De l'esprit des lois* is debt paid. Yet the uniqueness of Europe is here not only its freedom but nothing less than what Jaucourt himself had previously called *lettres*: The arts, belles lettres or literature, and the more "sensible utility" produced by arts—commerce and navigation above all.

Letters, then, define the glory, unity, and uniqueness of Europe. What is Europe, however, for Jaucourt? As the geographer of the *Encyclopédie*, Jaucourt had a very clear sense of the way in which geography, after Montesquieu, confused itself with history, thus forming a spatial chronology of humankind's progress. If France, with its *lettres*, was for him the unquestioned place of modernity, then Italy, on the contrary, as the entry on the country suggested, was a memento of a time that no longer is: "The good days of Italy have eclipsed, and its glory vanished. Its commerce is past, the source of its riches dried up" (Diderot 8.932). Under "Spain," not altogether differently, we read: "This beautiful kingdom, which once impressed great fear on the whole of Europe, has slowly fallen into such decadence that it can hardly overcome" (5.953). Undoubtedly, neither Italy nor Spain represented modernity. Voltaire had made a similar point: "Spain is the country with which we are no better acquainted than with the most savage parts of Africa, and which does not deserve the trouble of being known" (*Oeuvres complètes* 1:390–91; see also Salvio). Spain is, then, preyed on by the Inquisition, a place arrested in a time of savagery that precedes not only modernity but also history itself: no doubt, it does not deserve the trouble of being known. Also Italy, once glorious, fails to enter that very century of Louis XIV that, with Descartes and the lesson drawn from Bacon, brought Europe into modernity: in that century, writes Voltaire, "there was no longer taste (*goût*) in Italy" (*Oeuvres historiques* 10002). As Jaucourt then suggested in his article on Europe, being European meant to belong to a part of the world "more important than all because of its commerce, its navigations, its fertility, its intelligence and the industry of its peoples; because of its knowledge of Arts, Sciences." If neither Italy nor Spain, however, had participated in this progress of letters, could they be said to be Europe at all?

In the same way in which Montesquieu had theorized history, climate, and freedom as a way of theorizing Europe, Voltaire and Jaucourt were now theorizing letters, literature, and the arts and sciences to theorize the

Republic of Letters. Such a republic coincided with Europe, and at the same time was smaller, limited to the *Occident septentrional*, and bigger, universal, than the mere geography of Europe. Montesquieu's geopolitical argument—Europe is the difference of north and south—was reconverted by Voltaire and Jaucourt into a geocultural one (Dumont-Wilden 76): Europe was defined by its culture—in this sense, it was a Republic of Letters, a "grand republic divided into various states" (Voltaire *Oeuvres historiques* 620); but this culture had its heart in France. Its past, instead, was to be found between Italy and Spain. European culture as the culture of modernity was, then, the historic progress of letters from south to north, from Greece, through Rome, to the French age of Louis XIV, unveiled from France as the future of humankind.

A promising future indeed. Yet once southern countries had been dismissed as remnants of the past, and once France had been patriotically elevated to the rank of the "legislator of Europe"—once these steps had been taken, the universalistic claim of the *Encyclopédie*'s cosmopolitanism was doomed to encounter the diffidence of any parts of humankind, let alone Europe, that did not feel exactly French. Was it possible that, in order to become cultured, modern, and European, one had to become, also, French? Napoleon had not yet written that "all men of genius and all who have gained respect in the republic of letters are French, no matter what their country" (qtd. in Hazard, *Révolution* 116); but already by midcentury the sense was that the rhetoric of the arts and sciences was becoming the voice of French hegemony trying to define Europe in its image.

In 1750, Jean-Jacques Rousseau had already moved his attack against the arts and sciences with his "Discours" for the Academy of Dijon. The thesis of his speech was unequivocal: arts and sciences, taking humankind out of a "happy ignorance," had corrupted its morals while introducing "luxury, dissolution, and slavery" (*Oeuvres* 3:15), and damning Europe in an undesirable modernity. Already there, Rousseau's was not so much an attack against letters, but one against the *philosophes'* understanding of the letters as the bearer of a certain kind of progress for humankind—Jaucourt's "polishing the spirit, perfecting taste, and giv[ing] grace to sciences." All this polishing, taste, and grace was seen by Rousseau as an attempt to transform women and men into Parisians—affected, unnatural, and artificial.

In a letter addressed to D'Alembert in 1758, the argument was recapped on the occasion of D'Alembert's suggestion—in the article on

"Geneva" for the *Encyclopédie*—to open a theater, similar to the ones in Paris, in Rousseau's hometown. The suggestion was not received well by Rousseau, citizen of Geneva. Since the time of the revocation of the edict of Nantes (1685), Calvinist Geneva (along with Protestant England) had become a myth (Ramat) in Europe, standing for religious freedom and all northern, anti-Catholic virtues. As I noted in the chapter on Montesquieu, Catholicism and southern despotism were seen as two sides of the same coin. Paris, after Richelieu and Mazarin, was seen as nothing less than a betrayal of the northern cause for freedom—religious or otherwise. Although Montesquieu had tried, in *De l'esprit des lois*, to remind France of its northern and Protestant duties, the image of France one could draw from André De Murault's *Lettre sur les Anglois et les Francois* (1761) or from Voltaire's *Lettres écrits de Londres sur les Anglais et autres sujets* (1734) was that of a reactionary bulwark of anti-Calvinism. Calvinist Geneva, on the contrary, stood as the positive model of a modernity threatened by Catholic Paris.

Speaking as "a good citizen of Geneva" moved by "love of country," Rousseau, in the letter, simply argued that the imposition of anything French would be pernicious for the moral tempter of the Protestant people of Geneva. If the Republic of Letters was centered on Catholic Paris, then it was high time to dispel the myth of its universality:

> To ask oneself if Spectacles are good or bad in themselves, is to ask oneself a question that is too vague to answer. . . . Spectacles are for the people . . . there is, between one People and another People a prodigious diversity of habits, temperaments, and characters. Man, I agree, is one: but man modified by Religions, Governments, laws, habits, prejudices, climate, becomes so different from himself that one should no longer look for what is good for man in general, but what is good in a specific time and place. (*Oeuvres* 5:16)

In other words, such theaters could be good for Paris, but not for the people of Geneva. The literary standards set in Paris around the *Encyclopédie* were not, for Rousseau, necessarily the same as the norms that existed elsewhere.

Peculiar, in this context, was Rousseau's reevaluation of the south as the place of an original ancientness and of the past. No longer the commonplace of Montesquieu's Catholic despotism, but, rather, the incarnation of a nostalgia for an older way of living that modern Europe, with its arts and sciences, had long forgotten to remember, the original south, before being corrupted by the religion of the pope, was fragment of a paradise lost: "In the south the first familial ties were formed; there the first rendezvous between the two sexes occurred. . . . There were the first festivals; the feet were restless with joy . . . . [And] the voice accompanied that joy with passionate accents. Pleasure and desire melted together, and made themselves audible. There was, in the end, the true cradle of humankind" (*Essai sur l'origine des langues* 107). In Rousseau's reevaluation of the south, there was the implicit attempt to theorize the essence of Europe again—after and against Montesquieu and the *philosophes*. The south, which Montesquieu, Jaucourt, and Voltaire had seen as the limit of Europe's Republic of Letters, became for Rousseau, along with northern and Calvinist Geneva, a positive utopia. Yet in Rousseau as in Montesquieu, the south remained a distant fantasy of primitivism against which modern and northern Europe, with nostalgia or with pride, could still theorize itself. It remained the antithesis— nature; the past—posited by the spirit of a modern north eager not only to define itself but also to overcome its own discontents in some superior synthesis, or in a return to a hypothetical origin. In the meantime, however, the south was not silent and was writing its own theory of Europe to claim its own place, viva voce, in the Republic of Letters. If Voltaire, Montesquieu, and Jaucourt had theorized some kind of Europe in which certain standards of the arts and sciences immediately disqualified the southern countries, then a rehabilitation of the south could not be thought of without a rethinking of those same standards. Moreover, Voltaire, Montesquieu, and Jaucourt had theorized a Europe defined by its progress. Such a Europe was the modernity of history—its present and its end. Of this Europe, the south was at the same time margin and internal antithesis—its past. To reclaim the Europeanness of the south, to theorize a Europe not simply shaped in the image of Paris but capable of including the southern difference, what was necessary was, first, a rethinking of the arts and sciences, and, second, a new theorization of history. In other words, the south, striving to enter Europe with its Republic of Letters, needed now not only a new and more elastic and comprehensive theory of Europe but a new theory of history and of the arts and sciences within it. An expatriate Spanish Jesuit took this task on himself. It may have scared Hercules, but Father Juan Andrés did not seem to think that anything was too big for him.

Juan Andrés: A Spanish Jesuit in Italy

> If a great number of talents and learned men in all sciences had
> not come in exile to Italy from the last borders of Europe!
> —VINCENZO MONTI, *Per la liberazione d'Italia*

Juan Andrés renounced his right of primogeniture on Christmas Eve
1754 in order to wear the robe and become a Jesuit. He could not have
chosen a worse time. Since the order had been founded in 1540 with the
implicit (though never stated) intent to stop the Protestant Reformation,
Europe had already witnessed an ideological divide between Reformation and Counter-Reformation, Protestantism and Catholicism, Molin-
ism and probabilism that had typically set Jansenists and Protestants
against the Jesuit order.

Especially relevant for these pages were the quarrels concerning the
status, limits, and ends of knowledge—quarrels that had immediate
practical relevance in the restructuring of schools and educational systems all over Europe. As Alasdair MacIntyre has suggested, the Protestant Reformation had brought about a fairly new conception of what
knowledge is: "Reason can supply, so these new theologies [Protestant-
ism but also Jansenist Catholicism] assert, no genuine comprehension of
man's true end; that power of reason was destroyed by the fall of man."
In other words, these new conceptions consider knowledge of humankind's ultimate meaning an aporetic impossibility and limit the reach of
human knowledge to some kind of "practical" reason capable only to
assess "truths of fact and mathematical relations but no more" (53–54).
Luther's interpretation of Romans 1:17, concerning the justice of God,
precluded any possibility for human reason to understand and know
such justice. The latter could be acquired not by reason, studying, and
knowledge, but by grace—and, to a lesser extent, faith—only. As the
second article of the *Large Catechism* put it, "although the whole world
with all diligence has endeavored to ascertain what God is, what He has
in mind and does, yet has she [humankind] never been able to attain to
[the knowledge and understanding of] any of these things" (Luther 601).
Luther thus limited the reach of reason, as Mark Painter echoes Mac-
Intyre, "to manage earthly affairs of survival, state and law. But it is
completely inadequate when applied to affairs of the spirit. With Luther
reason becomes observational, calculative, managerial and limited to the
working out of practical matters" (6). It becomes, then, a prelude to

Immanuel Kant's practical reason, or, put differently, to Max Weber's Protestant spirit of capitalism.

As for the consequences all this had for pedagogy, these are clear to be seen: post-Lutheran Europe soon began to witness the emergence of two separate educational projects. On the one hand, the Jansenists' "small schools" of Port-Royal, whose model spread across "central and northwest Europe" (Ong, *Ramus* vii); on the other, the "colleges" of the Jesuits, which "produced a southern, Italy-centered 'Christian Humanism'" (Scaglione 48). What knowledge was or meant arguably constituted the core of the endless controversies between the two pedagogical models. For Jansenism, knowledge, unable to attain metaphysical truths, had to be limited to the pragmatics of social living—it became knowledge of what constituted perfect citizenship; for the Jesuits, instead, knowledge could not be limited to pragmatics, but had to provide a metatheory of knowledge aimed at understanding the presuppositions that generated, in the last analysis, practical knowledge. In other words, on the one hand, we have the practical dialectic (*dialectica utens*) of the Jansenists, aimed at merely explaining what one knows, for instance, in medicine or law; on the other, there is the teaching dialectic (*dialectica docens*) of the Jesuits, which wanted to teach the pupil not *what* we know, but *how* we know what we know (Ong, *Ramus* 162).

What I have been calling the Jansenist model had its heyday in the small schools of Port-Royal and was already becoming hegemonic in Voltaire's Republic of Letters. In 1763 (the same year, incidentally, of Rousseau's *Émile*), Louis-René de La Chalotais published his truly influential *Essai d'éducation nationale* that rehearsed many of the Jansenist pedagogical tenets in a climate of general enthusiasm for reforms. For La Chalotais, education, to begin with, had to be national, modern, secular, against the "vice of monasticity" (read the Jesuits), and run by the state. Second, and in line with Luther's distrust for papal Latin, schooling had to be done in vernacular French.[3] Third, education's goal was to form good citizens and to do so had to teach *practical* subjects, not the antiquated and useless humanities. Fourth, knowledge, being practical, was a commodity, produced by the school against the student's tuition, and always quantifiable and measurable through *written* examinations (the "document" that begins the "humanist assault on oral disputation"; Ong, *Ramus* 155), grades, and promotions.

Two things must be noticed about La Chalotais's influential model: first, that despite what his contemporaries saw in it, this model was less a *rationalization* than a *secularization* of post-Lutheran pedagogy. Already Jean Duvergier de Hauranne, abbé de Saint-Cyran, founder of Port-Royal, had claimed that the goal of education was service "not only for God, for Jesus Christ and His Truths but also for the common good, and for the interests of the Kings of the land . . . because if Jesus Christ died for men, it is just that men will die not only for Jesus Christ but also for other men" (qtd. in Sirignano 25). And Luther (in the *Discourse on the Utility of Sending Children to School*) had attacked humanistic education for being antiquated and largely pagan. The second point to be made is that the *Essai*'s polemical adversary was most evidently Jesuit education. It was Jesuit schools that stuck to a predominantly humanistic curriculum—Cicero's *Familiares*, Erasmus's *De copia*, Martial, Caesar's commentaries, Aesop, Aristotle, Livy, Lucia, Homer, Isocrates, and Virgil —with little interest, in fact, in the "morality" or Christianity of the books (Scaglione 78). Jesuit schools kept recommending, with disregard for national languages, that "all, especially the students of the humanities, must speak Latin" (Farrell 96). And Jesuit schools, always refusing the written test, with their endless discussions (the oral *disputatio*), with their "pedagogy of the spoken word" (Sirignano 82), and with their obsession with rhetoric and eloquence (Codina 40; O'Malley), were the major obstacle to the commodification and the measurability of knowledge. What is worse, the Jesuits' refusal to perceive direct tuition, their willingness to have 60 to 65 percent of their students from "sons of the working class," were at the same time inflating the price of the knowledge commodity, and establishing a true monopoly over it (the statistics are by Scaglione 118; for a different take on Jesuit schools' elitism, see Martin).

The issue of education was in fact not marginal to the Jesuits' first expulsion from a European state. In 1750, Sebastião José de Carvalho y Melo, the Count of Oeyras and future Marquis de Pombal, blamed the Jesuits for exercising economic control in the colonies, of accumulating immense (and untaxed) riches in Uruguay, of fomenting Indios' revolutions in Paraguay, and, last but certainly not least, of monopolizing education in the home country. As Franco Venturi summarizes, Pombal had basically accused the Jesuits "of opposing the will of the mercantilist state, which had now [in its attempt to overcome its economic crisis] decided to control the economy and education, religion and culture" of the country ("Church" 224).

The Jesuits were expelled from Portugal in 1758. In France, in the meantime, they were being accused not only of protecting their "feudal" privileges but also faced criticism for perpetuating a useless, backward humanistic culture hindering the modernization of the state (Northeast). As Robert Palmer noticed in a clever essay of 1940, the expulsion of the Jesuits in France coincided with a growing interest on the part of school reformers to create a modern and national educational system for the preparation of *citoyens*:

> Their general message was that education should be nationalized, and its object be to form citizens. Reformers complained that the schools were too secluded from civil life, that teachers in religious orders lacked patriotic spirit, that children were taught to see their true country in another world, and to place their allegiance too exclusively in God and religion. The old humanistic and literary education was condemned as useless in itself . . . . La Chalotais held, against the cosmopolitan and humanistic tradition of the Jesuits, that education should conform to the national character, be controlled by the government, and conducted by men who, "not renouncing the world," practiced the civic virtues that they taught, and had interests the same as those of the country. ("National Idea" 101–2; see also Mortier).[4]

In 1762, the Jesuit Order was expelled from France. The secularization and state control of both economic planning and national education was also central in the decision of Carlos III to expel Andrés' order from Spain in 1767. Fanatically pious when in Naples (where he was king, too), Carlos III was a rabid secularizer in Spain. He had very good economic reasons (e.g., the expropriation of their lands) to expel the Jesuits from Spain (Renda *Espulsione* ; Renda *Bernardo Tanucci*). He also had fairly convincing "cultural" motives for the expulsion: the Jesuits' attempt— 669 colleges, 176 seminaries, and a lot of private tutoring for young aristocrats (Domínguez Moltó 21)—to organize education against state monopoly (Brizzi 189). With the expulsion of the Jesuits, in other words, the traditional war of religion had translated into a new educational quarrel between the ancients and the moderns—between an idea of economic and cultural modernization centered on state schooling, on the one hand, and, on the other, the Jesuit Order as the perceived surplus, if not obstacle, to that modernization. An integral part of such a *querelle* was to promote, pretty much in Jaucourt's vein, the development of useful sciences. The Jesuits, identified with an old intellectual order still busy studying an old, unmovable tradition based on the lesson and imitation of the ancients, were perceived as the obstacle for a modern innovation of the curriculum requested by the new emerging bourgeois classes (Valero 192). Central to the political decision of expelling the Jesuits—in Portugal, France, and Spain—was, then, the cultural "question of national education" (Palmer, "National Idea" 100)—the choice, namely, between a pragmatically utilitarian national culture for the sciences and trades, on the one hand, and the Jesuits' humanistic and cosmopolitan (if not otherworldly) culture on the other.

When the decree of expulsion was promulgated in Madrid on April 2, 1767, Juan Andrés had to leave his teaching position at the Royal and Pontifical University of Gandía, the first Jesuit college that, in 1546, was forced by the insistence of the population to open its doors to non-Jesuit students. Andrés had been teaching there, for three years, courses in Latin, Greek, and Hebrew under the general rubric of rhetoric. Education in Gandía followed the *Ratio studiorum*: "The disciplines were divided in the traditional manner: first the Humanities . . . beginning with advanced Grammar . . . Rhetoric, languages (Latin, Greek, and Hebrew) . . . . Then Logic . . . and on to Philosophy proper" (Scaglione 70). Andrés left Gandía in the early days of April. Without food or clothing, he was put on a boat with other Jesuits from all over Spain. They were denied permission to land in Civitavecchia, Italy, and finally landed in Bonifacio, Corsica, where the patriots led by Pasquale Paoli, in the midst of their never-ending revolution for self-determination, fed the Jesuits and granted them temporary refuge. Andrés left Corsica for the more tranquil Italian mainland in 1768, when Pope Clement XIII, starting a full-fledged diplomatic war against Portugal, Spain, France, and the Kingdom of the Two Sicilies, decided to offer asylum to the Jesuits in the Papal State.

Here, in Ferrara, he lived for five years, until, on August 15, 1773, the new pope Clement XIV, in the attempt to reconcile the papacy with the foreign powers (and "advised by the Holy Spirit"; qtd. in Del Rio 143), suppressed the order from his lands.[5] Once he left Ferrara, Andrés moved to Mantua, where he arrived in January 1774. He stayed until the arrival of Napoleon in 1796. Here, in "that center of Italian learning and culture" (Mazzeo 39), Andrés achieved a rather prominent European status as a learned person and as citizen of the international Republic of Letters: he was visited by the likes of Johann Gottfried von Herder and Johann Wolfgang von Goethe, exchanged opinions and courtesies with learned Italians, befriended other Jesuits in exile, and carried out his research to write his magnum opus.

The way in which the conditions offered by Mantua helped Andrés to put together his learned and cultured work is obviously hard to quantify. Although it might be a bit of a stretch to call Mantua *that* center of learning and culture,[6] the city had witnessed, under the enlightened rule of empress Marie Therese of Austria, a significant cultural "reawakening" after the collapse of the Gonzagas (Quazza 229–30). Academies were being founded and financed—the Virgilian in 1752; the Theresian of Beaux Arts in the same year; the Philarmonic in 1761. Middle schools and universities, many under Jesuit control, had been reformed and modernized with a series of decrees between 1760 and 1761.[7] The city library had been constructed with the marbles (and a few books as well) salvaged from the destroyed villas of the Gonzagas. In sum, although not a center of frenetic intellectual life, Mantua, like the nearby Milan ruled by the same tolerant absolutism of Marie Therese, had witnessed a number of political and cultural reforms that had introduced some measure of modernization while keeping at bay the more revolutionary implications of the French enlightenment.[8]

It was in this climate of moderate Lombard reformism, in which trans-Alpine revolutionary ideas had been mixed with conservative Italian ones, and where great energies were employed for "the reorganization of the schools, of the universities, of culture in general" (Venturi, "Church" 218; see also Venturi, *Utopia*), that Andrés found his new home. Mantua was quite open to the new philosophies of modernization coming from beyond the Alps; and, at the same time, it appeared tolerant enough of the Jesuits, who were cherished for their cultural prestige and employed, both by the state and by private patrons, for the reorganization of the educational system: "There are so many Spaniards of merit here, that is impossible for me to list them one by one," wrote Andrés to his brother Carlos (Andrés, *Cartas familiares* 1:4). A Voltairian Jesuit, Saverio Bettinelli (1718–1808), was the venerated cultural symbol of the town. In other words, the incandescent and polarized atmosphere of Rome, Naples, or Venice—where Jesuits and so-called modernizers were at each other's throat (Del Rio 126–28, 136–37)—was far enough from Mantua to allow Andrés the intellectual distance necessary to absorb the lessons of Montesquieu, Voltaire, and, above all, Rousseau; it was so far, on the other hand, that acceptance of enlightened principles did not need to be unconditional to the point of fanaticism. Mantua was the perfect meeting place for different ideas and diverging national prejudices to meet and discuss (see Menéndez y Pelayo). It was a little republic of letters whose enrichment of Italian culture has perhaps been underestimated and in which Spanish Jesuits showed "a wonderful capacity to adapt" (Batllori 514).

In sum, Mantua offered the perfect atmosphere for an intellectual trained in the humanities, and one knowledgeable of the so-called practical sciences as well, to reconsider the presuppositions of both. From "this beautiful part of Europe" (Andrés qtd. in Mazzeo 17), Andrés then meant to attempt a general assessment of nothing less than all sciences. He wanted to look into their origins and foundations. Most important, he wanted to trace their history and progress. In doing just that, he found something at the same time hopeless and peculiar: what the *Encyclopédie* had theorized and canonized as *the* literature, was, after all, just a French local phenomenon hypostatized as universal. Still, there were other possibilities to retheorize literature: Andrés, the Spanish Jesuit in Italy, chose to retheorize from the south.

A Theory of Literary Historiography: Decentering Europe

Arguably the son of an encyclopedic age that "had its roots in [Roger] Bacon, the *Encyclopédie*, and the British *Universal History*" (Arato, "comparatista" 1), Juan Andrés was not kidding when he titled his magnum opus *Dell'origine, progressi e stato attuale d'ogni letteratura* (Of the Origins, Progress, and Present State of all Literatures). Echoing D'Alembert's program for the *Encyclopédie*—"to go back to the origins and generation of our ideas" (Diderot NA9)—but renouncing the collaborative framework of the Republic of Letters, Andrés, all alone, set out to study not only the origin of ideas but also their progress.[9] Proud of introducing an undertaking that "no other author, I believe, has conceived so far" (Andrés, *Dell' origine* 1:i), Andrés opened the first part of his seven-volume treatise, published from his Mantuan exile in 1782, with a master plan—"maybe too daring and bold" by his own admission —that would later gain him little of the glory he had dreamed of, but, instead, the unflattering nickname of "the presumptuous friar" (Carducci 2.45).[10] He should have seen it coming. The very incipit of *Dell'origine* was an invitation to brag-bashing—like that pretentious claim to be writing nothing less than "one critical history of the events that literature has suffered in all times and in all nations; a philosophical sketch of literature's [*letteratura*] progress from its origin to the present" (1:i).

Literature, first of all: what did this term mean for father Juan Andrés? His understanding of it was, to say the least, quite broad: it encompassed not only the belles lettres but also history, geography, chronology, archeology, grammar, mathematics, mechanics, hydrostatics, natural science, nautical science, acoustics, optics, astronomy, physics (general and applied), chemistry, botany, natural history, anatomy, medicine, philosophy, jurisprudence (secular and canonical), theology, biblical exegesis, and ecclesiastical history. Literature, in other words, was something reminiscent of (but, we will see, rather different from) Jaucourt's letters: not in the sense that Andrés saw the necessity to translate belles lettres into some "more sensible utility," but in the sense that literature represented for him the synthesis and totality of human knowledge.[11] Writing a history of the origin and progress of all of this was, one has to agree, quite a big task at hand. And then, "in all times and in all nations"!

It is easy to see how this gigantic effort, that only the daring few have claimed (and timidly at that) as the putative origin of comparative literature (e.g., Guillén 27), fostered in fact a whole thesaurus of self-righteous ironies. Esteban de Arteaga, for instance, another Spanish Jesuit in Italy, commented in 1785: "Yes, I confess I value myself only a literary pigmy, not a giant. I have not dared to face the Herculean task to cover the sciences and the literatures of all ages, all climates, and all nations. The Signor Abate Juan Andrés, bigger than me, and certainly more confident in himself, instead, has just done that" (Arteaga 1:178). To discuss all of this literature in all times and all nations, specialization in one field, to Arteaga's discomfort, obviously had to be sacrificed. As the apologist Ettore Guido Mazzeo puts it, Andrés "was in essence the opposite of the specialist" (Mazzeo 69). He liked to think broad, and was, by and large, a cosmopolitan scholar (Bérkov; Tejerina). Like that other cosmopolitan Voltaire, he could not accept a universe shrunk to Bossuet's Ile de France. True enough, Andrés's cosmopolitanism, when compared to that of Voltaire, seemed much more dictated by petty and practical reasons: it was because of the necessity of exile, not because of aspirations to become a man of letters, that Andrés had had to learn to master languages and cultures other than his native Spanish. It was the new historical reality of exile, not *studium*, which had faced Andrés with the comparatist's problem of understanding not one culture—if we follow Adolfo Domínguez Moltó's interpretation that " 'all literature' equals 'all culture' " here (67)—but, historically and critically, *all* cultures in relation with one another.[12] And it was, in the end, his allegiance to the Jesuit world with its ecumenical mission and its horizons "necessarily shaped by the supranational character of the Society" (Brizzi 188), not his commitment to the Republic of Letters, that had imposed on Andrés a cosmopolitan, transnational perspective, and perhaps a first understanding, however vague it might have been, of cultural differences.[13]

All, alas, to no avail. While Voltaire's universal history was canonized as the first true example of the genre (Fueter 358), *Dell' origine* remained, even for the comparatist, a monstrous work "with no sense" (Wellek, *Discriminations* 25) and an "excess of encyclopedic gusto" (Getto 99).[14] Such strong reactions are curious—not so much because I believe Andrés's was a better model for *Weltliteratur* than, say, Goethe's; but because, despite so much insistence on Andrés's alleged *encyclopédisme*, *Dell'origine* was the clear attempt, in more ways than one, to go beyond *encyclopédisme* and against all that the latter stood for. It is enough to see how Andrés, already in the first few pages of his preface, sets his tone of polemical *sprezzatura* against the *philosophes* in general and D'Alembert in particular. In the "Preliminary Discourse," the latter, following Bacon's taxonomy, had divided human knowledge into erudition (memory), belles letters (imagination), and philosophy (reason), as if one could be studied in itself and separated from the others. Also Jaucourt, as we have already seen, had divided knowledge between literature (belles lettres), philosophy (abstract), and (practical) sciences. Andrés responded:

> This kind of division is correct if we consider the relations of the various sciences with the faculties of our mind; but it is not very fruitful if we want to follow the progress that has been accomplished in those sciences.... Surely, natural history and ecclesiastical history are branches of historiography; but how can we separate natural history from physics, and ecclesiastical history from theology? In sum, such division . . . can serve those who want to examine the genealogy of sciences, but not those of us who want to write their history. (*Dell' origine* 1:iv)

In the *Encyclopédie*, the crisis of a traditional discursive system based on theological or Aristotelian notions of the unity of all knowledge had engendered a process of differentiation and fragmentation and produced a discreet series of self-regulating and autonomous disciplinary domains

(M. McKeon 17). As Voltaire had written in the *Encyclopédie* under "Belles Lettres," "universal knowledge is no longer possible to man: the true men of letters move their steps in different fields, since they cannot cultivate them all" (Diderot 7.599). The temptation to see Andrés as a conservative obscurantist trying to reclaim a lost and untenable unity is strong. What such prejudice would betray, however, is the assumption of the fundamentally progressive nature of the French *philosophes*, and the regressive one of their opponents.[15] Yet as José Antonio Valero suggests (187–89), Andrés's attempt to preserve a measure of connection between the literatures was no more regressive than the *Encyclopédie*'s own attempt to preserve a unitary perspective—D'Alembert's rational "system that is one" (Diderot NA9). The difference is that the unifying principle was no longer, for Andrés, the philosophes' universal reason.

Interestingly, if not surprisingly, such a unifying principle—which introduces an element of relativism to the otherwise objective universality of reason—is what Andrés called "critical history," or "philosophical history" (*Dell' origine* 1:i–v). Let us remember that history, for both Voltaire and Jaucourt, was a branch of the belles lettres (though for Voltaire the situation could be improved by applying "to the writing of history, what has already happened to physics"; see *Oeuvres historiques* 46). As such, history was not the end of knowledge, but just a key to the practical and useful sciences. Here, instead, it is history—Andrés's goal is "to write their [sciences'] history"—that appears as the *end* and ultimate summation of all knowledge. This does not mean that history is no longer a branch of the belles lettres: on the contrary, history remains similar to poetry in so far as "illusion has to be created in history just as in poems" (Andrés, *Dell' origine* 3:118); and it obeys the same narrative rules as the novella when its task becomes "to choose among the infinite facts only those that are worth narrating" (3:146). The difference between Jaucourt's and Andrés's history, instead, lies in the latter's capacity of synthesis and abstraction that only philosophy, the science of reason, possessed for Jaucourt and Voltaire. History is the ultimate philosophy for Andrés, not only because it can discuss the origin and progress of *all* sciences but also because its method is inherently a philosophical one: "Not the vast erudition, but the philosophical zest and spirit is the only force capable of forming, out of a confusion of materials, a fabric convenient to the wonderful richness of the world" (3:96). History, selecting those facts alone that are "worth narrating," is the only true philosophy.

Andrés's concern with history is interesting (and unsurprising), first of all because it follows what can be characterized as a general trend of literary studies in the eighteenth century. Earlier epochs had studied the corpus of a poetic tradition "not with a properly historical . . . interest, but from a rhetorical point of view" (Getto 2) by singling out authoritative examples, possibly to imitate, in a given literary tradition. Only in the eighteenth century is a predominant rhetorical interest abandoned in favor of a chronological organization (alternative, incidentally, to the arbitrarily alphabetical one of the encyclopedia). What Andrés thought to have found was that such novel interest in chronology was in fact not so general, and had instead its own geography: the French, under the spell of Cartesian reason and Montesquieu's general spirit, had failed to develop chronology into true history. Jean Pierre Niceron's *Mémoires pour servir à l'histoire des hommes illustres de la République* (1729–45), or Prosper Marchand's *Dictionnaire historique* (1758–59), were for Andrés mere fragmentary and itemized collections of biographical details. Even the *Histoire littéraire de France* (1733), developed by the Benedictines under the direction of Antoine Rivet de la Grange and Charles Clemencet, arguably "the model [of literary historiography] that other nations have taken on themselves to imitate," remained for him "farthest from the perfection that this kind of work requires. It is anyway mainly biographical; it follows with too much individuality the authors and their works; it fails to present with due precision the true picture of the general state of literature in the various ages it describes" (Andrés, *Dell' origine* 3:372).

A true sense of history, for Andrés, had to be found in Montesquieu's south—notably in his adoptive Italy, where history, not modernity, was the leading glory of the country; where the archeological excavations of Pompei and Ercolano (begun in 1748), not the modern marvels of Versailles (Ange Jacques Gabriel had completed the Petit Trianon in 1768) gave a sense of place; and where Gian Mario Crescimbeni, already in 1698, had produced an *Istoria della vulgar poesia*. Crescimbeni's history had been followed by the literary histories of Giacinto Gimma (1723), Francesco Saverio Quadrio (1739–52), Francesco Antonio Zaccaria (1750), and, last but not the least, by the *Storia della letteratura Italiana* (1772–82), by the "wise" Girolamo Tiraboschi (Andrés, *Dell' origine* 2:xiv). What attracted Andrés to these texts was that they all presented, through history, an explicit defense of Italian culture against the accusations of Dominique Bouhours's *Les entretiens d'Ariste et d'Eugène* (1671): that Italian modern poetry, starting with Petrarch's taste for the "embellishment," and more so under the influence of the Spanish baroque, had become "unreasonable" (on this, see Maugain; Fubini; Puppo 33–36). Girolamo Tiraboschi, for instance, had prefaced his work by saying that "the desire to add new glory to Italy, and to defend it still, if necessary, against the envy of some foreigners, convinced me to begin this general history of Italian literature from its most ancient principles to our own days" (1:v).

Anticipating Andrés, Tiraboschi had strategized his "defense" as a "history of the origin and the progress of Science in Italy" (1:x). Tiraboschi's historicist defense of Petrarch, and of his confluence in the rhymes of *Marinismo* and *Secentismo*, consisted in claiming that the significance of Petrarch had to be measured not on the basis of exogenous standards—say, reason—but as the manifestation of the particular cultural development of Italian literature in Petrarch's own epoch. The advantage of such a method was that it could be immediately applicable in the defense of Spain against French accusations of Spanish ignorance, lack of culture, taste, and letters. In other words, historicism might have appeared to Andrés as the best instrument to settle some accounts with the French.

It had been a Frenchman, after all, Marc Antoine Muret, who in 1588 had blamed the Hispano-Latin writers Seneca, Lucan, and Martial for the corruption of Latin letters and already prompted a response from Andrés in 1776 (see Mazzeo 23; Domínguez Moltó 70–71; Andrés, *Carta*). And it was not so much Bartolomeo de Las Casas's 1553 *Brevísima relación de la destrucción de las Indias*, but the "Huguenot translation" (Hanke 50; Keen) of the *Relación* in Dutch (1578) and French (1579) that had spread the "Black Legend" of Spain's (incidentally true) inhumanity in the service of France's colonial designs and against Spanish interests in the Americas.[16] In the eighteenth century, when the Spanish empire had already crumbled, Muret's indictment of Spanish aesthetics and the echoes of the Black Legend had persisted in the enlightened caricature of the Spaniard as inquisitorial, ignorant, uncultured, vain in the nostalgia of a lost empire, and religiously fanatical—the image, that is to say, of Spain's baroque excesses. What was at stake in this novel wave of Hispanophobia was obviously no longer colonial expansion, but France's hegemony as the cultural standard of Europe—as the center, any distance from which would be plain error.

Despite the fact that Italians were no less the victims of Bouhours's and Muret's Francocentric logics than the Spaniards were, the hegemony of the French discourse had offered Italian intellectuals the possibility (or scapegoat) of blaming Spanish influence for its own faults. The Mantuan Saverio Bettinelli, but also the much admired Girolamo Tiraboschi, had in fact promoted yet another *querelle*: whose fault was the crisis, if any, of Italian letters (see Palazón 16)? Andrés had answered with a polemical letter to the Italian "brother" Gaetano Valenti Gonzaga: significantly, the title with which the letter would be published in 1776 hinted at an alleged reason for the corruption of Italian taste. In short, the alleged Spanish influence had nothing to do with a crisis (alleged, too) of Italian literature. The arguments that Andrés found in the letter, and which later would become part of *Dell' origine*, certainly managed very well to "[defend] the honor of the [Spanish] Nation . . . from the offense that some Italians have advanced, when they have accused Her of having corrupted Italian taste" (*Carta* 4). Tiraboschi immediately retracted in front of Andrés's "good taste," and declared himself "sorry" for his own lack of judgment (Venturi, *Settecento* 1:262–66). Neither Saverio Lampillas nor Juan Francisco Masdeu, who had written with the same intentions as Andrés, had managed to achieve such retraction from the proud (and certainly authoritative) Tiraboschi. The fact is that Lampillas and Masdeu had advanced "a violent defense of the national cultural patrimony [of Spain] realized as an apologetic praise of Spanish literature said to have been an important contribution to Europe" (Micozzi 54); Andrés, instead, had forgone any apology and questioned the very logic—or "taste"—that allowed Muret, Bouhours, and Boilau—the French, that is—to order literature in a hierarchy in which France occupied the top, and Spain, *but also Italy*, the defective bottom. In other words, Andrés, differently than the virulent Lampillas and Masdeu, had managed to strike a strategic cultural alliance between the Spaniards and the Italians.

The strategy of the letter to Gonzaga was to produce the polemical backbone of *Dell' origine*. Rather than attacking the Italian despisers of Spain, Andrés saw both Italy and Spain as a brotherhood of victims of French prejudice. He then went directly to the source of that prejudice— and he found himself in the midst of Montesquieu's *Lettres Persanes*, whose seventy-eighth letter could, after all, be quoted in its entirety (it has already been done by José Cadalso) as a monument of French eighteenth-century Hispanophobia. An "invincible enemy of work" (Montesquieu, *Oeuvres* 2:249), Montesquieu's Spaniard constantly affects a culture that—be it clear to all!—he certainly does not possess:

"The eyeglasses [that all Spaniards wear] show demonstratively that the one who wears them is a man enlightened by science and a profound reader—so profound indeed that his eyesight has weakened. [In Spain] any nose adorned or weighed by [glasses] can be passed off, with no one daring to question, as a savant's nose" (2:248). For Montesquieu, the Spaniard's is an inferior intellect, and it is devoid of culture—culture being, of course, that essentially French attribute otherwise known as *raison*: "Surely you can find some intelligence and some commonsense people among the Spaniards; but don't look for any in their books. Take, for instance, their libraries, with their fantastic literature on one side, and the scientific works on the other. It is as if the whole thing had been arranged and collected by some secret foe of human reason" (2:250). Montesquieu's Spaniards, quite unflatteringly, are also excesses of hypocrisy. "So devout that you can hardly call them Christians," they possess "little formalities which in France would appear out of place; for example, an officer never strikes a soldier without asking his permission; and the Inquisition always apologizes to a Jew before burning him." Sure enough, these monstrous Spaniards, devoid of culture, empty of intellect, and clear of a moral sense, *must* have something to distinguish them, at least, from the beast. And in fact, Montesquieu concedes: "They are always in love. In dying of languor under their mistress's windows they have not their match in the world . . . . They are, firstly, bigots—secondly, jealous . . . . They allow their wives to appear with uncovered bosoms; but they would not have any one see their heels, lest hearts should be ensnared by a glimpse of their feet" (2:249–50). Yet passion, as we know already from *De l'esprit des lois*, only "multiplies crimes" and is hardly the decorous attribute of the reasonable *honnête homme*! To have a clear example of the latter, on the other hand, we only have to look at France, the "most ancient and powerful kingdom of Europe" (2:279), the center of a new reasonable sociability whose example needs to be extended to the whole continent: "One says that man is a sociable animal. In this sense, I believe the Frenchman is more a man than any other—he is the quintessence of man since it seems he acts only for society" (2:261).

It is not this immediate level of Montesquieu's Hispanophobia, however, that Andrés was determined to tackle. Compared to the *philosophes'* sclerotic insistence on a suprahistorical, universal reason, Montesquieu presented for Andrés the added danger of seeming capable of reconciling such universality with history. Climate had given Montesquieu opportunities both to theorize difference within Europe and to order difference hierarchically by measuring it against the standard of a French "good" weather. It is this "too strong influence of climate" (Andrés, *Dell' origine* 5:609), therefore, that Andrés had to eliminate as the effective cause of cultural excellence:

> It is quite common to attribute to climate an influence on everything, and especially on artistic taste and on the perfection of literature. I certainly agree that climate also has some role in all that pertains to the strength of the spirit. But to claim that the influence of climate determines the true origin and essence of the culture of various nations seems to me an assertion not backed by experience, and unconfirmed by facts. Under the same climate, with no great planetary change, the Greeks, brutes at first, became then for an extended period the wisdom of the world; and that same Greece, which was for many centuries the garden of Europe, has lately become a sterile [intellectual] desert. (Andrés, *Dell' origine* 1:26)

In other words, what Montesquieu—and, by implication, the French—had done, was more than attacking Spain. While hypostatizing their own men as "more men," they had indicted the whole south. The reason they had alleged for their indictment, once again, was climate: " 'Cold,' says Montesquieu, 'tightens the pores, and makes the body stronger; at the same time, makes the nutritional juices coarser, and the spirit becomes less lively.' The fame of the author would deserve a longer criticism than the one needed by the weakness of his reasoning. I would only like to ask Montesquieu if, France being colder than Spain, we should conclude that the French have stronger bodies and less lively spirit" (*Dell' origine* 1:27). In this sense, Montesquieu had little to do with universal reason, and was the mouthpiece, rather, of a merely French reason eager to declare itself superior and universal: *De l'esprit des lois*, for instance, "is not for other nations than France a reason to envy France" (Andrés, *Dell' origine* 6:385). Only the French, who gain from it, can see in Montesquieu's theory any universal truth: for the rest of humankind, "I have to say, I do not find that work too engaging, let alone instructive" (3:126).

For Montesquieu's climatological and spatial logic (whose alleged causality, in truth, Andrés had to exaggerate a bit), *Dell'origine* substitutes a historical one: there is hardly any "necessary relation"—no "law"—between natural and social facts; same climates and same places—say, Greece—have known different stages of success. The law of reason must be replaced by history, a critical understanding of differences in taste and habit that have little, if anything, to do with natural causes. And—just to hit the French where it hurts—submitting history to geography and climate is nothing less than *unreasonable*. History, which Andrés declares to have learnt from the Italian, thus emerges as the discipline capable of undoing French Europe from its climatological basis. As such, history is said to have a hermeneutic potential that no other science does: history can explain what climatology cannot.

Far from being the uncultured border of Europe, and far from representing only Europe's cultural past, the *present* south of eighteenth-century Italy became then for Andrés the very capital of Europe's most powerful science—history. The French have their climatologists, seemed to say Andrés; but Italy has, in the present of today, its literary historians: "Other writers have written biographies, have compiled factual details, have collected monuments, which have greatly served to enlighten literary history; but only Tiraboschi has given us a literary history. France and Spain have their literary histories, but theirs are still imperfect; only Italy has a complete and finished one—Tiraboschi's" (3:385). This was only marginally a praise of the Italians, as it was, in a deeper sense, the attempt to depict the south as a place in which culture was still active, and not merely a thing of the past. Most important, this was the attempt to find in history an alternative method to reason for the study of literatures.

This brings me to the second reason why Andrés's historical turn (so to speak) is at the same time interesting and unsurprising. In his 1948 Harvard lecture titled "Vico and Aesthetic Historism," Erich Auerbach had already observed that historicism "practically originated in the second half of the eighteenth century, as a reaction against the European predominance of French classicism" (185).[17] For Auerbach, historicism had emerged as "the conviction that every civilization and every period has its own possibilities of aesthetic perfection; that the works of art of the different peoples and periods, as well as their general forms of life, must be understood as products of variable individual conditions, and have to be judged each by its own development, not by absolute rules of beauty and ugliness" (183–84). In truth, we should not exaggerate the range of what Auerbach calls "every civilization and every period" here. Certainly born within Europe, and certainly short-circuited in the attempts to articulate "variations on a master narrative that could be called 'the history of Europe,'" as Dipesh Chakrabarty has maintained in *Pro-*

vincializing Europe, eighteenth-century historicism can hardly be seen as some kind of multiculturalism aimed at going beyond the strict confines of a Eurocentric universe: Europe, writes Chakrabarty, "remains the sovereign, theoretical subject of all histories" (27).[18] What the emergence of historicism signals, however, is that the very center of this Eurocentric vision becomes a contested site of theoretical discourse around the eighteenth century: against a fixed notion of European culture promoted by French classicism and rationalism, historicism pits its own alternative centers. The history of historicism is, then, the story of a battle for the definition of Europe and its culture that a homogenizing notion of Eurocentrism unfortunately runs the risk of obliterating.

Put bluntly, historicism had emerged, by the second half of the eighteenth century, as the ideology *and* methodology of a subaltern Europe—Vico's Italy, Herder's Germany, and Andrés's Spain—pitted against the unbearable hegemony of France.[19] Historicism was a theory of history radically opposed to the linear universal history of Montesquieu and Voltaire. Progress was not a line that went simply from east to west, or from south to north. For Andrés, who had Giambattista Vico's *Scienza nuova* under his belt, each place had a history of its own—and had to be judged on the basis of this local history, not from the perspective of a putative end of history located in a western and northern modernity.[20] "Progress" was to be understood not as a teleology of continuous perfectibility, but rather as the simple *passage* of cultural hegemony from one nation to another, after the new nation had "inherited" from the previous one the lights of its culture. For instance, if the Romans had come after the Greeks, and had inherited from them some ideas about rhetoric and metaphysics, this did not mean that the Romans had to be better: literature had "progressed" from Athens to Rome—but a comparative judgment of the two was simply beyond the point of history. Progress was for Andrés a movement *toward* a different place, not a movement *forward* to an ultimate end.

In this context we should understand Andrés's insistence that France had no histories: certainly, Bossuet had produced an entire *Discours sur l'histoire universelle*. Yet Bossuet's was only a pseudohistory, "monologic" (Greenblatt) and centered only on "what Europe is in the universe" and on "what Paris and the Ile de France mean within Europe" (Bossuet 4). Even Voltaire, who had avoided Bossuet's simplistic Francocentrism, and who Andrés had praised as a "Prometheus . . . who found a new way of treating Universal History" (*Dell' origine* 3:89), had been unable to produce more than a collection of "mostly false or altered chronicles, impious reflections, and scandalous doctrines" (3:90). Moreover, Tiraboschi's difference between *biblioteca* and *storia*—between the erudite collection of biobibliographical data, on the one hand, and a true history of origins and progress, on the other—was still valid for Andrés: French history, for him, remained "anyway mainly biographical." Yet Andrés was more willing than Tiraboschi to see anything positive in French historiography (Palazón 30).

Andrés's difference from Tiraboschi may be of some importance here: the Italian had denied France any historical sense—French histories were wrong and bibliographical. In this sense, Tiraboschi was applying an essentially French logic—there is one universal reason and therefore one reasonable way of doing history—against France itself. Arguably, Andrés was trying to go beyond Tiraboschi: France's spirit of scientific inquiry that Cartesianism had helped to promote was not necessarily antihistorical, but could establish, instead, some kind of empiricist historiography. This was the case, for instance, of Montesquieu's geographical and climatological history. In what ways did that history differ from the one Andrés was proposing? For Montesquieu, there was one reason, which took different shapes and degrees of perfection according to different geographies and climates. History was, then, the advancement of this single reason, and was, therefore, representable as a single line of progress from one place to another (Barraclough 84). For Andrés, instead, reason itself was historical, and relative, therefore, to a time and place. Each place, accordingly, had a history; and each place has some kind of historiography—even France. However, such admission of a French capability to write history constituted, paradoxically, a more radical criticism than Tiraboschi's of French rationalism: for the French, history was submitted to reason; for Andrés, reason had to be submitted to history.

Still, not France, but "Italy really leads . . . in literary historiography" (Andrés, *Dell' origine* 3:383). Historical relativism—I will come back to this point—did not preclude for Andrés the possibility of passing judgments and organizing hierarchies of value. While Italy produced historians, rationalist France could only produce a prescriptive and normative "modern code of good taste, not only in poetry but in the Belles Lettres in general" (2:204). Not that this was such a great achievement either. Nicholas Boileau's *Art poétique* (1674), to which Andrés was referring, had submitted literature to reason—verisimilitude, clear and distinct phrasing, normative rules of action and conduct, decorum of characters. This was for Andrés symptomatic of a more general, and utterly wrong, French attitude, theorized for instance by Jaucourt, to submit aesthetics—the key—to the superior relevance of practical sciences.

Andrés did not mind the progress of the sciences, which he considered, on the contrary, a "document of the sublimity, and I would dare say of the divinity of human spirit" (*Dell' origine* 4:1). Assuming the Jesuit's resistance to the new scientific spirit would mean to buy into the commonplace concocted for polemical reasons by the *philosophes* themselves. As Aldo Scaglione remarks: "The Jesuits were trying their best to teach both [science and the humanities]. Nonetheless, since the Jesuits' pedagogy has often been criticized for disregard toward the sciences and the practical or technical arts, it must be pointed out, as a symptomatic detail, that of the 130 astronomical observatories in existence in Europe in 1733, 30 belonged to the company" (87). In the specific case of Juan Andrés, it should suffice to say that he had been granted access to the Academy of Mantua thanks to his prizewinning dissertation on hydraulics. Neither ignorant of, nor predisposed against, the practical sciences, Andrés only minded the submission of the belles lettres to that scientific and mathematical language whose hegemony had been abundantly theorized in France by the likes of Bernard le Borier de Fontanelle and Maupertuis (Venturi, *Settecento* 1:355; Palazón 87–90):

> One could lament with good reason the promiscuity, and the abuse, that goes back and forth between these two kinds of literature [i.e., experimental sciences and belles lettres]. Perhaps, the determination to use the rhetorical figures of the belles letters in the sciences will spoil, eventually, the exactitude and just precision of the sciences; it is certain that the belles letters are already damaged by the habit of ruining them through the use of geometrical expressions and scientific idioms; and by the misuse of many words that are proper to mathematics, physics, chemistry, and other sciences into eulogies, academic prose, and even poetry. (*Dell' origine* 2:18–19)

Despite the lamenting tone, the defense of poetry against the practical sciences occupies here a philosophical, more than a merely polemical, dimension. The *encyclopédistes*, and D'Alembert in particular, were ready to see in the belles lettres the key to the superior practical sciences: the student-*citoyen*, as we have seen, needed to learn to read before being able to become a scientist. In this logic, the belles lettres occupied a subordinate, instrumental role vis-à-vis the practical sciences. To D'Alembert's pedagogical argument, Andrés added a genetic one: "The first written document extant to us belongs to history and poetry, not to philosophy" (*Dell' origine* 1:1). The argument, already familiar to sensism (Palazón 62), had been used in Italy by Vico as a way to show not the superiority, but the very limit of science. What did it mean, for Andrés after Vico, to declare poetry the origin of a literature that then progresses with science? It meant to illustrate the blindness of a science, stuck in its dependence on alleged empirical facts and observable certainties, to even face the *problem* of its origin. Can facts arise outside of the language that constitutes them? Can certainties exist outside the words that verify them? Can science ever escape its own origin in language?

Science had symptomatically marginalized the question of language as irrelevant for the purpose of "natural philosophy" (Chovillet). However, the fact remained that science had to use that very language to whose origin it remained programmatically blind. To say, as Cartesian formal logic did, that if A = B and B = C, then A = C, was to formulate something that could be true only within a linguistic convention in which the possibility that A "is" C was not a paradox but a "fact." The definition of a scientific law (as the Copernican one, which Galileo Galilei expounded in the rhetoric of a *dialogue* on world systems in 1632), or the very demonstration of a mathematical theorem, were as much a matter of syllogisms and enthymemes as they were of algebra (Goetsch 49–87). Andrés's "discovery" of the poetic origin of literature, echoing very closely Vico's project of a new science, seemed, then, to suggest the idea that all knowledge—Andrés's literature—originated as/through rhetorical figures. For both Vico and Andrés, whereas Cartesian and encyclopedic sciences had found their legitimization in the facts of the physical world, a new science was fundamentally a metaphysics, a science of the language that founded the knowledge of the physical world. Just as history had "to choose among the infinite facts only those that are worth narrating," so had science to choose, among the infinite epiphanies of the real, those that were worth considering as facts. We thus have Descartes, on the one hand, whom "the French want as the creator of a good physics"; and, on the other, Galileo, for whom "figures, numbers, and algebraic signs are the language of the Universe" and whose "profoundest reflections . . . give birth to metaphysics" (Andrés, *Dell' origine* 1:419, 1:490). Or, in another antithesis deriving from the same rhetorical structure, we have Isaac Newton's physics, on the one hand; and, on the other, John Locke, "the Newton of metaphysics," whose only goal was "to reflect over himself, and over his own thoughts" (6:326). This difference between adherence to the facts and linguistic (self-)reflection of what constituted a fact was fundamental for Andrés's elevation of literary historiography to a metaphysical, systematic theory of the "literatures of the whole world."

The rationalist paradigm is thereby inverted. It is not language that is subordinated to reason, but reason to language: "Contrary to popular belief, reason has more dependence on and greatest need of the faculty of the imagination; if philosophers want to make progress, they must, whether they want it or not, sit next to the poets" (Andrés, *Dell' origine* 1:41). The theoretical consequences are impressive: Boileau's submission of belles lettres to reason implied a universality of reason—the idea that "human nature was permanent and unchanging, wherever and when-ever it was found, and . . . therefore . . . norms could be prescribed to it" (Reiss 71). Such universality of reason, however, was untenable for An-drés, since reason itself depended on the original poetry of languages. Reason was, accordingly, relative to any specific language. What Boileau recommended as reason was therefore something originating within a French linguistic culture, which, in turn, was imposed by a hegemonic state on the periphery of Europe under the assumption of its own uni-versality. This was a rather original way of restating the question of the genius of languages, which had traditionally granted France the hege-mony of civilization: in Andrés's version of it, the genius of French language was not so much its propensity for *the* rational discourse, but rather, if tautologically, a propensity for a discourse perceived as rational only within the same language. In other words, neither reason nor en-lightenment were for Andrés "an impressively unified process across Europe, indeed a remarkable demonstration of the essential cohesion of European history" (Israel 137). There were many reasons, many enlight-enments, and many histories as well.

This left Andrés with a major problem: if historicism is the relativism of judging "each by its own development," how can a hierarchy between, for instance, the "good" histories of the Italians and the "bad" ones of the French still be maintained? More seriously still: once such a principle of relativism is introduced, how is it possible, even in eight quite lengthy volumes, to cover "the origin and progress of all literatures in all times and in all nations"? It is for this reason, I believe, that Andrés continu-ously qualified history with adjectives such as *critical* and *philosophical*.

To begin with, it is interesting that for Andrés *critical* and *philosophical* are not at odds with each other. In the article on "Belles Lettres" for the *Encyclopédie*, Voltaire had written that "criticism today is not necessary, and the philosophical spirit has replaced criticism" (7:599). Andrés insists, rather, that there is no philosophy without criticism.

What criticism meant for Andrés was the selection (*giusta censura*) of the representative works in each single literature. Critical was the interpretation of those works (*attenta lettura*) in the context of their place and time, and not according to allegedly universal criteria. Once its literature was then judged "each by its own development," what remained to be assessed was what, within each literature, had contributed to the general advancement of literature in the world. No matter how important a work or an author could have been in her or his historical and national context, what remained to be done was to select those that had contributed to universal language. The notion of universality thus reenters the theorization of literature, but is no longer limited to the geography of France or any other single nation: "Who on earth are Leon and Villages—Italians will say—compared to Costanzi and Speroni? And who cares about Philips and Canitz—will say the Spaniard—compared to Erera and Schilace? All nations will find my text lacking in promoting their own authors, and too prolix in discussing others. I beg the readers who will bring such an accusation against me to remember that I am discussing universally all literatures, and not particular national ones" (*Dell' origine* 2:xii–xiii). In order to assess which works and which authors were indeed relevant to universal literature, a *philosophy*, a unitary conception and idea of the progress of all literatures, was needed. *Philosophical*, in other words, described a principle of hermeneutic coherence, one opposed to the cumulative method of erudition and of national literature, that could trace the idea of progress ("che descriverà filosoficamente i progressi in ogni sua parte") in "such a cornucopia of facts" (1:v).[21] The philosophical was the power that could abstract, out of *all* the infinite literatures of all times and nations, *one* single, metaphysical history, with an origin and an end not yet in sight:

> In general, I believe that we can consider Asia as the true motherland, the cradle of literature. Because Asia was the first country to be populated after the Flood, it was the first to cultivate the sciences. It can also be said that the light of letters, like that of the sun, began to enlighten the Oriental quarters, following then its westward course, casting light first on

Egypt, and then on Greece, and after that illuminating our western regions [i.e., Europe]. God willing, this light will stay above us a little longer, or maybe will stop its course in our hemisphere, rather than keep moving toward the West transferring the splendor of sciences to America and leaving Europe in the same darkness of ignorance that nowadays casts a shadow not only on the Asiatic nations, but also on Egypt and on the eastern parts of Europe. (1:19–20)

A critical and philosophical history was, then, the key for Andrés to begin to "vindicate his native land" (Mazzeo 45), "oppose the implantation of the restraining Gallic literary tenets and precepts of the neoclassical school of thought . . . [and] counteract the influence of Encyclopedism" in Europe (Mazzeo 45).[22] Looking at literature not from Jaucourt's utilitarian perspective, but from a historicist one, Andrés had already achieved two objectives: first, his contemporary south emerged not as a cultural wasteland, but as the active producer of a vibrant historicist culture; second, southern literatures were different than the French ones (southerners write literary histories while Frenchmen compose the *Arts of Poetry*), and they could not be measured with the same standards. There was still one problem that literary historiography now needed to solve: where did modern Europe begin? Was it, really, in Montesquieu's Frankish woods that an ancient cycle of literature was historically transcended into modernity? Or did European modernity begin in the south after all?

The Discreet Charm of the Arabist Theory

But now, having brought to your attention this synthetic
picture, with its many details, I fear a question may be raised:
Is then all our civilization of Arabic origin?
—A. GONZALEZ PALENCIA, "Islam and the Occident"

Who were the fellow Muslims Abd al-Rahman found
in al-Andalus, and how had they come to be there?
What was that place, Europe, where they lived?
—MARIA ROSA MENOCAL, *The Ornament of the World*

The image of a light of culture moving from Asia to Europe as if following the sun and stationing over the Iberian peninsula before "moving toward the West transferring the splendor of sciences to America" sounds so enlightened and Voltaire-like, that the reader, who at this point is only at page 19 of *Dell'origine*, is almost led to believe in Andrés's *encyclopédisme*. Like Voltaire, Andrés was following the same biblical story of post-Adamitic civilization beginning in Asia, and then moving westward along with the sun. What Voltaire could not have possibly imagined was the Jesuit's (historicist) presentiment that the light of culture, perhaps, would not stay in Europe forever. Whereas history was for Voltaire a teleology leading to Europe, Andrés's historicism, instead, was based on the assumption that no place and no time was the ultimate end of history.

At any rate, in Andrés's account the light of literature has not yet transferred to America: it has just abandoned the eastern parts of Europe in the dark and is now moving toward the Atlantic.[23] Where do we find, then, the light of culture now? Without being exceedingly surprised, we find the light exactly around Spain and Portugal, where it is hesitating (and why would any light like to abandon beautiful Iberia!) to jump to the other shore of the ocean. The image is halfway jingoistic tastelessness and sheer beauty: by reclaiming the importance of Spain as the last Thule of Europe's culture before light would move to the New World, Andrés is already hinting at where modern literature really is. Paris is passé; New York may be the future. Madrid, no doubt, is the present.

The image does, in fact, summarize quite well the scope of the eight volumes of *Dell'origine, progressi, e stato attuale d'ogni letteratura*. As a transnational (and transcontinental) literary history, Andrés's book offers a look at various national literatures, but, above all, a chronology of the world's great literary epochs—those epochs in which the culture of one nation became patrimony of all literatures to follow. Briefly, this is Andrés's chronology, already sufficiently summarized by the cited image: the first great epoch of literature is in Asia after the Flood; literature then moves westward, first to Egypt (for the satisfaction of Martin Bernal), then to Greece, where it knows exemplary perfection (2:26–31). It then moves to imperial Rome; and then . . . . Then where? Chronology is of the utmost importance here because to understand where the light of literature moved after Rome meant nothing less than understanding in which language, and in which nation, resided the cultural origin of *modern* Europe. Voltaire had already said that "modern history . . . follows the decadence of the Roman Empire" (*Oeuvres complètes* 11:157); and August Wilhelm von Schlegel would soon canonize that same estimate for the Romantic generation: modernity, he wrote in the *Vorlesungen über dramatische Kunst und Literatur* (1809), is born out of the "encounter of Latin with the ancient German dialects," which, following the fall of Rome, inaugurates a "new European civilization" (13).

So, where does the light of culture find refuge after the fall of Rome? Montesquieu's answer had been unequivocal: after culture had but disappeared in the immediate and darkest years following the demise of the empire, it was in Charlemagne's Frankish schools and monastery that "Arts and Sciences seemed to reappear. One can say that the people of France was destroying Barbarity" (*Oeuvres* 1:1095). For Jaucourt, it was in French Provence that modern European culture begun: "In a word, all our modern poetry, comes from Provence" (Diderot 12:840).[24] Whether it was Charlemagne or the troubadours, one thing was certain: an origin of modern Europe was to be located somewhere in France.

It was this certainty that Andrés intended to demolish. First of all, *if* Charlemagne had managed to make anything reappear, it was only the pseudoculture of mediocre theologians, ignorant clerics, and illiterate priests (Andrés, *Dell' origine* 1:110): "Because in fact the Emperor, Alcuinus, Theodulf, and all those who were working for a reformation of studying had only one goal: service to the church. Accordingly, their great schools taught little more than grammar [useful only to read the psalms] and ecclesiastical singing" (1:108–9). In Frankish Europe, in other words, "Schools were created; but only to teach reading, singing, counting, and little more. Teachers were formed; but it was enough that they knew some grammar, and if one was ahead of his peers enough to know also a little bit of mathematics or astronomy, he was considered an oracle. But a Terence, a Cicero, a Quintilian did not exist in all France" (1:111).

Boileau had submitted literature to reason; Jaucourt to science; and Charlemagne to religion. They all had "drowned Europe in so much dialectical nonsense" (1:182). There *had* to be something rotten in France! Moreover, as we know from Aldo Scaglione, mentions of Alcuin's schools were often a veiled criticism of Jesuit education, accused of straying away, by teaching all the heathen Greeks and Romans, from proper knowledge (51). So if culture survived or revived in Europe, this could scarcely be the merit of Charlemagne and his educators.

As for the claim of a Provençal origin of modern literature, this was, as Andrés probably learnt from Vico, just the "arrogance" (*alterigia*) (Andrés, *Dell' origine* 2:11) and "pretentiousness of the French, who brag about monuments of superior antiquity both in prose and in verse"

(1:266).[25] First of all, Provençal, the idiom that "so much ado created all over Western Europe" (1:292), originally was not the French of Languedoc, but, in case, Catalan (1:294). Second, and more important, what has French Provençal poetry ever achieved if not much bragging about such a mediocre poem as the *Roman de la rose*, "where absolutely nothing happens but the picking of a rose" (1:338)? Rather than creating modern poetry, the French had drowned Europe in the darkness of scholasticism: "None of the first scholastics was a Spaniard. None of the early controversies that excited the scholastics excited Spain. And none of the early scholastic sects was born in those places. Spaniards got scholastics from the Gauls" (1:168).

If the French had not invented modern poetry, then who did? There was only one answer for Andrés: Arab literature had been the central influence in the rebirth of modern Europe (1:x). With a prose reminiscent of the *One Thousand and One Nights*, Andrés described Baghdad as the very light of modern culture—as the locus, namely, where a shift from classical languages to the vulgar ones "accessible to the people" had been transacted: "One sees hundreds of camels entering Baghdad, charged only with paper and books; and all the books, in whatever language they were written, were immediately translated into Arabic" (1:120). From Baghdad, the hegemonic center of the ninth century, literature had then been exported to the entire world—and had reentered Europe to cast some lights in its dark ages: "So, throughout the vast Arab domains, in all the three parts of the world [the ones known at the time: Asia, Africa, and Europe] where their empire had been extended, we see Saracen letters enter triumphantly, and dominate, like their armies, the globe. Since the ninth century of our era, the light of Arabic literature began to shine, and for six or seven centuries it kept glittering brightly" (1:124). Not unaware of the consequences of such an assertion, Andrés conceded that

> [this is] a truth that many will take as a ridiculous paradox; namely, that modern literature, not only in the sciences, but also in the Belles Lettres, recognizes the Arab as its mother. Paper, numerals, gunpowder, the compass came to us from the Arabs. Maybe also the pendulum and the law of gravity, and other recent discoveries . . . were known by them long before they came to our philosophers. Universities, astronomical observatories, academies, literary institutions do not think they have an Arab origin, and perhaps they will not be very grateful to me for having refreshed their memory with the remembrance of such an old event. (1:xi)

Accordingly, Andrés would devote to what will later be known as the Arabist theory the lengthiest and most problematic chapter of his entire treatise—a chapter he was not even sure how to title in order to render it more palatable to his European readers: vaguely, *Della letteratura degli arabi* (*Of Arabic Literature*) in the Parma edition; programmatically, *Dell'influenza degli arabi nella moderna coltura delle belle lettere* (*The Influence of the Arabs in the Modern Culture of Belles Lettres*) in the Venetian and Prato editions; hiding the Arab, *Dell'introduzione della lingua volgare nella coltura delle lettere, particolarmente nella poesia* (*The Introduction of Vulgar Languages in Literature, especially in Poetry*) in the Roman and Pisan editions.

Andrés was not the first to formulate the Arabist theory. In the seventeenth and eighteenth centuries, in fact, this theory was a rather common (if not uncontested) one (Menocal, "Pride and Prejudice" 67; Mazzeo 156–57; Monroe 67). In England, hermetics and Rosicrucians had already recognized Arabic as "the linguistic medium through which much of the Hermetic *corpus* had been transmitted to Europe in the medieval period" (Matar 89). Even in France the thesis of a Provençal origin of both rhymed poetry and the novel (*roman*) had been questioned in the name of the Arabist theory.[26] Pierre Daniel Huet, the bishop of Avranches, had begun his 1670 letter to Monsieur de Segrais by saying that "it is neither in Provence nor in Spain, as many believe, that one can hope to find the first beginnings of this pleasant amusement of honest relaxation [i.e., the *roman*]" (4). Such beginnings, instead, were "due to the Orientals— namely, Egyptians, Arabs, Persians, and Syrians" (11). Similarly, as far as modern poetry was concerned, "it is the Arabs, in my opinion, who have given us the art of rhyming" (15). But it was especially in Italy, where Andrés was exiled, that the question of an Arab influence in the development of European "wisdom" had been tackled—since Nicolò Cusano's *De docta ignorantia* (1440)—with the "patriotic" aim of pointing to Pythagoras's school of Crotone as the Italic origin of Western philosophy (Casini). Vico had impugned the same thesis, with clear anti-Cartesian intentions, in *De antiquissima italorum sapientia* (1710).

In the domain of the belles lettres, Giovanni Maria Barbieri, whose *Rimario* (1570) Andrés had read through Tiraboschi (Palazón 19), had already proposed an Arab origin of rhymed poetry: because the Arabs liked to sing more than write and recite poems, they had replaced Greco-Roman prosody, based on the length of the syllables, with the more musical rhyme.[27] Following Barbieri, Ludovico Muratori's *Dissertazioni sopra le antichità italiane* (1751) had singled out the much-despised Arabs as the unexpected preceptors of "our Elders"—the Tuscan Dante, Petrarch, and Boccaccio. Subsequent chronologies and histories of Italian poetry had thus seen the origin of a secular lyrical tradition not in the courts of Provence, but in the Sicilian school of Fredrick II, whose court "between 1225 and 1250, nearly two centuries after the Arabs had been politically deposed by the Normans, was as brilliant and refined a center of Arabic learning as any in the Middle East or in Spain" (Menocal, "Pride and Prejudice" 74). The Sicilian school had not only introduced the secular topos of love (Boase 62–75), which would later become central in the early-thirteenth-century *stil novo* (the new style) up to Dante and Petrarch; it had also brought rhyme in Italian versification, and, more important, the sonnet form, which was the likely modification of the *zajal*, an Arab stanza of six verses popular with the Arabs living in Sicily and rearranged in the final sextet of the Italian (not the later English) sonnet (Oppenheimer; Wilkins, "Invention"; Wulstan).[28] It is from this Italian tradition of patriotic Arabism, not from Huet or the Rosicrucians that, in my opinion, Andrés developed his own Arabist theory. His interest was not a philological but a (geo-)political one: to remove the centrality of France in the history of modern Europe.

For Andrés, it was "unreasonable [to suppose] that the use of rhyme began with the French, and from them was spread all over Europe" (*Dell' origine* 1:307). Instead, "both French and Provençal must recognize the Arabs as their teachers" (1:301). Arab was the "invention" of rhyme (2:35–38) and the origin of the *roman*: "Fantasy drove the Arabs to pleasant descriptions and gracious fables, and to every kind of works that come from imagination and good taste. The *roman* was particularly consistent with their genius, and they were received with such expectation from both learned men and the people that one commonly believes them born out of Arabic ingenuity" (1:139–40). In short, the Arabs had invented two of the pillars of modern European culture: "Maybe their language . . . presents to the creative genius words and expressions, which generate ideas" (2:8).

Arabic, also, was the origin of literary historiography (1:137), modern philosophy (1:141), mathematics (1:147), astronomy (1:148), medicine (1:150–51), and jurisprudence (1:153)—all of modern literature, in fact, with the only exception of modern theater, which originated instead in Europe's south between Italy (Angelo Poliziano's *Orfeo*) and Spain (Fernando de Rojas' *Celestina*), came to "us" from "Arabia": "Arabia, this

inglorious Asian peninsula; Arabia, barbarian country, place of ignorance and wilderness—Arabia gave shelter to the lost literature [of the
ancients], and offered sacred asylum to the gentile culture that Europe
had rudely cast away" (1:116).

As suggested above, Andrés did not invent the Arabist theory. He was,
however, taking it away from the restricted domain of Arabists, theorists
of national literature, and critics of literary genres. What for Huet was a
mere philological question had become for Andrés a more radical reorientation of the putative origin of modern Europe. By rearticulating
an old theory within a new comparative perspective, he was positing the
rather controversial hypothesis of a non-French, and non-European,
origin of Europe's modern culture—let alone the debt Christian Europe
had contracted with the Islamic world (Arato, *Storiografia* 437). The
question is how to interpret correctly Andrés's controversial proposi-
tion. In 1941, Ramón Menéndez Pidal had liquidated any opposition to
the Arabist theory as "a very rooted prejudice: the belief in the lack of
intellectual communication between the two worlds, the Christian and
the Islamic" (34). In more recent times, Maria Rosa Menocal has claimed
that the Arabist theory "first ceases to be discussed and then becomes
altogether taboo" in the second part of the nineteenth century, when "a
European sense of self emerged . . . which was the height of the colonial-
ist period, and the prevailing attitudes precluded, consciously or sub-
consciously, any possibility of 'indebtedness' to the Arabic world . . . it
would have been inconceivable or very difficult for most Europeans to
imagine, let alone explore or defend, a view of the 'European' as being
culturally subservient to the 'Arab'" ("Pride and Prejudice" 67–68).

The introduction to the present book has made clear (I hope) that a
European sense of self did not need to wait for the nineteenth century in
order to emerge. Moreover, I am inclined to believe that an attempt to
undermine the theory of an Arab origin of rhymed poetry begins in fact
long before Andrés's own theorization of such origin. Michele Amari,
for one, considered seriously the possibility that already the (Christian)
scribes and copyists of the thirteenth century, when transcribing the
early Arab-Sicilian rhymed poetry, were so ashamed of even quoting that
material that they minimized the Arab influence in that poetry (*Storia*
4:759). What needs to be added at this point is that it would be a gross
misreading of the Arabist theory (and of Andrés) to suppose that its
goal was to "view the 'European' as being culturally subservient to the
'Arab.'" Although Adolfo Domínguez Moltó imagines Andrés as an "ad-

mirer, defender, and popularizer" of Arab culture (73), nowhere does *Dell' origine* show much sympathy toward the Arab, that "itinerant and nomadic nation" (Andrés, *Dell' origine* 1:116), the pyromaniac of Alexandria's library, and the one bamboozled by Mohammad, "that famous impostor" (1:131). Arab literature, after all, often fell short of that "naturalness of feelings, simplicity of concepts, truth and propriety of figures" that characterized Andrés's own European standards of good taste: it lost its balance in "excessively daring metaphors," "endless allegories," and "excessive hyperboles" (1:134–35).

That Andrés was not concerned with the destiny of the Arab in particular, or with the destiny of multiculturalism in general, is evident from his total disinterest in trying to learn the language, and his reliance on the Spanish translations of the Escorial. Arab literature was treated by him only insofar as it meant something for the history and genesis of *European* culture. Not that Europe was for him, as for Bossuet and Montesquieu before, the necessary end of history. The progress of literature, however, was now "above us . . . in our hemisphere, [before] transferring the splendor of sciences to America." A philosophical history of literature had, then, to be written in view of such progress. Sure enough, Montesquieu's and Voltaire's Eurocentric prejudice was repeated here: it never occurred to Andrés that making present literature climax in Europe (though a more southern Europe than Montesquieu's and Voltaire's) could constitute a mere error of perspective. At any rate, Europe still represented modernity for Andrés—the nowadays of progress. Accordingly, Chinese and Indian literatures (Andrés, *Dell' origine* 1:13–14) could be liquidated in the space of one paragraph each because unimportant for the progress of literature. Besides the Arabs, only Caldeans "can stay in our memory, because from their doctrines the Greeks drew many notions" (1:14); and Egypt "only deserves, from the whole of Africa, our consideration, Egypt having been the school of the Greeks" (1:17).

Absolutely uninterested in establishing any "subservience" of Europe, disinclined to claim Arab literature as the origin of European modernity, Andrés only wanted to promote Spain, and, at most, southern Europe, as origins. What operated on Andrés was, in this sense, the *discreet* charm of the Arabist theory. The Arabs had sowed the seeds, but southern Europe made them bloom: "Where Arab science bloomed more, where the light of their knowledge shined brighter, where the reign of their literature got fixed, so to speak, was in Spain" (1:122). In sum, "the first flashes, which gave blinded Europe some light, came from Spain; therefore, we can reasonably say that the origin of modern literature derived from Spain" (1:174).

Answering the Hispanophobic prejudice, in Menocal's words, that "as an appendage of the Oriental world of Islam, the civilization of Spain did not constitute an integral part of Europe" ("Close Encounters" 50–51), Andrés restored the crumbled empire to its old position of glory. Spain, marginal south of a northbound Europe, came out of his pages as the synthesis of world culture—as the topos, namely, where east and west met. Spain was the last Thule, moreover, of European culture, before the light would move to the New World. Even more important, Spain was depicted as the very origin of *all* that is modern in Europe—the origin of rhymed poetry, of the *roman*, and of modern theater (*nuovo teatro*) (2:400). The paradigm of northern European hegemony was, at least in Andrés's intentions, flipped upside down: Pierre Corneille had to learn from Spain how to build "the magnificent edifice of French theater" (2:401); the modern epic had to be copied from "southern poetry" (2:134); and Spain was still to rule as the light of a new Europe.

Eager still to imagine itself as the ideal center of Europe, Spain was certainly ready to salute the work of its exiled child with the greatest euphoria: "Charles III, the very monarch who expelled the Jesuits from Spain, was so favorably impressed by the scope and quality of [Andrés's] work that he instructed the authorities at the Real Colegio de San Isidoro and at the University of Valencia to adopt it as the official text in the course of literary history given at those institutions, thus making them the first European centers of learning to offer a course on the history of universal literature" (Mazzeo 45). The work that was supposed to decenter a profoundly Francocentric Europe; the work that was supposed to undermine the presuppositions of a nationalistic way of looking at literature through the magic of a nascent comparativism—this same work became a nationalist monument to Spain's nostalgias and ambitions. In truth, only Andrés was to blame. Incapable of extending the implications of his historicism to a critique of *any* centralism, Andrés was in fact the historical product of Auerbach's "individual conditions" of his own place and time—a time, I will argue in the next chapter, during which ideas of Europe had started to merge, if not wane, into theories of nationalism.

A fundamental blindness had prevented Andrés from seeing the full consequences of both his historicism and of his Arabist theory: that historical relativism could hardly be reconverted into a theory of Spanish (or southern) centralism; and that the Arab origin of European poetry could hardly justify his commitment to keep east and west as cultural antitheses of each other. Southern Europe, it is true, was promoted by Andrés from Montesquieu's past of European history to the very origin of Europe's modernity. A south conceived as *causa prima* of Europe, however, was hardly a south understood as *causa sui*: the Europeanness of the south was still claimed as the putative beginning of what Europe is "today." In this, rather than representing any solution, Andrés remains for us the allegory of the problems and difficulties that we may still face when attempting to provincialize Europe from its interior borders— problems and difficulties, however, that should not justify any uncritical embracing of monolithic notions of Eurocentrism. As for the question of European studies, the prevalent assumption that Europe took permanent shape in the writings of Montesquieu and the *philosophes* should seriously be questioned, lest that Europe, which emerged from the historical circumstances of French hegemony, be not mistaken as a truth of universal validity. Against that Europe, Juan Andrés had begun, in 1782, to theorize a different one: it was a Europe seen from the south; it did not end "where Christianity ends," but began where the Orient began.

4   Mme de Staël to Hegel

> Germany, for its geographical location, can be considered the heart
> of Europe, and the great continental association will never be able
> to recover its freedom if not through the freedom of this country.
> —MADAME DE STAËL, *De l'Allemagne*

> Germany? But where is it? Here's a country I cannot find!
> —FRIEDERICH SCHILLER, "Das deutsche Reich"

The sort of nationalism that Juan Andrés had pitted against a Francocentric Europe was not a peculiarly Spanish or southern phenomenon.
In the second half of the eighteenth century, while Andrés was already
working on *Dell' origine*, the idea of the nation was affirming itself in
Europe against the cosmopolitan ideals of the Republic of Letters: "The
particular against the general, the individual against the universal. Exactly because the fear is that universality will suffocate individuality, and
that the general will suffocate the particular—for this very reason, the
promoters of national individuality hold a strong polemical attitude
against [Francocentric] Europeanism" (Chabod 122).

After the "Discours" of Dijon and the letter to D'Alembert, Jean-
Jacques Rousseau had penned some "Considérations sur le gouvernement de Pologne" in 1772. The "Considérations" had been occasioned by
the latest events in Poland's political history. At the opening of the
eighteenth century, Poland was still under the sphere of influence of its
powerful neighbors—Prussia, Austria, and, especially, Russia. In 1768,
local resentment against foreign influence had led to the formation of
the so-called Confederation of the Bar. For four years, the confederation
attempted to govern Poland as an independent nation, to protect its
constitution, and to make of Roman Catholicism, as opposed to orthodox eastern Christianity, the religion of the land. The confederation was

supported, at a distance, by both France and the Ottoman Empire. In 1772, however, Russian military intervention brought the experiment of the confederation to an end. Austria and Prussia, afraid of a complete Russian takeover, struck some deals with the czarina Catherine II, proposing to partition Polish land for the sake of continental peace. The proposal was accepted by Catherine II, who managed, however, to keep control of most of Poland. In 1772, therefore, the aspirations of an independent nation had been sacrificed at the table of European diplomacy. Who was to blame? The three powers, for sure; but in the "Considérations," Rousseau went as far as to blame the entire concept of Europe—a concept, elaborated in the salons of Paris, too quick to celebrate cosmopolitanism and universalism at the expense of any national spirit:

> Today, there are no longer Frenchmen, Germans, Spaniards, and English-men, whatever you call them—only Europeans. All have the same tastes, all the same passions, customs, because not a single one of them has received a national form by a distinctive legislation. In the same circumstances they would all do exactly the same things. They will all tell you how unselfish they are, and act like scoundrels. They will all go on and on about the public good, and think only of themselves. They will all sing the praises of moderation, and each will wish himself a modern Croesus. They all dream only of luxury, and know no passion except the passion for money; sure as they are that money will fetch them everything they fancy, they will all sell themselves to the first man who is willing to pay them. What do they care what masters they serve, or what country's laws they obey? Their fatherland is any country where there is money for them to steal and women for them to seduce. They are everywhere at home. (*Oeuvres* 3:960)

This was not the first time that Rousseau had expressed some distrust toward cosmopolitanism, and, more specifically, against Europeanism. Already *Émile*, in the eponymous novel of 1762, had been taught to "distrust those cosmopolites" (4:249) who try to better "Man" and fail to improve the citizen. *La nouvelle Héloise* (1761) had also praised the Englishmen, who "don't have the need to be Man" (2:216), for being nationalists and insular at heart. As I have suggested in the previous chapter, Rousseau's distrust for such concepts was largely motivated by his suspicion that behind them lurked the hegemony of some state powers—France, or even Russia in the case of Poland—which were arrogant enough to legitimate their interests, ambitions, and even ways of living as universal or European. Had not the partition of Poland, after all, been legitimated in the name of European peace?

At the risk of rewriting universal history against Montesquieu and Voltaire, the "Considérations" were a frontal attack against Europe first, and against *European* Russia, the archenemy of Polish nationalism, consequently. In *De l'esprit des lois*, Montesquieu had praised the czar Peter the Great (1682–1725) for "giving European customs and manners to a European nation" (*Oeuvres* 2:565). Voltaire, too, had offered a similar monument to Peter the Great, who transformed Russia, hitherto "scarcely known in Europe," into a great European Empire (69). In sum, for both Montesquieu and Voltaire, Peter had brought Russia to the eighteenth century—that is to say, to modernity—by bringing it to Europe: after that, Russia was no longer the "Orient"; it became a European empire. For Rousseau, instead, exactly because of that Europeanness conquered through Peter's love for the West, "the Russians will never be really civilized . . . Peter had the genius of mimicry; but not the true genius that creates and makes everything out of nothing . . . . He made [of his people] a German one, a British one, instead of starting to make of it the Russian people" (*Oeuvres* 3:386).

What was this abhorred Europe for Rousseau? In the *Extrait du projet de paix perpétuelle de M. l'abbé de Saint Pierre* (1761), Europe did not sound like such a bad deal after all:

> All the powers of Europe constitute, among themselves, some kind of a system that unites through the same religion, through the same set of laws, customs, letters, and commerce, and provides the necessary balance of forces. Add to this: the particular situation of Europe, which is more populated and more united than other continents; the continuous mixing of interests that ties of blood and of commerce, of arts and colonies, have instituted among European monarchs; the multitude of rivers and the variety of their courses, which make communications easy; the restless mood of its inhabitants, which makes them travel incessantly, and brings one in the country of the other; the invention of the printing press, and the common taste in the arts, which has made possible the sharing of scholarship and knowledge; and finally, the multitude and small size of the European States which, interdependent in their common need for luxury and in the difference of climates, has always made each people necessary to all others. All these causes together make of Europe not only,

like in Asia or Africa, an ideal collection of peoples that only have one name in common, but a real society with its religion, its habits, its customs, and even its laws, which no single people can break without immediately causing some danger to the others. (*Oeuvres* 3:567)

Yet, as it is already implicit in the *Extrait*, this "real society," perhaps exactly because it *is* real, remains quite distant from any ideal: this system of Europe, capable only of satisfying "luxury" and the "sharing of scholarship and knowledge," careful only about its internal "balance of forces" that had led to Polish partition, was a perennial threat to the "originality" of its single parts. Hence the inherent dissatisfaction in *all* notions of Europe, including those that aimed for a perpetual peace. Perpetual peace, once obtained through the European balance of forces, when detrimental to national originality, was capable of leading only to its exact contrary: "The perpetual dissent, brigandage, thrones usurped, revolts, wars, homicides which daily sadden this respectable home of the Wise, this brilliant asylum of the Sciences and the Arts . . . the pretended fraternity of the Peoples of Europe is a name to be laughed at, a name, 'fraternity,' that expresses with irony their mutual animosity" (*Oeuvres* 3:567–68). A repressed sense of nationalism, sacrificed at the altar of a common and supposedly balanced Europe, returns through the symptoms of perpetual dissent and war. This is all that can be achieved in the name of Europe.

It is in this sense that Rousseau was said to close an old, cosmopolitan epoch in order to father a new one—called Romantic and hinging on the question of national specificities. Against the uniformity of Europe, the nation starts affirming itself as the true center of a true fraternity: freedom, which for Montesquieu was the end of European history, begins now with a savage "disdain of European pleasures" (Rousseau, *Oeuvres* 3:182), and with a recuperation of more local, national desires. Rousseau, along with Andrés, contributes to the logic that at the eve of the French Revolution starts undoing, rather than consolidating, the very idea of Europe.

Yet the distance between the old and the new, between doing and undoing, should not be overestimated here: Does such novel logic of nationalism truly undo the idea of Europe? Or is it, rather, a reformulation of it—a denial of cosmopolitan Europe, that is, advanced in the name of a new Europe of nations? The rhetoric of Rousseau's logic is so explicitly and blatantly critical of Montesquieu's Europeanism that it is easy to miss in it that rhetorical unconscious that still ties the Polish considerations to *De l'esprit des lois*. With an echo of Machiavelli, Montesquieu had written that "in Europe the natural divisions of the terrain form a plurality of States . . . . This forms, in turn, a spirit of freedom" (*Oeuvres* 2:529). Twenty-four years later, Rousseau similarly located in "the multitude and small size of the European States" the reason for a return to national freedoms—but also, as a matter of paradoxical facts, the very Europeanness of nationalism.

The Unbearable Europeanness of the French Revolution

> In the eyes of Europe, we can be the model.
> —MAXIMILIEN DE ROBESPIERRE, *Discours*

> Should the Revolution only be French, just as
> the Reformation was Lutheran?
> —NOVALIS, "Die Christenheit oder Europa"

"What is a nation?" asked Ernest Renan in 1882. First of all, he answered, a nation is *not* "the vast agglomerations of men found in China, Egypt or ancient Babylonia, the tribes of the Hebrews and the Arabs, the city as it existed in Athens and Sparta, the assemblies of the various territories in the Carolingian Empire" (9). Montesquieu's "extended territories" are thus not only "despotic" (*Oeuvres* 2:362): "Vast agglomerations," adds Renan, are also "without a *patrie* [homeland]." Europe, the land of Montesquieu's freedom, is therefore also the land of Rousseau's "nations, such as France, England and the majority of the modern European sovereign states" (Renan 9). In truth, it is not simply Europe that functions as the homonym of nation: neither the Greek city-states of Athens and Sparta nor the Roman Empire were nations in any sense of the word. Only *modern* Europe, as it were, has nations: "Nations . . . are something fairly new in history" (9). In European history, that is, if such specification is still needed after Montesquieu. The newness of history began for Renan with yet another echo of Montesquieu: when "the Germanic invasions . . . introduced into the world the principle which, later, was to serve as the basis for the existence of nationalities" (9). One sees the slow work of construction of the idea of Europe, the unfolding of its rhetorical unconscious here: feudalism, private property, and freedom were for Montesquieu the beginning of a modern Europe brought about by the German Franks. Renan also adds to the picture of German achievements the introduction of nationalism in modern European history. That modern history had begun with Montesquieu's Gallic feudalism: it had climaxed, however, only with the revolution of 1789. "France," declares Renan with the clearest sense of *patrie*, "can claim the glory for having, through the French Revolution, proclaimed that a nation exists of itself. We should not be displeased if others imitate us in this. It was we who founded the principle of nationality" (12).

In a way, Renan was attributing nothing less than everything to the French Revolution, and theorizing, once and for good, the intimate relation between nation and revolution. The syllogism went like this: the nation is the highest embodiment of a people's freedom; freedom is a will of law and self-determination that pits a people against the old order of empire and absolute authority; ergo, the nation is the product of a revolution. By ultimately realizing what the Germans had "introduced" in the history of the universe, 1789 was thus for Renan the climax of a modern Europe united no longer by the spirit of cosmopolitanism but by its plurality of nations. "Africa . . . and Asia," had written Machiavelli, "have always been one or two empires at most . . . ; only Europe has had a few empires, and an infinite number of republics" (*Opere* 585). "In Europe," had echoed Montesquieu, "the natural divisions of the terrain form a plurality of States" (*Oeuvres* 2:529). Renan could then conclude: not unity, but national difference is the essence of Europe. Nationalism is not the undoing of Europe, but the final realization of a modern Europe spurred by the French Revolution.

It may sound curious that such a modern Europe of nations is made to begin in 1789, and not, for instance, in 1776. In that year, on July 4, on the other side of the Atlantic, the U.S. Declaration of Independence had already mentioned "citizens" and "their Country"—let alone equality and liberty—thirteen years before the Jacobeans would utter those same words again. The fact is that inheriting the Enlightenment's belief in the universality (and originality) of French values, it could only be France, not the thirteen United States of America, that could paradoxically see in French nationalism not a peculiarly French desire, but, paradoxically, a European one. As the count Honoré de Mirabeau told the National Assembly after the fall of the Bastille: "The influence of such a nation [France] will undoubtedly conquer the whole of Europe" (qtd. in Davies 713).

And conquer it did. "After 1789 everyone knew that the world could be turned upside down, that determined men could mobilize the social forces and psychological motors which underlay the surface of the most tranquil society" (Davies 713). More important, after 1789 everyone seemed to know that modern Europe was defined neither by Voltaire's letters nor by Montesquieu's feudal institutions, but by national revolutions. Take William Blake's *Europe: A Prophecy* of 1794, for instance, where Europe is the apocalypse of revolutionary hubris—"in the vineyards of red France appear'd the light of his fury" (66)—liberating itself from the yoke of paltry reason, petty religion, and ancient regimes. Or take William Wordsworth's 1804 poem entitled "French Revolution as It Appeared to Enthusiasts at Its Commencement": from France to the British Isles, Europe entire sings the Revolution's "pleasant exercise of hope and joy" (1:636).

Certainly, not everybody was enthusiastic about this new revolutionary Europe of nations. Edmund Burke, for one, in the *Reflections on the Revolution in France* (1790), lamented the end of a once-glorious Europe, and the beginning of a petty bourgeois one: "The age of chivalry is gone. That of sophisters, economists, and calculators, has succeeded; and the glory of Europe is extinguished for ever. Never, never more shall we behold that generous loyalty to rank and sex, that proud submission, that dignified obedience, that subordination of the heart, which kept alive, even in servitude itself, the spirit of an exalted freedom" (126).

In *Considerations sur la France* (1796), Joseph de Maistre went so far as to interpret the revolution as God's punishment against France, whose monarchy had betrayed its providential mission, thus leaving Europe, demoralized, in the hands of *philosophes* and libertines:

> Every nation, like every individual, has a mission which it must fulfill. It would be futile to deny that France exercises a dominant influence over Europe, an influence she has abused most culpably. Above all, she was at the head of the religious system, and it was not without reason that her king was called *most Christian*: Bossuet has not overstressed this point. However, as she has used her influence to pervert her vocation and to demoralize Europe, it is not surprising that terrible means must be used to set her on her true course again. (50)

This was neither Burke's time, however, nor Maistre's. It was the time of revolution, and Nabulione General Bonaparte was antonomasia and personification of this very revolution.

On May 5, 1789, the reunion of the General Estates in Versailles had opened a new cycle in the history of France by converting the old regime into a constitutional monarchy. On August 10, 1792, the monarchy was overthrown and, on September 21, France was declared a republic—an event symbolized by the spectacular beheading of the king and queen. Monarchic Europe had obviously followed the French events with increasing preoccupation. Already in 1789, revolutionary forces, inspired by the French example, had declared a United States of Belgium and overthrown Joseph II, the emperor of Austria. In 1791, the Poles demanded once more a national constitution and independence from Russia; in 1794, led by Tadeusz Andrzej Bonawentura Kociuszko (who had just come back from North Carolina where he fought against Britain under General Nathaniel Greene), the Poles started their own national revolution. In Germany, resentment against Prussian hegemony was on the rise in all the other states. Since 1791, the *Patriote français*, edited by Jacques Pierre Brissot de Warville, had started a crusade for the military liberation of the peoples of Europe—"only Robespierre," observes Stuart Woolf, "asked himself to what extent those peoples would welcome the French as their liberators" ("Storia" 152–53).

The coalition that Austria, Prussia, Russia, Holland, and England formed against France could not do much to halt the spread of revolutionary ferments. Worse, it could not do much to stop its military advance in Europe. In 1796, the Directorate of the Revolution had planned a strategy of simultaneous wars for the liberation of Europe: General Lazare Hoche was to invade Ireland; the generals Jean Victoire Marie Moreau and Jean Baptiste Jourdan Germany; and the young debutant Napoléon Bonaparte had to start the Italian campaign with the putative goal of freeing Italy from the Austrian yoke, and the more concrete economic objective of having Italian taxes pay for the reconstruction of postrevolutionary France. In a few months, Napoléon liberated Milan, besieged Mantua, and broke the Austrian lines in Rivoli. It was an astounding beginning of his career.

"Ce n'est qu'un début," went the Parisian slogan of 1968, "this is only the beginning." In a period in which the principle of a "revolutionary expansion" of France, theorized by Larevollière Lepaux and legalized in 1792 by the Republican Convention (Ricceri 57), was becoming some kind of Frenchman's burden, Italy truly was nothing more than a beginning for Napoléon Bonaparte: "You [Italians] are the *first* example . . ." (qtd. in Woolf, "Storia" 162; emphasis mine). What was the end, then? A perfect reintegration and novel Europeanization of Europe. The historian Stuart Woolf describes Napoleonic integration in these words: "If the Orient was 'orientalized,' as Said argues, Europe had been 'Europeanized' by the construction of a unifying grid of civilization, against which all cultures could be measured and classified" ("Construction" 89). What this meant, in Napoléon's own words, was "to found a European code, a supreme Court for all Europe"; and to make of Europe "a single European people . . . a truly united nation [so that] everybody, no matter where he traveled, would always have been in the common fatherland of all." Focused on such a modernizing mission, Napoléon, who may have read *De l'esprit des lois*, certainly shared with Montesquieu the idea of a Frankish origin of Europe fathered by Charlemagne. Asking to be crowned in Aix-la-Chapelle, once the capital of Charlemagne's reign, Napoléon presented himself as the new father of a new Europe. Just as Charlemagne had reunified and regenerated the Roman Empire, so was Napoléon to reunify and regenerate the Holy Roman Empire into, so to speak, the new revolutionary French Europe: "There is not enough sameness among the nations of Europe. European society needs regeneration. There must be a superior power which dominates all the other powers, with enough authority to force them to live in harmony with one another—and France is best placed for this purpose" (qtd. in Thompson 38–39).

Europe, in turn, seemed quite eager to be regenerated by the example of revolutionary France: the Swiss were ready to declare the Helvetic Republic, in 1798, against the aristocratic cantonal governments; and the Italians themselves, in large measure, were quite enthusiastic that the revolution was entering, with Napoléon, Italy as well. This state of euphoria, however, was not to last long. If the welcoming of the French liberators had been quite triumphal, the following fiscal pressures (someone had to pay for all these liberations!), the military draft, political interferences, and the fundamental disinterest of the French in Italian nationalism quickly turned the Italians against the rescuers of their freedom (Banti, *Risorgimento* 18–31). The French, wrote Vincenzo Cuoco, who was certainly not a conservative of the likes of Burke and Maistre, had brought a revolution that was "too French and scarcely Neapolitan" (qtd. in Casini 244). "The French have deluded themselves about the nature of their revolution, and believe to be universal what is, in fact, the product of the specific political circumstances of the French nation" (Cuoco 37). Other peoples, like "the stupid Belgians and the bestial Germans" (in the words of the directorate, qtd. in Woolf, "Storia" 161), were not much happier than the Italians about this liberation imposed through the means of military occupation. Especially in Germany, which was at the time a collection of small states under the control of Prussia, the project had become that of the construction of a German nationalism far from the French model. Robespierre might have been right, after all: Why would people welcome unconditionally the French as their national liberators?

The limits of wars of liberation are certainly a hot topic today. In the time we are discussing, even hotter was any mention of the archenemy of Napoleonic imperialism—Anne Louise Germaine Necker, married de Staël. "Bonaparte had so persecuted her that people said in Europe one had to count three Great Powers: England, Russia and Mme de Staël," offered Mme de Chastenay (qtd. in Isbell 6). England had not won Waterloo yet (Napoleon's chief of police, at any rate, would blame Mme de Staël, not Wellington, for the fall of Napoléon); and Russia had scarcely come out unscathed from the Polish quagmire. Mme de Staël, instead, in the small town of Coppet, Switzerland, was already starting to dismantle Napoleonic Europe: anti-French, national, Romantic—the sort of Europe imagined by her was undoubtedly a novel one. Most notably, cultural hegemony had shifted from France to Germany. Yet even this new Europe kept being divided, just as in the times of Montesquieu, between north and south.

German Europe Considered in Her Relation to Religion

> Marriage: Europe owes once more to the church
> the small numbers of good laws it still has.
> —CHATEAUBRIAND, Génie du christianisme

The product of a revolutionary age, and written by an active participant in the revolution—first as a Girondist moderate republican, then as a constitutional monarchist, and finally as an outlaw of Robespierre's Directorate—Anne-Louise Germaine Necker Madame de Staël's De la littérature considérée dans ses rapports avec les institutions socials was in its own right a revolutionary work.[1] To begin with, this was the first work proposing to study literature not simply in itself but according to the "influence that religion, customs, and laws have on literature, and the influence that literature has on religion, customs, and laws" (Staël, Littérature 64). For the first time, literature was caught in a dialectics with society and was said to be, in some sort of Gramscian way, not only a product (representation) but also a producer (creation) of social institutions.

Just as revolutionary was Staël's message: concluding *De la littérature* with a peculiar praise both of medieval Christianity and the Enlightenment culture of the ancien régime, Mme de Staël depicted revolutionary France as a moment of corruption in European history—one in which the humanism of Christianity and the Enlightenment had turned into the culture of fear called the Age of Terror or of the guillotine. Moreover, against the model of the French Revolution, *De la littérature* had begun to praise a different one—that of a bourgeois Germany centered not on the militaristic cult of heroic revolutions, but on that of "domestic happiness" (171). Staël would later develop this thesis in *De l'Allemagne* (1810), a true call for a new Europe with the "German race" (1) at its center. Germany, according to Staël, was the nation in which "men are the most learned and most meditative of Europe" (23) whose universities were "the most knowledgeable of Europe" (244), and whose "influence on thinking Europe dates from the times of Protestantism" (67). Already with the publication of *De la littérature*, however, Staël's move against Francocentrism—if not blunt anti-Gallicism—and in the direction of a German Europe quickly aroused the anger of the Directorate of the Revolution, which decreed the arrest of Mme de Staël in 1796. After having avoided prison for the intervention of her husband, in May 1800, less than one month after the publication of *De la littérature* and the vehement attacks from the French press, Staël decided to leave Paris for her husband's estate in Coppet, Switzerland. There she formed a salon frequented by the likes of Benjamin Constant, Simonde de Sismondi, Charles Victor de Bonstetten, and August Wilhelm von Schlegel.

In spite of its political daring, however, *De la littérature* was quite a conservative book in some respects. Although its attention to the social relevance of literature (and its attention to gender) made of *De la littérature* a breakthrough in literary theory, the idea Staël seemed to have of literature was, after all, hardly a revolutionary one. It was downright parochial, in fact, when compared to previous works such as Andrés's *Dell' origine*, or even when measured against Voltaire's opening, in the *Essai*, on the literary world of China, India, and Arabia. Both Andrés and Voltaire had spent pages on the great literatures of the Orient. One paragraph on Mohammad (inspired perhaps by a premature vision of Samuel Huntington and Silvio Berlusconi) instead sufficed for Staël: "Mohammad . . . gave birth to a fanaticism with the most astonishing insouciance . . . . His religion was destined only for the people of the south, had as its only goal to stir a military spirit by offering compensations for military exploits. This religion created conquerors, but did not bring any seed of intellectual development . . . Islam was stationary in its effects: it halted the human spirit" (167). According to Mme de Staël, both literature—which rather canonically comprehended "poetry, eloquence, history, and philosophy" (91)—and its progress were a European prerogative. Hardly any word needed to be spent to justify such a Europeanist assumption. "I believe that we can consider Asia as the true motherland, the cradle of literature," had said Andrés. For Staël, instead, literature had begun, more simply, in Greece: "One can consider the Greeks, as it concerns literature, as the first nation [*peuple*] that has ever existed" (93). Literature, in other words, was the unfolding of nothing else than the "moral and political Europe" (61). Staël's study of literature, in turn, was becoming yet another theory of Europe.

Even less revolutionary than her blunt Eurocentrism was Staël's unassailable faith in the idea of history as continuous progress. Inherited from Montesquieu, and filtered through the *philosophes*, the postulate of an infinite "perfectibility of the human species" (Staël, *Littérature* 59, 87) shaped the entirety of her narrative. "My goal," she assertd, "is to observe the progress of the human spirit, and only philosophy can indicate such progress with certainty" (120). Certainly, also the southern Andrés had talked about progress—but not as an ideal of linear perfectibility; and not as something that "only philosophy," without the aid of a critical spirit, could indicate with certainty. Mme de Staël, however, *seemed* (I will come back to my word choice soon) not to have ever heard of such Andrés.

Literature, instead, was for Staël a story of continuous perfectibility that went, more or less, like this: literature began in Greece, the "childhood of civilization" (*Littérature* 94). The foundation and origin of literature, the Greeks "could not imitate anyone" before them. They were thus rough but pure (or pure but rough, depending on the point of view). "Having only nature as a model," the Greeks began literature as pure representations of nature (111). One of the limits of their art, especially in the theater, was "the exclusion of women" (117). Exit the Greeks. The Romans enter in Mme de Staël's literary theater of universal (European) history: "The Greeks gave the impulse to literature and the fine arts. The Romans marked the world with the traces [*empreinte*] of their own genius" (128–29). The Romans, in other words, were the first trace of progress in the infinite betterment of literature that the Greeks had only begun: the Romans reached "an authority of expression, a gravity of tone, and a regularity of periods" (131) that easily surpassed anything Greek. They did not, however, reach ultimate perfection. For that, we must patiently wait for their fall and for the inauguration of a new and most beautiful era—modernity—heralded by "the invasion of the Peoples of the North, the establishment of Christianity, and the Renaissance of the Letters" (162).

We have seen in the previous chapter how Andrés had rescued the Middle Ages, the Dark Ages, from their canonical image of gloominess and decline and promoted them as the origin of a modern Europe starting from Al-Andalus. Staël's palimpsest, however, was not Andrés, but Montesquieu. Like Montesquieu, Staël saw the Middle Ages as a period of inexorable progress and the beginning of a modern Europe initiated not by the Muslims of Al-Andalus, but by "our German fathers":

> People count in history more than ten centuries in which one usually believes that the human spirit regressed. This would be a strong objection against the system of progress [*système de progression dans les lumières*], if such a long period, if such a considerable portion of time known to us, had seen the great work of perfectibility recede. But this objection, which I would consider very seriously, if it were founded, can be refuted in a very simple manner. I do not think that the human species regressed in this period; I believe, on the contrary, that giant steps were made in the course of these ten centuries, both for the spread of knowledge [*lumières*], and for the development of intellectual faculties. (163)

What were these "giant steps" that knowledge made in the Middle Ages? Put simply, they were the entry of "the nations of the North" into "civilized society."

When the northern nations entered civilized society, however, they did not come in timidly knocking at the door. They shattered a Roman Empire. They ended an epoch, and ushered in a new one—modernity. It was an age no longer complacent in the imitation of nature: "Imitation does not allow . . . for infinite perfectibility" (179), since nature, after all, remains (for Staël at least, before Hegel) always the same. What Montesquieu's "German fathers" brought in was a "new development of sensibility and a deeper knowledge of human character." The much-admired Friedrich Schiller had mentioned something similar, also in 1800, in *Über naive und sentimentalische Dichtung*: the poetry of the ancients was naive contact with and imitation of nature; "our" modern art instead, "because nature has disappeared from our humanity" (Schiller 194), was a sentimental art, swallowing in the melancholia of what was lost.

Once again, we can easily see the influence of Montesquieu on Staël's idea of Europe: progress is the transgression of "the laws that God has established" and the overcoming of a natural state. The end of this progress is the establishment not only of human laws but of human literature as well—a "philosophical" literature disentangled from the mere imitation of God's creation. As in Montesquieu, moreover, the spirit of Europe, after dispensing with any comparison with the Orient, became for Staël a dialectic of north and south: "There exist, I believe, two completely distinct literatures: those that come from the south and those that descend from the north; those for which Homer is the first source, and those of which Ossian is the origin" (*Littérature* 203). The only difference to Montesquieu—quite substantial, in fact—is that France no longer constituted the north, but the border of a south ending before Germany, the new *caput mundi*, the real heart of Europe, and the ultimate antonomasia of the north (212–16).

At any rate, for Staël there was one literature with "two completely distinct" origins—Homer, and Ossian, the "primitive" and "Germanic" poet that James Macpherson had completely fabricated, unbeknownst to Mme de Staël, in 1765 (see Haywood). The progress of literature, then, coinciding with a progress of Europe, was a movement from the ancient south—Greece, Italy, and the Iberian peninsula (Staël, *Littérature* 193)— to a modern north. As the idea of progress implied the idea of the inferiority of the origin, Staël coherently announced that "Greek tragedies are, then, I believe, much inferior to our modern tragedies" (110); and "it is not less true that the moderns, in metaphysics, ethics, and sciences, are infinitely superior to the ancients" (121). In short, "I have given my preference to the literature of the North over that of the South" (54).

There was one thing, however, in which the ancients, that is, the southerners, excelled—to the point that they were better at it than the northerners ever were: history. What about progress then, one might ask! Does not the admission that something was better in ancient times contradict the whole idea of necessary progress? Staël was genuinely at pains when trying to explain this apparent contradiction, to the point that one wonders why, rhetorically speaking, she even mentioned history if it threatened to disrupt her entire logical edifice. Was she trying to respond directly to someone in particular—say, Andrés—who had claimed the superiority of the south in works of history? We cannot know with certainty. We can agree, instead, with Staël—once she had mentioned the southern superiority in history, she owed some explanation:

> I must present here some reflections on the causes of the superiority of the ancients in the genre of history. I believe that these reflections will prove that such superiority is not in contradiction with the following progress of thought. There are histories that are accurately called philosophical histories; there are others whose merit consists in the truthfulness of their pictures, in the warmth of their narrative, in the beauty of their languages. It is in this last genre that Greek and Latin historians have excelled. One needs a more profound knowledge of man to be a great moralist than to be a good historian . . . . In ancient history one finds neither the philosophical analysis of moral impressions, nor the unperceived symptoms of the soul's affections. (152–53)

So even if southerners would claim that they were better at histories, this did not compromise, but actually reinforced, the thesis of the south's inferiority vis-à-vis the north: southerners could be better historians because they had not progressed as philosophers. Progress—Mme de Staël could now conclude after this most arduous test—was the prerogative of the north; and philosophy, pace Andrés, had nothing to do with history.

After literature was presented as the unfolding of a progress of the "moral and political Europe," Europe returned, then, in *De la littérature*, as the very same dialectic of north and south that Montesquieu had originally proposed in 1748. The history of Europe was the story of its progress from Montesquieu's amoral south—"The peoples of the south . . . fiery tempers, easily duped, easily fanatical, suffered all the superstitions and crimes that reason ever suffered" (Staël, *Littérature* 168)—to a north "born from the morality of sentiments" (116). The north, then, was modernity, the climax of a progress that defined Europe. The south constituted the past of that same Europe—purer, yes, but hardly perfect. In Schiller's formulation: "They *are* what we *were*" (180).

De la littérature thus reestablished "such a difference of character between those of the north and those of the south" (Staël, *Littérature* 167) that the whole idea of Europe ran the risk of obliterating. There was not one Europe, but, at the very least, two: north and south. This did not mean that two Europes could not be reconciled into one: just as literature was one—going from the ancient naive one of Homer to the modern and sentimental one of the German Romantics—so was Europe one, from south to north. What kept the two Europes together? Not new to doubting, but unaccustomed to despair, the intrepid Mme de Staël had the right answer for all: literature, obviously, was an element that bonded the modern northerner, Ossian in hand, with his southern ancient brother (the sisters, after all, though inspirations to their men, "have not composed truly outstanding works"; Staël 171–72). Yet even more and above literature, it was religion that had made Europe one: "Christian religion has been the bond that has united the peoples of the north with those of the south; it has melted, so to speak, in one opinion two opposed customs . . . [northerners and southerners] have ended up becoming nothing else than one single people disseminated in different countries of Europe. Christian religion has contributed powerfully to that" (168–69).

"If you go from one end of the continent to the other, what is it that says you are in Europe?" asked recently, in December 2003, Italy's deputy prime minister Gianfranco Fini when the Polish delegation was denied a substantial reference to Christianity in the preamble of the Constitution of the European Union. "The presence of the Church" was Fini's answer—and Staël could not have agreed more. Mohammad may have given birth to fanaticism, but the fundamentalist idea of Europe as Christianity is born here, in the impossibility to keep "such a difference of character" together if not through the invocation of God.

Both north and south, for Mme de Staël, were Christian, and this was enough—pace all atheists, Jews, Gnostics, and residual Muslims of Europe—to make the continent one. Religion, in the end, operated the miracle that kept north and south together as Europe. Staël's confessional idea of Europe was not a total novelty in 1800. The German poet Friederich Leopold von Hardenberg, otherwise known as Novalis, had already celebrated the Christian unity of Europe in 1799, with *Die Christenheit oder Europa: Ein Fragment*. Novalis's was not too far removed from Staël's: Christianity and the Roman papacy, in the Middle Ages, had ended years of European wars through the invocation of a common faith in Christ. In 1798, however, the French armies of Marshal Berthier had marched against the pope, deposed him, destroyed Rome, transformed the Papal States into a republic, and taken Pius VI prisoner to Paris. Just a few weeks before the writing of the Novalis's fragment, the pope had died in exile, and the Directorate of the Revolution had forbidden electing a new one. Novalis's nostalgia for Christian Europe was thus perfectly in tune with Staël's enmities toward revolutionary France, which both saw as the greatest danger to the unity of Europe. Christianity was the only power capable of a "reconciliation of north and south" (Staël, *Littérature* 170); revolutionary France could only colonize, as an empire, north and south, but it could hardly reconcile them.

Mme de Staël's discussion of Christianity marked in yet another way her epochal desire to move away from a Francocentric to a new, Germanocentric Europe. For her, the cementing force of Christianity could no longer be Novalis's papacy, but, rather, Protestantism. And where was Protestantism to be found in the year 1800? Cardinal Mazarin had made of France a Catholic country; the revolution had secularized its institutions. If, "in general, what gives the modern peoples of the north a more philosophical spirit than the one possessed by the peoples of the south, is the Protestant religion" (Staël, *Littérature* 211), then France had become, pace Montesquieu, a miserably southern country: Catholic and despotic. Its literature, accordingly, would be discussed by Staël with the southern ones; its classicism demoted to a mere imitation of the models of Greece and Rome. Once the modern project of Protestantism had been betrayed by Mazarin's France and by Napoléon's revolution, Germany was not only the climax of progress but also the Protestant engine of European union. The *trait d'union* between Montesquieu's French Europe and a new German one, on the other hand, was Madame de Staël's salon in Coppet.

The Law of Marriage and the Order of Desire: Theorizing Sex

> There were two great systems conceived by the West for governing sex: the law of marriage and the order of desire.
> —MICHEL FOUCAULT, *The History of Sexuality*

> It continually resurfaces as a question of either/or: freedom or servitude, the liberation of desire or its subjugation.
> —MICHAEL HARDT AND ANTONIO NEGRI, *Empire*

> Open the seraglios of Africa, of Asia, and of this southern Europe of yours.
> —DONATIEN ALPHONSE FRANÇOIS DE SADE,
> *La philosophie dans le boudoir, ou les instituteurs immoraux*

The project that Mme de Staël began with *De la littérature*, and which she tried to complete at Coppet, was, properly speaking, one of translation. Montesquieu's idea of a dialectical Europe—north and south, Protestant and Catholic—had to be translated from a French to a German center. Montesquieu's German *fathers*, moreover, had to be translated into a new theory of gender (see Tenenbaum) attempting to look at the "changes that have been operated in literature at the epoch in which women have started to become part of the moral life of man" (Staël, *Littérature* 101). Undoubtedly, *De la littérature* was led by an unprecedented attention to the question of gender in the context of literary studies: what did it mean—asked Staël—"to write and think as a woman" (64)? What was the role of women in the development of literature? The question raised an even larger one: What had gender and sex to do in the constitution of a theory of Germanocentric Europe?

Already in his *Lettres persanes* Montesquieu had shown a great interest in questions of gender, and had offered what has been called "a typology of political relationships between men and women" (Mosher 25). Gender relations represented different typologies of government. Europe, besides being associated with a particular kind of politics (freedom against Oriental despotism) was also associated with a particular kind of gender politics. The *Lettres persanes* were an epistolary novel that described, through the ironic perspective of Persian voyagers, the peculiarities of European culture. Many were the differences—as we can expect from the pen of Montesquieu—between free Europe and the despotic Orient; but one was more striking than any other: the social and familial role of women. Montesquieu symbolized the position of women in the Orient through the figure of the harem—a model of despotism without limits. In the harem, the one male master—symbol of the absolute monarch—demanded a constant subjection, control, and isolation of his citizens/women (see Grosrichard). How different, the fictional voyagers observed, was the social role of women in the West! "To the peoples of Europe," they noticed, "all the wise precautions of the Asiatics —the veils that cover the women, the prisons [i.e., the harem] where they are detained, the vigilance of the eunuchs—seem more proper means to increase the activities of this sex, than to restrain them" (Montesquieu, *Oeuvres* 1:211–12). In Europe, according to the Persians imagined by Montesquieu, women were, for good and for bad, "free." In Asia—this was Montesquieu's unspoken conclusion—they were instead enslaved.

An important subplot of the *Lettres persanes* was thus the revolt that the preferred wife of the male despot, Roxanne, organized in the harem while the master was still in Europe. Montesquieu suggested that the problem with the political model of the harem—a model, I repeat, of monarchic absolutism—was not that it was patriarchal. As we have seen in the discussion of feudalism (chapter 2), patriarchy and patriarchal inheritance were in fact the very foundations of European freedoms. The problem with the harem model, instead, was that its very excess, its absolute and hyperbolic subjection of women to their patriarch, *threatened* patriarchy with the constant possibility of revolt. The governmental model of the harem, in other words, was "ruined by its own internal vice" (Montesquieu, *Oeuvres* 2:357), a vice of excess and immoderation.

What the *Lettres persanes* offered, then, was the presentation of two antithetical models of authority exemplified through the simile of gender relations: Oriental (patriarchal) authority was the complete subjection of women and citizens alike; European (patriarchal) authority granted instead some measure of liberty to its subjects—citizens and women—in turn creating a guarantee of social order. The isolation of the women in the harem, their dependency on the sexual desire of one single male, quickly engendered dissatisfaction. The desire to escape one's gender role transformed the seraglio into a sanctuary of sexual transgressions. The slave wife Zelid had begun by having an affair with the white eunuch Cosrou (1:208). Even Roxanne, the most faithful of the wives, had in the end "seduced your eunuchs" (1:372). By the last part of the novel, the frantic letter of the chief eunuch to his master hinted with despair at the spread of homosexuality in the harem: "Things have gotten to an unsustainable point: your women have thought that your departure [for Europe] has left them in a state of complete impunity. Horrible things are happening here" (1:362). *De l'esprit des lois* had reached similar conclusions: "Possession of many women—who could have guessed! —leads to that kind of love that nature disavows" (2:513); that is, the only way to satisfy sexual desire in the constrictive structure of harem relations is homosexuality.

Whereas the smallest unit of European society, the family, was thus built on the binary of male and female, the smallest unit of Oriental society, the harem, threatened social order not only through excessive despotism but also through a continuous proliferation of gender roles that reacted to such excess. The paradox was quite curious for Montesquieu ("who could have guessed!"): the most despotic regime, that of the harem, was so extreme that it became, ironically, impossible to maintain. By promoting a perpetual desire to escape one's gender role, it engendered a proliferation of such roles. In the West, both men and women could find freedom and satisfaction by observing the limits (laws?) of their gender roles. In the Orient, they simply could not, and they had to find new, deviant roles. Men needed to invent, so to speak, the eunuch as the guardian of women's virtue. Women had to discover homosexuality to compensate for the sharing of the husband's sexual services.

The greater freedom that Europe gave to its women, concluded Montesquieu, was, then, the guarantee of its social order. This did not mean that Europe was immune from this kind of Oriental disorder: in ancient Greece, *De l'esprit des lois* reminded the reader, "love took a form one does not dare mention" (2:342); in the Roman Empire, "young boys were priceless" (2:335) to older men; in contemporary Italy, the castrati looked to Montesquieu like horrendous monsters (2:1261); and even in England —free and constitutional England—women were so scarce that men "throw themselves into debauchery" (2:580). What this meant, therefore, was that Europe, *in theory* was a social order of men and women. Yet in practice, this Europe, too, was still on the way to final perfection.

Also the *Encyclopédie*, in its unmistakable jargon of scientific authenticity, left the practice of gender out of its theoretical framework. Homosexuality, for one, did not even appear. And here is the usual, indefatigable Jaucourt (also the author, incidentally, of the entry on "Sex"): "Woman (Natural law). In Latin, *uxor*. Female of the man, considered as long as she is united to him by the bond of marriage [*considérée en tant qu'elle lui est unie par les liens du mariage*]. Look then under Marriage and Husband" (Diderot 6:471). Like north and south were the two parts of that perfect and self-contained idea that was Europe, so were male and female the two complementary elements to be synthesized in marriage. At the entry "Marriage," still considered by Jaucourt under the heading of "natural law" and described as an "institution of nature," we read a praise of Montesquieu's remark that the perfectly "natural" union is that of (one) man and (one) female. In this resided for Jaucourt the "natural freedom" of the woman.

Natural or not, however, this union was also said, in the same *Encyclopédie*, to be specific to Europe only. The curator of the entry argued that marriage was an institution established by Christianity, which brought "in all European countries" a new social model of compassionate patriarchy. Before Christianity, and still in non-Christian lands, men, according to cultural "prejudices," were considered superior to women. This prejudice legitimated, for instance, the enslavement of women in the harem. Christianity, instead, was an "exception" to this otherwise general prejudice: in Europe, it "established . . . a real superiority of man, and yet preserved for the woman the rights of equality . . . . Domestic servitude of women and polygamy made Orientals distrust the fair sex, and, eventually, made the fair sex distrustful" (Diderot 6:468). In sum, for Europe the real inferiority of women—as opposed to the inferiority sanctioned by mere prejudice—never signified for the latter a loss of liberty: women, within Christianity, were *objectively* inferior, but not slaves. Quite an interesting way of justifying patriarchy in the West, one might argue: the specter of Oriental prejudice legitimated European discrimination of women as a benign—let alone realistic—form of paternalism. What had European women to complain about, when their fate was measured against that of a commonplace Orient concocted by the fantasy of Montesquieu! European women had to be quite grateful of being still free, despite their "real" inferiority.

Compared to the *Encyclopédie*, Montesquieu had advanced a more secular hypothesis concerning the difference of European sexual mores arising along with, but not necessarily because of, the spread of Christianity. The sort of chivalric conduct sung in the chanson de geste and in the chanson d'amor had represented, perhaps invented anew, a novel relationship between the sexes in which "our [man's] connection with women is founded . . . on the desire of pleasing them, because they are quite enlightened judges of personal merit" (Montesquieu, *Oeuvres* 2:822). With similar intentions, Jaucourt had suggested (as mentioned in chapter 2) that the chanson Provençal and the chivalric romance had opened the age of modernity in Europe: the kind of modernity introduced by the chanson entailed a new relationship between the sexes. Women had now an authority of judgment, and the cavalier attitude of men was informed by a code of courtship and an expectation of refusal. Above all, love as a ritual of courtship had been formed. As an example of the gender relations appearing in the chanson, let us read, at random, from an anthology of troubadour poetry:

> Midons que te mon cor gatge
> prec, si com cel que merceia,
> que no m'aia cor voltage,

ni fals lauzengiers no creia

de mi, ni s'albir

qu'eu vas autram vir

que per bona fe sospir

e l'am ses enjan

e ses cor truan;

qu'eu non ai ges tal coratge

com li fals drut an

que van galian,

per qu'amors torna en soan

[As someone who asks for grace,

I pray you my lady,

who keep my prisoner of love:

do not be inconstant in your love to me,

and do not trust false rumors about me,

or do not suppose that I turn my attention toward any other woman.

Because I suffer in good faith,

loving you without deceit and without disloyalty:

my heart is not like the one of lying lovers,

who cheat and make love becomes debased.]

(Sansone 327)

The chanson by Gaucelm Faidit, circa 1180, was quite typical of the genre and of the time: the speaker was a male poet, and prayed a woman, elevated to the status of judge (to use Montesquieu's word) and almost to that of an earthly divinity, to accept his plea of love. The woman had the power of making the male poet either happy or forlorn. The male poet's love was not sexual eros, but an almost spiritual—platonic—form of desire. This love, moreover, was without disloyalty, in the sense that it was monogamous. Any different kind of love, any polygamous one, would be debasing of the very word. This was, arguably, the kind of love that Jaucourt found at the center of Christian ethics; but it was also a kind of love that, from Montesquieu's secular perspective, set the parameters for the kind of gender relations—monogamous and heterosexual—that both the *Lettres persanes* and *De l'esprit des lois* considered as the basis of modern Europe. Against the objectification of the woman in the Oriental harem, the European society predicated by Montesquieu did preserve a patriarchal hierarchy between the sexes—the male is still the privileged author-poet and his reader-interlocutor—but without objectifying the woman, who was elevated, instead, and even venerated, as the judge of manly courting.

Much of Madame de Staël's often-celebrated recuperation of the Middle Ages was, if we look carefully at it, exactly a recuperation of Montesquieu's promotion of woman as a subject in the context of the chanson and the chivalric romance. The Middle Ages of chivalry, in fact, offered Staël an alternative model to the despotic one of Napoléon's France. The sort of French imperialism that Napoléon had begun with the Italian campaign in 1976 smacked too much, for Staël, of Oriental despotism. Napoléon had crowned himself in Aix-la-Chapelle, but he was no Charlemagne—he was, actually, the new Saladin. As the despotism of the Orient was based on the enslavement of women in the harem, so was postrevolutionary despotism based on the increasing marginalization of women: "Since the Revolution, men have thought it politically and morally desirable to reduce women to the most absurd mediocrity" (Staël, *Littérature* 335). What's worse: she was right. After the coup d'état of the eighteenth Brumaire of 1799, Napoléon had been quick to declare that "since women have no political rights, it is not appropriate to define them citizens"; and the Napoleonic code, architected by that paladin of family values that was Jean Etienne Marie Portalis—"good fathers, good husbands, and good sons make good citizens"—had marginalized the social role of women to mere "obedience" (Bock 108–9). So, while this Napoleonic revolution was proposing itself as the model for a new Europe, Staël recuperated the Christian model of the Middle Ages as an alternative version of Europe—one in which the putative freedom of women stood for the more general freedom of society at large.

Within Christian Europe, women were never the authors of "truly superior works," warns Staël (171). They did not write chivalric romances, nor (pace Bogin) the poetry of the troubadours; "nevertheless, women have not served [in that time] the progress of literature in lesser ways than men, as they have inspired men an abundance of thoughts on the kind of relations they are to entertain with those beings [women] so mobile and delicate" (171–72). What Staël meant, simply, was that the almost complete totality of troubadour poetry in fact presented itself as inspired uniquely by the (male) poet's love for a most beautiful, lofty, and unreachable woman—a woman that only in the later traditions of the Italian *stil novo* and Petrarchism would start acquiring a proper name: Beatrice, Laura . . . . For Staël, then, Christianity entered Europe to dispel "the odious institution of [familial] slavery" and to institute "conjugal love" between one man and one woman (170–71). The *roman*, "varied production of the spirit of the moderns" (179), was but the literary equivalent of the religious institution of Christianity—what the Catholic critic C. S. Lewis once called the "allegory" of Christian, monogamous love and marriage.

European modernity, in other words, was produced, for Mme de Staël as for Montesquieu, by a set of epochal transformations that occurred after the fall of the Roman Empire. First, the nascent hegemony of the German tribes introduced in Europe "a respect for women that is unknown to the people of the south" (Staël, *Littérature* 211)—a respect parallel to the new "spirit of a free people" (206). Second, the spread of Christianity replaced an ancient (and southern) culture of sensual pleasure, war, "vengeance and passion" (202), exemplified by Homer's epics, with a new culture (Ossian's) concerned with "the brevity of life, the respect of the dead" (205), and the cult "of domestic happiness" between husband and wife (171). Third, as the new literature created a new role for the woman, who was now both free and responsible for domestic happiness, it also discovered a new idea of love. The latter was no longer understood as immediate sensual pleasure, but as the celebration of the almost mystical courtship and union of man and wife. In this epochal transformation, Europe ultimately realized itself—qua freedom—as a new internal dialectics not only of north and south but of female and male as well. Just as the dialectics of north and south had served Montesquieu the necessity to theorize a Europe "that cannot be compared to anything else," this new dialectics of male and female served Staël to eliminate the Orient, with its unruly gender confusion and its despotism, from the scene of European literature.

The picture of Staël's Eurocentric universe was thus clear: the "new, dreamy, and profound sensibility, which is one of the great charms of modern literature" (*Littérature* 181), began in (northern) Europe with the emergence of woman as the subject of poetry and as the judge of man's love. Modernity, ergo, was once again a European success story from which the Orient was once more excluded. One problem, however, arose at the moment in which Staël decided to argue that the index of European difference could be found in its modern literature of love. In other words, if the great epochal shift of modernity consisted in a turning toward love, was one to assume that no other time and place but modern Europe had such a notion of love? First, one had to eliminate the poetry of Sappho, singing Lesbos's poetess's love already in the sixth century BC—not a big problem, arguably, since such poetry hardly fell within the strictures of heterosexual love imposed by Staël. Second, one had to eliminate the Kama Sutra (sixth century AD) and the *ars amatoria* of Ovid (ca. 2 AD) for being too materialistic—being about sex, in other words, rather than about loftier forms of love. Third, and more problematically, one had to eliminate the whole tradition of Arab love poetry, devoted to the poet's quite monogamous love for a most beautiful, lofty, and unreachable woman: "I have Allah as my only Lord, oh Abda, / So I have gotten to take your face as my one Lord," wrote for instance Bassar ibn Burd (qtd. in Galmés de Fuentes 18) in the seventh century AD. Was not the love for Abda as heterosexual, monogamous (as for the one God), and spiritual as the love of Gaucelm Faidit? As Simonde de Sismondi would observe in 1813, in the midst of the dispute fired by Staël's thesis of the fundamentally European nature of love,

> this delicacy of the sentiments of the troubadours, this mysticism of love, has a more intimate relationship with Arab poetry than one would think, given the vicious jealousy of the Muslims and the cruel persistence of polygamy. The women of Muslims are divinities in their eyes, and slaves at the same time. The seraglio is at the same time a temple and a prison. The passion of love has, among the peoples of the south, a livelier ardor, a greatest impetuosity than in our Europe. (1:95)

The main problem for Staël's thesis was that the Oriental tradition, which was supposed to work as the antithesis of Europe, presented, in fact, remarkable similarities to what was supposed to be the uniqueness of Europe. Was Mme de Staël so sure that the uniquely European poetry of love of the Middle Ages did not come from preexisting Arab models? We are thus back to the very problem raised by Juan Andrés's Arabist theory: was modern poetry—in rhymes and about love—a *European* invention? Or did the Arabs bring it to Europe? Andrés's doubt, in the meantime, started concerning not only the origin of modern European literature but, more radically, the origin of European gender relations, which were symbolic, in turn, of social and power relations. In other words, if the Arabs had developed such a notion of love in their poetry, the whole edifice of European freedom as the antithesis to Oriental haremlike despotism was in danger of crumbling. In truth, Staël never mentioned Andrés—but she still had to face his theory, and argue, at the very least, that the Arabs did not bring modern poetry to Europe. On the contrary, the Arabs only learned love poetry from the Europeans: "The Moors established in Spain borrowed from chivalry and its *romans* their cult of women. Such cult did not exist in the national customs of the Orient. The Arabs who remained in Africa were not similar, from this point of view, to those established in Spain. The Moors gave the Spaniards their spirit of magnificence; the Spaniards inspired the Moors their love and their chivalric honor" (*Littérature* 193). So if the Arabs learned love poetry from the Spaniards, where did the southern Spaniards learn it from? No doubt from "the northern peoples, [who] judging from the traditions that are still remnant and from the customs of the Germans, have always and in all times had a respect for women that is unknown to the people of the south" (211)! If this chronology—modernity begins with the Germans, who spread it to Spain, whence it is picked by the Andalusian Moors—sounds too much like a bilious response to Juan Andrés's Arabist theory, that is because, quite likely, it really was.

Europe from Coppet

> Coppet is the headquarters of European opinion.
> —STENDHAL, "De l'amour"

The group that from 1766 to 1817 met at Staël's salon in Coppet seemed to be quite concerned with the question raised by Juan Andrés's Arabist theory, which threatened to comprise at its core the attempt to theorize Europe as the moral and political place of love. François Raynouard, who would begin the publication of the *Choix des poésies originales des troubadours* only in 1816, had already introduced the work of Juan Andrés to the members of Coppet in 1801, when he had started his correspondence with Simonde de Sismondi. For the collection he was preparing, Raynouard wanted to defend the thesis that Jean-Baptiste de Sainte-Palaye had elaborated in *Mémoires sur l'ancienne chevalerie* (1753) and in the *Histoire littéraire des troubadours* (1774). Sainte-Palaye's theory was quite similar to the one Mme de Staël had elaborated concerning the origin of love poetry in the European Middle Ages (see Passerini 211–30). For that reason, arguably, Raynouard had developed an interest in the work of the Coppet group and was curious to know how they would handle the recently translated work of Juan Andrés. The *Histoire des sciences et de la littérature depuis les temps antérieurs à l'histoire grecque jusqu'à nos jours* (this was the curious French title of *Dell' origine*, 1805) seemed to confirm the hypothesis of Thomas Warton's *History of English Poetry* (1774), which had already claimed, but without strong arguments, that love poetry had entered Europe through the Arabs and was not a specific European invention. Andrés, arguing as we have seen, that the Arabs brought a totally novel idea of poetry—syllabic, in rhymes, *and* about love—into Europe, offered textual and stylistic confirmation to Warton.

Sismondi was the first one in Coppet who faced the problem of Andrés's Arabist theory in a direct way. In 1813, after a long correspondence with Raynouard, he published *De la littérature du midi de l'Europe*. The book began with a short summary of Staël's and Sainte-Palaye's argument: chivalry and Provençal poetry had been born together under the influence of Christianity; they had both engendered a new cult of woman and love. In more ways than one, Sismondi's project was homage to and the ideal continuation of Mme de Staël's *De la littérature*. As the latter had established the distinction between "two completely distinct literatures," so was Sismondi certain he could "detach [southern people] from the people of the north" (1:ii–iii), and "romance languages from Germanic ones" (1:10). As Staël had studied the "influence that religion, customs, and laws have on literature, and the influence that literature has on religion, customs, and laws," so did Sismondi want "to show the pervasive reciprocal influence that the political and religious history of peoples has had on their literatures" (1:ii). And as Staël had promoted the Middle Ages as the origin of Europe's modernity, so was Sismondi's study intentioned to posit a medieval origin of modern German Romanticism. What stood between Sismondi and the realization of all of these goals was none less than the friar Juan Andrés.

Sismondi's first mention of Andrés occurs in the very first chapter of the *Littérature du midi*—in fact, in the first note to the entire book. Its ambiguous tone of praise and scorn sets from the very outset the relation of mock respect that Sismondi wants to assume vis-à-vis his predecessor:

> I only know of two works that comprehend the history of this entire part of literature [that of the south of Europe]. The first, with an even wider scope, is that of Andrés, Spanish Jesuit, Professor in Mantua: *Dell' origine e de' progressi d'ogni Letteratura* . . . . He overviews the history of all human sciences in all the languages and in the entire universe; and with a vast erudition, he develops in philosophical fashion the general march of

the human spirit; but since he never gives one example, never analyzes the particular taste of one nation, and only gives rapid judgments scarcely motivated, he does not leave any clear idea of the writers and works whose names he has assembled together. (1:14–15)

Better, then, the other of the two works, incidentally, Friedrich Boutterwerk's *Geschichte der schönen Wissenschaften*, 1801–10, which Sismondi judges at least "credible" (16).

Despite such exordium, Sismondi drew quite liberally from *Dell' origine*. Call it a tribute to Andrés, here is, for instance, what Sismondi wrote in his chapter entitled "Literature of the Arabs": "One sees hundreds of camels entering Baghdad, charged only with paper and books; and all the books that men of letters thought worthy of being brought to the people, in whatever language they were written, were immediately translated into Arabic" (1:47).

Here, instead, is what Andrés had written in *Dell' origine*: "One saw hundreds of camels entering Baghdad, charged only with paper and books; and all the books thought to be proper for public education, were immediately translated into Arabic to be accessible by everyone" (1:120). Plagiarism!—denounced Andrés's biographer (Mazzeo 87–90). Plagiarized from Andrés's book, in fact, could also be Sismondi's indictment of Arab poetry, which for Andrés was filled with "excessively daring metaphors . . . endless allegories . . . excessive hyperboles" (1:134–35), and for Sismondi relying "on too daring metaphors, endless allegories, and excessive hyperboles" (1:60).

Yet Sismondi's thesis was, rather than plagiarism, a total rewriting of Andrés's theory. On the one hand, it is true, Sismondi agreed with Andrés's claim that "Arabia gave shelter to the lost literature, and offered sacred asylum to the gentile culture that Europe had rudely cast away" (1:116). In Sismondi's words, the Arabs, "who had contributed more than any other nation, with their conquest and fanaticism, to destroy the cult of sciences and letters" (1:40), were the ones who revived in Europe a love for Aristotle and the classics when the whole "West was drowned in barbarity" (1:39). To Arabia, Sismondi's Europe, in a clear echo of Andrés, also owed "the invention of paper" for books (Sismondi 1:73), the inventions of gunpowder, the compass, and the numerals "without which the science of calculus could not have been pushed to the stage we know today" (1:74). Still following Andrés, Sismondi also argued that rhyme entered Al-Andalus with the Arabs (1:104). Seemingly contradicting Mme de Staël and confirming Andrés, Sismondi even went as far as declaring that "it is from them [Arabs] that we have received . . . this drunkenness of love [*enivrement d'amour*], this tenderness, this delicacy of sentiments, this religion, this cult of women, which have had such influence on chivalry, and which we find in all southern literature, which, because of these traits, has an Oriental character" (1:66). In short, "Arab [literature] gave an altogether new impulse to literatures in Europe" (1:10), and "modern Europe [was] formed at the Arab school and enriched by it" (1:10).

Was Sismondi, then, to conclude, following Andrés and against his hostess at Coppet, that the Arabs (or Spain) were the origin of modern Europe? Not so fast. First, asked Sismondi, "What has left of so much glory?" (1:76). The question, as well as the answer to it—"the vast regions where Islam dominated or dominates still are now dead for all sciences" —was less naive than one might think at first glance. To say that Arab culture, once glorious, was dead at present meant to situate that culture, once again, in the *past* of the European telos of progress: "This immense wealth of Arab literature, of which I have given only some glimpses, no longer exists in any Arab country, or in any of the countries where the Muslims dominated" (1:77). Arab culture, in other words, was the last stage of the ancient world, a continuation of the Aristotelian legacy (1:70)—something that, at any rate, no longer *is*. Modernity, instead—European modernity—began *after* that, and, to some measure, indifferent to the great discoveries of the "ancient" Arabs.

Andrés's mistake, from the point of view of Sismondi, was that he had considered literature as a whole, as *one* organism progressing in history and moving from one nation and continent to another. Accordingly, modern literature had begun for Andrés with the Arabs, who had introduced it to Al-Andalus. From there, literature had enlightened Spain, and, in the end, the whole of modern Europe. For Sismondi, instead, there was not one but *two* literatures. Mme de Staël had been clear: there are "two completely distinct literatures." Accordingly, Sismondi could distinguish between a southern literature, revitalized by the Arabs, and a northern one, "like" the Arab in some respects, yet "easily distinguishable" from it. Andrés, for instance, had maintained that rhyme had been brought to Europe from Arabia. For Sismondi, instead, "Arab poetry is rhymed *like* ours" (1:60; emphasis mine), but it was Andrés's mistake to believe that Arab rhyme was the model followed by the Provençal poets of France. Rather, the European troubadours developed rhyme like the Arabs did, but independently from them. Also the *roman*, Andrés had suggested, was Arab in origin. Though similarities between Arab storytelling and the European romance also existed for Sismondi, "Arab imagination, which sparks in all its brilliance in these tales [*A Thousand and One Nights*] is easily distinguishable from the chivalric imagination" (1:64).

The influence of the Arabs was, then, in Sismondi's last analysis, limited to the literatures of the south: "The people of the south . . . formed their poetry at the school of the Orientals" (1:10); and "Oriental style . . . spread to all romance languages" (1:42). Germanic languages, on the other hand, seemed free from such Oriental origin. That is why, since Germany was the essence of Europe, Spanish literature was not entirely "European: it is Oriental" (1:42). And that is why southern literature presented itself as the very antithesis of the austere, ethical, and Protestant European literature: "Studying the literature of the south, we have often been surprised of the subversion of morality, the corruption of all principles, of the social disorganization that this literature indicates" (4:19); reading such southern literature, "we will then be happy to breathe, in a language close to ours [Spanish], the scents of the Orient and the incense of Arabia; happy to see, in a faithful mirror, the palaces of Baghdad . . . and to comprehend [*comprendre*], in a European people, this brilliant Asiatic poetry, which created so many marvels" (4:179).

Happily and gleefully, Sismondi could then make Asia and Arabia disappear from his theorization of modern Europe: not only because the love that Staël singled out as constitutive of Europe was "easily distinguishable" from Oriental love poetry; but also, and more important, because Europe contained within itself its own Oriental Other. As for Montesquieu, the Oriental was comprehended within Europe's south and spoke its romance languages. Quite cunningly and brilliantly, Sismondi started from (or plagiarized) Andrés's Arabist theory to claim exactly the opposite of what Andrés had claimed: not that the south was the heart and origin of Europe's modernity, but that the south was, as Montesquieu had already declared, its internal antithesis (on Sismondi's north and south, see also Rosset).

Compared to such cunning, the other members of Coppet had a much more pedestrian way of dealing with Andrés, the south, and Arabist theory. With the exception of Benjamin Constant—"I don't like our ancient poetry, nor our chivalry" (qtd. in Duranton 349)—everybody at Coppet argued, at one time or another, on the question of medieval romance, chivalric poetry, and the question of Arab influence. August Wilhelm von Schlegel, in *Observations sur la langue et la littérature pro-vençales* (1818), steadfastly rejected the Arabist theory while declaring himself shocked that someone (Andrés) could think that such a cruel and misogynist people as the Arabs could have invented a form of poetry based on the adoration of women. Even if, Schlegel contended, the Arabs had invented the use of rhyme, they most certainly did not invent love: "Muhammad's sect has never had the slightest influence on anything that constitutes the original genius of the Middle Ages" (67–69). The founder and editor of the journal *Europa*, Friedrich von Schlegel, would, like his brother August, in the end radicalize Sismondi's thesis: not only was Arab influence limited to Al-Andalus—even the Spanish "muse of old Castile is . . . free from Arabic or oriental admixture" (Schlegel 247); moreover, the evolution of northern (European) literature was radically distinct from the literature "of Catholic countries, such as Spain, Italy, Portugal" (246; see also Duranton; Cometa). Even more fundamentalist was Charles Victor de Bonstetten's *L'homme du midi et l'homme du nord*, published as late as 1824. Europe, for Bonstetten, was divided into two climates. What *L'homme du midi* added to Montesquieu was the racial ramification of climatology—there were two distinct races of "man"— and more than an echo of the Coppet discussions about troubadour love: "In the South Love appears to the senses, and through them be-comes inconstant. In the North it drifts into dreaminess, and oftentimes constitutes the destiny of a whole life" (87).

The sort of Europe that Montesquieu had started imagining in 1748 sedimented in the literary theories of Coppet. Asia, to begin with, was not essential to define the culture and literature of Europe. Its influence, if any, was limited to the south. A definition of Europe proceeded in-stead, dialectically, from the antithesis of north and south—an antithesis that, dialectically indeed, was imagined as a spiritual progress *from* an old past *to* a modern north. This dialectic was sustained by the religious unity of Christian Europe, which provided the fundaments for its cul-ture. Even this unity—Christianity—was in turn dialectically split be-tween Protestantism and Catholicism.

In this definition of Europe, the emergence of a new continental hege-mony, and of new levels of subalternity, were already visible. Greece had almost disappeared from these discussions about Europe, except to re-turn in mentions of ancient and classical literature—a primal origin, in other words, too remote to still be of any significance. Neither Turkey nor Malta was even suspected of being part of Europe. Eastern Europe—Russia, Poland, Bulgaria, and the Slavic states—was so marginal as to be unworthy of any discussion. Sismondi, exemplary of all this, had maintained that there were "three distinct races [in Europe]: the Latin, the Germanic, and the Slav"; but his plan was to discuss only "Romance literature and Germanic literature," which alone comprehend the totality of "civilized Europe" (1:iii). Southern Europe was Italy, Spain, and Portugal: it was Romance, somewhat Oriental, "ancient," and Catholic. Northern Europe was England, Helvetia, Scandinavia, and above all, Germany: it was Germanic, Western, modern, and Protestant. The status of France, uncertain between north and south, was that of an eclipsed hegemonic power. Now it was *Deutschland über Alles*.

Dialectics, or Europe

> They see themselves at the end of a long European dialectic.
> —THOMAS PYNCHON, *Gravity's Rainbow*

Montesquieu's understanding of Europe as a self-contained system—"history cannot compare it to anything else"—divided into two complementary parts—north and south—was, then, as *Europe (in Theory)* has suggested so far, the beginning of a Eurocentric approach to universal history that the Romantics of Coppet simply reformulated in a Germanic (rather than Frankish) key. As Enrique Dussel suggests, this Eurocentric position, which "reinterpreted all of world history," ultimately cohered in the Germanocentric philosophical system of Georg W. F. Hegel, "for whom the 'Orient' was humanity's 'infancy' (*Kindheit*), the place of despotism and unfreedom from which the Spirit (*Volksgeist*) would later soar toward the West, as if on a path toward the full realization of liberty and civilization" (Dussel, "World-System" 221).

The *Vorlesungen über die Philosophie der Geschichte* (published posthumously in 1822) was perhaps Hegel's most coherent attempt to theorize Europe as the center of the world. The centrality of the German Confederation (*Deutscher Bund*) in the new Europe, after all, was but the political outcome of the recent Congress of Vienna, which in 1815 has restructured Germany on the imperial model of Charlemagne. Hegel's text, in a way, only wanted to theorize, after the fact, this already existing Germanocentric Europe. It also wanted to systematize the entire European " 'periphery' that surrounds that center" (Dussel, "Eurocentrism" 65). Hegel's periphery, following Montesquieu, was "Europe's own Iberian peninsula," and, more generally, Europe's own south: Greece, Malta, Portugal, Spain, southern France, and Italy (65–71). Hegel's recentering of postrevolutionary Europe on the Germanic world (see Thompson 58) needed to theorize systematically what had remained just an implicit suggestion in Montesquieu: the idea of Europe's historical progress, that is, as *dialectics*. A full-fledged theory of dialectics, in other words, was what Hegel wanted to add to Montesquieu's Eurocentric position.

What this meant was that the negativity of the south, theorized from Montesquieu to Coppet, and contrasted only by the unsuccessful challenge of Andrés and his southern historians, was not just an accident of European theory. In other words, the negativity of the south was not theorized because, accidentally, the south in 1748 or in 1800 happened to be an economic and political margin of Europe. The negativity of the south, on the contrary, was the *necessary condition* for all these Eurocentric theories of Europe. If Eurocentrism is the tendency to explain history "without making recourse to anything outside of Europe" (Dussel, "Europe" 469–70), then Eurocentrism *needs* a figure of antithesis internal to Europe itself—it *needs* to posit a south as the negative moment in the dialectical progress of the spirit of Europe. In sum, what a theory of Europe needed, and what Hegel provided, was a full-fledged theory of dialectics. Montesquieu had theorized "a kind of balance between the southern and the northern nations [of Europe]"; Staël had theorized "two completely distinct literatures" and their "melting" together through the bond of Christianity; and both had theorized Europe as a progress from south to north. What Hegel needed now to theorize was the very connection between progress and the much-discussed difference of north and south.

The stated aim of the *Philosophie der Geschichte* was to provide a philosophical history of the world—philosophical in the sense that, rather than being concerned with mere facts, such history would divine the transcendental significance of history and give meaning to each single event. Hegel's assumption, accordingly, was that world history, or universal history, was a rational theodicy—a succession of events that *made sense*: "The history of the world . . . presents us with a rational process" (Hegel 9). This was the premise Hegel asked his reader to accept: "In beginning the study of Universal History, we should at least have the firm, unconquerable faith that Reason *does* exist there; and that the World of intelligence and conscious volition is not abandoned to chance, but must show itself in the light of the self-cognizant Idea" (10; original emphasis). The idea that history was a rational process of continuous betterment— from savagery to the law—was, of course, Montesquieu's. Hegel, certainly not accustomed to praise anybody but himself, for once was ready to acknowledge the debt: "It is only a thorough, liberal, comprehensive view of historical relations (such as we find in Montesquieu's 'Esprit des Loix [*sic*]'), that we can give truth and interest to [history]" (6–7). The *Philosophie der Geschichte* was therefore concerned exactly with finding such "thorough" and "liberal" historical relations among disparate world events and facts. These relations, in turn, were to show that universal history had to be ultimately coherent and aiming toward a single end: "The History of the world is none other than the progress of the consciousness of Freedom" (19). The echo of Montesquieu—freedom is the end of history—is certainly audible yet again. Also in Hegel's treatment of the despotic Orient the reader should have no problem to trace the logic back to *De l'esprit des lois*:

> The Orientals have not attained the knowledge that Spirit—Man *as such* —is free; and because they do not know this they are not free. They only know that *one is free.* But on this very account, the freedom of that one is only caprice; ferocity—brutal recklessness or passion, or a mildness and tameness of the desires, which is itself only an accident of Nature—mere caprice like the former.—That *one* is therefore only a Despot; not a *free* man. (18)

If freedom was unattainable for the Orientals, it was, then, to Montesquieu's "German fathers" that Europe owed the knowledge of freedom: "The German nations, under the influence of Christianity, were the first to attain the consciousness that man, as man, is free" (Hegel 18). This was, arguably, Montesquieu filtered through the religiosity of Coppet (whose sense of Christianity Hegel praised in some footnotes devoted to the Schlegel brothers; see Hegel 58 and 160). Also influenced by the discussions of Coppet seemed Hegel's interest in patriarchy as "the primary form of conscious morality, succeeded by that of the State as its *second* phase" (41). Despite this Coppet-like religious patriarchalism, however, the project of the *Philosophie der Geschichte* remained Montesquieu's more secular one: freedom, said Hegel, was not found in a state of nature or given by a transcendental God; rather, "to the Ideal of Freedom, Law and Morality are indispensably requisite . . . . Society and the State are the very conditions in which Freedom is realized" (41). The spirit of the law, in other words, was the realization of freedom. Freedom, in turn, is what "tirelessly transgresses," as Montesquieu had written, the natural laws that God has established. The difference, noticeable indeed, was that Montesquieu's spirit of the laws had become, in Hegel's postrevolutionary age of nationalism, a spirit of the state.

All these similarities between the *Philosophie der Geschichte* and *De l'esprit des lois*, however, are just barely relevant when compared to a much more essential one: the way, that is, in which Hegel understood history exactly on Montesquieu's geographical basis. "The Geographical Basis of History" is in fact titled the central section of Hegel's course on world history. For Hegel, history was not simply a chronological issue but one of space, too: history "falls under the category of Time as well as Space" (79). History happened in places, and chronology could best be described as the advancement of the spirit (of freedom) from one site to another: "The History of the World travels from East to West, for Europe is absolutely the end of History, Asia the beginning" (103). The plot traced by true history, moreover, was the climatological advancement of the spirit from a "torrid" south to a "temperate" north: "The true theatre of History is . . . the temperate zone; or, rather, its northern half, because the earth there presents itself in a continental form, and has a broad breast, as the Greeks say. In the south, on the contrary, it divides itself, and runs out into many points" (103).

As Massimo Cacciari and Franco Cassano have separately observed, the division of the south meant here the southern inability to cohere into a nation-state—an inability overcome, of course, by the nascent German nation (Cacciari, *Arcipelago* 20; Cassano, *Pensiero* 22). History was thus a movement from east to west; but, in fact, its "true" theater was a movement limited only to Europe, and going from south to north. After eliminating America and Australia (Hegel 83), too immature and "new" to be part of true history (Gerbi 582–614), the *Philosophie der Geschichte* also got rid of Asia and Africa from the true theater of history. Africa, to begin with, "has remained—for all purposes of connection with the rest of the World—shut up" (Hegel 91). It could then be no part of world history. Sure enough, Carthage and North Africa had their moment of glory; but "this part [of Africa]," said Hegel, "was to be—*must* be attached to Europe" (91). So, Hegel could quickly leave Africa, not to mention it again. For it is no historical part of the World; it has no movement or development to exhibit. Historical movements in it—that is in its northern part—belong to the Asiatic or European World . . . . What we properly understand by Africa, is the Unhistorical, Undeveloped Spirit, still involved in the conditions of mere nature, and which had to be presented here only as on the threshold of the World's History. (99)

Once he crossed the threshold and got to Asia, "the region of origination," Hegel soon informed his reader that "in Asia arose the Light of the Spirit, and therefore the history of the World" (99). This concession to be an origin, however, could not guarantee Asia a much better fate than the one Hegel had just administered to Africa: because the "empire of fanaticism" (100) failed to develop, as it were, "in a really historical form." The "beginning of history may be traced to them"; but "*they* have not attained an historical character." In other words, even if Asia "presents the origination of all religious and political principles . . . [only] Europe has been the scene of their development" (101).

Europe thus remained as the sole stage for Hegel's true theater of history. Not that this was a limitation! The loss of Asia, Africa, Australia, and America was not, after all, a major one or to be lamented: "Europe [is] the mingling of these several elements" (103); by itself, Europe was synthesis of the *whole* of world history. In a sense, even Europe was too much for Hegel to deal with. An entire part of it had still to be eliminated. Hegel's Europe was divided not in two (north and south) but, rather, in three parts: southern Europe, "looking towards the Mediterranean" and including "Greece also"; the "heart of Europe," of which "France, Germany and England are the principal countries"; and "the north-eastern States of Europe—Poland, Russia, and the Slavonic Kingdoms." My reader should not worry, however, that the whole idea of a Europe (in theory) predicated on the antithesis of north and south would come to a halt here: northeastern Europe was, for Hegel, de trop. "These people [from eastern Europe] did, indeed, found kingdoms and sustain spirited conflicts with the various nations that came across their path . . . . Yet this entire body of peoples remains excluded from our consideration, because hitherto it has not appeared as an independent element in the series of phases that Reason has assumed in the World" (350). In other words, eastern Europe, along with Asia, Africa, America, and Australia, was dispensable too. Europe—or world history, which is to say the same—only needed two, and no more than two parts: north and south.

The way in which Hegel could be so confident that a history of the whole world needed no more than a look at a small part of Europe is certainly striking. Yet Hegelian history *did* happen in such a small theater. And a theater it was. Like a modern comedy, it had four acts—which Hegel, theatrically indeed, gave the more scientific name of "phases." Asia was the "first phase" of history, but a phase "really unhistorical" (105–6); the "Greek World" truly began history by positing, against Asiatic despotism, the idea of "individualities forming themselves" (106–7); "the third phase is the realm of abstract Universality (in which the Social aim absorbs all individual aims): it is the Roman State" (107–8); its fourth and "ultimate result" was the "Germanic World," the moment of the spirit's "perfect maturity and strength" when freedom is founded not on despotism (first stage), individuality (second), or empire (third), but in the state, understood as the perfect, Montesquieu-like synthesis of individual and communal needs (108–10). Europe was, then, the history of a progress from the absolute negativity of despotism to the final (and a bit Hollywood-like) happy end of conquered freedom. In fact, the moment of despotism (Asia) was not even part of this progress—it was merely the origin and prologue through whose *negation* history could truly begin.

What was peculiar about Hegel's understanding of Europe was not the idea of its self-sufficiency, progress, historicity, or, even, of its north-south difference. All these ideas we have repeatedly encountered—in Montesquieu, Voltaire, Jaucourt, Staël, Sismondi, Bonstetten, and the Schlegels. What was peculiar was the way in which *all* these elements cohered now into a philosophical system, one Hegel could, and *did*, call Europe. In such a system, history and progress were produced by internal differences and antitheses: each of the four stages of Hegel's world history, in other words, was not just a process of linear evolution but a process of negation of the preceding stage. History began when the Greek individual affirmed itself as a negation of despotic authority: the individual found subjective freedom. The Roman state, in turn, was the negation of the individual self-sufficiency and its alienation into the superior good of the republic: it was the moment in which the objective freedom of the state triumphed. The fourth and last stage of Europe/history—the Germanic world—was the moment in which this alienation was negated, and the individual found itself free in the state: the moment, in other words, when subjective and objective freedom coincided. I am free because what I want is what the state wants:

> This is the point which consciousness has attained, and these are the principal phases of that form in which the principle of Freedom has realized itself;—for the History of the World is nothing but the development of the Idea of Freedom. But Objective Freedom—the laws of real Freedom—demand the subjugation of the mere contingent Will—for this is in its nature formal. If the Objective is in itself Rational, human insight and conviction must correspond with the Reason which it embodies, and then we have the other essential element—Subjective Freedom— also realized. (456)

If Montesquieu had theorized Europe as the modernity of universal history, Hegel was now theorizing Europe as a process of historical dialectics—a process that was certainly unique to Europe:

> Universal history . . . shows the development of the consciousness of Freedom on the part of Spirit, and of the consequent realization of that Freedom. This development implies a gradation—a series of increasingly adequate expressions or manifestations of Freedom, which result from its Idea. The logical, and—as still more prominent—the *dialectical* nature of the Idea in general, viz. that it is self-determined—that it assumes successive forms which it successively transcends; and by this very process of transcending its earlier stages, gains an affirmative, and, in fact, a richer and more concrete shape. (63; original emphasis)

Africa was nature. Asia was the prehistorical unfreedom of despotism. Only Europe "developed" toward freedom, and such development was of a "dialectical nature." What this meant is that the idea of freedom "advances to an infinite antithesis" (Hegel 26) by constantly negating and "transcending . . . earlier stages" of freedom toward an ever-richer Germanic one. No antithesis, no progress. The south was, then, the necessary antithesis that Hegel's Germanic north had to imagine in order to imagine itself as progress and modernity—in order, namely, *to be* Europe. Put differently, the south had to occupy the place of negativity (the "immaturity" of history), lest Europe, as progress, would stop existing once and for all as modernity.

5 Orientalism, Mediterranean Style

THE LIMITS OF HISTORY AT THE MARGINS OF EUROPE

And you advise me to write history? To record the outrageous
crimes of the men by whom we are still held down?
—MARCUS TULLIUS CICERO, "Letters to Atticus"

When Edward Said denounced the whole of Oriental studies in 1979 as
"a conspiratorial system of domination and exploitation of the east"
(*Orientalism* 1), the world of academia found itself divided, in Aijaz
Ahmad's rather unappreciative words, "between inordinate praise and
wholesale rejection" (168). Many have since subscribed to Said's hypothesis and investigated supplementary ways in which academic knowledges
such as Orientalism frame, legitimate, and at times produce systems of
dominance and power (e.g., see Marrouchi). Others have defended the
field from Said's "politicization" and insisted on at least some versions of
Orientalism that are not "singularly informed by a colonial administrative objective," but rather by cultural and literary interests (Rice 236).[1]

It might be worth noticing, however, that such a divide has been
scarcely noticeable in southern European receptions of Said, where *Orientalism* has instead most often been received with the highest degree
of enthusiasm. Jane Schneider, editing a volume entitled *Italy's "Southern Question": Orientalism in One Country* in 1995, was quick, for instance, to declare that southern Europe, too, "was certainly affected by
Orientalism" (5), and more eager still to adapt Said's paradigm for the
understanding of the southern European context. As if following Gyan
Prakash's suggestion that "it is up to the scholars . . . including Europeanists" to use the theoretical frameworks of postcolonial and subaltern studies ("Subaltern" 1490; see also Prakash, "Writing"), southern
Europeanists seem to have found in Said a new lexicon to discuss the old
facts of Europe's internal colonialism. Franco Cassano's *Southern Thinking* (*Pensiero meridiano*), 1996, opened with a clear echo of Said's notion

of the "objectified" Orient: "Southern thinking means, fundamentally, to give back to the south its ancient dignity as subject of thought; to interrupt a long sequence in which the south has been thought as an object by others" (3). Also Franco Piperno, in *Elogio dello spirito pubblico meridionale* (1997), denounced the prejudice of southernism (*meridionalismo*)—its reduction of the south to a "premodern relic of the past" (13)—in a way that was quite reminiscent of Said's indictment of the Orientalist prejudice that "primitiveness . . . inhered in the Orient, *was* the Orient" (*Orientalism* 231).

Historical reasons to see similarities between Said's Orient and the European south are certainly not lacking. In chapter 2 of the present book, I have noticed the way in which nineteenth-century ethnographies of the European south (Lombroso, Niceforo, etc.) had been historically inspired by, if not directly modeled on, previous notions of what constituted the Orient. The Italian poet Giuseppe Goffredo has discussed a more recent Orientalism of the south, at work still in the European Union's policies of the "two Europes" (two-lane, two-speed, and all variations thereof): "The Orientalists represent the South as an estranged fetish, crystallized in a chronic backwardness, arrested in a ruined present" (66). This has not necessarily been a European attempt at colonizing postcolonial studies, but a more genuine search to frame theoretically an old southern feeling (which precedes the development of postcolonial and subaltern studies), historically expressed from both the Left and Right of the political spectrum (Alianello; Galasso). It is this feeling that has made southern scholars seek in Said's *Orientalism* a way to express and codify some of their own anxieties.

Admiration and usability, however, should not prevent us from understanding why a bunch of southern Orientalists who want "to separate themselves from their predecessors of the north" and who refuse to "align themselves with the European Arabists of the north" have started to sound frankly aggravated at that book, "in which both British and French cultural hegemony are affirmed in their relation to the Orient," and in which all other Orientalisms are so cavalierly dismissed and "denied [their] rightful place" (Jubran 8). Let us refresh our memory with the beginning of Said's book:

> The French and British—less so the Germans, Russians, Spanish, Portugese, Italians, and Swiss—have had a long tradition of what I shall be calling Orientalism . . . . The Orient is not only adjacent to Europe; it is

also the place of Europe's greatest and richest and oldest colonies, the source of its civilizations and languages, its cultural contestant, and one of its deepest and most recurring images of the Other. In addition, the Orient has helped to define Europe (or the West) as its contrasting image, idea, personality, experience. Yet none of this Orient is merely imaginative. The Orient is an integral part of European material civilization and culture. Orientalism expresses and represents that part culturally and even ideologically as a mode of discourse with supporting institutions, vocabulary, scholarship, imagery, doctrines, even colonial bureaucracies and colonial styles. (1)

The fact remains that, despite having a shorter tradition, these other Orientalisms may have been just as important as the British and French ones to "help . . . define Europe (or the West)." They should, then, be important to me, at least, in the writing of a book called *Europe (in Theory)*. This does not mean that politics and knowledge live on different grounds, but simply that other Orientalist traditions can give us a less reified version of such a relationship. Is it too simplistic to suppose that there may be a "bad" Orientalism (in the service of colonial exploitation) and a "good" one that does not legitimate the structures of European domination, and dismantles instead its theoretical system?[2] In addition, some of the minor Orientalist traditions that Said brackets away did live an Oriental identity that was all but "merely imaginary": the Russians *were* the Orient of Europe, and may still be; the Spaniards fought against their Oriental self in 1492 to become Europeans; and southern Italians, as I will discuss below, lived an Oriental experience that in some sort of reevaluation of all values, was itself a system of domination and exploitation (sometimes enriching, sometimes merely brutal) *from* the east.

This chapter thus begins with a hypothesis and a paraphrase, both from Walter Mignolo's *Local Histories/Global Designs*. The hypothesis is that, after all, "I am where I think" (both geographically and historically speaking); the paraphrase, hence, is a question: How can you be a southern European Orientalist without twisting the very concept of Orientalism?

In truth, much more than Orientalism may be twisted in this southern operation: the very theory of Europe as antithesis to the east (discussed in chapters 1 and 2) and a theory of historiography that, according to Gyan Prakash, "projected [Europe] as History" ("*Subaltern*" 1475), may come out irremediably perverted. This is not to suggest that an Orientalism from the south necessarily constitutes the antithesis of Said's French and British Orientalism—a strategy of liberation, for instance. On the contrary, this intends to be an illustration of a *problematic* kind of "border gnoseology," a "critical reflection on knowledge production from . . . the interior borders of the modern/colonial world system" (Mignolo, *Local Histories* 11). And since the interior border I will discuss here is not Mignolo's Spain—displaced "from hegemonic position by England"—but Sicily—that had nowhere to be displaced from—it will be important to maintain an internal distinction even between Spanish and Sicilian Orientalisms. If the former was understood as "a branch of national culture" (Américo Castro, qtd. in Jubran 12), Sicilian Orientalism emerged ambiguously in the mid-nineteenth century (Marchianò) as a branch of nationalism, a branch or Europeanism, and as the crisis of both.

The following pages will be devoted to the work of Michele Amari—if not the founder, certainly one of the most influential and interesting figures of Italian Orientalism. Italy had a respectable history of Oriental studies before Amari. Already in imperial Rome, interest for the Orient was alive, and it continued uninterruptedly throughout the Middle Ages. The model for humanistic education in fifteenth-century Rome and Florence required the knowledge not only of Latin and Greek but also of Hebrew, Arabic, Chaldean, and Aramaic, The teaching of Hebrew, Arabic, and Chaldean was institutionalized in Rome in 1481, under the Studium Urbis of Pope Sistus iv. In the sixteenth century, Rome was the European capital for Oriental studies, and other languages such as Coptic and Armenian were taught in the university.

A figure of considerable importance for the knowledge about the Orient he provided to Europe was Leo Africanus. G. J. Toomer writes:

> A Spanish Muslim who had migrated to Fez at an early age, and was moderately well educated there, he was captured by Christian corsairs in 1518, and brought to Rome, where he was handed over to Pope Leo X. After a two-year imprisonment, during which he was allowed to use the Arabic manuscripts in the Vatican Library, he was baptized, changing his name from al-Hasan b. Muhammad b. Ahmad al-Wazzan to Johannes Leo, in honour of his patron the Pope. After his release he lived in Italy for a while, where he taught Arabic to Cardinal Aegidius of Viterbo, before eventually returning to Morocco and Islam. He wrote a number of

works in and on Arabic, including a grammar. Most of these have not survived, but a version of his "Description of Africa," which he composed in Italian, was republished many times, in Latin and other languages, in the sixteenth and seventeenth centuries, and long remained a principal source for European knowledge of the Islamic world. (21)

The presses of Italy were among the first in Europe to publish in Arabic. The first book printed in Europe with Arabic moveable types was the *Book of Hours* published in Fano in 1514. In 1538, the complete Koran was published in Venice, a city tied by an age-long commercial relationship to the Orient. In 1584, Giovan Battista Raimondi, a teacher at La Sapienza University in Rome, opened a press devoted to the exclusive study of the Orient, the Stamperia Orientale Medicea.

In the seventeenth century, the Vatican bought the Arabic moveable types of the Orientale Medicea—and scholarly interest in the Orient quickly transformed into missionary zeal. The Sacra Congregatio Propaganda Fide, founded in 1622 with the intent of spreading the Christian faith in the world, became probably the biggest European producer of books in Arabic, "but the types of literature published [by the Congregatio] were very circumscribed, being principally liturgical and homiletic. This was in accordance with the missionary and apologetic goals of those who controlled the presses; rigid supervision and censorship by the ecclesiastic authorities stifled any tendencies to further enquiry" (Toomer 24).

In the eighteenth century, interest in the Orient was not limited to the Arab countries. In 1732, the *Collegio de' Cinesi*, or Chinese College, was inaugurated in Naples to become one of the very first centers of sinology in Europe. Italian Orientalism, at any rate, remained focused on the Arab world. In the meantime, however, British and French colonial interests in the east had made such investments in the study of the Orient that no Italian state could ever hope to match. While institutes and departments of Oriental study multiplied in England, France, and (for different reasons) Germany, no Oriental school was instituted in Italy until 1903, when Celestino Schiaparelli (1841–1919), a disciple of Michele Amari, would open the Orientale of Rome. Until then, Hebrew and Arabic were taught merely as languages in the universities, while Coptic, Chaldean, and Aramaic had but disappeared. When Michele Amari was appointed professor of Arabic at the University of Pisa in 1859, his intention was that of reforming completely not only the study of Arabic but also that of Orientalism. Caught in some kind of Orientalism envy, Amari wanted to promote Italian universities to the rank of European ones: put bluntly, if Paris, London, and Berlin had their Oriental schools, a city in Italy also had to create its own. The kind of Orientalism Amari had in mind, however, was hardly one "informed by a colonial administrative objective." Orientalism was not, for Amari, the study of a faraway object to be known, colonized, exploited, and administered. It was, rather, the study of his own history and a reflection on the place that his native Sicily, the most marginal and southern province, occupied in Italy and in Europe itself.

The General Law of Europe: Vienna, 1815

In the first half of the nineteenth century, Sicily was technically a Spanish colony. Practically, it was a European one. After the storm of the revolution and of the Napoleonic wars, the Congress of Vienna had opened, in 1814, with the stated objective of "restoring the general law of Europe" (Charles Maurice de Talleyrand, qtd. in Duroselle 313). The territories that had been "unlawfully" occupied by Napoléon were now to be returned to their legitimate sovereignties. These had to be found largely among the four main allies responsible for the defeat of Napoléon: Britain, Russia, Austria, and Prussia. Or better: it is not that legitimate sovereignties had to be found in Britain, Russia, Austria, and Prussia *as nations*. If one thing was clear to the participants in the congress, it was the necessity to declare the age of nationalism over. Careless of the protests of the nascent "German Nation" (Fichte), utterly uninterested in the "ardent[ly] love[d] fatherland" of the Poles (Rousseau, "Government" 31), and certainly impatient with Italian calls for national unification, the participants in the congress, in a "spirit of cheerful cynicism" (Davies 582), divided, shared, and exchanged among themselves the lands that the spirit of nationalism had conceived as one.

The logic of Vienna was simple: sovereignties, neither national nor popular, were legitimate sovereignties of the monarchic families that had ruled Europe for centuries before. In short, this is what happened: small kingdoms and principalities were preserved within their confines; the part of central Europe that once constituted the core of Charlemagne's empire was divided and organized into a German confederation of thirty-nine states, of which four were free cities, and the rest belonged to one or the other monarchic families of Europe; King Frederick William III of Prussia expanded his territories to Saxony, Westphalia, the Rhine, and a small partition of Poland; George I of the German House of Hanover, the ruler of England and Ireland, obsessed now with overseas colonies, was content with just the small islands of Malta and Helgoland (and with the promise that no one would interfere in his affairs in Ceylon, Cape Colony, and the West Indies); the Hapsburgs, the hosts of the Congress, got their share of Poland (the lot of it went to the Russian czar Alexander I) and most of northeastern Italy, which was divided among various branches of the family; the House of Bourbons, after Louis XVI had been guillotined, was sat back in France (Louis XVIII) and Spain (Ferdinand VII), and confirmed, with greatest consequences for both history and this chapter, as the ruler of both southern Italy and the island of Sicily.

Starting from Fürst Metternich's assumption that "Italian affairs do not exist," and from Count Angeberg's assurance that Italy was but "a combination of independent states, linked together by the same geographical expression," the congress had been less than charitable to the aspirations of the Italians. Not only had Hapsburgs and Bourbons divided between themselves most of Italy, leaving only Rome to the pope and Piedmont to the House of Savoy; moreover, the Bourbons had decided, trampling on any Sicilian feelings of autonomy, to unite the Kingdom of Naples (southern Italy) and the Kingdom of Sicily into the single Kingdom of the Two Sicilies, with Ferdinand its first king and Naples its capital. For the urban bourgeoisie of Palermo, until then the capital of the Kingdom of Sicily, the annexation of Sicily to Naples sanctioned by Vienna meant not only the loss of an independence that "had a long and jealously guarded tradition of political and administrative autonomy" (Riall 31); it also meant, more pragmatically, the loss of administrative jobs and an outflow of tax revenues. To make things worse for the Bourbons, middle-class resentment only added to the aristocratic one. Eager to keep under check the power of a distrusted aristocracy, the Bourbon reforms of 1815 aimed at creating "a new class of non-noble landowners in the countryside" (Riall 33) through the eradication of feudal and church property, the establishment of communal lands, and the redistribution of the estates. Such reforms had obviously fueled the hostility of the upper classes at a moment in which the loss of Sicilian autonomy prevented the middle classes to be euphoric about land redistribution (Barone, Benigno, and Torrisi 86). Last but not the least, even the peasants, in part stirred up by the nobility, in part animated by grievances of their own (see Riall 57), were becoming part of the Bourbon problem.

Practical recriminations of Sicily's various classes were, to say the least, amplified by a general attitude of dismissal and sufficiency that had become politically operative with Vienna (Natoli 252). Already at the congress, Sicilian requests were welcomed with utter indifference: in the words of a Swiss delegate, "One does not seem to be willing to listen to them, although they say that they can neither harm nor help the European equilibrium, and although they promise not to be ambitious" (qtd. in Straus 94). Immediately after Vienna, Sicilians had not been heard when their parliament was dissolved; their opinion had not been asked when their flag was abolished; and the fact that freedom of the press and assembly had been suppressed did not seem to be a concern, according to either Ferdinand or Metternich, for Sicilians themselves (Mack Smith 2:352–53). To paraphrase William Roscoe Thayer: Were Sicilians satisfied? "No. Had they been consulted? No. Did their dissatisfaction matter? No. That generous but deluded knight, Don Quixote, once mistook a flock of sheep for a hostile army; Metternich, the champion of the Old Régime, mistook the human populations of Europe for sheep" (121).

It is not altogether clear whether the Sicilian sheep *really* turned into an army. But on July 14, 1820, the fourth day of the celebrations of the patron saint Rosalia, a popular insurrection exploded in Palermo at the cry of "Long Live Santa Rosalia! Long live Sicily! Long live freedom!" Governmental offices were burnt down, officers killed, and their heads paraded around the town. The requests, unsurprisingly, were for a constitution like the one of Spain, and for the political autonomy of the Sicilian nation from Naples. Although the revolt failed to move outside of Palermo, Ferdinand's fear must have been such that he sent a whole division headed by General Florestano Pepe to quench the insurrection; and then a second one, in February 1821, led by Pietro Colletta, who, incidentally, combined his military career with that of a historian.

The insurrection of 1820 was subdued on March 26, 1821: sixty people were tried, and eleven put to death. Only those who had participated in public lynching were executed, the others merely imprisoned. The hatred for Ferdinand of the Bourbons, and for the European order sanctioned by the Congress of Vienna, in the meantime, was growing: as one insurrection was being repressed, a new one was being prepared in Palermo, one that was supposed to take to the streets on January 12, 1822.

It was uncovered before anything happened, and on January 23, its four-teen organizers were arrested, tried, charged, and sentenced to death. The roster of the fourteen nationalists, an example in itself of the inter-classist reach of anti-Bourbonism in Sicily after 1815, included priests (Buonaventura Calabrò, Vincenzo Ingrassia, and Giuseppe La Villa), menial workers (Giuseppe Candia, Antonino Pitaggio, Natale Seidita, Michele Teresi), a poet (Giuseppe Lo Verde), members of the middle class (Dr. Pietro Minnelli and the notary Gaetano Di Chiara), and noble-men (Salvatore Martinez, Gioachino Landolina, Gerolamo La Manna, and Michele's father, Ferdinando Amari). The latter group would have their sentence commuted to life in jail—partly because of their social status, and partly because of some alleged collaboration with the police.

At any rate, not even these arrests could stop the Sicilians' enmities toward the king, nor their opposition to the new European order sanc-tioned by Vienna. But in truth, Vienna was not the only obstacle for the Sicilians. Sure enough, Metternich could never allow Sicily—"a people, half barbarous, superstitious without limits, fiery and passionate like the Africans" (qtd. in Aymard and Giarrizzo 684)—to be considered at the same rank as a European state. The major problem, however, was that not even the European revolutionaries were ready to accept any part of Italy, let alone southern Sicily, as a modern European nation.

Ideas of freedom, brotherhood, and equality soon arrived from revo-lutionary France, and proliferating Masonic lodges had made Jacobin-ism a presence all over Italy. Yet the aspirations of the Italian Jacobins soon met the skepticism of the European Jacobins themselves. On No-vember 19, 1792, the Republican Convention of revolutionary France had published a declaration granting "fraternity and help" (qtd. in Woolf, "Storia" 153) to any people fighting for liberty. Revolutionary France had been eager to help the patriots of Belgium, Holland, and Renania in their respective struggles for self-determination. It had been even more eager, later in 1822, to help the "descendants of the wise and noble peoples of Hellas, we who are the contemporaries of the enlightened and civilized nations of Europe" (Greek patriots, qtd. in Woolf, "Construction" 91).

French revolutionaries, however, had been more reticent when con-sidering whether to encourage French ideas of freedom and nationality in Italy too. The *citoyen* François Furcade, in 1790, had recommended "not even to think about making Italy a Republic. Its people is not disposed in the least to receive liberty—nor would it be worthy of it" (qtd. in Venturi, "L'Italia" 1127). In 1796, when the French foreign minister Charles de Gontant Delacroix asked his agents in Italy about the possibility of encouraging a revolution there, he got back a unanimous answer: the Italians were not mature enough for freedom. One of the agents, François Cacault, wrote: "One should not trust at all the extreme petulance of the vivacious youth of Italy, moved and transported by the ideas borrowed from our revolution, and who want to stir up a new state of things without knowing how, without knowledge . . . . One would need, coming to Italy, men truly mature for liberty. But the evaporated men [*l'homme évaporé*] of this country are just stupid" (qtd. in Woolf, "Storia" 158–59). The curious metaphor of evaporation was in fact plainly understandable, in this context, for anyone who had Montesquieu under his belt: how could one expect men from the heated south to be mature enough for freedom? So when Napoléon came to liberate Italy in the spring of 1796, liberation was achieved through military conquest and military control over the territory. "We have given you liberty," proclaimed publicly Napoléon (qtd. in Woolf, "Storia" 162). Privately, however, he concurred with the judgment of his council: "All information we have gathered about the spirit of the Italians, announces that they are not mature for freedom" (qtd. in Woolf, "Storia" 178).

If maturity was lacking in Italy, it was certainly nonexistent in its southernmost part, which, by the time Ferdinando Amari was arrested, had been labeled by Hegel's philosophy as the "immature" part of world history (see chapter 4). Between 1794 and 1795, the dispatches of the French diplomats in Italy continuously remarked on how much worse southern Italy was than the north: "Its people are more corrupted . . . and more prone to crime"; the south is a "very vicious country"; in short, it is no material for freedom and revolutions. Sure enough, as Jaucourt had written under "Sicile" in the *Encyclopédie*, "all the revolutions that Sicily has suffered make the history and the description of this island interesting" (Diderot 15:165). But the word *revolutions*, in the *Encyclopédie*'s pre-1789 contest, merely meant, as it is clear from Jaucourt's short history of the island, nothing more than a continuous change of dynastic successions (on the vague use of the term before 1789, see Goulemot, Masseau, and Tatin-Gourier 185–86). At any rate, even those revolutions were history now: "Sicily has nothing of interest today, except its mountains and the tribunal of the Inquisition" (Diderot 15:165). Or, as Alexis de Tocqueville put it in a less known work on revolutions and democracy, "You [Bourbons] have bastardized her [Sicily's] heart, replacing her desire of fame with courtly ambition, her desire for merit and courage with the power of favoritism" (*Voyage* 158). Sicily, "denatured by oppression, [its national character] crushed," is no place for a revolution; it is no nation either (59). Whether because of its southern climate or because of its history of oppression, Sicily hardly qualified as a revolutionary subject in 1820. As the northern Italian Francesco Trinchera observed: "It does not take much intelligence or insight to understand that a people that is so profoundly degraded . . . cannot think seriously about freedom, cannot understand it, want it, die for it" (qtd. in Moe 145). The Milanese Gian Rinaldo Carli, a collaborator of *Il caffè*, reiterated the point by going back to the origin of the dichotomy in *Della disuguaglianza fisica, morale e civile fra gli uomini*: "As Montesquieu has judiciously remarked, northern men are more courageous than southern men" (qtd. in Berselli Ambri 175).

No understanding of freedom, no understanding of nation either. Was not a nation, after all, the by-product of a people's revolution—like that of 1789—that had broken with the past of monarchical inheritances and restituted the state to the free sovereignty of the citizenship? Had Sicily ever had such a revolution? Were not sectarian interests—such as, for example, the split between Palermo and Messina in 1820—the symptom of the Sicilian inability to agree on a specific political project for a revolution (on this issue, see Aymard and Giarrizzo 675–83)? The Sicilian historian Francesco Renda, almost apologetically, recounts the ways in which the avowal of a Sicilian nation was reiterated "as a peculiar way for the island to participate in the profound movements of renovation and freedom, common at the time in a great part of Europe" (*Storia* 31). Nicolò Palmeri, writing about the Sicilian vesper in the *Saggio storico-politico sulla costituzione del Regno di Sicilia* (1817), had mentioned a "nation recomposing itself" already at the time of the Angevins; Giovanni Evangelista Di Blasi, in 1821, had presented his *Chronological Storia of the Viceroy* of Sicily as a tribute of "love for the country and the nation"; and Rosario Gregorio, in the *Introduction to the Study of Sicilian Public Law*, published five years after the French Revolution, had reiterated the existence—since the time of the Normans!—of a Sicilian nation (qtd. in Renda, *Storia* 27–28). So much insistence was meant to respond to the accusations, for instance, of the anonymous French pamphleteer of 1804 quoted by Benedetto Croce, who found that people in the south "do not have a national character, and possess instead qualities diametrically opposed to it." It was to counteract the idea that, in the south, "the concept of nation, in general, has no political consistency" (Giuseppe

Maria Galanti, qtd. in Croce, *Storia del regno* 278–79). Yet insistence notwithstanding, the commonplace was well set: Sicilians, stolid in their heated climate, were unable to prepare a modern revolution. Ergo, Sicily and nationhood remained oxymoronic terms in the thesaurus of revolutionary Europe.

So while father Ferdinando languished in the royal jails of Palermo for having taken part in a nationalist revolution that few Europeans were ready to accept as a national one (or, for that matter, as a revolution), the son Michele, at age twenty-six, was working hard trying to solve the problem that had obsessed him since the night of the arrest: how to promote an undeniably Sicilian revolution—without, of course, ending up in jail.[3] The solution adopted was, so to speak, a generational one: with the increased police control brought about by the repression, the Sicilian revolutionary youth could only opt for either the underground or for the "participation in literary circles that were, apparently, not immediately political" (Banti, *Nazione* 27). The second alternative had the unquestionable advantage of being less risky; perhaps more important, it was also capable of imagining, even for people who had not read Benedict Anderson, the symbolic elements necessary for the different communities of, say, Messina and Palermo to feel part of one nation. The tactic had already started having impressive results on the peninsula: Ugo Foscolo, just writing novels (*Jacopo Ortis* is from 1798) had done more to inspire the patriotism of the likes of Giuseppe Mazzini than any Bourbon abuse (Banti, *Nazione* 38). Not to speak of Vittorio Alfieri, whose fiery *Rime* of 1789 made for compulsory reading for the cadres of the Italian resistance.

Also in Sicily, the questions of Sicilian patriotism and independence had to become, at least for a while, less a matter of throwing stones at the police than of singing Sicilian patriotism with epic tones. Lionardo Vigo had written, for instance, about Sicily's preeminence in southern European history (*Atlantide*, unpublished), and, more poignantly, about Sicily's love for freedom and independence (*Ruggero*, 1822). Following the same route, young Michele Amari thus determined he would serve history, to use his expression, by becoming a "hero of ideas," and not, like the unfortunate father, one of deeds.[4] Put bluntly, in 1832 Michele Amari had decided to bequeath to the written word the responsibility to deliver revolutions—a less hazardous way of doing politics in Sicily, indeed, and a respectable compromise between revolutionary hubris and instincts of self-preservation.[5] A translation in Manzonian decasyllabic blank verse

(!) of Walter Scott's *Marmion* was Amari's Trojan horse, a Maussian gift surreptitiously published in the citadel guarded by the unsuspecting Bourbon censorship.[6] From the outside, *Marmion* was the usual great-literature stuff—bouncy couplets, profundity galore, and the loftiness of so-called universal experience: "And come he slow, or come he fast / It is but death who comes at last." But inside this hollow belly, the true and insidiously revolutionary meaning resided, ready "T' invade the town, oppress'd with sleep and wine" (Virgil 2:347): not only was Walter Scott the token of a new liberalism that reconciled Voltaire and Rousseau to David Hume, William Robertson, and Lord Byron (Amari, *Appunti* 16).[7] Moreover, the Scottish patriot and bard had written *Marmion* in 1797, while organizing a resistance against the French . . . . Get it? The problem is that actually no one, with the possible exception of the biographer in search for the usual early signs of a committed youth (for example, Bonfigli), *ever* got it.[8] The Sicilian cultural jet set, including the Bourbon one, even accorded Amari a respectable position in society (Amari, *Appunti* sheet 21). In spite of all this success, it did not want to be a book for "that cancer of the barons" (quel canchero dei baroni), for the "aristocratic scum" (canaglia aristocratica), and not even for "middle class libertines, who wanted bigger reforms and were swindled or swindlers by the word freedom" (i libertini del ceto medio i quali aspiravano ad una maggiore riforma ed erano ingannati o ingannatori col nome di libertà). *Marmion*'s ideal reader, at least in Amari's hopes, had to be the popular masses, the people, the revolutionary "third estate" (*terzo stato*; Amari and Palmeri xxix) that Augustin Thierry, by then sick and blind, would only later theorize in the *Essai sur l'histoire de la formation et des progrès du tiers état* (1853). This people was a more secular entity than the multitudes of Mazzini, always driven by God's Providence; and most certainly it was not the Francophile middle class that François Pierre Guillame Guizot, in his courses at the Sorbonne, was theorizing in those years as "the spark of European civilization" (qtd. in Verga 39). The antithesis of a bourgeoisie "with a big belly, rosy-cheeked, with champagne and pâté de foie gras in their hands, and a constant fear of socialism" (Amari and Palmeri 18), Amari's people was the Romantic idea of a potentially revolutionary subject that alone could construct the nation still to be realized (Peri 39–42). The problem, and a serious one at that, was that this third estate did not have the foggiest idea of what, politically speaking, *Marmion* was supposed to mean. Untrained in the art of allegorical reading, it could scarcely imagine that, mutatis mutandis, Scott's

French stood for the Bourbon colonists and Scotland's freedom was to mean Sicily's. In other words, *Marmion* was no popular success.

It was not a political success either. For that, a more explicit subject was needed. Amari's friend Salvatore Vigo, with arguable wisdom, "advised me to drop poetry and all the Marmions of the world" (Amari, *Il mio* sheet 28), and pushed Amari, instead, in the direction of political pamphleteering and political historiography. So Amari tried with some scholarly *Observations* against the Neapolitan historiographer Giuseppe del Re (1833)—they only "gave him some trouble, also from some liberal circles" (Tommasini 288); with a history of the 1820 revolution—obviously too risky and aborted (Peri 31–32); with the *Sicilian Political Catechism* (1839)—all too explicit about independence, published underground, anonymously, and a big distribution hassle. In sum, Amari was starting to realize that he had to find the *very* delicate balance between getting to the people and avoiding censorship at the same time—or, as he once put it, to hail revolution without getting caught ("gridare la rivoluzione senza che il vietasse la censura"; Amari, *Guerra* 1:xxvi).

With this end in mind, he was left with, roughly, one possible topic, and two options on how to deal with it. The topic—of this, at least, Amari was certain—could no longer be allegorical. If Amari wanted to speak to, or simply move to action, a potentially revolutionary Sicilian third estate, he could not talk about Scotland and Celtic lore. The topic had to be a Sicilian one. The so-called Sicilian Vesper of the twelfth century was a famous-enough Sicilian revolution, so that deciding to write about it must have proven a relatively easy choice. The story was already a best-selling topic, avidly consumed by both Italian revolutionaries and Sicilian autonomists:

> [Fausto] Niccolini wrote about it in 1831, in *Giovanni di Procida* . . . but already in 1822 Francesco Hayez had represented the scene of the rebellion in a painting commissioned by the Marquise Visconti d'Aragona, second wife of the Marquis Alessandro Visconti d'Aragona, who was investigated for the Milanese plot of 1821 . . . . The painting had been replicated in 1835 by Hayez for a commission of Francesco Arese, who had just been liberated from the Spielberg jails after a sentence for his participation in the insurrection of 1821; the painting was then replicated once more in 1844–46. (Banti, *Nazione* 84)

Once the topic was chosen, what remained now to decide was how to write about it. Given the advice "to drop poetry," only two options were left to Amari: "The form of the historical novel was the one he chose at the beginning. Francesco Domenico Guerrazzi had used it to write his relevant *Una grande epoca della storia italiana*, which celebrated the resistance of Florence against the invader. Guerrazzi had said: 'I wrote this book because I could not fight!' Amari, similarly, wanted to write a book that could amount to a battle" (Tommasini 289–90). Brandishing historical novels had other illustrious precedents: the usual Scott, but also Alexandre Dumas, the hero of the Parisian revolution of 1830, who had recently come to Sicily to cure himself from some disease or another, look for action, and bring the message of revolutionary Giuseppe Mazzini's Young Italy to the island (Bonfigli 4–5).[9] It had also the advantage of being a popular-enough genre to read: it converted historical reality, as Georg Lukács famously said, into "mass experience" (23). It was pedagogically useful for the education of the masses.

The second and last option was to write a straightforward history book. The advantage would have been its closer adherence to facts. A "greater quantity of historical circumstances" (Manzoni 2:1737), in other words, could render the pedagogical message of the book, rhetorically at least, more credible. Leopold von Ranke was already discrediting the novel's "fantastical reconstructions" to the point that writing novels always ran the risk of making one's work less relevant in political terms. That is why in revolutionary Italy, fostered by ideals of national independence, there was a clear tendency "to professionalize history, historiography, and historians" (Verga 48–50)—to sell the words and messages written in a history book as hard, undeniable facts; and, possibly, as examples for the future. History was thus being subdivided in the Italian academy into various hyperprofessionalized and hyperspecialized fields. The number of specialized journals was multiplying accordingly. The institution of the *deputazioni di storia patria* (the first in Turin in 1833), which were ministerial think tanks devoted to collecting national documents and to publishing for the glory of the country, was making abundantly clear the impressive strength of historiography in concocting national myths—no matter if the nation in question was Piedmont, Italy, or Sicily. It is not that the belles lettres, and the historical novel in particular, were being completely dethroned: Massimo d'Azeglio, for instance, a rather institutional figure in the future Piedmontese parliament and already a promoter of Italian unification, kept publishing best-selling and outright patriotic historical novels still in 1833 (*Ettore Fieramosca*) and 1841 (*Niccolò de' Lapi*). Also Francesco Domenico

Guerrazzi and Silvio Pellico—to name only people from what has been called the canon of Italy's insurrectional youth (Banti, *Nazione* 45)—were staying the course of the historical novel. Yet the epochal trust in the superior relevance of history seemed to have made the decision for Amari: "It is well known that the author of the *Vesper* pondered seriously whether to write a novel or a researched history. The second option was chosen in the end: although Amari held in high regard works of imagination, he considered history now as the knowledge of the people's consciousness to be achieved through the research of a collective memory" (Marcolongo 8). In short, Michele Amari found himself a historian.

The Europeanization of Sicilian History

> Europe invented historians and then made good use of them.
> —FERNAND BRAUDEL, *Civilization and Capitalism,*
> *15th–18th Century*

> The greatest of Italian historians is Amari.
> —HENRY FURST, "A Controversy on Italian History"

> But history was not his purpose.
> —ILLUMINATO PERI, *Michele Amari*

As he began his new book, Amari then made his intention quite explicit: he wanted "to make history, not novels" (*Guerra* 1:xix). This did not mean that the temptation of the historical novel had completely disappeared. After all, as Alessandro Manzoni had written in a letter to Monsieur Chauvet, historiography had the despicable tendency of erasing the point of view of the vanquished ones, and of registering only the actions, not even the thoughts, of those who have won: "All that is sacred and profound in defeat [*sventura*]" escapes historiography (qtd. in Raimondi 107). Accordingly, it was not certain that history, *magister vitae* for some, could be the best teacher in downtrodden, subaltern, and ultimately colonized Sicily: the Manzonian thoughts, hopes, and the disillusionment of the Sicilian people had to be reconstructed, whether archival evidence was enough or not.

Literary and narrative in its style and concern, the history that Amari published in Palermo in 1842, initially titled *Un periodo delle storie siciliane del tredicesimo secolo* (*A Period of the Sicilian Histories of the Thirteenth Century*), was arguably a hybrid narrative attempt, still under the shadow of *Waverley* and *Queen Margot*, to translate revolutions into a popularly accessible mass experience: "I have, then, decided, being Sicilian, to narrate the change of domination that happened in my island at the end of the thirteenth century, in the face of an excess of tyranny that very rarely one has seen the like" (Amari, *Guerra* 1:2). In narrating his *storia*, in presenting himself as a character with thoughts, hopes, and disillusionments, Amari constantly supplemented the archive with flights of rhetorical fantasy—as in the reconstruction, for example, of the climactic scene:

> On the eve of Easter, the streets of the capital [Palermo] were covered in mirth; the porticos, the temples, the palaces adorned with different designs of gold drapes and silks; the lamps spread the light of day on all quarters; in the cathedral, where the vesper was being celebrated, the dazzle of endless candle, as big, writes Speciale, as columns, was blinding; the noise of trumpets, horns, and drums, symbols of the war that deafens peace, was won by the harmony of more delicate instruments and by the cheerful songs of the people. They were to spend the entire night in such amusements. At the break of the day, which was the twenty-fifth of March, Fredrick was anointed and crowned king of Sicily. (2:288–89)[10]

Amari's story, which closed on March 25, 1296, with the coronation of Fredrick III of the house of Aragon, had begun at the hour of the vesper on March 30, 1282. At that highly symbolic time when the sun sets, sparked by the offense of an Angevin soldier who had begun a legendary body search ending in the breasts of an abundantly virginal and most beautiful woman (1:194), a popular insurrection broke out. It was the end of the tyrannical rule of Charles I of Anjou, who had taken Sicily away from the Hohenstaufens (who had replaced the Normans, who had conquered the Arabs . . .) and subjected it to Frankish rule.[11] The above-mentioned notoriety of the episode within insurrectional circles; the pathos of the Italian (or Sicilian) honor trampled on by the foreigner; the epic of the popular revolt—these elements had made the history of the vesper a very attractive topic for the engaged historian. What better subject than this already realized Sicilian revolution to celebrate and salute popular revolts to come! After all, this was an event that had "shaken the whole of Southern Europe" (Amari, *Guerra* 1:5); it had had a much better ending than the 1820 insurrection;[12] and it even illustrated the necessity to take that most serious business of revolutions away from disorganic intellectuals and give it back to the people, "sole foundation for equality and a free life" (1:6), Romantic *Volk* giving foundations to the putative Sicilian nation: "Sicily owes to its people, not to its dominant classes, that revolution, which saved her in the XIII century from extreme shame and misery" (1:xix–xx).[13]

What better subject than this, indeed! As Amari once reminisced, "One could not find a better subject for my goal: it had five centuries of antiquity to oppose to censorship; yet it illustrated the way to prepare, I believed, a terrible and victorious revolution" (1:xxvii). Moreover, by depicting the Spanish Fredrick III as the liberator of Sicily against French brutality, Amari could well hope the Bourbons would mistake a call to arms against them for the historical praise of their past service to Sicily. In sum, the same rhetorical *translatio* that in *Marmion* had substituted the Scots for the Sicilians and the French for the Bourbons, was, in part, still at work here: the evil Angevins of the *Vespro* were to be read as metaphorical precursors of the Bourbons; but the historical subject of the revolution—the Sicilian people—was here historically coinciding with the real thing. The message was clear: the Sicilian people had a glorious revolutionary past. It was now time to recall it with historical precision, without rhetorical artifice.

As history, Amari's book was an unprecedented success. Its author must not have regretted the *Marmion* left behind. Unhindered by tropes or "fantastical reconstructions," and not dulled by too many flights of belles-lettrism, the true meaning of the work came across, this time, loud and clear (Marcolongo 70; Giuffrida xvi; Tommasini 298): popular revolution was the only way to Sicilian freedom.

The Bourbon police, unfortunately, soon noticed the clarity of the message, too: "Palermo, October 24, 1842. Dear Don Leonardo [Vigo], my work has been prohibited; the copies of the book have been requisitioned; I have been suspended from my clerical duties and called to Naples to be interrogated; the three censors who had licensed my book have been fired" (Amari, *Carteggio* 3:11). Amari, who knew well the ways of the police, never went to the "interview" in Naples and fled to Paris instead, where he rented at 48, rue de Luxembourg. There he was canonized—the first Sicilian, perhaps, to make it big in Paris—with the French translation of his book. With the translation, the title changed into *La guerre des vêpres de Sicile* (*The War of the Sicilian Vesper*), and the sense widened considerably to become a manual not for Sicilian insurrections only, but for Italian and even European ones.

The first revolution the book meant to prepare was, obviously, the one against the Bourbons—and a manual to prepare terrible and victorious revolutions the *Vespro* certainly was. It taught lots of very useful things— such as how to organize an informal army for a war of maneuver; ways to isolate the enemy militarily and politically; the art of strategic alliances with foreign powers; and the bitter necessity, too, of violence and death (Amari, *Guerra* 1:219). Above all, however, and from the very first words (echoes of Machiavelli), the book was a celebration of the people's power: "The reputation of strength, through which the sovereign controls the State, is a very delicate balance; it therefore happens that, at the very moment in which control of public life seems to be lost, power is restored, either by the virtue of the prince, or by the impetus of the people. Then, great events will shine: injurious foreign ties will be broken, corrupt political orders will crumble, and the State will strengthen itself through healthy reforms" (1:1). The power and strength of the constituted order, in other words, is all "reputation," in the eyes of the beholder: the people *can* break that balance. And, with an echo of the discussions on natural law that had fired the eighteenth century (Hof), sometimes the people *ought* to break it through revolutions, for example, when sovereigns failed to operate "healthy reforms" and break the social contract with their subjects.

The central role of a revolutionary people in the events of the vesper seemed to be, in fact, the very point of Amari's book. Until now, Amari suggested, historiography of the vesper had confined itself within a simple plot:

> John of Procida, for love of country and personal revenge, decides to take Sicily away from Charles of Anjou; he offers it to Peter, king of Aragon . . . ; conspires with Peter, with the pope, with the emperor of Constantinople, with the Sicilian barons. When all is ready, the conspirators give a sign; kill the French; raise Peter to the Sicilian throne. This has been, more or less, the history of the Sicilian Vesper. In truth, some modern historians, mostly from the other side of the Alps, have doubted such a vast, secret, and successful conspiracy; but this theory of the Vesper has always been the prevalent one, and the majority of the historians, especially the Sicilian ones, have repeated it over and over again; and history has built on the conspiracy. (*Guerra* 1:xix)

Refuting the theory of Sicilian historians, and building instead on the skepticism of a few historians "from the other side of the Alps," Amari's book then rewrote the old story by making courtly conjurors and "individual protagonists shrink, and the people grow bigger" (1:xxx).[14]

It may be easy to understand why historians, "especially Sicilian ones," may have insisted on the theory of the vesper as a war of dynastic succession. After all, these were intellectuals coming from, and writing on behalf of, the baronial classes of Sicily (Casarrubea). They had no sympathy, obviously, for insurrections beyond their class's control. A more European perspective was thus needed by Amari to rinse Sicilian history from its baronial legacies. Yet as Denis Mack Smith suggests, "Some people [other than Sicilian historians] had an interest in maintaining that John of Procida and Aragon had been the chief actors all along: the Angevins needed to ascribe their defeat to more than a civilian mob, and it suited the Aragonese to take credit for everything" (1:73). European historians, in other words, were still looking at the vesper not as a revolution, but as a war of dynastic succession. For Amari, instead, the fact that the betrayed vesper *ended* with a dynastic succession, and yet another colonization of Sicily, did not mean, *post hoc, ergo propter hoc*, that dynastic succession was the motive of the revolution: "The revolution was born from the people, and popular was its beginning; as soon as the aristocracy infiltrated it, the old laws of monarchic restoration came back" (*Guerra* 2:479–80).

What seems at stake here is not only the political question of whether a "civilian mob" can become the "people" and subject of its own destiny but also the geopolitical question of whether the Sicilian mob in particular could ever conceive of the idea of freedom or concoct a revolution.[15] Could it be casual, for instance, that the hero of historians, "John [of Procida,] was an Italian from the mainland" (Mack Smith 1:71), and not a Sicilian? There can be little doubt that Michele Amari, in the reevaluation of his people, was yielding to a certain provincial *pietas*. Yet it is my impression that he was also doing a little more than that. To start illustrating this "little more," I will begin from the end of the *Vespro*. In its concluding chapter—the one supposed to "show my political and philosophical beliefs" (Amari, *Guerra* 1:ix)—Amari implied that this Sicilian event of the thirteenth century may have not only anticipated the "storm of the French Revolution" but that it should have—though it did not—helped Sicilians to "correct" (*correggere*) that storm when it came to Italy (2:490). In what sense could the experience of the vesper, retold by Amari, correct the French Revolution? Amari's very insistence on the people, and his lack of squeamishness *vis-à-vis* revolutionary violence certainly do not authorize an interpretation of this correction in anti-Jacobean and conservative function (see Bollati 62–70; Marcolongo 8).

It seems to me that what Amari was doing when elevating an episode of Sicilian history to the status of national revolution, and, even, as an "example for Scotland, the Flanders, and Switzerland" (*Guerra* 2:484), was not so much writing a history of a revolution or a theory of revolutions in general. Rather, he was operating a true revolution—a correction indeed—of *theory*. I am referring, of course, to that theory of Europe that we have been trying to follow since chapter 1 of the present book. According to such theory, freedom *is* the genius of Europe: "In Europe, the natural divisions [between states] forms, year after year and in the perpetuity of the centuries, a spirit of Freedom. On the contrary, a spirit of servitude reigns in Asia, and never quits that region" (Montesquieu, *Oeuvres* 2:24).[16] If freedom is the ultimate goal of universal history, imagined, for instance, by Immanuel Kant as the teleological approaching of "a perfectly just civic constitution" (*Our History* 16), then Europe is also the very subject of universal history.

Montesqueiu's theory of freedom, as we have already seen, coincides with a theory of Europe. But Europe, in this theory, is a difference between a positive north, "free and independent" (Montesquieu, *Oeuvres* 2:793), and a negative south incapable of the "daring action" that fosters revolutions and engenders freedom (2:475). Freedom, in this sense, remains the spiritual endowment of Europe's *north*—a north, that is, with Paris at its center. As the Italian revolutionary Giuseppe Mazzini, once noticed: "Today we judge freedom, equality, and association on the sense given to these words in France. At the origin of such prejudice is the idea, which we believe is false despite its almost universal hold, that France is the mover of the European continent" (*Opere* 2:550–51).

Montesquieu's theory of a Europe moved by French freedom is not subverted, but only supplemented, by the myth of the French Revolution as the epiphany of progressive freedom—the latter being, as François Cacault wrote, one of those "ideas borrowed from *our* revolution," and that no *alleged* other revolution could have envisioned before. Bertrand Barriére made it clear: France was the origin of European freedoms, and French language "that which first consecrated the rights of man and citizen, the language whose task is now to transmit to the world the most sublime thoughts of freedom" (qtd. in Hazard, *Révolution* 121). Cacault's and Barriére's is the theory, as James Blaut calls it, of "diffusionism": events (modernity, revolution, liberation, etc.) like history originate in

Europe, and are then "diffused" from there as from the center. What we may add to Blaut, is that Eurocentric theory is supplemented by yet another internal center, an ideal north, where all originates and from where all is diffused. Sicily, in this supplementary theory of Europe, is margin and periphery.

It is according to this theory, arguably, that a contemporary historian of the stature of Denis Mack Smith, like the historians against whom Amari revolted in 1842, still needs to deny the vesper as a "*political* revolt." Against the very cosmopolitan spirit that animated the *philosophes*, the vesper, for Mack Smith, is expression of the "most violent feelings of xenophobia [vis-à-vis the French]," lacking all constructive aims. In the end, Sicilians remain spiritually incapable of Montesquieu's daring actions: they "submitted without difficulty to the rule from Spain"; and "this proves that the rebellion of 1282 cannot have been against foreign domination as such" (Mack Smith 1:71, 1:75). For Mack Smith, in conclusion, nothing else than chauvinism has "made it possible for a horrible massacre to be magnified [by Amari] into the most glorious event in Sicilian history" (1:72). Not altogether differently, Amari's interpretation of the vesper as a popular revolution is for Steven Runciman the sign of the chauvinism of the Sicilians, "a proud and not a modest people" (291).

Sure enough, Amari's gesture can be said to be exaggeratedly chauvinistic, embodying even a sense of the cultural superiority of Sicily (first true revolutionary of Europe) vis-à-vis the rest of the world. But is this sufficient to dismiss the whole of Amari's gesture, as if the puerility of this intellectual from the margins who evokes his own version of origins were not comparable to the puerility and chauvinism of a hegemonic center resting on the unquestioned certainty of being the origin of all?[17] The fact remains that such a gesture, chauvinistic or not, is quite more radical than Mack Smith and Runciman are willing to acknowledge. Besides claiming a Sicilian origin for revolutionary Europe, it also aspires to contextualize such a revolution, well beyond "Sicilian history," as a glorious event in *universal* history—exemplary indeed, beyond Sicily, "for Scotland, the Flanders, and Switzerland." Antonio Gramsci had already grasped this tension between "local history and universal designs" (to paraphrase Mignolo, *Local Histories*) as the very kernel of Amari's *sicilianismo*. Is Sicily a subject of universal history or is its history, as Croce famously put it, "not ours, or ours only in small part" (qtd. in Gramsci, *Risorgimento* 169)?[18]

In other words, Amari intends here to claim Sicily as a place in which freedom originated independently from the French version of it, which equals to say that Sicily is for Amari neither the past nor the immaturity of European history, but rather an integral part of its modernity. Freedom, to begin with, is not immanent to Europe, but rather "suffocated by Europe's political order" (Amari, *Guerra* 1:xxiv)—a political order that clearly refers to the Congress of Vienna. Besides denying the French Revolution the status of origin (diffusionism), Amari engages Montesquieu's Franks, reduced to the evil caricature of the tyrant Charles, in an intertextual game whose stake is the very relocation of freedom. For Amari, reminiscent here of Juan Andrés, freedom did not originate among the Franks, but in Sicily. Not so naive to "forget the imperfections of those ancient parliaments" (Amari, *Guerra* 1:102), Amari saw in the Sicilian constitution prepared after the vesper exactly what Montesquieu had located up north—balance and separation of powers directly resulting from the division of property:

> In the old Sicilian constitution, principality and aristocracy balanced each other; barons did not have unlimited power on people, nor on their livelihoods; peasants were less serfs than elsewhere—no country worker was a serf; bourgeois and city dwellers, also those from feudal lands, felt their freedom, and protected their immunity. Judicial power, depending directly on the prince, did not serve all the wants of feudalist barons. Taxes were acceptable; services were mild; universal levies were very rare; and only parliaments could impose them. (1:67–68)[19]

A division of power had thus been realized in Sicily—thereby making the island a part, if not the origin, of the European sphere of freedom. The constitution, albeit "imperfect" and still relying on the good will of the prince, was "unknown in the continent, while it had existed in Sicily for seven centuries, until the Bourbons stole it from our parents, giving them in exchange Napoleonic despotism minus Napoléon's power and glory" (1:xxiv).

From quotations such as this, it already becomes clear that the strength of the *Vespro* is also, however, its major limitation. In creating the image of a constitutional, revolutionary, freedom-seeking Sicily, Amari was clearly trying to counteract the (Montesquieu-like) commonplace of a savage, backward south, which preunification Italy knew well from the pages of Augustine Creuzé de Lesser, who claimed, in 1806, that "Europe ends at Naples and ends there quite badly. Calabria, Sicily, all the rest belongs to Africa" (qtd. in Moe 37). Against such claims, Amari's intention was to give Sicily a bond with the rest of Europe (see Peri 37)—both methodologically, by using the methods of documentary historiography, and ideologically, by measuring its degree of civilization on the constitutional standards set by Montesquieu, Voltaire, Edward Gibbon, and Hume. Far from being local history, the story told by the *Vespro* was one of Anjou and Provence, of Aragon and Catalonia, France and Spain, and of popes and emperors from the east and west. This Sicilian story was not only an example for Switzerland, the Flanders or Scotland; it was a paradigmatic tale for a whole Europe that, after a revolution, the Terror, and Napoléon, was still reflecting on the themes of political freedom, despotism, and national and popular self-determination.

Echoes of the European debate on democracy (see Mastellone)—from Alexis de Tocqueville's *La démocratie en Amérique* (1835–40) to Giuseppe Mazzini's *Pensieri sulla democrazia in Europa* (1847)—are felt in Amari's discussion of liberty and freedom. The stress on constitutionalism, far from being incomprehensible outside of Sicily, was common currency in a Europe more and more disillusioned about the prospects of enlightened absolutism and moving already toward forms of liberal representation. The epic of a people erupting into terrible and just violence against tyranny, moreover, breathed the same European air as did Thomas Carlyle's *French Revolution* (1837) or Jules Michelet's *La peuple* (1846), which had made of revolution the best-selling topic of the age.[20] Even the question of a putative Sicilian nation was very much in line with a general European feeling, moving beyond Voltaire's cosmopolitanism into an era of "imagined communities" (B. Anderson). This was a story, in other words, focused on Sicily—but about and for Europe. Benedetto Croce, for one, understood it very well: the *Vespro*, he wrote, was "the first [Sicilian] work that, at the time, seemed worthy to be placed near foreign ones" (*Storia della storiografia* 228).

And placed near foreign ones it was—in the French Librairie Européenne: the flair of the revolutionary who had defied censorship first, and later the panache of the exile, had given Amari a European notoriety that no other Sicilian writer had ever enjoyed before. Amari, in sum, made it to Europe. The problem, however, was that Amari and his Sicily were joining the European table as the parvenu, the Giovannino-come-lately at an already busy banquet. Or, to put it more earnestly, Sicily was entering universal history, but only because it was said to have reached some standards of freedom and civility that were set, judged, and measured, as Mazzini had noticed, "on the sense given to these words in

France." I am not thinking so much of Gyan Prakash's "foundational" traps here—that Amari, namely, failed to "displace the categories framed in and by [European dominant] history" ("Writing" 399) and legitimated them instead. I am talking of the much simpler desire of the wannabe—to imitate and please, and shun difference from a putative standard as the worst of shames.[21] As his friend Salvatore Vigo once wrote to Amari, "foolish is that nation that, in Europe, does not take part of Europe's modes and orders" (qtd. in Amari, *Carteggio* 3:65). And, lest Amari's Sicilian nation would be taken for foolish, the writer of the *Vespro* had made it part of such European modes and orders. Sicily *was* part of Europe because it was proved to be a national *Volk* like Herder's Germany; because it had a revolution not altogether different than the French one; because it had now a history of its civilization (Amari's) comparable to Voltaire's *Age de Louis XIV*; and, last but not the least, because its political order had been as good as the much celebrated English model theorized by John Locke's *Two Treatises of Government* (1690) and hypostatized as exemplary (suggests Hof 195) by Enlightenment Europe: "Both the English and the Sicilian constitutions had a common origin [i.e., balance of power], and the Sicilian was reformed on the basis of the English one in 1312" (Amari, *Guerra* 1:xxiv).

Especially this last point had already been rehearsed by another Sicilian, the legal historian Rosario Gregorio. In *Considerazioni sopra la storia di Sicilia dai tempi dei Normanni sino ai presenti* (1805), Gregorio had proposed the theory that the Normans, after "freeing" Sicily from the non-European Muslim domination, had established an administrative organization on the model of the system of William the Conqueror of England: Norman Sicily's system of taxation, the *duana de secretis* had consisted of two divisions, one supervising accounts and the other collecting taxes and paying expenses. This structure was seen as fundamentally similar to the organization of the exchequer of England, which consisted of the upper and the lower exchequer. Gregorio's thesis had achieved some authority in Europe, and even in England (see Takayama 61–62). It is thus understandable that Amari, at the epoch of the *Vespro*, was still willing to stick to it as a way of granting Sicily its passport as a modern European nation. The problem of Gregorio's thesis as inherited by Amari, however, was that it made the prerequisites for Sicily's dignity still dependent on a putatively northern wind of freedom. In fact, the whole reevaluation of Sicilian history that operated in the *Vespro* depended on notions of constitutionalism deriving from northern enlightenment: the civility of a people had to be measured on the basis of its historical progress toward freedom, which, in turn, was based on its capacity to generate a revolution. Answering the sort of revolution envy that had haunted Europe after 1789, Amari, like Nicola Palmieri before him, could then propose that "the maturity of France only came one century after the English one, around two centuries after the Dutch, and five centuries after the maturity of the Sicilians" (qtd. in Giarrizzo 356). Yet it was not *iuxta propria principia* that Sicily had acquired dignity on the European scene, but because it was shown to fit a theory of revolutionary Europe that saw civilization as political maturity, progress toward the liberal freedoms of the rights of "man," and readiness for a revolution (on the fundamentalism of liberal principles, see Cassano, *Pensiero*). With the *Vespro*, Amari was thus widening the confines of Europe to include his Sicily, but he was not widening a theory of Europe.

He might have achieved exactly that in his next major historical work, when, against Gregorio, he argued, for instance, that Sicilian constitutionalism, and the *duana de secretis* in particular, had little to do with the exchequer or other forms of European constitutionalism: it derived, instead, also etymologically, from the Arabic administrative organization of Sicily, and specifically from the *dîwân at-tahqîq* (Amari, *Storia* 3:324–31). Before Amari could look outside of Europe for new symbols of Sicilian dignity, however, a disillusion with Europe had certainly to occur. In 1848, exiled in Paris in the revolutionary days of the fall of Louis Philippe and the creation of the Second French Republic, Amari had followed with renewed hopes the events of the coeval Sicilian revolution, which had begun on January 12 (King Ferdinand's birthday). The revolution was not limited, this time, to Palermo, but involved the whole of Sicily, cities and countryside alike. With joy, he had read in the French papers about the provisional government of Palermo, and of the efforts to adopt the Sicilian constitution of 1812. With republican pleasure, he had learned from his friends' letters that the new government had dethroned King Ferdinand II, and crowned and sworn to the constitution Alberto Amedeo of Savoy. But then, on May 15, 1849, the mood of the news swung like a pendulum: the Sicilian armies had been defeated by Ferdinand's, France and England had refused to help, Catania and Messina were in rubble, the parliament had been dissolved. And then, on December 2, 1851, the eighteenth Brumaire, the imperial mantle finally fell on the shoulders of Louis Bonaparte, and the epoch of revolutionary France was closed once and for good. It was at this climax of disappointment that hopes in French models—revolutions, constitutions, and the like—seemed to wane. Amari grew "weary of walking in the boulevards rather than in Montepellegrino; of attending soirées rather than hunts; of drinking tea rather than wine; of speaking French or English, not Italian; and of living in a country from which we expect generous political thoughts, and where we find only the idiocy of the market, or worse" (*Carteggio* 3:55).[22] At this point, when all over Europe the forces of the restoration came back triumphantly and with a vengeance, Amari needed to look outside of France, and perhaps outside of Europe too, in order to find a feasible model, or perhaps a founding myth, for the hope of a democratic Sicilian nation. In other words, the issue that was to legitimate a Sicilian revolution could no longer be the insistence that Sicily, too, was a European nation; but that Sicily, exactly because Other and not merely European, may have the seed to escape the history of Europe's present barbarity. In the prophetic words of the *Vesper*: "While in the rest of Europe the northern brethren had lost the virtues of the barbarians, and preserved their vices only, Sicily, like Spain, lived under the domination of the Arabs, who were at least learned if not civilized" (1:9). What learning did the Arabs leave to Sicily, and to Europe as well, to oppose the ultimate failure of European civilization?

The Other Europe of Michele Amari

> And all rulers are the heirs of those who conquered before them.
> —WALTER BENJAMIN, "Theses on the Philosophy of History"

The idea to write "of the wandering of Sicilian Arabs, and of other Arabs that navigated the Mediterranean, too" (Amari, *Carteggio* 3:28) had come to Michele Amari around 1843, while he was living at number 48, rue de Luxembourg (Henry James, living in the same street at number 29, wrote instead of one navigated American in 1875). It would take eleven years for Amari to publish the first book of what he already thought would be his masterpiece, and eighteen more years (no tenure clock ticking, obviously) to issue the last, and fourth, volume in 1872.

Historically, a book about the Arabs of Sicily would have reconstructed pretext and context for the revolution of the *Vespro*: the Angevins, after all, had been given Sicily by Pope Clement IV (in 1266), who wanted to Christianize an island that still "looked Muslim to all the good Christians of the West" (Amari, *Storia* 3:731). Politically, a book about the Sicilian Arabs might have worked as the continuation of the *Vespro*'s celebration of the people; it was to suggest, also, a revision of the previous autonomist tendencies. By pointing to, for instance, the Muslims' disunity—tensions among Arabs, Berbers, and Persians—as the very cause for their decline (3:150), Amari wanted to suggest the need for unity between Sicily and all the rest of Italy.

Much had happened, in the twenty-nine years between the conception of this work and its final conclusion, for Amari to be able to keep the idea of Sicilian autonomy at play. For one, the failed revolution of 1848 must have convinced autonomists that a strategic alliance in the name of Italy's liberation (from Austria in the north, the pope in the center, and the Bourbons in the south) had become a political necessity. Finished was the viability of fragmented resistances carried out for the sake of some identity politics.[23] On February 20, 1848, when things were still going well for the revolutionaries, and the Bourbon King was ready to grant them a constitution fashioned on the French one of 1830, Giuseppe Mazzini, arguably the most authoritative voice of the Italian revolution, had warned Sicilians of the dangers of autonomy in an open letter to their leaders: "Local individualism," he wrote, would eventually let "Europe decide for you" (*Opere* 2:372). When a restoration of European powers—the balance of Power—punctually happened, and the Sicilian revolution was crushed once again, it became quite difficult for Amari and the autonomists not to swallow Mazzini's pill—"you belong to us [Italy]" (voi siete nostri)—and to accept that "only a religion of Unity can give glory, mission, and purpose to Sicily . . . in Europe" (Mazzini, *Opere* 2:370–71).

According to Mary Poppins's principle that just a spoonful of sugar helps the medicine go down, Amari had thus gulped Mazzini's unity down with the sugar of its eventual success, which he remembered in 1872, concluding his magnum opus: "I started this hard toil as a Sicilian yearning freedom for a small State. I conclude it hoping that all Italians will become one bigger and bigger family; hoping they will see in unity and liberty the well-being and honor of all and each one" (*Storia* 3:922). Accepting the process of national unification, and the promotion of Sicily to an Italian province in Mazzini's Europe, did not mean, however, that Sicily was to accept passively the modality in which such an imagined community was built. A tension between the historical necessity of unity and the will to difference opens up for Amari after 1848 (and explains, perhaps, the contradictions noticed by Peri). It is perhaps the very abandonment of political autonomism, in fact, that exasperates the need to assert cultural diversity: whereas the *Vespro* had claimed a European place for Sicily as a modern constitutional nation, the new work was now to insist on the difference that Sicily marked in any preconceived ideas of Europe. The criteria for a composition of Europe could no longer be identity with a set of standards, but the acceptance of difference. Sicily's culture and history, in other words, had to become part of an amended theory of Europe capable not of assimilating Sicily, but of recognizing it in its difference.

The story that Amari started telling in 1843 was quite straightforward, almost classical in its simplicity: one place (Sicily) and one (Braudelian!) *long* time spanning from the seventh to the thirteenth century. The action—a kind of national-popular mixture of historical and detective novel framed by the documentary evidence of philological historiography—was that of the Arab conquest of Sicily (year 827); of the establishment of a very rich Muslim civilization on the island (next century); of the decline and fall of the Muslim colonial power by Norman hands (1060–91); and of the survival, maybe flourishing, of Muslim civilization in Sicily still at the court of Fredrick II (1197–1250). The detective-like spin concerned the way in which the annals of history had completely lost the memory of these five centuries of Muslim presence in Europe, five centuries that—as Andrés had already suggested to us, and Amari will never tire to repeat—were in fact *fundamental* for the creation and establishment of European civilization itself.

The Mystery of the Missing Muslim, à la Eugène Sue or Arthur Conan Doyle, would have made for good sales. But Amari, despite being unemployed, almost destitute, and supported financially by his friends, was certainly not interested in financial success: "Readers will judge if my work stinks of market," he wrote in the preface to Ibn Zafer's *Political Consolations* (Muhammad ibn Abd ix). He found academia, instead, less stinky, and trying to land a job in either Pisa or Florence, he opted for the arguably more bookish title of *Storia dei Musulmani di Sicilia* (*History of the Muslims of Sicily*). The result, despite a misleadingly academic title, was the greatest Sicilian epic ever.

Amari's epic, however, did not begin in medias res. Sicily, after all, had been a land of conquest long before the Arabs had arrived there. Amari thus began with the Greeks, good colonists (with some recorded exceptions), who had made the island glorious and *magna*; and then the

Romans, who had exploited it as if it were their "big estate" (Amari, *Storia* 1:108); after that the "Northern barbarians," who had finished transforming it into a wasteland with no social institutions, and nothing, alas!, worth mentioning (1:117). The Byzantine Empire had but continued this long litany of abuses, until, a little tongue-in-cheek, redemption had come from high for the battered Sicilians:

> If we were to rely on pious local legends, Christianity had early and splendid beginnings in Sicily. Saint Peter, so we are told, quickly sent to Sicily bishops from Antioch in the year 44. And all those bishops, persecuted and persecutors alike, tear down pagan temples, silence oracles, kill dragons; the Bishop Marciano, hiding in the subterranean labyrinths of the capital, builds an altar with the image of the Virgin Mary, and is strangled by the Jews. Mary and Teja face martyrdom in Taormina to defend their chastity; and near their tombs is erected the first monastery for women in the whole Christian world. (1:119)

Despite the anticlericalism he had learned from Father Quattrocchi, a "revolutionary and atheist," and from his other teachers, "all unbelievers and liberal priests" (Amari, *Il mio terzo esilio* sheets 7–8), Amari was not trying here to dismiss Christianity, but rather to recognize its historical (albeit secular) relevance as the carrier of moral, social, and political aspirations of the people (*Storia* 2:264–65).[24] Besides dragon hunting and virginal ecstasies, Amari meant, Christianity's *original* role in Sicily had been that of "fighting the lively strength of principality, aristocracy, and learned classes; all these social groups together, feeling threatened by the new power that was rising in the world, did all they could to combat it" (1:121). Early Sicilian Christianity, in other words, had been a popular mass movement from below—not altogether different than the one of the vesper—rebelling against the barbarity of the powerful, the privileged, and the courtesan intellectual.

With the writing of the *Storia dei Musulmani di Sicilia*, Amari, at the same time, was trying to go beyond the mere writing of historical events. His attempt was to organize the disparate facts of history into some kind of unitary vision—into a universal or philosophical history, namely, that would avoid, however, the pratfalls of Montesquieu's theory of progress from an ancient south to a modern north. He had thus started looking at the past from within the intellectual frame of Vico's philosophy of history, which offered the clear advantage of undoing the teleological line of positivist historicism (which divided the universe and Europe between backward and modern nations), through "the famous *corsi e ricorsi* that are Vico's form of the cyclical pattern of the succession of civilizations" (Berlin 85). As a matter of fact, not only in Vico, but also in Ibn Khaldun —"who widened the scopes of the philosophy of history even more than Giambattista Vico" (Amari, *Storia* 1:180–81)—Amari had found a cyclical vision (or philosophy) of history that was capable of undermining the foundations of Montesquieu's linearity of progress. Civilization, for Vico and Ibn Khaldun, was not a teleology that moved from south to north, but rather a cycle that repeated itself in every place, north and south alike.

From Vico and Ibn Khaldun, Amari took the idea of the three stages of every civilization. The first was an age of barbarity (Ibn Khaldun) or "of the Giants" (Vico), in which force ruled and poetry was the form that gave sense to the world: "Common vices are superstition, preying, revenge, and cruelty; everybody possesses quick intelligence, clever words, propensity to eloquence and poetry" (Amari, *Storia* 1:143).[25] There were, after that, heroic ages (1:145), when chivalrous heroes—Muhammad for Ibn Khaldun, the princes for Vico—instituted the law. Finally came human and democratic ages, in which natural equity naturally reigned in the free commonwealth. After that, the cycle began once again. Invariably, the return of barbarity coincided for Amari with a newly formed ruling class betraying the people. In the *Vespro*, a revolution "born from the people" had become monarchic restoration (the dynastic succession of the Aragons to the Anjou) "as soon as the aristocracy infiltrated it" (2:479–80). In the case of Christianity, not altogether differently, an initially popular fight against "the lively strength of principality, aristocracy, and learned classes" came to a halt as soon as a new hierarchy—new principality, aristocracy, and learned classes—was formed from within the same once-popular church: "As the Sicilian church grew old, a hierarchy emerged from it. Hence, the ecclesiastical order shaped itself in the image of the empire's administrative order. And we clearly see, by the beginning of the fifth century, that the bishop from Rome exercises metropolitan power on the island" (*Storia* 1:123).

Realigned with Byzantium, the church restored social hierarchies; landed property reemerged; Sicily, which had freed itself from its subjection to metropolitan Byzantium through the church, became again a margin of the metropolitan center of Rome; and the old Byzantine estates were shared among the church's high officers.

Through Vico and Ibn Khaldun, a first tenet of European historiography, progress, was thus denied. At any rate, it was in this Christian Sicily, ordered in the image of the empire, hierarchically divided, and preyed on by the new barbarians in papal robes, that the Arabs came to inaugurate a new heroic age that would, slowly but surely, lead up to the *ricorso*, a new cycle of democracy. It would have been "a frightening challenge to Christian Europe" (Mack Smith 1:3). Christian Europe, however, was too busy to notice: "It was busy arguing a very subtle and otiose theological question: if the works of God made man in Jesus Christ were led by two wills—one divine, one human—or by a single will, which Monotelites called 'teandric,' meaning divine-and-human-at-the-same-time" (Amari, *Storia* 1:188).

Between Christian distraction and the vagueness of Arab chronicling (1:195), the only thing certain is that the Arabs must have made it to Sicily on *a* morning, approximately between October 31, 649, and June 17, 653:[26]

> At any rate, the extant writings of Pope Martin and the accounts of the Pontifical Book that are not unacceptable by criticism, confirm without doubt the incursion, which must have happened between the end of October, 649, and June 17, 653, or actually between 650 and 652, because the first and last year should be eliminated, since it is not credible that a thousand men would venture on a naval expedition in a season other than the summer. And the year 652 sounds quite convincing. (1:194)

The battle which took place on that morning without a certain date had to be the first in a long series, which, after more or less one century and a half, would finally give Sicily to the Muslims. Their victory would eventually free a "people whose mind suffered between the chains of the monks and those of the emperor, and whose body under the whip of emperor and militaries. In one word, Sicily had become Byzantine in and out; sick with the phthisis of a decaying empire. So, when we look at the poor conditions of this people, we cannot complain about the Muslim conquest, which shook and renewed Sicily a bit" (Amari, *Biblioteca* 349).

The similitude between this Muslim conquest and the history of the vesper is worth noticing. Once again, canonical historiography had read the Muslim invasion of Sicily as the story of a courtly plot (Amari, *Storia* 1:367) aimed at nothing more than a dynastic succession (this time with some more exotic characters). Sicilians, now as always, were incapable of Montesquieu's freedom and only gave themselves to this or that ruler in some kind of historical variation of the game of musical chairs. Also Arabs, incidentally, were incapable of real conquests according to the canonical historiography that Amari had consulted: history, after all, was the history of European aristocracy and principalities determining the fate of the world. Once again, Amari refuted these canonical interpretations and proposed one in which popular resentment, not courtly or invisible hands, prepared the conditions for the new Muslim regime to come. What Amari saw in Sicily at the eve of the Arab invasion was a true popular ferment that determined the fall of Byzantium's rule.

Arab domination, in turn, became a continuous alternation, according to Ibn Khaldun's and Vico's cycles, of barbaric rule (Ibrahim ibn Ahmad, 875–901), popular insurrections (the Palermo uprisings of 912, 913, and 1019), and attempts, like Ibn Qurhub's in 913, "to order Sicily into a legitimate and stable government, with all the liberty that was conceivable for orthodox Muslims" (Amari, *Storia* 2:175). After that, it is yet more cycles of counterrevolutions (916), barbarity (the sack of Palermo in 917), and joys. The latter climaxed, in the year 351 of the hegira (962 A.D.), in the Great Circumcision staged with due pomp and circumstance in the public square of Palermo: "Starting with the son and brothers of the emir Ahmad, and then on from the nobles to the lower classes, reaching a total of fifteen thousand circumcised boys" (2:295–96).

The Arabs, too, then fall into that pattern of universal history that Amari had drawn from Vico and Ibn Khaldun. The fact would be in itself relevant, but what it actually signals is that history, in this case, no longer coincides with, or is limited to, Europe. In European history, "Islam is confined to the past and qualified as 'oriental' which means antihistoricistic, while the West proves through this acquisition its entry into modernity, a lay modernity based on historical becoming" (Scarcia Amoretti 172). In Amari's *Storia*, instead, the "Orientals" are agents and subjects of history too. In fact, when compared with the Byzantine-Christian cycle, the Arab one seems definitely more fruitful for the history of Sicily: "As the population grew, and the wars of conquest ceased, learned studies began to grow, and even to put some leaves and fruits. Research was favored also by a more familiar contact with the vanquished population, by a more liberal education and doctrine that the African Muslims had brought, and by the example set by the jurists sent to order the judicial system in Sicily" (2:253). And, ah!, what wonders these Arabs brought to the desolate island that had once been of the pope! Far from being the barbarians depicted by many, and despite the Montesquieu-like "scorching climate and a dried-out soil" (Amari, *Storia* 1:134) from which they came, Amari's Arabs land in Sicily as the bearers of civilization. *They* give Europe, contrary to any theory of European diffusionism, and long before Montesquieu's celebrated Franks (who, after all, brought only Charles to Sicily), a spirit of the law, the sharia or Islamic law, "of the same kind as the European one of many centuries later" (1:152).

In Ibn Khaldun's *Muqaddimah* (1377), which translates as *Introduction to History*, Amari had found, first and foremost, a way to correct Montesquieu's climatology. In the second prefatory discussion to the *Muqaddimah*, Ibn Khaldun, following Aristotle through Averroës and Ptolemy, had divided the known world into seven zones—*iqlîm*, from Greek *klima*, or climate—going from north to south. The Mediterranean, in the fourth and median zone, blessed by a temperate climate, was the very Aristotelian middle between nature and civilization:

> The north and the south represent opposite extremes of cold and heat. It necessarily follows that there must be a gradual decrease from the extremes towards the center, which, thus, is moderate. The fourth zone (i.e. the Mediterranean) is the most temperate cultivated region . . . . Therefore, the sciences, the crafts, the buildings, the clothing, the foodstuffs, the fruits, and even the animal that comes into being in the [Mediterranean] are distinguished by their temperate character. The human inhabitants of these zones are more temperate in their bodies, colour, character qualities, and general conditions . . . . They avoid intemperance quite generally in all their conditions. Such are the inhabitants of the Maghrib, of Syria, of the two Iraqs . . . as well as of Spain . . . . The Iraq and Syria are directly in the middle and therefore are the most temperate of all. (Ibn Khaldun 1:167–68)

Although Ibn Khaldun's geometric sense of the world had omitted to mention another country "in the middle," Sicily, this was enough for Amari to declare that in the Mediterranean, not in the north, was to be found the true cradle of civilization.

Reminiscent of the southernist polemics that had crossed Italy in the late eighteenth century, and which I have recalled in chapter 2, Amari summons up Juan Andrés's Arabist theory and adds that a genius of their language (Amari, *Storia* 2:610) made philology and poetry flower among the Arabs (1:147, 2:526). Coming from Asia, Africa, and Al-Andalus, the Muslims gave Sicily, therefore, the honor of developing a new form of troubadour poetry, rhymed and sung, that would later "infiltrate the whole of Europe" (3:729–31).[27]

Amari, in fact, is quite close to believing that *all* sciences flourished with the Muslims of Sicily in an age when they were getting lost in the rest of medieval Europe. For instance, "as the darkness of barbarism fell, geography became idiotic in Europe, like every other science; it was reduced to shapeless scribbles, to summaries of summaries" (3:683). Idrisi's *Garden of Civilization*, with its most compelling descriptions of Sicily, was "the first book worthy of the name 'general geography'" (1:49) ever published in modern Europe. More important, Ibn Khaldun, "the most ancient writer of the philosophy of history, properly speaking" (1:84), gave Europe that first theory of history.

Amari saw his book on the Muslims of Sicily not simply as local history but as a veritable history of the origin of modern Europe. As he later explained to the German Orientalist Friedrich Arnold Brockhaus, "the age of Muslim Sicily was one of the causes of the rebirth of sciences and letters in the whole of Europe" (Amari, *Carteggio* 119). In this regard, "the Muslim wars in Sicily from the seventh through the twelfth centuries can be divided into two orders of events: one is the material for a local history, but not the other" (Amari, *Storia* 1:29). In other words, if the conquest of Sicily was material for local history, the civilization of Muslim Sicily, on the other hand, was material for nothing less than a universal *storia dell'umanità*—a history of humankind (1:178).

Besides giving modern Europe its arts and sciences, its first geography and philosophy of history, Muslim Sicily, as opposed to Montesquieu's Franks, introduced in the continent a new spirit of the law, the "basis of any civilization" and the very cause of "European civilization" in particular (2:255). The law, in fact, had such devout followers among the Muslims of Sicily that, for instance, "professor Abù Said Luqman ibn Yùsuf, martyr of exegesis, is said to have died of a wound he grew on his chest from the corner of the desk where he used to write his commentaries" (2:257). No wonder jurisprudence had in Islam "greater civic and literary influence than in either the heathen or the Christian West" (2:255)!

Besides greater influence, the law had in Islam "wider borders" (2:255) than in Europe, as it covered not only the (national) citizen and the powerful but the foreigner and the weak as well: "A Qurayshi [i.e., someone belonging to one the leading families of Mecca] had taken away, with no qualms, all the goods of a foreign merchant. Many generous people, among whom Muhammad, still twenty-five years old, gathered and tried to devise ways to protect, in the city of Mecca, the weak, the foreigner, free men and slaves—anybody from anybody else, from whatever family they were" (1:152). It is from this law protecting the weak from the powerful, not from the French Revolution with its rights of man caring for citizens and private property only,[28] that true democracy and freedom, suggests Amari, originated: "It was social democracy, as we would call it today. Its form fit quite well the fundamental principles of Islam: equality and fraternity. It was the realization, rare in the world, of a sovereign people" (1:171).

Amari's thesis is clear: Sicily has nothing to learn from the northern nations and has known *liberté, fraternité, égalité* from Islam—long before any other European country. The first problem with such a thesis was, of course, that it ran counter to the historiographic *doxa*: that the revolution of 1789, namely, "was really the first time that a state, embodying the entity called 'the nation,' issuing from a clean political break with the past, produced a *novus ordo seculorum*: democracy or the government of the people" (Englund 89). Such *doxa*, for Amari, who might as well have had in mind Walter Benjamin's "Theses on the Philosophy of History," was but an act of suppression that the victorious Norman chroniclers had perpetrated against the vanquished Muslims: along with a "true and grim religious persecution" of the Arabs (Amari, *Storia* 3:444–47), Amari wrote, Christian chroniclers had operated another, "concealed and slow" form of persecution (3:541): they had cleansed European history from the Arab presence.

In short, to argue that Sicily did not need the benevolent authority of Europe to know democracy, historiography was, at best, insufficient. At most, it was *the* obstacle. To remove such obstacle, and recuperate what had been cleansed and concealed by history, Amari thus resolved to supplement "those few studies that Europeans have done so far" about Sicily (3:863) with nothing less than the work of "our . . . Orientalists" (2:17): Orientalism was called on to compensate for the deficiency of historiography; Orientalism, not history, singled out in Islamic law— a mixture of prescriptions from the Koran, pronouncements of the Prophet, and corollaries of the doctors—the very reason for an Arab (as opposed to a European) propensity for *liberté, fraternité, égalité*. Orientalism, moreover, could be capable of demolishing the whole edifice of a

European philosophy of history—with its prejudices, presumptions, and half truths—in which freedom was theorized as a "climate" frankly and ultimately unattainable for Sicily.

Through Orientalism, finally, those same words—*liberty, fraternity, equality, democracy*—which had defined modern Europe since at least the French Revolution and which had, in Mazzini's expression, the "sense given to these words in France"—could acquire a new and original meaning. Relying on the archive of the Oriental writers themselves, the *Storia* not only erected Muslims Sicily as the origin of those concepts but retheorized them as well. Montesquieu, for instance, had famously made freedom—the pillar of Europe's identity—coincide with the "individual right to own the property that civil laws give him" (*Oeuvres* 2:768). The European notion of freedom, if not "entirely derived from this concept of possession . . . [was] powerfully shaped by it" (Macpherson 3). Freedom as freedom to property had been the basis for the two revolutions that had shaped the very identity of the modern West in the eighteenth century—the French (Barnave) and the American (R. McKeon). The Declaration of the Rights of Man, cited here in Thomas Paine's translation, summarized the principle in its third article: "The end of all political associations is the preservation of the natural and imprescriptible rights of man; and these rights are liberty, property" (115).

Amari, on the contrary, saw an inescapable contradiction between the right to liberty and the right to property. Freedom began for him with Islamic law's kind of social democracy—with the alienation of property, that is, onto the figure of the transcendent that grants the true rights of man. Human beings are not the owners of natural resources. God has simply entrusted them with a "viceregency" (*khilafa*) of his creation (see Moosa 196). Summarizing the point that Ibn Khaldun had made in the twelfth discussion (on Islamic jurisprudence) of his introduction, Amari made community, cooperation, and shared property—that is, *asabiyah* (for a discussion of the term, see Baali)—the pillars of the perfect Islamic society: "For sure, since Muslims admitted the existence of a Creator, they had to make Him lord of his own creations; but they thought He had left the land, and also water, air, fire, and light for universal use to all his creatures—not only to Muhammad, and even less so to the caliphs that were his successors" (Amari, *Storia* 2:18–19). The palimpsest of John Locke's *Second Treatise of Government* is still readable here: "If it be difficult to make out 'property' upon a supposition that God gave the world to Adam and his posterity in common, it is impossible that any man but one universal monarch should have any 'property' upon a supposition that God gave the world to Adam and his heirs in succession, exclusive of all the rest of his posterity" (Locke 5:115). Yet Locke had concluded that "to make use of [property] to the best advantage of life and convenience" God had let individuals "appropriate" nature for the benefit "of any particular men" (5:115–16); Amari, instead, left property public, as the very foundation of a sort of collective state. This did not mean, incidentally, that the Arabs lacked the famous idea of property, which just as famously Locke (like Rousseau after him) had conceived of as the beginning of civil society. It meant, rather, that the Prophet "tempered with wisdom and sometimes with humanity the exercise of that beastlike right" (Amari, *Storia* 2:21).[29]

Whereas Locke had posed an unenforceable limit to private property, coinciding with a vague notion of personal need—"as much as any one can make use of to any advantage of life before it spoils" (5:117)—Amari celebrated instead the Islamic system of taxation that redistributed the benefits of private usage among civil society as a collective entity:

> Koran and Sunna recognize the full property of cultivated land, as they recognize the use property of any other assets. Property is taxable: ten percent on the produce of the land, and two and a half percent on cattle and other assets. Muhammad had the sublime idea of calling this tax *sadaqât*, that is to say, goodwill offer; and *zakâh*, which is translatable as "purification": purification, he meant, of the sin that the rich would be judged for if he were to let the poor die of hunger, and the State treasury shrink. (2:19)

It was a kind of purification, indeed, which could redeem society from that very Marxian original sin that is accumulation. At any rate, once community rights overruled private property rights, as Amari suggested through his reading of Islamic law, the rights of man as formulated by Paine seemed now less universal and more the historical product of Western needs and circumstances. Aside, or even against them, another kind of rights of man, drawn from Islamic law, could in fact be imagined (similar controversies are recently addressed by Arkoun 106; Moosa; An-Na'Im).

If freedom was the essence of Europe, this essence, first of all, came from the Orient. More important, from the Orient came also the necessity to redefine that very essence of Europe, and to disentangle it from the structures of private property. In other words, Europe, like freedom, could now be retheorized anew through the archives of Orientalism. As a matter of fact, not only freedom but also the notion of identity—be it a European or an Italian identity—had now to be retheorized starting from "Oriental" Sicily. If a politics of identity—Sicilian national identity; identity of Sicily with the norms of Europe—had been the goal of the *Vesper*, the *Storia*, instead, seemed now weary of exactly that notion.

Just as the Normans had forced the populations of Sicily to Christianize, says Amari, their historiography had Europeanized Sicily: a sense of ethnic identity, in other words, was thrust on Sicily; the island's plurilingual (Amari, *Storia* 1:322–24), plurireligious (3:541–43), and pluriethnic (2:458) vicissitudes were erased, along with any trace of its Arab and Jewish history. The memory of the Oriental past, at best, was kept as a memento of a fundamental Sicilian imperfection that only European intervention, in the form of blonde warriors "whose language, complexion, and social order confirmed their Germanic origin" (3:18), could be capable of correcting. Sicily, corrupted and de-Europeanized by the Muslims, was at the receiving end of history—the history of freedom that, as in Montesquieu, was diffused from a Germanic north. To understand the forcefulness of this rhetoric of Europeanization concocted by early Norman historiography, and to imagine the resilience of such a rhetorical unconscious in the historiography of the island that spans across the centuries, it is enough to remember what Rosario Romeo, the authoritative historian of Sicily, would still write in 1950: "During the High Middle Ages, Sicily remained almost completely extraneous to the life of the West. What operated, instead, was . . . Arab influence . . . . Only with the Normans' intervention Sicily was reconquered to Europe; in fact, . . . the reconquest was achieved only some centuries after the Saracens were expelled from the island" (*Risorgimento* 11).

Amari's interest in making of Sicily a proper subject in the history of the West, and of relegitimating it to Europe, however, had ended with the *Vesper*. The stake was now higher: Sicily was part of Europe and universal history not because it has been reconquered to it, but, simply, because it was. The original laboratory of social democracy, the experiment of some kind of exchequer of Muslim Sicily, the island had little to envy or to learn: it required to be part of universal history not because it adhered to some putative European standards, but because of its unique history and its difference.

Although Amari's Sicily declared itself ready to join the Italian revolution, and although it sounded eager to enter Europe as a free subject—

one that had known freedom since the Arab conquest—Sicily did not join as sameness. Like Mazzini in "The Present Conditions and the Future of Europe" of 1852, Amari also believed that "the map of Europe must be redrawn" (Mazzini, *Opere* 2:521)—at the very least, to include Sicily as subject, not object, of continental politics. Yet whereas Mazzini believed that European "unity is necessary," and that "unity of faith, of mission, of intents" had to be reached within Europe (*Opere* 2:545), Amari's redrawing of the map shunned any such concept of unity: "Contrary to the Byzantine society that left Sicily, the Muslim one that took its place brought elements of activity, progress, and discord" (*Storia* 2:1). It was this element of discord that a theory of Europe had to be made to accept: discord in the sense of Attilio Scuderi's "physiological cultural conflict," which is not the intolerance of ignorance, but the "only way to construct multiple identities." The *Storia* thus introduced, as facts, the multiethnic presence of Muslim Sicily as an element of discord in the Europe of standards. Methodologically, Orientalism, supplementing history, sounded a quite discordant note in the otherwise monotonous theorizations of Europe's freedom. In the end, Orientalism, not history, could make of Sicily a part of Europe, and claim, at the same time, its difference. Or could it?

A Sicilian *Muqaddimah*

The day Amari woke up to find himself an Orientalist, he was an exile in Paris. His Orientalist education had been suspiciously French and imperial—under "the living legacy," as Said would have it, of Antoine Isaac Silvestre de Sacy and his disciples.[30] Noël Des Vergers's 1841 French translation had introduced Amari to Ibn Khaldun; the classes of Joseph Toussaint Reinaud, the successor of Sacy at the École des Langues Orientales Vivantes, to Arabic; and the Bibliothèque Impériale to the archives. Yet the *Storia dei Musulmani di Sicilia* had very little intention of continuing any legacy at all—nor had its author the usual timidity of the parvenu in a new academic field. While declaring himself "forced," with sarcastic confidence, to having to reject the usual authorities (Amari, *Storia* 1:18), Amari entered the field of Oriental studies with the clear intent of subverting it—the same way he, "hero of ideas," had been wanting to subvert the Bourbon monarchy for years. The intention was not lost on his readers. The Italian Orientalist Isidoro Carino, in a review for the *Archivio storico siciliano*, 1873, soon noticed that "Amari rejects the authority of this writer [Rampolli, author of the *Muslim Annals*], which on the contrary had been fundamental for the critical works of his predecessors; he lends authority, instead, to more than eighty Arabs, whom he studied in their printed works and in the manuscripts they have left in various libraries; he then compares them to Western chroniclers" (224–25). Pace Carino, what Amari was doing was nothing more than what many Orientalists and historians suppose they *ought* to be doing: work the archives and compare the sources. He had announced quite candidly: "I compared the texts [of Western scholars] with the original codes; I collected historical fragments, geographical descriptions, biographies, and both the prose and the poems of the Sicilian Arabs, or at least the titles of the works that had been lost—all that had been written in Arabic" (*Storia* 1:19). But of course one does not need to beg the authority of Said to realize that Amari was really *not* doing what Orientalists used to do: for the latter, the Muslim was a document, not a historian. A Muslim voice had been silenced by European Orientalism as the voice of an exotic Other so alien to the logic and rigor of (European) scholarship that it could only be studied and catalogued like the flora and fauna, but not engaged in conversation. In short, using Oriental sources as *historical subjects*, as writers (not merely objects) of history, or as a perspective on historical facts, was nothing short of a theoretical revolution for Amari and his public.

Just as European historiography had obscured the Arab as an accident and obstacle in the giddy progress of universal history, so had Orientalism obscured the Muslims of Sicily as something that could disturb the predetermined image of absolute difference and exoticism that any Muslim was supposed to embody. For Orientalism, in short, Muslim Europe could not have possibly ever been: "Despite all the intellectual culture the Muslim colonies of Spain and Italy contributed to European civilization, it has happened that their history has long remained obscure and neglected, as if it were the history of barbarian people" (Amari, *Storia* 1:1). As Carino noticed for us once again, Amari, after supplementing history's deficiency with the knowledge of Orientalism, was now operating a "complete rewriting" of Orientalism itself (277).

In Amari's privileging of the "eighty Arab writers" there was, therefore, not only a retheorization of historiography but also a retheorization of Orientalism in which the Arab had undergone a quite radical transformation—from object of study to subject of history, from document to speaker. The authorities that Amari was challenging, in the last analysis, were those of instituted Orientalism itself. If, so far, the Orient, the Oriental, and "Orientalism belonged . . . to European scholarship" (Said, *Orientalism* 130), it started looking as if *Europe*, for Amari, could now belong to Arab historiography.

As I reach this felicitously subalternist conclusion, I would like to take advantage of the sense of accomplishment I have thus acquired and go back to that murkier and most ill-defined morning between the years 649 and 653 when the first Muslim battleship approached Sicily. This is an important morning, quite obviously, as it stages a first encounter between Sicilians and Muslims, between Europe and the Orient. But it is a morning of which we still know next to nothing: How was this first intercultural experience? Was it love at first sight? Certainly not on European accounts: "European memoirs all agree that they irrupted with great fury" (Amari, *Storia* 1:216). Benedictine monks, exaggerating as usual, "made the Muslims invade Sicily one century before Muhammad, and savagely kill Saint Placid along with thirty monks and nuns who lived in his monastery in Messina" (1:220). No doubt, according to Amari, we should not rely on European history. And we cannot rely on Orientalist scholarship either. On the other hand, Arab memoirs say—nothing. They do not really seem concerned with what was seen, from Muslim eyes, as yet another military triumph. In a variation of the Catholic "tell the sin but not the sinner," they sometimes mention *a* victory, but not the vanquished (1:217), so that, were we to rely on them, we would never be sure whether we were reading a history of Tripoli or of Syracuse.

What Amari figures out is that Sicily, in truth, was not a major goal for the Muslims. At most, after the conquest of Spain (after 711), they looked at Sicily as a potential bridge with the African colonies. Here, some very pesky Berbers were keeping the Muslim war machine so busy, and the Arab chroniclers so focused—one relentless insurrection after another— that any conquest of Sicily could neither be accomplished nor narrated for a few centuries still. Even long after 652, when Byzantine Sicilians and Muslims seemed more and more divided by religion, and kept together by commerce only (1:359); when warfare between the two nations became a daily affair; when the possibility to colonize the island, taking advantage of the people's unhappiness with Byzantium, seemed close at hand—even then a conquest of Sicily was not on Arabs' minds:

In early 827, the Muslim forces discussed the utility of a Sicilian campaign. When another faction proposed to raid Sicily without remaining there and creating colonies, one Sahnûn ibn Qâdim got up to dissent: "How far is Sicily from Italy? he asked. "You can go back and forth two or three times from dawn to sunset," was the answer. "And between Sicily and Africa?" And the answer: "One day and one night travel." "Oh, even if I had wings, I wouldn't fly to that island," concluded Sahnûn, punning on his name that is given in Africa to a very cunning bird. At any rate, the witticism did not work. The majority, speaking in one voice, deliberated in favor of the war. But it had to be a war for the booty, not for a colonial conquest. (1:390)

Not only was Sicily nowhere to be found on the Muslims' strategic plans; the battering of Sicilians was not in their chronicles either:

In the end, Sicily endured an incursion, of which we only know it happened in the year 204 of the hegira (between June 28, 819, and June 16, 820); that the attack was led by Muhammad ibn 'Abd Allâh ibn al-Aglab, cousin of the Aghlabite prince Ziyadat Allâh; and that the Muslims, once they made enough prisoners, went back to Africa. It must have been, then, just a raid, or the venting of religious rage in some kind of punitive mission. (1:359)

So, *comme un boucher*, like a butcher, with no particular hatred or intention but a vague desire to "vent religious rage," these Arabs, these future saviors and bearers of a new heroic age, would hit Sicilians, take them prisoners in Africa, and enter barely enough information in their chronicles to satisfy ordinary administration.

When the Muslims finally do conquer Syracuse in 827, helped by "a disgruntled general in the Sicilian army who led a mutiny and asked for help from the Aghlabids of Kairouan" (Mack Smith 1:3), the nonchalance of Arab chroniclers is only comparable to the partisanship of the Europeans. The latter, led by Tommaso Fazzello, a Dominican monk who wrote in 1560 the most voluminous Sicilian chronicle ever—*De rebus siculis decades duae*—were certainly eager to highlight the infidels' ontological inhumanity. They reported with self-righteous indignation, for instance, of how "Halbi (that's how they misspelled names and confuse chronology) would have sent forty thousand Saracens to Sicily, led by Fazzello, upon landing in Mazara burned his own ships, and conquered Selinunte, captured its citizens, and, to give an example to the whole of Sicily, cooked them in copper cauldrons. As evidence of such events, Fazzello mentions Muslim annals and Leo the African, but does not explain who wrote, who translated, and who published such annals" (Amari, *Storia* 1:360–61). Leo the African, on the other hand, writing his memoirs at the court of Pope Leo X, to whom he had been given as a gift by some pirates from Djerba, was not the most reliable source either. Part of it was that he had to please Christendom, to which religion he had recently converted (until he had enough of popes, Eucharists, and holy cities, converted back to Islam, and disappeared from Europe forever). Even if he had never written a line about the cooked people of Selinunte, his writings had the newly convert kind of bias. Worse, the only documents he could find in the pope's library were in fact Christian ones—hardly an alternative point of view to European histories. To supplement those documents, the well-learned Leo only had his Muslim memories—the ones from before the pirates, the abduction, and the holy water. And this is what *really* annoyed Amari about the African: in those memories, much like in Arab memoirs, there seemed to be no place for the conquest of Sicily. Here is Amari:

> It is likely that Leo, mixing up clear memories with murkier speculations, must have heard the name of Alcamo while in Rome. Or perhaps he heard it from the Berbers. In any case, he must have put that name together with that of Assad—the only name he was certain had something to do with Sicily, so little had he read about it. As proof of the fact he knew that little about the Sicilian conquest, suffice it to read the short paragraph where he mentions it en passant. (1:363)

These "few lines" that Leo knew about the conquest of Sicily were not so much proof of the African's scholarly negligence as of the fact that there was next to nothing in the whole of the Arab chronicles, the *ta'rikh*, the histories, or whatever you want to call them, about the conquest of Sicily.

Sure enough, Amari the historian compares imperial compilations with Arab sources (this was his trademark Orientalist retheorization of historiography, after all). He even finds Oriental records more "genuine" (1:373) than the European ones. And yet, even forgiving the Orientals for relying sometimes on second- and thirdhand sources (1:376–77), or for exaggerating things "with the excuse that 'so is said,'" (1:377) how can one ever excuse the sated nonchalance with which they mistake the day that forever changed Sicily and Europe—and the blood, and death, and Sicilian suffering—for "yet another one"?

Our heart was trembling—an Arab chronicler writes—trembling for old captain Assad, when, after praying, he suddenly turned to us: "These are the same barbarians you have found in the northern coast of Africa. They are your slaves! Do not fear them, oh Muslims!" So, he ran down the middle of the battlefield, and found himself soon caught up with the enemy. He came out of it all drenched in blood, blood dripping from the spear, blood through the arm, blood down to the armpit—so tells us the narrator, astounded by the bravery of the old warrior! The bravery of all other Muslims, courage being such an ordinary virtue among them, is never mentioned. All the chroniclers have to say is that this was a day like hundreds of others: heavy fighting, God on our side, great Muslim conquest, excellent loot, exemplary massacre of the Infidels. (1:398)

The Muslim conquest of Sicily, the event that Amari wants to inscribe in the annals of universal history, is but "a day like hundreds of others"! The whole chronicles of the conquest repeat this gesture of marginalization over and over again: "Byzantine chroniclers say nothing of the event, for fear of shame; the only record is preserved by the Arabs, but brief and vague" (1:469). From a different perspective hinging on the Arabocentrism of someone who "condemns as physical and moral vices all characteristics that are unusual to him" (2:353), the geographer Ibn Hawqal "pontificates: Palermo has no intelligent people, no learned men, no wits, no religion. There are no dumber people in the world, nor more odd. They are utterly uninterested in virtue, and quite eager to learn more vices" (2:351). But he does not even take the time to understand—in Amari's historicist variation of Ludwig Andreas Feuerbach's "Der Mensch ist was er isst" (A person is what he eats)—that "at the roots of so much iniquity is the fact that they are reduced to eat uncooked onions, lunch through supper, whether they are rich or poor" (2:351).

Ibn Khaldun does not do better, either, writing five centuries later, when he overlooks again the exploitation and poverty of the Sicilians and remembers one abuse "with hurry, as customary" (Amari, *Storia* 1:199), another massacre "briefly and vaguely" (1:440n). So, "lucky the one who can find a reference to the situation of the people of Sicily during the Muslim domination" (2:33)!

One starts understanding the frustration of Amari: the history that he is trying to rescue from obliteration has been caught between the rock of European falsifications and the hard place of Arab satiety. It is a history lost between two dominances—the old Arab and the new European one—that, to draw from Ranajit Guha's arguably parallel experience, ruled Sicily without hegemony: their histories, in other words, did not need to create any consensus about either domination in Sicilian consciousness (see Guha). The question is: How to write a history of such consciousness lost in the memory of all who conquered? How to write the story of "a bunch of men who, after all, could devote themselves to culture for one century or so, were subjugated as soon as they would start harvesting their first intellectual fruits, and then persecuted and cast away the next century. What is astounding is that, after all this, little bits of literary memories of them exist at all" (Amari, *Storia* 2:527). And how to find, in those "little bits of literary memories," the traces for a history with no center and no ethnos, made by "the ferment of the many heterogeneous elements that together formed the people of Sicily, and above all of Palermo: many races; Islam and latent or living remnants of Christianity; unequal civil rights, wealth and misery, war and industry; tower of Babel where arrogance, resentment, abjection, and endless social sores would grow" (2:353)?

All these questions, once the Orientalist supplement had revealed itself to be insufficient, had to remain unanswered by Amari. His *Storia dei Musulmani di Sicilia* was, then, more than a history, the narrative of an impossibility. The Mediterranean perspective on universal history that Amari's Orientalism had introduced certainly looked at things from a different angle than the one of hegemonic European historiography. Sicily could now even be claimed as a discordant part of Europe. And even the concept of Europe, at this point, could be retheorized again, to make it not the antithesis of the Orient, but an integral part of its history and civilization. This was thus a good story to tell. Yet even such a Mediterranean perspective could hardly give a history and an image to subaltern Sicily. It could, at its very best, summarize its disappearance between Europe, on the one hand, and the Orient, on the other. "I conclude," Amari wrote at the close of his book, "moved by an irresistible urge to look into obscurity" (4:921). As if the history of Europe from the perspective of the PIGS, in the end, could not possibly be told.

Notes

1 The Discovery of Europe

1. In Santiago, in the north of Spain, Catholic resistance against Islam was formed around the twelfth century. The Christian Reconquest of Iberia made the cult of Saint James (Santiago) and the pilgrimage to his site a major symbol of Christian mobilization against the east. After the final defeat of the Moors in 1492, the symbol of Santiago Matamoros (Saint James the Moors Killer) became the figure of national unity for Catholic Spain under Ferdinand and Isabelle. While proposals to include Christianity as the religion of Europe abound around the project of a European constitution, it might be worth noticing that "for the Council of Europe, what is now a signposted routeway—the *Camino de Santiago*—becomes a symbol of European cultural itinerary, a symbol of the ideal of European integration" (Graham 26).

2. By this I mean a post-Bismarckian kind of political science. For Bismarck, we remember, "anyone who speaks of Europe is wrong." Peregrine Horden and Nicholas Purcell suggest that this assertion, scribbled on the back of a telegram form 1876, only meant "that designations such as 'Europe' are empty and arbitrary" (15).

3. "Claiming to speak in the name of intelligibility, good sense, common sense, or the democratic ethic, this discourse tends, by means of these very things, and as if naturally, to discredit anything that complicates this model. It tends to suspect or repress anything that bends, overdetermines, or even questions" (Derrida, *Other Heading* 55).

4. History is understood here in the sense of Marc Bloch's "historical semantics" (*Craft*) and Antonio Gramsci's philological "history of terminology," as "a study of words [that] can help us understand the very limit of words, and avoid that metaphors materialize themselves, almost mechanically, [into truth statements]" (Gramsci 85).

5. This is a theory, incidentally, that became instrumental in the eighteenth century to claim not so much a Christian, but a Frankish origin of Europe: Charles Martel's Europe of Poitiers, maturing in Charles's grandson's, Charlemagne, Holy Roman Empire, would be, according to such theory, the origin, kernel, and truest essence of Europe. In chapter 3 of this

book, I will discuss the way in which Juan Andrés will question the Franco-centrism of this theory and will propose another with Arab Spain at its center.

6. Or, in the pseudo Aretino's less orthodox version: "Per Europa godere, in bue cangiossi / Giove, che di chiavarla avea desio; / e la sua deità posta in oblio, / in più bestiali forme trasformossi" (Aretino 189).

7. If we accept Momigliano's theory—that since the Greeks started talking about Europe, they must have also begun it—then it follows the recurrent claim that "the forerunner of European civilization . . . is to be found in the Hellenic world" (e.g., Likaszewski 40). Not that such claim, trite as it may sound, will (or should) be without contention: as we will see by the end of this introduction, such a Mediterranean beginning of Europe (Said's "A") will be quite inconvenient when the objective is to argue (B) a more northern essence of Europeanness on the part of, say, the French *philosophes* of the eighteenth century. For that, Robert Bartlett's Charlemagne (or Bernard Lewis's Charles Martel) will undoubtedly do much better.

8. Edith Hall identifies Aeschylus's *Persians* as "the first unmistakable file in the archive of Orientalism, the discourse by which the European imagination has dominated Asia ever since by conceptualizing its inhabitants as defeated, luxurious, emotional, cruel, and always as dangerous" (99). Thomas Harrison warns, however, that "the assumption of a continuous tradition of the Orient—and a corresponding idea of Europe—may indeed play into the hands of those who ascribe very different values to East and West, who believe . . . that . . . the Western community is nevertheless . . . called upon to lead the world" (42). It should be remarked, however, that Aeschylus does not use the term *Europe* himself and that such discussions, in the last analysis, may be more revealing of *our* concerns about Europe than of the Greeks'.

9. "Europe, in Strabo's definition, included Iberia, Celtica (between the Pyrenees and the Rhine), and Brittany. In the east, it was divided by the Danube. On the left bank were the Germans, the Getae, the Tyregetae, the Bastarnae, and the Sarmatians; on the right bank were Thracia, Illyria, and Greece. . . . Strabo had practically no knowledge of Scandinavia (since he confused the Baltic with the Ocean) or of the huge plain which stretches between the lower Baltic and the Don" (Duroselle 64–65).

10. "The *limes*, the 'frontier line', was a vital feature of the Empire's defence. It was not, as is sometimes supposed, an impenetrable barrier. From the military point of view it was more of a cordon, or series of parallel cordons, which, whilst deterring casual incursions, would trigger active countermeasures as soon as it seriously breached. It was a line which normally could only be crossed by paying *portaria* and by accepting the Empire's authority. It was, above all, a marker which left no one in doubt as to which

lands were subject to Roman jurisdiction and which were not. Its most important characteristic was its continuity. It ran up hill and down dale without a break, and along all frontier rivers and coasts. In places, as in Britain, it took the form of a Great Wall on the Chinese model. Elsewhere it might carry a wooden stockade atop earthworks, or a string of linked coastal forts, or, as in Africa, blocks of fortified farmhouses facing the desert interior" (Davies 185–88).

11. "The medieval 'T-O' maps represent the earth schematically divided into three by the Nile and Tanais running north and south forming the head of the 'T,' the Mediterranean running West from the juncture of the 'T,' sometimes marked as the site of Jerusalem in the center of the world, and the whole thing inscribed in the circle of 'the Ocean.' These maps express the blend of the classical and biblical heritages characteristic of the West. They superimpose onto the three sons of Noah—Sem, Ham, and Japheth, iconic ancestors of the world's races—the divisions devised by the Ionian historians and geographers, who took the Aegean to be the fulcrum of meaningful contact and conflict. The inner sea, ever since Isidore of Seville called the Mediterranean such, is the upright leg of the 'T,' the axis around which this universe revolves" (Moulakis 16).

12. "Can other aspects of Europe's distasteful recent past be reconciled with the notion of European identity? Europeanness has to embrace the unacceptable: Srebrenica and Auschwitz as well as High Gothic cathedrals, romantic castles, utopian Renaissance town planning and symphonic music. The memorable history of Europeans embraces pogrom, persecution and prejudice, near-continuous internecine war, oppression and genocide. The twentieth century has seen mass death, carpet-bombing of cities and, above all, the Jewish Holocaust of 1933–45. This remains archetypically 'European' heritage, and arguably the most serious challenge facing contemporary European society in creating a sense of common identity. European Jews—ironically the principal European people not nationally defined— were deported and murdered by Europeans in Europe in pursuit of a European ideology" (Graham 44).

13. "*Medium Aevum*, 'the Middle Age,' was a term first used by devout Christians who saw themselves living in the interval between Christ's first and Second Coming. Much later it was taken up for different purposes. Renaissance scholars began to talk in the fifteenth century of the 'Middle Age' as the interval between the decline of antiquity and the revival of classical culture in their own times. For them, the ancient world stood for high civilization; the Middle Age represented a descent into barbarism, parochiality, religious bigotry. During the Enlightenment, when the virtues of human reason were openly lauded over those of religious belief, 'medievalism' became synonymous with obscurantism and backwardness. Since then,

of course, as the 'Modern Age' which followed the Middle Age was itself fading into the past, new terms had to be invented to mark the passage of time. The medieval period has been incorporated into the fourfold Convention which divides European history into ancient, medieval, modern, and now contemporary sections. By convention also, the medieval period is often subdivided into early, high, and late phases, creating several successive Middle Ages. Of course, people whom later historians refer to as 'medieval' had no inkling of that designation" (Davies 291).

14. Just to avoid possible misunderstandings deriving from my sometimes synonymic use of *Frank* and *German*: the Franks were, according to the *Oxford English Dictionary*, one of the "Germanic nation, or coalition of nations, that conquered Gaul in the 6th century."

15. "It is true that Christians are made—by baptism—not born, but the vast majority of those born in Christian Europe . . . underwent baptism as a matter of course. They could easily think of themselves, not as voluntary recruits to a particular community of believers, but as members of a Christian race or people. . . . The ethnic sense of 'Christian' can be found repeatedly and perhaps increasingly in the High Middle Ages. The term 'the Christian people' (*populus Christianus*), which was common, implies no more than 'the community of Christians'; but when the Saxons were forcibly converted by Frankish arms in the decades around the year 800, adoption of the new religion made them 'one race, as it were (*quasi una gens*), with the Franks'" (Bartlett 251).

16. "Medieval Europeans commonly referred to Muslims as 'Saracens,' an epithet derived from the Arabic word *sharakyoun* or 'easterner'" (Davies 258).

17. According to William of Malmesbury, however, the pope himself claimed, when preaching the Crusade in 1095, that nothing less than "Europe" was at stake (see Hay 30–31).

18. Parataxis being, according to the *Oxford English Dictionary*, "the placing of propositions or clauses one after another, without indicating by connecting words the relation (of co-ordination or subordination) between them."

19. "April 1215 . . . is the first time that the word *universitas* is attested as a description for the collected academic world in Bologna. Perhaps this date can be regarded as the birthday of the universities, though this is a slightly misleading interpretation, as there was nothing special in the word *universitas*. This was a purely technical term taken from the doctrine of corporations in Roman law. . . . It has no special ideological content and is used quite neutrally of the total mass of teachers and students at the Bologna law schools. It was only much later that the word acquired a specially philosoph-

ical meaning: in the middle ages *studium generale* was and remained the official term of the university" (Pedersen 144–45).

20. "Certain doctrines of Aristotle's writings did not harmonize with Christian revelation: namely, his judgments concerning the eternity of the world, the immortality of the soul . . . and, lastly his concept of a Supreme Being who took little account of the world and the men in it. . . . Perhaps for reasons like [these], the bishops of the dioceses near [the university of] Paris met in a local synod and decided to forbid 'books of Aristotle on natural philosophy . . . .' " Yet the 1255 curriculum of Paris "was very heavily weighted in favor of Aristotle. The very books forbidden by the provincial synod some forty years before now formed part of the ordinary lecture materials" (Daly 82–83). On the Europeanness of Aristotle, Nicolas Bakhtin had to say: "Europe was always essentially Aristotelian. Also it still is in so far as it remains truly Europe" (qtd. in Botz-Bornstein 179–80).

21. "Crusader, linguist, philosopher, ornithologist, patron of the arts, protector of Jews, and master of a harem, Fredrick II was twice excommunicated by the Pope for disobedience and officially condemned by a General Council as a heretic. He ruled in the south as a despot, imposing an efficient, centralized administration on Church and State alike. He even encouraged an imperial cult of his own person. He presided over a brilliant, cultured court at Palermo—a magnificent blend of Latin, German, Jewish, Greek, and Saracen elements. To his contemporaries he was quite simply the *stupor mundi*, the 'wonder of the age' " (Davies 351).

22. Hay talks instead of a "confusion" between Christendom and Europe: "From 1400 to 1700, and in certain areas and contexts perhaps beyond this terminus, the new unity was confounded with the old" (96).

23. "In Abraham Ortelius's *Thesaurus geographicus* (1578) we have a telling entry under the word 'Christiani': 'vide Europaei' " (Hay 109).

24. One should keep in mind, however, that a difference between name and adjective may not have been perceived with the same intensity by Enea Silvio as it is by us. Fourteenth- and fifteenth-century grammars (Thomas of Erfurt, Nicholas Perotti, Aldo Manuzio, Antonio de Nebrija) see the *nomen adiectivum* as a mere modal variation of *nomen substantivum*. A real separation between the two classes of words will not be achieved until the eighteenth century (see Scarano 12).

25. What becomes increasingly inaccurate to maintain, as *Europe (in Theory)* intends to show, is that there is such a thing as a Romano-Germanic unity of Europe: "The Romano-Germanic world was itself by no means homogeneous. Differences arising from their different backgrounds had deeply marked the various societies of which it was composed. Yet, however pronounced these differences may have been, how can we fail to recognize,

over and above them, the predominant quality of a common civilization—that of the West?" (Bloch, *Feudal* xx). Such a theorization of Europe as "the West," which relies on the bracketing away of differences between north and south in the name of a "predominant" yet indemonstrable "quality of a common civilization," is exactly what *Europe (in Theory)* means to question, looking instead at the crisis between north and south in the theorization of Europe.

26. The quotation marks hope to indicate my relative position regarding the use of the term *discovery* as it is applied to America: more explicitly, I stand between Edmundo O'Gorman, who suggests that *discovery* is a misleading term since "Indians" already knew the continent quite well, and Alphonse Dupront, who reevaluates the term *discovery* as the necessary European false consciousness that could legitimate and even entail conquest.

27. According to Federico Chabod, Machiavelli's would be "the first formulation of Europe as a community which has distinctive features beyond mere geography, with characteristics that are purely 'earthly,' 'secular,' nonreligious" (48).

28. Whereas previous ages had not privileged a single orientation for their maps, the north was now definitely "up" in *all* European maps, as "the result of historical process, closely connected with the global rise and economic dominance of northern Europe" (Turnbull 8).

29. On the small size of Europe, already Pierre de Ronsard had noticed that "L'Europe est trop petite" (Europe is too small) (1:299).

30. "Historians . . . have tended to pay little attention to what Marx regarded as the second major source of primary accumulation, namely, colonial plunder. Such indifference is unfortunate; for it is not possible to imagine how a credible history of capitalism can be reconstructed without comprehending colonialism . . . the Spanish mining of silver with forced labour in the Americas; the forcible transfer of millions of Africans as slaves across the Atlantic; and the levying of tribute on Asian shipping and land. England came in time to be the major beneficiary from all these three practically simultaneous processes of forcible subjugation and destruction of non-European economies" (Habib 21).

31. As a persona, Europe also had *one* story to tell, and *one* history to unfold: "The sixteenth century also marked the beginning of an endless series of histories of Europe leading off with the Florentine Pier Francesco Giambullari's *Historia dell'Europa* (1566) and the Spanish Alfonso Ulloa's *Historia de Europa* (1570)" (Mikkeli 41).

32. Lusitania was the old Roman province comprising today's Portugal and part of Spain.

33. "The point of this contrast—which from every point of view is extreme—lies surely in the nature of the Dutch achievement: its entirely practical

nature. And this in turn brings to mind its overwhelmingly prosaic character; beginning with sieges and dikes and ending with sermons and paintings.
'Prose' is not a term of contempt or denigration: there can be a poetry of
prose. But consider; is it even imaginable that this society should, like Spain,
produce a picaresque novel? (In 1600 Amsterdam is indignantly suppressing
vagrancy, if necessary, by shutting up the offenders.) Or a Don Quixote?
There are no two ways about it; there is no context in the life of the Dutch
Republic in which Don Quixote, with his strain of lofty and pathetic ideal-
ism as well as his ridicule, could have a meaning in relation to perceived reality around Holland: whether in his capacity as the socially aimless, crazed
hidalgo subject to endless delusion (forget the unfamiliarity with windmills)
or as a symptom of some deep cultural want" (Lehmann 166).

34. Since then, "the cardinal problem in defining Europe has centered on
the inclusion or exclusion of Russia" (Davies 3).

35. Also Curzio Malaparte sees the Reformation as the crisis dividing
north and south that begins modern Europe: "The Reformation is not the
birth of a critical modern spirit proper of Western and Northern civilizations, but the separation of such spirit from catholic dogmatism, which
belongs instead to Eastern and Southern civilizations, and which is the
essence of Latin civilization. When these two contrary tendencies finally
separate, and when the former escapes the control of the latter, and becomes
in turn the hegemonic one, what happens is a crisis. The history of Europe is
contained, in its entirety, in this irreconcilable contrast" (358–59).

36. In 1642, the French statesman Demarets de Saint-Sorlin had dramatized a similar line of thought in his play *Europe*: "*Europe* was not a successful play, but it is none the less symptomatic that a statesman should interest
himself in propagating his hostility to Spain (the 'Ibere' of the play) in terms
which some generations earlier would have seemed purely mythological.
'Europe', the princess, is full of concern for all her children (and it is stressed
that all the nations are of common stock) but chooses to be defended by
'Francion.' It was a programme of a European peace in which peace would
be kept by an alert and powerful, but beneficent and disinterested, France"
(Hay 119).

37. Ideas of peaceable federations, in fact, go well beyond the chronological limits I suggest: already Dante, in *De Monarchia* (1308), had for instance
theorized the possibility of a unity of different principalities under the *prin-
ceps unicus*, the pope. At the other end of my chronology, Winston Churchill
and Franklin D. Roosevelt made some references to Sully (Rougemont 93),
and their project of an Atlantic Charter was explicitly inspired, at the end of
World War II, by Sully's one for perpetual peace. The European Union,
fantasized by and realized in the Treaty of Rome (Savinio), is another fruit
growing in Sully's plant.

38. According to Paul Hazard, however, the east retained a fundamental role as the antithesis of Europe and the mirror of her identity: "Of all those regions which competed for her [Europe's] attention, she responded most readily to the East. It was an East gravely distorted by the European view of it; nevertheless, it retained enough of its original impressiveness to loom forth as a vast agglomeration of non-Christian values" (*European Mind* 28).

39. This reevaluation of the Greek and Roman past was part of a more general trend: "The seventeenth century also saw a departure from established cultural patterns. Knowledge of some Greek, but particularly Latin, continued to be required in all schools above the primary level, but little writing was done in Latin after 1600 except in international law, natural science and Roman Catholic theology. . . . Outside the academy, new approaches in science began to emphasize empiricism and induction, rather than the essentially deductive reasoning that the earlier religious orientation of education had required. . . . Even in literature the ancients were revered more in terms of themselves and as adornments of an educated person than as practical guides, and they certainly had little impact on creative activity" (Nicholas 430).

40. To complicate the whole matter, Europe was not only the end of history but also, more often than not, its beginning: a new interest in the chronology of world epochs (Hazard, *European Mind* 41–48) began, with a clear intention to disprove the claims, supported by Egyptology and sinology, that Chinese and Egyptian societies were not only older than European ones but even older than the three thousand years proposed by the Bible as the age of post-Flood civilizations. For the most complete treatment of these chronological controversies, see Paolo Rossi's work. For the ways in which the claimed anteriority of Europe vis-à-vis the so-called New World legitimated, in turn, claims of Europe's (colonial) superiority, see Antonello Gerbi.

2 Montesquieu's North and South

1. A more recent return of the atavist theory can be found in Banfield; Putnam, Leonardi and Nanetti; and Fukuyama. It must be kept in mind, however, that 1870 is the year of Italy's unification: as north and aouth are united, in theory, for the first time, theory starts articulating internal differences and disunities.

2. Similarly, Benjamin Disraeli notices the "legacy of oriental sires" still remnant in Mediterranean Europe (Pemble 146).

3. The inspiration of the Argentinean criminal code of 1921, Enrico Ferri's *Sociologia criminale* (1884) argued for the necessity to couple punitive mea-

sures with preventive ones: among these, physical education was a remedy for crime.

4. Already in a public lecture to the Academy delivered on August 25, 1720, titled "Of the Causes for the Transparency of Bodies," Montesquieu had been clear about the ineptitude of the Greeks in tackling the most serious problems facing modern science: "At first sight, it would seem as if Aristotle knew what transparency was, since he defined light as *the act of transparency as transparency*; in truth, however, he knew nothing of either transparency or light" (*Oeuvres* 1:27). And in the *Pensées* (number 1458), he wrote: "The majority of the ancients' reasonings are not exact" (1:1345).

5. Trying to open a trading route with the east, Jean Baptiste Colbert had failed, first, to found a colony in Madagascar. He had managed, instead, to establish ports in Bourbon and Île-de-France (now Réunion and Mauritius), but by 1719, despite such success, the French Eastern Company was already near bankruptcy. The company would finally be dissolved in 1769, when it was clear to everybody that it was unfruitful to maintain.

6. In fact, a look at book 8, chapters 15–20, also informs us of the political and social dangers of territorial expansions. Prefacing the discussion with the assertion that "I cannot be understood until you have read the four chapters that follow" (2:362), Montesquieu tells his reader that "a small territory" is more proper to a republic, and an "average extension" to a monarchy. Only despotism can guard over huge territories: "Do not even think to counteract my argument by mentioning Spain here; Spain only proves what I have already said. To control America, it did worse than despotism itself: it destroyed the inhabitants" (2:362–64). And despotism, as we know, is not a properly European form of government.

7. The war of the Spanish succession (1701–14) was precipitated in 1700 by the death of King Charles II of Spain, the last of the Spanish Hapsburgs. Charles II had died without heirs and had named the grandson of King Louis XIV of France, Philip, as his successor. The prospect of united Spain and France led Britain to form an alliance with the Austrian Hapsburgs and to declare war on France and Spain.

8. In C. B. Macpherson's more skeptical understanding of the issue of property limits, "Locke's astonishing achievement was to base the property right on natural right [nature's fruits are originally given by God to man] and natural law [man needs to appropriate nature for his living], and then to remove all the natural law limits from the property right" (199). This elimination of all limits, which would open the alley, theoretically speaking, to capitalist accumulation, would be done not only by claiming the supposedly vacant lands of the Americas but also by the introduction of money: as "gold and silver do not spoil; a man may therefore rightfully accumulate unlimited

amounts of it" (204). On these issues, see also Tully, "Aboriginal Property" 58-62; and, including a discussion of the limits and legacy of Macpherson, Tully, *Approach* 71–136.

9. Although Montesquieu is correct here, and although, by 1830, three quarters of European commerce is in fact intercontinental, it can be noticed, against Montesquieu, that the products from the colonies provide a very substantial, and economically integral, part of eighteenth-century inter-European commerce (see Goodman and Honeyman 53).

10. Also the "Causes that Can Affect the Spirit" insists on this division of Europe: "In our Europe, there are two kinds of religions: the Catholic one, which demands submission, and the Protestant one, which wants independence. The peoples of the north have embraced Protestantism from the beginning; those of the south have defended Catholicism" (Montesquieu, *Oeuvres* 2:62).

11. Etymologically, the word *Sirocco* connects the south with the east again: according to the *Oxford English Dictionary*, *Sirocco* derives from the Arab *sharq*, east—the same root for the word *Saracen*. Under this wind, southern Europe is "Saracen."

12. On how much that "almost" could cover, interpreters have fervidly fought: criticizing R. N. Stromberg's indictment of "Montesquieu's monstrous and historically barren error in attributing all human differences to geographic environment," Roger B. Oake has, for instance, stressed that "even 'savages' are stated only to be *almost* entirely dominated by 'climate' " (59; original emphasis).

13. "In the last analysis, only Europe seems to know the mutability of time. . . . Here's Europe, then: a geographical and historical space" (Goldzink 145).

14. Originating from Isocrates (see chapter 1), the commonplace of the coincidence of the history of Europe with a history of freedom is central, for instance, in François Guizot. In the *Cours d'histoire moderne* (see Verga 38–47), a series of lessons he gave at the Sorbonne in 1828, the palimpsest of Montesquieu is clearly visible: France is the center of Europe because it is its most modern and progressed nation; France's progress, which is central to European progress, is the progress of freedom, which coincides with a modernization of the law (and a progressive privatization of natural resources). As we will see in chapter 4, also German historiography and philosophy—from the Schlegel brothers to Hegel—makes Europe coincide with a concept of freedom. Against Montesquieu and Guizot's faith in progress—as progress of continuous civilization—the Schlegels and Hegel seem to think in terms of destiny: it is the destiny of Europe to realize freedom.

15. Jacob Grimm's *Deutsche Grammatik* (1819–37) had not only confirmed the derivation of French from Latin but also its fundamental un-

Germanness: whereas Germanic languages, in the course of their evolution, had seen the transformation (the so-called Grimm's Law) of unvoiced consonants (*p, t, k*) into their aspirate equivalents (*ph, th, kh*), French instead, along with the other Romance languages, had remained extraneous to such changes. Latin *pater* had, for instance, changed to the German *Vater* and the English *father*; but in Romance languages, there had been no shift from the *p* to the *ph* sound: there was the French *père*, the Italian and Spanish *padre*, and the Portuguese *pai*. With Grimm's Law, the destiny of French southernness, of its belonging to an un-German Romance margin, would for ever be sealed. Montesquieu's German aspirations, however, had absolutely no premonition of all this.

16. "The individual, it was thought, is free inasmuch as he is proprietor of his person and capacities. The human essence is freedom from dependence on the will of others, and freedom is a function of possession. . . . Society consists of relations of exchange between proprietors. Political society becomes a calculated device for the protection of this property and for the maintainance of an orderly relation of exchange" (Macpherson 3).

3   Republics of Letters

1. The *Encyclopédie*, which would soon start defining a whole epoch, had started as the simple idea of the printer André Le Breton to translate Chambers's English *Cyclopedia* into French. Denis Diderot, nominated by Le Breton as the editor in chief for the project, transformed the original idea, with the help of D'Alembert and Jaucourt, into a more ambitious attempt at creating a true synopsis of knowledge. The seventeen volumes of the *Encyclopédie*, which were distributed and read throughout most of Europe, were published between 1751 and 1772; supplements were added in 1777 and 1780. The initial subscription for the text counted five thousand people.

2. However, already in the "Discours sur les motifs qui doivent nous encourager aux sciences" (1725), Montesquieu had argued that Europe's difference from savagery (in the specific case, America) consisted in the fact that Europe had (European) arts and sciences, whereas savage nations did not (*Oeuvres* 1:53).

3. Such a linguistic shift certainly fit well the nationalist ambitions, for instance, of Gallican Protestantism. It also reflected, as Mark Painter has pointed out, a profound crisis of traditional linguistics, most notably, the Augustinian faith in a coincidence between Word and World, between sign and thing. In this sense, "The very question of knowledge seems already caught up in the dynamics of language" (6). The belief of pre-Lutheran theology is that the word, as possessed by humankind, is a reflection of God's order—or, in the terms of classical philosophy, of *logos*. A word carries with

it an ontological significance. The word not only brings humankind closer to God but it also offers a way of knowing God's creation as *logos*. Humankind finds itself in an ordered cosmos, and language, separating humankind from nature, gives access to and knowledge of that order. But since, in Lutheran theology, God's order is ultimately unknowable, language, the guarantor of such knowledge, loses its privileged position. Incapable of accessing the theologized *logos*, language remains bound to knowing only earthly matters. Neither Latin nor Greek or Hebrew are thus any way closer to knowing the will of God. National languages, at least, have the advantage of knowing the will of the state!

4. Curricular changes suggested by D'Alembert in the entry "Collège" for the encyclopedia included: "Close study of French grammar; substitution of French for Latin composition, since study of Latin is for the single purpose of reading the texts of great authors; introduction of foreign language into the curriculum; development of history courses, a study that should be done *à rebours*, that is to say with the contemporary period as the point of departure (an idea that D'Alembert considers 'very just and philosophical'); precedence of philosophy over rhetoric, 'for, after all, one must learn to think before one writes'; moral instruction based on Seneca, Epictetus, and the Sermon of the Mount; early training in geometry and experiments in physics" (Mortier 65). For a concise summary of Cartesian modern education, exemplified in the *Logique de Port-Royal*, see Perkinson. On the reformation of European schools to meet the requirement of usefullness, the institution of curricula in engineering, accounting, and modern medicine, see Hof 215–16.

5. "[After the decision] people say the Pope is haunted by visions. People say he strolls around the Papal rooms, screaming he has been forced to sign the decree of suppression: 'Compulsus feci! Compulsus feci!' He suffers a herpes that deforms his face . . . . After a long agony, he dies on September 22, 1774. Rumor has it that he has been poisoned . . . . Obviously, the assassins are the Jesuits" (Del Rio 145).

6. It may be a stretch, especially when compared to the nearby and arguably more lively Milan where Cesare Beccaria had published *Of Crime and Punishment* (1764) under the influence of *De l'esprit des lois*; where the Verri brothers had disseminated the ideas of the French Enlightenment through the journal *Il caffè* (1764–66); and where Giuseppe Parini had begun to divulge his antiaristocratic sentiments in the *Gazzetta di Milano* since 1769. At any rate, the historian Carlo Denina, in *Le rivoluzioni d'Italia* (1793), compared the Mantua of Andrés and Bettinelli to the cultural wealth of Weimar: "where Wieland, Goethe, Herder, and Berthuch live" (qtd. in Carpanetto and Ricuperati 393).

7. Mantua had become a safe haven for many exiled Jesuits, including

Andrés's archenemy Esteban Arteaga. Andrés, however, did not pursue a career in state education, and, more traditionally, became preceptor of the Marquis Bianchi's family (the stipend being supplemented by a pension still coming from Madrid). Andrés studied mostly in the Bianchis' library, and, through the marquis, he got to know, in quite typical Italian fashion, the Mantua that counts, which introduced him to a membership in the local Accademia Reale di Scienze e Belle Lettere.

8. "Differently from what happened in France, where the *philosophes* formed, although not without internal contrasts, a front opposed to government, the academics of Milan . . . starting with Pietro Verri, devoted their entire careers to public office, and collaborated with the government to implement reforms" (Bonora 97).

9. "Therefore, we declare that we did not dare facing all alone a task bigger than our own strengths. Our role as editors has then consisted merely in giving order to the materials in great part provided by others" (D'Alembert) 75.

10. An eighth volume was added to the 1785 Parma edition (printed by Bodoni); it is the one on which I am basing this study. For a history of the text's various editions and translations, see Mazzeo 78–79, 194–96.

11. "Regarding *literature* in eighteenth-century literary historiography, it is a known fact that the term was understood in the pre-modern sense, as a term whose meaning covered the entirety of human knowledge in written form, and not only the belles letters" (Valero 171).

12. "The discipline of comparative literature . . . is unthinkable without the historical circumstances of exile" (Apter 86). Also: "It does not seem casual . . . that the first contemporary scholar of what he calls 'the Andrés case', is an exile of the last civil war, Francisco Giner de los Rios" (Palazón 16).

13. "Jesuit and other missionary activities raised two problems to which Europe was very alive even at the end of the eighteenth century. One of these problems was how to reconcile a new religion [Christianity] with a traditional culture. This led men like De Nobili to identify themselves totally with the local culture. They recognized the differences between the two cultures and the danger of asking the Indians to give up their way of life while embracing a new religion. This was perhaps the first understanding, however vague it might have been, of the problems of imposing one culture upon another" (Mukherjee 10).

14. Wellek's resistance to Andrés can be easily explained through Wellek's aporetic resistance to historicism, which, as I will discuss in a moment, is the very basis of Andrés's method. For Wellek's hostility to history, and for his notion of the work of art as "monument, not document," see Wellek, "Review" 254–55.

15. Already in 1939, Robert Palmer warned the scholar of the eighteenth

century about seeing "two distinct groups . . . pitted against each other, a group of *philosophes* who favored new and enlightened ideas and another group, mostly clerical and frequently Jesuit, who stood directly across the path of intellectual development. This view of the matter is essentially that of the *philosophes* themselves" ("French Jesuits" 44). The kind of opposition to enlightenment I am arguing here is in no way an obscurantist maneuver, but a chapter in the readjustment of the idea of Europe that included also, but not exclusively, those who had remained faithful to the Roman Church.

16. In 1969, Benjamin Keen complained: "References to the Black Legend almost invariably proclaim foreign rivals' envy of Spain's American riches and their desire to take over the empire as the principal reasons for the creation and diffusion of the Legend." This amounted, for Keen, to absolving Spain from its historical actions in the Americas, whereas other, and more authentic reasons, were behind the fortune of the Black Legend: alongside imperial interests, also "nationalist aspirations and religious and other ideological conflicts with Spain of the Counter-Reformation, sometimes even an authentic humanitarianism . . . all played their part" (713–14). Without absolving Spain, and without questioning "authentic humanitarianism," I would, however, insist on the weight imperial designs had in the spread of the legend.

17. Since my English spell-checker keeps flagging *historism*, let me move to *historicism* by first reminding my reader that only by the 1940s the latter term, fashioned after Benedetto Croce's Italian *storicismo*, started competing with, and finally replacing, the former, inherited instead by the German historiographical tradition of *Historismus*.

18. Abdesselam Cheddadi insists on the Europeanness of history—and the instrumental way in which the Islamic *ta'rikh* is often translated as "history" only to establish a comparison whereby the Eastern *ta'rikh* would appear as faulty history. See Ibn Khaldun and Cheddadi. For Giovanna Calasso, who draws from Cheddadi, a supplementary difference between *ta'rikh* and an eminently European sense of historiography consists in the fact that in "the '*ta'rikh*' by Arab authors, we find no trace of the concept of 'universal history'" (205).

19. Georg Iggers (who sees the emergence of historicism in Friedrich Schlegel's 1797 "Of Philology") similarly claims that historicism had introduced in the analysis of human events an "orientation which recognized individuality in its 'concrete temporal-spatiality' . . . distinct from a fact-oriented empiricism," as well as from an objective Cartesian reason (130).

20. Viconian is for instance Andrés's claim (*Dell' origine* 1:1) that poetry (not reason or philosophy) is the first language: "The first writings that came to us from antiquity are historical and poetical, not philosophical." Also in

tune with Vico is the attempt to "diminish" the alleged antiquity of some non-European cultures—Chinese, Egyptian—to some kind of national pride (1:3–4), what Vico had called "boria delle nazioni." On some of these points in Vico, see Dainotto.

21. "When, in the second half of the eighteenth century, one advocates a 'philosophical perspective,' what is meant by the term implies, in general, the defense of the new critical method, from which a complete vision of all knowledge can be built. . . The new literary history, in its attempt to give a totalizing and integrated view of all knowledge, coincides then with en-cyclopedism" (Valero 183–84). On the opposition between philosophical method and erudite method in the context of eighteenth-century literary historiography, see Guglielminetti 14–15.

22. Another Spanish Jesuit in Italian exile, Francisco J. Llampillas, had already devoted to the anti-Gallic and pro-Spanish cause the volumes of his *Saggio storico apologetico della lettratura spagnola* (1778–81), another exam-ple of Italian Jesuit literary historiography.

23. On Andrés's albeit partial and tentative reevaluation of Russia as part of Europe, see Bérkov 461–69.

24. As late as 1942, Provençal poetry still defined Europe. During the Congress of the European Youth, held in Vienna in that year, Baldur von Schirach spoke: "The song that once upon a time filled the valleys of Prov-ence; that same song that is today the triumphal song of Europe and its civilization; the song of the troubadours as expression of those superior sentiments that distinguish us from the Jews and from Black American's jazz—that song is something that the Jewish mind will never be able to understand" (qtd. in Lipgens 103).

25. That the French liked to claim a French origin for everything was a fact that Andrés really took at heart to dispute time and again. As if the question of poetry and the *roman* were not enough, also the invention of a language for deaf-mutes had been claimed by the French for their Abbée Apée. An-drés, however, could not let the lie pass and explained to the whole world who the real (and un-French) inventor was (see Andrés, *Lettera dell'origine*).

26. "The influence of Arab culture was so pervasive that it was hardly nec-essary to leave Occitania to hear the melodies of Andalusia and Arabia. Much of southern France had been conquered by Moslem invaders in the mid-eighth century. Although the Saracens, as they were called, did not maintain their hold for long, they left their mark in place names, and, undoubtedly, in the folk imagination. Toward the end of the eleventh century refugees from southern Spain began to settle in the area of Nîmes and Montpellier, bringing Arabic and Arab culture once again to Occitania" (Bogin 46).

27. Barbieri's is the often-cited book, incidentally, that Girolamo Tira-

boschi reprints in Modena in 1790, in the midst of the Arabist polemics, with the new programmatic title *Dell'origine della poesia rimata*. On this, and the general controversy, see Eusebi.

28. Wilkins would later retract his theory of the invention of the sonnet by claiming, arguably not very convincingly, that the idea of the sextet came to the Sicilian Giacomo from Lentini in a burst of sheer inspiration. See Wilkins, *Invention of the Sonnet* 35.

4 Mme de Staël to Hegel

For the quite adventurous biography of Mme de Staël (interesting but beyond the scope of this chapter), see Balayé; Diesbach; and Winegarten.

5 Orientalism, Mediterranean Style

1. Said himself, however, found in Raymond Schwab's writing "the avoidance of ethno- and anthropocentric attitudes" and "an interest in oriental literature for its own sake" (Schwab xv). It is hard, on the other hand, not to see *Orientalism*'s point. A collusion of knowledge and power in that discipline was certainly not lost, for one, on the founder of the British Asiatic Society, William Jones, who wrote in 1771: "Since a variety of causes which need not be mentioned here give the English nation a most extensive power in that kingdom [India] . . . the languages of Asia will now perhaps be studied with uncommon ardour . . . the limits of our knowledge [will be] no less extended than the bounds of our empire" (qtd. in Mukherjee 80). Also, Italian fascism did not miss the nexus of colonialsm and Orientalism. Discussing Italy and the Orient in the Florentine *Fascist Studies*, Carlo Capasso wrote in 1932: "The Great Powers have always had stakes in the Orient. It is therefore natural that, in all the major European countries, a voluminous literature on the Orient has been produced. . . Italy has come last in this interest for the Orient" (v–vi). For a panorama of reactions to Said, see Marrouchi 210–14.

2. Lest my point is mistaken for a simplistic variation on the National Rifle Association theme that "it's not guns that kill," let me drop a more theoretically appropriate allusion to Antonio Gramsci's discussion of Caesarism, which "can be both progressive and reactionary" (Gramsci, *Selections* 217).

3. "To hail revolution while avoiding censorship" is revealed to be, a posteriori, in a preface of 1851, the very program, and problem, of Michele Amari's first historical book (*Guerra* xxvi).

4. "History needs heroes of ideas as well" (Amari, *Guerra* 2:323). Accordingly, this chapter assumes a fundamental discrepancy between Amari's deeds and ideas: whereas his deeds move from initial positions of radical

democracy to the moderate Cavourism of his later years, his ideas grow toward a rather heroic opening of the very concept of Europe.

5. These included the financial support of the fatherless family, which meant, in turn, a humiliating clerical job for the Bourbon secretary of state that put thirty-five monthly ducats into Amari's pockets—barely enough for "a piece of bread" (Bonfigli 3).

6. "The gift is . . . something that must be given, that must be received and that is, at the same time, dangerous to accept" (Mauss 215).

7. "The feeling of veneration for the past, which in the pages of Hume and Gibbon had already become value and meaning of national history, was given by Scott all the power of imagination" (Romeo, "Michele Amari" 160).

8. So, for instance, Alessandro D'Ancona sees *Marmion* as a gift of love to the unreciprocating Agatina Peranni, while Renata Pucci Zanca views it as a vague hymn to heroism to compensate for the father's cowardice. See Amari, *Carteggio* 315–97; Pucci Zanca 254–55.

9. For those interested in biographical details, there is actually a little mystery concerning Amari's personal knowledge of Dumas before 1842. At any rate, it is certain that in 1842 Amari held Dumas in such consideration as to send him a copy of his new book. See Marcolongo 66n.

10. Indebted to the style of Scott and Dumas, Amari's story is also strikingly similar to the Arab humanists' notion of *akhbar*, or narrative history, as opposed to chronology history, or *ta'rikh*. For Arab humanists and scholastics, "*akhbar*-history is . . . one of the three divisions under prose composition, along with applied rhetoric, i. e. letter-writing and speech-writing" (Makdisi 170).

11. Amari alludes later to the commonplace (and historic problem) of Sicily as "eternal colony": "From early histories to recent ones, many foreign peoples came to walk on the soil of Sicily: Carthaginians, Vandals, Goths, Byzantines, Germans, French, Spaniards. . ." (*Storia* 1:105). The citation of a pathetic Sicilian prince is at this point de rigueur: "We are old, Chevalley, very old. For more than twenty-five centuries we've been bearing the weight of many superb and heterogeneous civilizations, all from outside, none made by ourselves, none that we could call our own. We are as white as you are, Chevalley, and as the Queen of England; and yet for two thousand and five hundred years we've been a colony" (Tomasi di Lampedusa 170).

12. The parallelisms between the insurrection of the vesper and the failed one of 1820 had already been established in Michele Palmieri's 1834 *Customs of the Court and the People of the Two Sicilies*, published in French in Paris. See Giarrizzo.

13. "Nationalism usually conquers in the name of a putative folk culture. Its symbolism is drawn from the healthy, pristine, vigorous life of the peasants, of the Volk" (Gellner 57).

14. In this, one can detect Amari's skepticism regarding the usefulness of secret plots in revolutionary action—and a very direct attack against the underground sects of Freemasons and *carbonari*, who, in Amari's mind, were usurping the people's historical place.

15. Hints of that can be found in Leonardo Sciascia: "And I must say that, of all the reasons he [Amari] offers against the theory of the courtly plot. . . the most convincing remains the one he adduces as a Sicilian who know Sicilians" (979).

16. Also Said identifies the nexus freedom-Europe as "an idea that will acquire [after the Crusades, and climaxing in Chateaubriand] an almost unbearable, next to mindless authority in European writing: the theme of Europe teaching the Orient the meaning of liberty" (*Orientalism* 172).

17. "The passion with which native intellectuals defend the existence of their national cultures may be a source of amazement; but those who condemn this exaggerated passion are strangely apt to forget that their own psyche and their own selves are conveniently sheltered behind a French or German [or British] culture which has given full proof of its existence and which is uncontested" (Fanon 209). "Before Said, Fanon, his *maître à penser*, recognized that in the triangular dialogue between the settler, the native, and the native intellectual, there is 'a prominent confrontation on the phantasmatic plane.' Versions of origins are offered and resisted in a continuing dialectic" (Marrouchi 288).

18. Back to Gramsci's Caesarism. Like it, *sicilianismo* "can be both progressive and reactionary" (Gramsci, *Selections* 217). On "reactionary" and "progressive" *sicilianismo*, see Marcolongo 9.

19. Amari was, however, more cautious when writing for a French public: "Sicily is the only Italian state which has possessed for a long time this form of monarchic and representative government that is called today 'constitutional.' The Sicilian people has been the first in Italy to use this word, 'constitution,' rather than the more abstract 'reform.'" (*Quelques observations* 1).

20. As Giuseppe Mazzini put it in 1852: "The literature of Europe in the last few years has been largely political, revolutionary, made for war. Out of ten historical works, seven at least discussed, whether favorably or not, of a realized or an unfinished revolution; out of ten polemical, economical, or political works, no less than seven welcome or reject the symptoms of an imminent revolution" (*Opere* 2:541).

21. As in Alessandro Manzoni's authentic horror of diversity: "Haven't you heard, great and good Lamartine, that there is no worse word to throw at Italy than diversity? And that this word only reminds Italy of a long time of suffering and decay?" (qtd. in Bollati 61).

22. On the French "genius of the market," an ironic variation on the theme of the genius of the French language mentioned in chapter 2, Giuseppe

Mazzini wrote: "French intelligence creates little, but assimilates a lot; led by a manufacturing instinct, it always receives its raw materials from abroad. Quick, agile, active, and full of self confidence; naturally inclined to monopoly, and helped by a clear and distinct language, the French genius takes ideas, embellishes them, and puts them into circulation. Often, to make things easier, French intelligence dismembers ideas, reduces them into little fragments. . . In all this lies the life and the importance of the French genius" (*Opere* 2:552). I should mention, without meaning by this a dismissal of the Italian anti-French polemics as simply fascist, that much of this fervor against France, which is also a redimensioning of the French Revolution as the event that changed the world forever, will become central in Italian fascism's understanding of its own (alleged) revolution.

23. On January 12, the birthday of King Ferdinand II, the Sicilian revolution takes Palermo, then all of Sicily. Once again, the requests are for autonomy and a constitution. The insurrection soon moves to the Italian mainland, and then to France, Austria, Hungary, and Germany. Ferdinand's bombing of Messina and Palermo earned him the nickname of King Bomba, by which he is known in the annals of American literature (Melville).

24. On the problems Amari had to face because of his anticlericalism, see Carino 279. For a sample of Amari's anticlericalism, the following: "Everybody knows that the curia is not an aristocracy, but the fattest part of the middle and lower bourgeoisie" (*Biblioteca* 1:324–25).

25. Like Vico's "giants," Amari's early Arabs "They are tall, robust, lean, pure caucasian visages, moderate beard, strong teeth, self-assured, penetrating eyes" (Amari, *Storia* 1:141).

26. Mostly from the Aghlabid families from Kairouan (in today's Tunisia), it is unclear who these Arabs really were, or from where they came. They were probably a coalition coming from different places, including Africa (Berbers as well), Spain, and Asia. Also, their social extraction was quite varied. From around the year 948, the rule of the Sicilian colony goes to the Kalbite families from Syria (and possibly of Yemeni descent).

27. On the Arabic derivation of troubadoric poetry and of the very word *troubadour*, see Menocal "Close Encounters."

28. On the "xenophoby" of French nationalism, see Vovelle (18–19). At this point of his narrative, however, Amari had to bracket away the way in which Christians and Sicilians did not enjoy, in fact, equal rights in Muslim Sicily: non-Muslims were, as Amari will acknowledge only in the last chapters of the *Storia*, "protected persons" (*dhimmi*), "barred from enjoying some crucial liberties that are available to Muslims" according to a strict interpretation of Islamic law (Moosa 202).

29. " Terrible and perhaps unnecessary right" was property right for Beccaria (71).

30. "The living legacy of Sacy's disciples was astounding. Every major Arabist in Europe during the nineteenth century traced his intellectual authority back to him. Universities and academies in France, Spain, Norway, Sweden, Denmark, and especially Germany were dotted with the students who formed themselves at his feet" (Said, *Orientalism* 129).

Works Cited

Abrahamian, Evrand. "Oriental Despotism: The Case of Qajar Iran." *International Journal of Middle East Studies* 5.1 (1974): 3–31.

Abu-Lughod, Ibrahim A. *Arab Rediscovery of Europe: A Study in Cultural Encounters*. Princeton, NJ: Princeton University Press, 1963.

Adorno, Theodor W. *Minima Moralia: Reflections from Damaged Life*. Trans. E. F. W. Jephcott. London: Verso, 1978.

Agamben, Giorgio. *Infanzia e storia: Distruzione dell'esperienza e origine della storia*. 2nd ed. Turin: Einaudi, 2001.

——. *Stanze. La parola e il fantasma nella cultura occidentale*. Turin: Einaudi, 1977.

Ahmad, Aijaz. *In Theory: Classes, Nations, Literatures*. London: Verso, 1992.

Ali, Tariq. *The Clash of Fundamentalisms: Crusades, Jihads, and Modernity*. London: Verso, 2002.

Alianello, Carlo. *La conquista del sud: Il Risorgimento nell'Italia meridionale*. 1972. Milan: Rusconi, 1994.

Althusser, Louis. *Montesquieu: La politique et l'histoire*. Paris: Presses Universitaires de France, 1959.

Amari, Michele. *Appunti autobiografici*. Palermo: Fondo Michele Amari.

——. *Biblioteca arabo-sicula, ossia Raccolta di testi arabiciche toccano la geografia, la storia, le biografie e la bibliografia della Sicilia*. Leipzig: F. A. Brockhaus, 1857.

——. *Carteggio di Michele Amari, raccolto e postillato coll'elogio di lui, letto nell'Accademia della Crusca*. Ed. Alessandro D'Ancona. 3 vols. Turin: Roux Frassati, 1896.

——. *La guerra del vespro siciliano*. 9th ed. 3 vols. Milan: Hoepli, 1886.

——. *Il mio terzo esilio*. Palermo: Fondo Michele Amari.

——. *Quelques observations sur le droit public de la Sicile*. Paris: 1848.

——. *Storia dei musulmani di Sicilia*. 4 vols. Florence: F. Le Monnier, 1854.

Amari, Michele, and Niccolò Palmeri. Introduction to *Saggio storico e politico sulla costituzione del regno di Sicilia infino al 1816 con un'appendice sulla rivoluzione del 1820*. Lausanne: Francesco Carini, 1848.

Amartya, Sen. "Democracy as a Universal Value." *Journal of Democracy* 10.3 (1999): 3–17.

Ammendola, Teresa, and Pierangelo Isernia. "L'Europa vista dagli italiani: I primi vent'anni." *L'Europa in Italia: Élite, opinione pubblica e decisioni.* Ed. Maurizio Cotta, Isernia, and Luca Verzichelli. Bologna: Il Mulino, 2005. 117–69.

Anderson, Benedict. *Imagined Communities: Reflections on the Origin and Spread of Nationalism.* London: Verso, 1983.

Anderson, Perry. *Lineages of the Absolutist State.* 1974. London: Verso, 1979.

Andrés, Juan. *Carta al Sig. Commendatore Fra Gaetano Valenti Gonzaga sopra una pretesa cagione del corrompimento del gusto italiano nel secolo XVII.* Cremona, Italy: L. Manini, 1776.

———. *Cartas familiares del Abate D. Juan Andrés a su hermano D. Carlos, dándole noticias del viaje que hizo a viarias ciudades en el año 1785, publicadas por el mismo D. Carlos.* 8 vols. Madrid: Sancha, 1787–93.

———. *Dell' origine, progressi e stato attuale d'ogni letteratura.* 2nd ed. 8 vols. Parma, Italy: Stamperia reale, 1785–1822.

———. *Dissertatio de problema hydraulico ab Academia Mantuana proposito ab anno MDCCLXXIV.* Mantua, Italy: Typis Haeredis A Pazzoni, 1775.

———. *Lettera dell'origine e delle vicende dell'arte d'insegnar a parlar ai sordi e muti.* Vienna: Alberti, 1793.

An-Na'Im, Abdullahi. "What Do We Mean by Universal?" *Index on Censorship* 4.5 (1994): 120–28.

Apter, Emily. "Comparative Exile: Competing Margins in the History of Comparative Literature." *Comparative Literature in the Age of Multiculturalism.* Ed. Charles Bernheimer. Baltimore: Johns Hopkins University Press, 1995. 86–96.

Arato, Franco. "Un comparatista: Juan Andrés." *Cromohs* 5 (2000): 1–14.

———. *La storiografia letteraria nel Settecento italiano.* Pisa: ETS, 2002.

Aretino, Pietro. *Dubbi: Altri dubbi e sonetti lussuriosi.* Ed. Francesca Alberini. Rome: Editori Associati, 1966.

Ariosto, Lodovico. *Orlando furioso.* Ed. Lanfranco Caretti. Turin: Einaudi, 1992.

Aristotle. *The "Art" of Rhetoric.* Trans. John Henry Freese. Ed. G. P. Goold. Vol. 22. Cambridge, MA: Harvard University Press, 1939.

———. *Politics.* Trans. H. Rackham. Cambridge, MA: Harvard University Press, 1998.

Arkoun, Mohammed. *Rethinking Islam: Common Questions, Uncommon Answers.* Trans. Robert Deemer Lee. Boulder, CO: Westview, 1994.

Arteaga, Esteban de. *Le rivoluzioni del teatro musicale italiano dalla sua origine fino al presente.* 2nd ed. 3 vols. Venice: Stamperia di C. Palese, 1785.

Ascherson, Neal. *Black Sea.* New York: Hill and Wang, 1995.

Auerbach, Erich. *Mimesis: The Representation of Reality in Western Literature.* Trans. Willard R. Trask. Princeton, NJ: Princeton University Press, 1974.

———. "Vico and Aesthetic Historism." *Scenes from the Drama of European Literature*. Minneapolis: University of Minnesota Press, 1984. 182–98.

Aymard, Maurice, and Giuseppe Giarrizzo. *La Sicilia*. Turin: Einaudi, 1987.

Aziz, Miriam. *The Impact of European Rights on National Legal Cultures*. Oxford: Hart, 2004.

Baali, Fuad. *Society, State, and Urbanism: Ibn Khaldun's Sociological Thought*. Albany: State University of New York Press, 1988.

Bacon, Francis. *Ideal Commonwealths, Comprising More's Utopia, Bacon's New Atlantis, Campanella's City of the Sun and Harrington's Oceana*. Ed. Henry Morley. Rev. ed. New York: P. F. Collier, 1901.

Balayé, Simone. *Madame de Staël: Lumières et liberté*. Paris: Klincksieck, 1979.

Balibar, Étienne. *We, the People of Europe? Reflections on Transnational Citizenship*. Trans. James Swenson. Princeton, NJ: Princeton University Press, 2003.

Ballard, Roger. "Islam and the Construction of Europe." *Muslims in the Margin: Political Responses to the Presence of Islam in Western Europe*. Ed. W. A. R. Shadid and P. S. Van Koningsveld. Kampen, Netherlands: Kok Pharos, 1996. 15–51.

Bamyeh, Mohammed A. "Frames of Belonging." *Social Text* 39 (1994): 35–55.

Banfield, Edward C. *The Moral Basis of a Backward Society*. Glencoe, IL: Free Press, 1958.

Banti, Alberto Mario. *La nazione del Risorgimento: Parentela, santità e onore alle origini dell'Italia unita*. Turin: Einaudi, 2000.

———. *Il Risorgimento italiano*. Bari, Italy: Laterza, 2004.

Barnave, Antoine. *Power, Property, and History: Barnave's Introduction to the French Revolution and Other Writings*. Trans. Emanuel Chill. New York: Harper and Row, 1971.

Barone, Giuseppe, Francesco Benigno, and Claudio Torrisi. *Elites e potere in Sicilia: Dal medieovo ad oggi*. Catanzaro, Italy: Meridiana libri, 1995.

Barraclough, C. "Universal History." *Approaches to History: A Symposium*. Ed. H. P. R. Finberg. Toronto: University of Toronto Press, 1962. 83–109.

Bartlett, Robert. *The Making of Europe: Conquest, Colonization, and Cultural Change, 950–1350*. Princeton, NJ: Princeton University Press, 1993.

Baruzi, Jean. *Leibniz et l'organisation religieuse de la terre*. Paris: F. Alcan, 1907.

Bassand, Michel. *Self-Reliant Development in Europe: Theory, Problems, Actions*. Aldershot, UK: Gower, 1986.

Batllori, Miguel. "Jyan Andrés y el humanismo." *Revista de filologia española* 29 (1945): 121–28.

Battiato, Franco. *La voce del padrone*. EMI Records, 1981.

Beccaria, Cesare. *Dei delitti e delle pene*. 1764. Ed. Alberto Burgio. Milan: Feltrinelli, 1991.

Benjamin, Walter. "Theses on the Philosophy of History." 1942. *Illumina-tions: Essays and Reflections*. Trans. Harry Zohn. Ed. Hannah Arendt. New York: Schocken, 1969. 253–64.

Berenger, Jean. "Conscience européenne et mauvaise conscience à la cour de Mathias Corvin: La naissance du mythe de Dracula (1462–1465)." *La con-science européenne au xve et au xvie siècle: Actes du colloque international organisé à l'École Normale Supérieure de jeunes filles, 30 septembre–3 oc-tobre 1980*. Paris: l'École, 1982. 8–22.

Bérkov, P. "Don Juan Andrés y la literatura rusa (Estudio de historiographía sobre la literatura rusa)." *Rivista de archivios, bibliotecas y museos* 3.51 (1930): 461–69.

Berlin, Isaiah. *Three Critics of the Enlightenment: Vico, Hamann, Herder*. 1960. Ed. Henry Hardy. Princeton, NJ: Princeton University Press, 2000.

Bernal, Martin. *Black Athena*. Vol. 1, *The Fabrication of Ancient Greece, 1785–1985*. New Brunswick, NJ: Rutgers University Press, 1987.

Bernier, François. *Travels in the Mogul Empire, a.d. 1656–1668*. 1663. Trans. Archibald Constable. Ed. Vincent Arthur Smith. London: Oxford Univer-sity Press, 1916.

Berselli Ambri, Paola. *L'opera di Montesquieu nel Settecento italiano*. Flor-ence: L. S. Olschki, 1960.

Berthold-Bond, Daniel. "Hegel's Eschatological Vision: Does History Have a Future?" *History and Theory* 27.1 (1988): 14–29.

Bhabha, Homi K. *The Location of Culture*. London: Routledge, 1994.

Bhabha, Jacqueline. " 'Get Back to Where You Once Belonged': Identity, Citi-zenship, and Exclusion in Europe." *Human Rights Quarterly* 20.3 (1998): 592–627.

Blake, William. *The Complete Poetry and Prose of William Blake*. Ed. David V. Erdman. 2nd ed. Berkeley: University of California Press, 1988.

Blaut, James M. *The Colonizer's Model of the World: Geographical Diffu-sionism and Eurocentric History*. New York: Guilford, 1993.

Bloch, Marc Léopold Benjamin. *Feudal Society*. Trans. L. A. Manyon. Chi-cago: University of Chicago Press, 1961.

——. *The Historian's Craft*. Ed. Joseph Reese Strayer and Peter Putnam. New York: Vintage, 1953.

Blom, Hans W. "The Republican Mirror: The Dutch Idea of Europe." *The Idea of Europe: From Antiquity to the European Union*. Ed. Anthony Pag-den. New York: Woodrow Wilson Center Press, 2002. 91–115.

Boase, Roger. *The Origin and Meaning of Courtly Love: A Critical Study of European Scholarship*. Manchester: Manchester University Press, 1977.

Bock, Gisela. *Le donne nella storia d'Europa: Dal medioevo ai nostri giorni*. Bari, Italy: Laterza, 2001.

Bogin, Magda. *The Women Troubadours*. New York: Norton, 1980.

Bollati, Giulio. *L'italiano: Il carattere nazionale come storia e come invenzione*. 1983. Turin: Einaudi, 1996.

Bonfigli, Luigi. Preface to *Pagine scelte da la guerra del Vespro siciliano e da la storia dei mussulmani di Sicilia*. Florence: La Voce, n.d. 3–12.

Bonno, G. "Le modernisme de Montesquieu." *French Review* 14.4 (1941): 288–93.

Bonora, Ettore. *Parini e altro Settecento: Fra classicismo e illuminismo*. Milan: Feltrinelli, 1982.

Bonstetten, Charles Victor de. *The Man of the North and the Man of the South; or, The Influence of Climate*. 1824. New York: F. W. Christern, 1864.

Borzel, Tanja A. "Why There Is No 'Southern Problem': On Environmental Leaders and Laggards in the European Union." *Journal of European Public Policy* 7.1 (2000): 141–62.

Bossuet, Jacques-Bénigne. *Discours sur l'histoire universelle*. Paris: S. Mabre Cramoisy, 1681.

Bots, Hans, and Françoise Waquet. *La république des lettres*. Paris: Belin and De Boeck, 1997.

Botz-Bornstein, Thorsten. "Europe: Space, Spirit, Style." *European Legacy* 8.2 (2003): 179–87.

Bouhours, Dominique. *Les entretiens d'Ariste et d'Eugene*. 4th ed. Paris: Sebastien Mabre-Cramoisy, 1673.

Boyes, Roger. "Sober North Vies with Siesta South: Fault Lines of Europe." *Times*, March 17, 1999.

Braudel, Fernand. *Civilization and Capitalism, 15th–18th Century*. Trans. Siân Reynolds. 3 vols. Berkeley: University of California Press, 1992.

Braunstein, Philippe. "Confins italiens de l'empire: Nations, frontières et sensibilité européenne dans la seconde moitié du xve siecle." *La conscience européenne au xve et au xvie siècle: Actes du colloque international organisé à l'École Normale Supérieure de jeunes filles, 30 septembre–3 octobre 1980*. Paris: l'École, 1982. 35–48.

Brizzi, Gian Paolo. "The Jesuits and Universities in Italy." *European Universities in the Age of Reformation and Counter Reformation*. Ed. Helga Robinson-Hammerstein. Dublin: Four Courts Press, 1998. 187–98.

Brugmans, Hendrik. "Europe: One Civilization, One Destiny, One Vocation." *Europe: Dream, Adventure, Reality*. Ed. Brugmans. New York: Greenwood, 1987. 11–39.

Bufalino, Gesualdo. *Opere: 1981–1988*. Ed. Maria Corti and Francesca Caputo. Milan: Bompiani, 1992.

Bugge, Peter. "Asia and the Idea of Europe: Europe and Its Others." *Kontur: Tidsskrift for kulturstudier* 1.2 (2000): 3–13.

Burke, Edmund. *On Taste; On the Sublime and Beautiful; Reflections on* the French Revolution; A Letter to a Noble Lord. 1790. New York: P. F. Collier, 1909.

Byatt, A. S. "What Is a European." *New York Times Magazine*, October 12, 2002, 46–51.

Cacciari, Massimo. *L'arcipelago*. Milan: Adelphi, 1997.

——. *Geo-filosofia dell'Europa*. Milan: Adelphi, 1994.

Cadalso, José. *Defensa de la nación española contra la carta persiana LXXVIII de Montesquieu*. Ed. Guy Mercadier. Toulouse: Institut d'études hispaniques hispano-américaines et luso-brésiliennes, 1970.

Calasso, Giovanna. "Universal History, Local History, National History: Recent Theoretical and Methodological Contributions on Islamic Historiography." *The East and the Meaning of History: International Conference, 23–27 November 1992*. Ed. Biancamaria Scarcia Amoretti. Rome: Bardi, 1994. 199–218.

Camões, Luís de. *Os lusiadas*. Ed. Frank Pierce. Oxford: Clarendon, 1973.

Campanini, Massimo. Introduction to *Al-Farabi: La città virtuosa*. Milan: Rizzoli, 1996. 1–43.

Capasso, Carlo. *Italia e Oriente*. Florence: La Nuova Italia, 1932.

Caraccioli, Louis Antoine. *Paris, le modèle des nations étrangères ou l'Europe française*. Paris, 1777.

Carducci, Giosue. *Lettere*. 5 vols. Bologna: Nicola Zanichelli, 1938.

Carino, Isidoro. "Recensioni." *Studi Amariani*. Eds. Andrea Borruso, Rosa D'Angelo, and Rosa Scaglione Guccione. Palermo: Società siciliana per la storia patria, 1991. 221–302.

Carpanetto, Dino, and Giuseppe Ricuperati. *L'Italia del Settecento: Crisi trasformazioni lumi*. 1986. Bari, Italy: Laterza, 1990.

Carravetta, Peter. "La questione dell'identità nella formazione dell'Europa." *La letteratura europea vista dagli altri*. Ed. Franca Sinopoli. Rome: Meltemi, 2003. 19–66.

Carrithers, David W. "Introduction: Montesquieu and the Spirit of Modernity." *Studies on Voltaire and the Eighteenth Century* 9 (2002): 1–34.

——. "Montesquieu's Philosophy of History." *Journal of the History of Ideas* 47.1 (1986): 61–80.

Casarrubea, Giuseppe. *Intellettuali e potere in Sicilia*. Palermo: Sellerio, 1983.

Casini, Paolo. *L'antica sapienza italica: Cronistoria di un mito*. Bologna: Il Mulino, 1998.

Cassano, Franco. *Modernizzare stanca: Perdere tempo, guadagnare tempo*. Bologna: Il Mulino, 2001.

——. *Il pensiero meridiano*. Bari, Italy: Laterza, 1996.

Céard, Jean. "L'image de l'Europe dans la littérature cosmographique de la Renaissance." *La conscience européenne au XVe et au XVIe siècle: Actes du*

*colloque international organisé à l'École Normale Supérieure de jeunes filles,
30 septembre–3 octobre 1980*. Paris: l'École, 1982. 49–63.

Cervantes Saavedra, Miguel de. *Don Quijote de la Mancha*. 2 vols. Ed. Martín
de Riquer. Barcelona: Galaxia Gútenberg, 2001.

Chabod, Federico. *Storia dell'idea d'europa*. 1961. Bari, Italy: Laterza, 1995.

Chakrabarty, Dipesh. *Provincializing Europe: Postcolonial Thought and Historical Difference*. Princeton, NJ: Princeton University Press, 2000.

La chanson de Roland. Ed. Pierre Jonin. Paris: Gallimard, 1979.

Charlemagne [pseudo.]. "The Players Do Better than the Politicians at Making Europe Loved." *Economist*, May 31, 2003, 55.

——. "Rendezvous in Versailles." *Economist*, January 22, 2003, 13.

Chateaubriand. *Génie du christianisme*. 1802. Ed. Pierre Reboul. 2 vols. Paris:
Gallimard, 1966.

Chovillet, Jacques. "Descartes et le problème de l'origine des langues." *Dix-
huitième siècle* 4 (1972): 39–60.

Cicero, Marcus Tullius. *Letters to Atticus*. Trans. Bailey Shackleton. Ed. L. C.
Purser. 4 vols. Cambridge, MA: Harvard University Press, 1999.

Cocks, Peter. "Towards a Marxist Theory of European Integration." *International Organization* 34.1 (1980): 1–40.

Codina, Gabriel. "The 'Modus Parisiensis.'" *The Jesuit Ratio Studiorum:
Four hundredth Anniversary Perspectives*. Ed. Vincent J. Duminuco. New
York: Fordham University Press, 2000. 28–49.

Collingwood, R. G. *The Idea of History*. 2nd ed. New York: Oxford University
Press, 1956.

Cometa, Michele. "Friederich Schlegel tra Oriente e Occidente." *Medioevo
romanzo e orientale: Il viaggio dei testi*. Ed. Antonio Pioletti and Francesca
Rizzo Nervo. Venice: Rubbettino, 1999. 61–78.

Commission on Human Rights. *Racism, Racial Discrimination, Xenophobia,
and All Forms of Discrimination: Situation of Muslims and Arab Peoples in
Various Parts of the World in the Aftermath of the Events of 11 September
2001*. New York: United Nations, 2003.

Courtois, Jean-Patrice. "L'Europe et son autre dans *l'Esprit des lois*." *L'Europe
de Montesquieu: Actes du Colloque de Gênes (26–29 mai 1993)*. Ed. Alberto
Pstigliola and Maria Grazia Bottari. Naples: Liguori, 1995. 309–28.

Cowell, Alan. "Seven European Nations Form a Passport-Free Zone." *New
York Times*, March 27, 1995.

Croce, Benedetto. *Storia della storiografia italiana nel secolo xix*. Bari, Italy:
Laterza, 1947.

——. *Storia del regno di Napoli*. 1924. Milan: Adelphi, 1992.

Cunliffe, Barry W. *The Oxford Illustrated Prehistory of Europe*. Oxford: Oxford University Press, 1994.

Cuoco, Vincenzo. *Saggio storico sulla rivoluzione di Napoli*. 1801. Ed. Fulvio Tessitore. Naples: Itinerario, 1988.

Curcio, Carlo. *Europa, storia di un'idea*. Florence: Vallecchi, 1958.

Dainotto, Roberto M. "Vico's Beginnings and Ends: Variations on the Theme of the Origin of Language." *Annali d'italianistica* 18 (2000): 13–28.

D'Alembert, Jean Le Rond. "Discours préliminaire." *Encyclopédie, ou dictionnaire raisonné des sciences, des artes et des métiers*. 1751. Vol. 1. Ed. Alain Pons. Paris: Flammarion, 1986. 74–184.

Daly, Lowrie John. *The Medieval University, 1200–1400*. New York: Sheed and Ward, 1961.

Damrosch, David. *What Is World Literature?* Princeton, NJ: Princeton University Press, 2003.

Davidson, Peter. *The Idea of North*. London: Reaktion, 2005.

Davies, Norman. *Europe: A History*. Oxford: Oxford University Press, 1996.

De Béthune, Maximilien. "Le projet politique." *L'Europe une: Les philosophes et l'Europe*. 1662. Ed. Jean Pierre Faye. Paris: Gallimard, 1992. 71–91.

Defoe, Daniel. "The True-Born Englishman: A Satyr." 2001. Blackmask Online. August 31, 2003 http://www.blackmask.com/books63c/trueborneng.htm.

Del Rio, Domenico. *I Gesuiti e l'Italia*. Milan: Corbaccio, 1996.

De Luca, Erri. *Aceto, Arcobaleno*. 10th ed. Milan: Feltrinelli, 2005.

De Romilly, Jacqueline. "Isocrates and Europe." *Greece and Rome* 39.1 (1992): 2–13.

Derrida, Jacques. *Dissemination*. Trans. Barbara Johnson. Chicago: University of Chicago Press, 1981.

——. *Of Grammatology*. Trans. Gayatri Chakravorty Spivak. 2nd rev. ed. Baltimore: Johns Hopkins University Press, 1998.

——. *The Other Heading: Reflections on Today's Europe*. Trans. Pascale-Anne Brault and Michael Naas. Bloomington: Indiana University Press, 1992.

Descombes, Vincent. *Le même et l'autre: Quarante-cinq ans de philosophie française (1933–1978)*. Paris: Minuit, 1979.

Dibon, Paul. "L'Université de Leyde et la république des lettres au 17ème siècle." *Quaerondo* 5 (1975): 4–38.

Dickie, John. *Darkest Italy: The Nation and Stereotypes of the Mezzogiorno, 1860–1900*. New York: St. Martin's, 1999.

Diderot, Denis. "Encyclopédie, ou dictionnaire raisonné des sciences, des arts et des métiers, par une société de gens de lettres." 2001. Ed. ARTFL Project, PhiloLogic Software, and University of Chicago. http://www.lib.uchicago.edu/efts/ARTFL/projects/encyc/.

Diesbach, Ghislain de. *Madame de Staël*. Paris: Perrin, 1983.

Domínguez Moltó, Adolfo. *El abate D. Juan Andrés Morell (un erudito del siglo* XVIII). Alicante, Spain: Instituto de Estudios Alicantinos Diputación Provincial de Alicante, 1978.

Donne, John. *Selected Prose.* Ed. Neil Rhodes. Harmondsworth, UK: Penguin, 1987.

Donoghue, Denis. *Reading America: Essays on American Literature.* New York: Knopf, 1987.

Duchet, Michele. *Anthropologie et histoire au siècle des lumières: Buffon, Voltaire, Rousseau, Helvétius, Diderot.* Paris: F. Maspero, 1971.

Dumont-Wilden, Louis. *L'évolution de l'esprit européen.* Paris: Flammarion, 1937.

Dunford, Michael. "Economies in Space and Time: Economic Geographies of Development and Underdevelopment and Historical Geographies of Modernization." *Modern Europe: Place, Culture, and Identity.* Ed. Brian Graham. London: Arnold, 1998. 53–88.

Dupront, Alphonse. *Spazio e umanesimo.* Trans. Gigliola Fragnito. Venice: Marsilio, 1993.

Duranton, Henri. "L'interprétation du mythe troubadour par le Groupe de Coppet." *Le Groupe de Coppet: Actes et documents du deuxième Colloque de Coppet, 10–13 juillet 1974.* Ed. Simone Balayé and Jean-Daniel Candaux. Geneva: M. Slatkine, 1977. 349–73.

Duroselle, Jean Baptiste. *Europe: A History of Its Peoples.* Trans. Richard Mayne. London: Viking, 1990.

Dussel, Enrique. "Eurocentrism and Modernity (Introduction to the Frankfürt Lectures)." *Boundary 2* 20.3 (1993): 65–76.

——. "Europe, Modernity, and Eurocentrism." *Nepantla: Views from South* 1.3 (2000): 465–78.

——. "World-System and 'Trans'-modernity." *Nepantla: Views from South* 3.2 (2002): 221–44.

Dvornik, Francis. *The Ecumenical Councils.* New York: Hawthorn Books, 1961.

Eisenstein, Elizabeth L. *The Printing Press as an Agent of Change: Communications and Cultural Transformations in Early Modern Europe.* Cambridge: Cambridge University Press, 1979.

Elliott, J. H. "The Discovery of America and the Discovery of Man." *Facing Each Other: The World's Perception of Europe and Europe's Perception of the World.* Vol. 1. Ed. Anthony Pagden. Aldershot, UK: Ashgate/Variorum, 2000. 159–83.

Elton, G. R. "Europe and the Reformation." *History, Society, and the Churches: Essays in Honour of Owen Chadwick.* Eds. Derek Edward Dawson Beales and Geoffrey Francis Andrew Best. Cambridge: Cambridge University Press, 1985. 89–104.

Engels, Friedrich. *The Origin of the Family, Private Property, and the State.* Ed. Lewis Henry Morgan. New York: Pathfinder Press, 1972.

Englund, Steven. "The Theater of French Democracy." *A History of Democracy in Europe.* Trans. Nicholas Y. A. Bradley. Ed. Antoine de Baecque. Boulder, CO: Social Science Monographs, 1995. 88–112.

European Task Force on Culture. *In from the Margins: A Contribution to the Debate on Culture and Development in Europe.* Strasbourg, France: Council of Europe, 1997.

"Europe: Those Fuzzy Frontiers." *The Economist*, December 11, 1997, 32.

"Europe's Southern Shadow: Immigration from North Africa Is the Problem of the Coming Decade." *Newsweek International*, October 18, 2004, 40.

Eusebi, Mario. "Andrés, Arteaga, Tiraboschi e il contrasto sulle origini della poesia rimata." *Spanische Literatur; Literatur Europas.* Ed. Frank Baasner. Tübingen, Germany: Max Niemeyer, 1996. 332–36.

Fanon, Frantz. *The Wretched of the Earth.* 1961. Trans. Constance Farrington. New York: Grove, 1991.

Farrell, Allan P., ed. and trans. *The Jesuit Ratio Studiorum of 1599.* Washington, DC: Conference of Major Superiors of Jesuits, 1970.

Ferri, Enrico. *Criminal Sociology.* London: T. Fisher Unwin, 1895.

——. *Delitti e delinquenti nella scienza e nella vita.* Milan: n.p., 1889.

Fichte, Johann Gottlieb. "Addresses to the German Nation." 1806. *The Nationalism Reader.* Ed. Omar Dahbour and Micheline R. Ishay. Atlantic Highlands, NJ: Humanities Press, 1995. 62–70.

Fischer, Jürgen. *Oriens, Occidens, Europa: Begriff und Gedanke Europa in der späten Antike und im frühen Mittelalter.* Wiesbaden, Germany: Franz Steiner, 1957.

Folkierski, W. *Entre le classicisme et le romantisme: Étude sur l'esthétique et les esthéticiens du XVIII siecle.* Kraków: Académie polonaise des sciences et des lettres, 1925.

Foucault, Michel. *Histoire de la folie à l'âge classique: Folie et déraison.* Paris: Plon, 1961.

——. *The History of Sexuality.* 1978. Trans. Robert Hurley. New York: Pantheon, 1990.

Fournier, Vincent. "Les grands clivages de l'Europe." *Précis de littérature européenne.* Ed. Béatrice Didier. Paris: Presses Universitaires de France, 1998. 97–104.

Fubini, Mario. *Dal Muratori al Baretti: Studi sulla critica e sulla cultura del Settecento.* 3rd ed. Bari, Italy: Laterza, 1968.

Fueter, Eduard. *Geschichte der neureren Historiographie.* Munich: R. Oldenbourg, 1925.

Fukuyama, Francis. *Trust: Social Virtues and the Creation of Prosperity.* New York: Free Press, 1995.

Furst, Henry. "A Controversy on Italian History." *New York Times Book Review*, June 3, 1934, 8–10.

Gabriel, Astrik L., and the University of Notre Dame Mediaeval Institute. *Garlandia: Studies in the History of the Mediaeval University*. Notre Dame, IN: Mediaeval Institute, University of Notre Dame, 1969.

Galasso, Giuseppe, ed. *L'altra Europa: Per un'antropologia storica del Mezzogiorno d'Italia*. New rev. ed. Lecce, Italy: Argo, 1997.

Galmés de Fuentes, Álvaro. *El amor cortés en la lírica árabe y en la lírica provenzal*. Madrid: Cátedra, 1996.

Gates, Warren E. "The Spread of Ibn Khaldun's Ideas on Climate and Culture." *Journal of the History of Ideas* 28.3 (1967): 415–22.

Gearhart, Suzanne. "Reading *De L'Esprit des Lois*: Montesquieu and the Principles of History." *Yale French Studies* 59 (1980): 175–200.

Geary, Patrick. *The Myth of Nations: The Medieval Origins of Europe*. Princeton, NJ: Princeton University Press, 2003.

Gellner, Ernest. *Nations and Nationalism*. Ithaca, NY: Cornell University Press, 1983.

Gerbi, Antonello. *La disputa del Nuovo Mondo: Storia di una polemica (1750–1900)*. 1955. Milan: Adelphi, 2000.

Getto, Giovanni. *Storia delle storie letterarie*. 4th ed. Florence: Sansoni, 1981.

Giarrizzo, Giuseppe. "Note su Palmieri, Amari e il Vespro." *Archivio storico per la Sicilia orientale* 69.2 (1973): 355–59.

Gibbon, Edward. *The History of the Decline and Fall of the Roman Empire*. Ed. David Womersley. London: Allen Lane, Penguin, 1994.

Giuffrida, Romualdo. "Michele Amari tra lotta politica, ricerca storica e attività parlamentare." *Michele Amari: Discorsi e documenti parlamentari (1862–1882)*. Ed. Giuffrida. Palermo: Accademia nazionale di science lettere e arti di Palermo, 1989. ix–xlii.

Gnisci, Armando. *Da noialtri europei a noitutti insieme: Saggi di letteratura comparata*. 3rd ed. Rome: Bulzoni, 2002.

Goethe, Johann Wolfgang von. *Italian Journey: Et in Arcadia Ego*. Trans. W. H. Auden and Elizabeth Mayer. Harmondsworth, UK: Penguin, 1962.

Goetsch, James Robert, Jr. *Vico's Axioms: The Geometry of the Human World*. New Haven, CT: Yale University Press, 1995.

Goffredo, Giuseppe. *Cadmos cerca Europa: Il sud fra il Mediterraneo e l'Europa*. Milan: Bollati Boringhieri, 2000.

Goldzink, Jean. "Montesquieu et l'Europe." *L'idée de l'Europe au fil de deux millénaires*. Ed. Alfred Grosser and Michel Perrin. Paris: Beauchesne, 1994. 141–49.

Góngora y Argote, Luis de. *Las soledades*. Madrid: Ediciones del Arbol, 1935.

González Palencia, A. "Islam and the Occident." *Hispania* 18.3 (1935): 245–76.

Goodman, Dena. *The Republic of Letters: A Cultural History of the French Enlightenment*. Ithaca, NY: Cornell University Press, 1994.

Goodman, Jordan, and Katrina Honeyman. *Gainful Pursuits: The Making of Industrial Europe, 1600–1914*. London: Arnold, 1988.

Goscinny, René, and Albert Uderzo. *Asterix le Gaulois*. 1959. Paris: Hachette, 1998.

Goulemot, Jean Marie, Didier Masseau, and Jean-Jacques Tatin-Gourier. *Vocabulaire de la littérature du XVIIIe siècle*. Paris: Minerve, 1996.

Graham, Brian. "Introduction: Modern Europe; Fractures and Faults." *Modern Europe: Place, Culture, and Identity*. Ed. Graham. London: Arnold, 1998. 1–18.

Gramsci, Antonio. *Il materialismo storico e la filosofia di Benedetto Croce*. Turin: Einaudi, 1948.

——. *Il Risorgimento*. Ed. Valentino Gerratana. 3rd ed. Rome: Editori Riuniti, 1996.

——. *Selections from the Prison Notebooks of Antonio Gramsci*. Trans. and ed. Quintin Hoare and Geoffrey Nowell-Smith. New York: International Publishers, 1971.

Graves, Robert. *The Greek Myths*. 1955. 2 vols. Harmondsworth, UK: Penguin, 1960.

Greenblatt, Stephen. "Introduction." *Genre* 15.1–2 (1982): 239–42.

Grosrichard, Alain. *Structure du sérail*. Paris: Seuil, 1979.

Guglielminetti, Marziano. "Storia delle storie letterarie." *Fare storia della letteratura*. Ed. Ottavio Cecchi and Enrico Ghidetti. Rome: Editori Riuniti, 1986. 11–28.

Guha, Ranajit. *Dominance without Hegemony: History and Power in Colonial India*. Cambridge, MA: Harvard University Press, 1997.

Guillén, Claudio. *The Challenge of Comparative Literature*. Trans. Cola Franzen. Cambridge, MA: Harvard University Press, 1993.

Guizot, François Pierre Guillaume. *Histoire de la civilisation en Europe depuis la chute de l'Empire romain jusqu'à la rèvolution française*. Paris: Didier, 1828.

Habermas, Jürgen. *Theory and Practice*. Trans. John Viertel. Boston: Beacon, 1973.

Habib, Irfan. "Capitalism in History." *Social Scientist* 23.7–9 (1995): 15–31.

Hale, John. *The Civilization of Europe in the Renaissance*. New York: Touchstone, 1993.

Hall, Edith. *Inventing the Barbarian: Greek Self-Definition through Tragedy*. Oxford: Clarendon, 1989.

Hanke, Lewis. *Bartolomé de las Casas, Bookman, Scholar, and Propagandist*. Philadelphia: University of Pennsylvania Press, 1952.

Hardt, Michael, and Antonio Negri. *Empire*. Cambridge, MA: Harvard University Press, 2000.

——. *Multitude: War and Democracy in the Age of Empire*. New York: Penguin, 2004.

Harrison, Thomas. *The Emptiness of Asia: Aeschylus' "Persians" and the History of the Fifth Century*. London: Duckworth, 2000.

Hartog, François. "Fondamenti greci dell'idea d'Europa." *Idee d'Europa*. Ed. Luciano Canfora. Bari, Italy: Dedalo, 1997. 17–29.

Hay, Denys. *Europe: The Emergence of an Idea*. Edinburgh: Edinburgh University Press, 1957.

Haywood, Ian. *The Making of History: A Study of the Literary Forgeries of James Macpherson and Thomas Chatterton in Relation to Eighteenth-Century Ideas of History and Fiction*. Rutherford, NJ: Fairleigh Dickinson University Press, 1986.

Hazard, Paul. *The European Mind: The Critical Years, 1680–1715*. Trans. J. Lewis May. New Haven, CT: Yale University Press, 1953.

——. *La révolution française et les lettres italiennes, 1789–1815*. Paris: Hachette, 1910.

Hegel, Georg Wilhelm Friedrich. *The Philosophy of World History*. 1822. Trans. John Sibree. Buffalo: Prometheus Books, 1991.

Herodotus. *The Histories*. Trans. A. D. Godley. Cambridge, MA: Harvard University Press, 1920.

Hobbes, Thomas. *Leviathan; or, The Matter, Forme, and Power of a Commonwealth Ecclesiasticall and Civil*. 1651. London: Penguin, 1985.

Hof, Im. *L'Europa dell'illuminismo*. Trans. Alessandro Califano. Bari, Italy: Laterza, 1993.

Horden, Peregrine, and Nicholas Purcell. *The Corrupting Sea: A Study of Mediterranean History*. Oxford: Blackwell, 2000.

Hotman, François. *Franco-Gallia; or, An Account of the Ancient Free State of France, and Most Other Parts of Europe, before the Loss of Their Liberties*. Trans. Robert Molesworth. 2nd ed. London: E. Valentine, 1721.

Huet, Pierre-Daniel. *Traité de l'origine des romans*. 1670. Stuttgart: Metzler, 1966.

Hugo, A. "Ce que nous entendons par l'Orient." *Revue de l'Orient: Bulletin de la Société Orientale* 1.1 (1843): 6–8.

Hulliung, Mark. *Montesquieu and the Old Regime*. Berkeley: University of California Press, 1976.

Huntington, Samuel P. *The Clash of Civilizations and the Remaking of World Order*. New York: Simon and Schuster, 1996.

Ibn Khaldun. *The Muqaddimah: An Introduction to History*. Trans. Franz Rosenthal. 3 vols. New York: Pantheon, 1958.

Ibn Khaldun, and Abdesselam Cheddadi. *Peuples et nations du monde: Extraits des Ibar*. Paris: Sindbad, 1986.

Iggers, Georg G. "Historicism: The History and Meaning of the Term." *Journal of the History of Ideas* 56.1 (1995): 129–52.

Iiritano, Massimo. *Utopia del tramonto: Identita e crisi della coscienza europea*. Bari, Italy: Dedalo, 2004.

Introvigne, Massimo. "La Francia contro il 'modello turco.'" *Il Domenicale: Settimanale di cultura* 3.39 (2004): 25.

Isbell, John Claiborne. *The Birth of European Romanticism: Truth and Propaganda in Staël's De l'Allemagne, 1810–1813*. Cambridge: Cambridge University Press, 1994.

"Is Europe Corrupt?" *The Economist*, January 23, 2000.

Israel, Jonathan Irvine. *Radical Enlightenment: Philosophy and the Making of Modernity, 1650–1750*. Oxford: Oxford University Press, 2001.

Jordan, William Chester. *Europe in the High Middle Ages*. Harmondsworth, UK: Penguin, 2002.

Jubran, Carl I. "The Europeanization of Spain: Orientalism and Hispano-Arabist Philology, 1880–1920." *The Image of Europe in Literature, Media, and Society*. Ed. Will Wright and Steven Kaplan. Colorado Springs: University of Southern Colorado, 2001. 8–17.

Kamm, Thomas. "Snobbery: The Latest Hitch in Unifying Europe: Northerners Sniff as 'Club Med' South Clamors to Join New Currency." *Wall Street Journal*, November 6, 1996.

Kant, Immanuel. *On History*. Trans. Lewis White Beck, Robert E. Anchor, and Emil L. Fackenheim. Ed. Beck. Indianapolis: Bobbs-Merrill, 1963.

——. "To Perpetual Peace: A Philosophical Sketch." 1795. Trans. Ted Humphrey. *Perpetual Peace and Other Essays on Politics, History, and Morals*. 1983. Indianapolis: Hackett, 1992. 107–44.

Kapuscinski, Ryszard. *Lapidarium: In viaggio tra i frammenti della storia*. Trans. Vera Verdiani. Milan: Feltrinelli, 1997.

Keen, Benjamin. "The Black Legend Revisited: Assumptions and Realities." *Hispanic American Historical Review* 49.4 (1969): 703–19.

Keene, Donald. *The Japanese Discovery of Europe: Honda Toshiaki and Other Discoverers, 1720–1798*. London: Routledge and K. Paul, 1952.

Kormoss, I. B. F. "The Geographical Notion of Europe during the Centuries." *Europe: Dream, Adventure, Reality*. Ed. Hendrik Brugmans. New York: Greenwood, 1987. 81–95.

Kriesel, Karl Marcus. "Montesquieu: Possibilistic Political Geographer." *Annals of the Association of American Geographers* 58.3 (1968): 557–74.

La Chalotais, Louis-René de Caradeuc de. *Essai d'éducation nationale; ou, Plan d'études pour la jeunesse*. Paris, 1763.

Lampillas, Saverio. *Ensayo historico-apologetico de la literatura española con-*

tra las opiniones preocupadas de algunos escritores modernos italianos. 2nd ed. 7 vols. Madrid: Marin, 1789.

Le Goff, Jacques. *La civilisation de l'Occident médiéval.* Paris: Arthaud, 1965.

Lehmann, A. G. *The European Heritage: An Outline of Western Culture.* Oxford: Phaidon, 1984.

Le Rider, Jacques. *Mitteleuropa: Storia di un mito.* Trans. Maria Cristina Marinelli. Bologna: Il Mulino, 1995.

Lewis, Bernard. *The Muslim Discovery of Europe.* New York: Norton, 1982.

Lewis, C. S. *The Allegory of Love: A Study in Medieval Tradition.* New York: Oxford University Press, 1936.

Lewis, Martin W., and Kären E. Wigen. *The Myth of Continents: A Critique of Metageography.* Berkeley: University of California Press, 1997.

Likaszewski, Jerzy. "Europe: The Origins and Endurance of a Dream." *Europe: Dream, Adventure, Reality.* Ed. Hendrik Brugmans. New York: Greenwood, 1987. 40–73.

Lindberg, Leon N., and Stuart A. Scheingold. *Europe's Would-Be Polity: Patterns of Change in the European Community.* Englewood Cliffs, NJ: Prentice-Hall, 1970.

Lipgens, Walter. *A History of European Integration.* Oxford: Clarendon, 1982.

Locke, John. *The Works of John Locke.* 2nd ed. 10 vols. London: Thomas Tegg, 1823.

Lombroso, Cesare. *Delitto, genio, follia: Scritti scelti.* Ed. Delia Frigessi, Ferruccio Giacanelli, and Luisa Mangoni. Turin: Bollati Boringhieri, 1995.

Lombroso, Cesare, and Rodolfo Laschi. *Il delitto politico e le rivoluzioni.* Turin: n.p., 1890.

Longino, Michèle. *Orientalism in French Classical Drama.* Cambridge: Cambridge University Press, 2002.

Lowenthal, David. "Book I of Montesquieu's *The Spirit of the Laws.*" *American Political Science Review* 53.2 (1955): 485–498.

Lukács, Georg. *The Historical Novel.* Trans. Hannah Mitchell and Stanley Mitchell. Lincoln: University of Nebraska Press, 1983.

Luther, Martin. "Large Catechism." *Triglot Concordia: The Symbolical Books of the Ev. Lutheran Church.* Ed. F. Bente and W. H. T. Dau. St. Louis: Concordia Publishing House, 1921.

Lützeler, Paul Michael. *Europäische Identität und Multikultur: Fallstudien zur deutschsprachigen Literatur seit der Romantik.* Tübingen, Germany: Stauffenburg, 1997.

Lyser, K. J. "The Concept of Europe in the Early and High Middle Ages." *Past and Present* 137.1 (1992): 25–47.

Machiavelli, Niccolò. *Opere.* Ed. Corrado Vivanti. Turin: Einaudi-Gallimard, 1997.

MacIntyre, Alasdair. *After Virtue: A Study in Moral Theory.* 2nd ed. Notre Dame, IN: University of Notre Dame Press, 1984.

Mack Smith, Denis. *A History of Sicily*. 2 vols. New York: Dorset, 1968.

Macpherson, C. B. *The Political Theory of Possessive Individualism: Hobbes to Locke*. London: Oxford University Press, 1964.

Maistre, Joseph de. *The Works of Joseph de Maistre*. 1965. Trans. Jack Livel. New York: Schocken, 1971.

Makdisi, George. *The Rise of Humanism in Classical Islam and the Christian West: With Special Reference to Scholasticism*. Edinburgh: Edinburgh University Press, 1990.

Malaparte, Curzio. *L'Europa vivente e altri saggi (1921–1931)*. Ed. Enrico Falqui. Florence: Vallecchi, 1961.

Malek, Abdel Anwar. "Orientalism in Crisis." *Diogenes* 44. (1963): 105–23.

Manzoni, Alessandro. *Tutte le opere*. Ed. Mario Martelli. 2 vols. Florence: Sansoni, 1973.

Marchianò, Grazia. *La rinascenza orientale nel pensiero europeo: Pionieri lungo tre secoli*. Pisa: Istituti Editoriali Internazionali, 1996.

Marcolongo, Bianca. "Le idee politiche di Michele Amari." *Studi Amariani*. Ed. Andrea Borruso, Rosa D'Angelo, and Rosa Scaglione Guccione. Palermo: Società siciliana per la storia patria, 1991. 63–106.

Mariani Zini, Fosca. "Mille di queste notti: L'influenza del racconto orientale nell'estetica francese del XVIII secolo." *La rinascenza orientale nel pensiero europeo: Pioneri lungo tre secoli*. Ed. Grazia Marchianò. Pisa: Istituti editoriali e poligrafici internazionali, 1996. 19–67.

Marino, Adrian. "Histoire de l'idée de 'littérature européenne' et des études européennes." *Précis de littérature européenne*. Ed. Béatrice Didier. Paris: Presses Universitaires de France, 1998. 13–17.

Marramao, Giacomo. *Passaggio a Occidente: Filosofia e globalizzazione*. Turin: Bollati Boringhieri, 2003.

Marrouchi, Mustapha. "Counternarratives, Recoveries, Refusals." *Boundary 2* 25.2 (1998): 205–57.

Martene, Edmond, and Ursin Durand. *Veterum scriptorum et monumentorum historicorum, dogmaticorum, moralium, amplissima collectio*. 9 vols. Paris: Apud Montalant, 1724.

Martin, A. Lynn. *The Jesuit Mind: The Mentality of an Elite in Early Modern France*. Ithaca, NY: Cornell University Press, 1988.

Masdeu, Juan Francisco. *Historia crítica de España y de la cultura española*. 20 vols. Madrid: Sancha, 1783–1805.

Mastellone, Salvo. *A History of Democracy in Europe: From Montesquieu to 1989*. Trans. and ed. Iain L. Fraser. Florence: Centro Editoriale Toscano, 1995.

Matar, N. I. *Islam in Britain, 1558–1685*. Cambridge: Cambridge University Press, 1998.

Maugain, Gabriel. *Boileau et l'Italie*. Paris: H. Champion, 1912.

Maurer, Armand A. *Medieval Philosophy*. 2nd ed. Toronto: Pontifical Institute of Medieval Studies, 1982.

Mauss, Marcel. *The Gift: The Form and Reason for Exchange in Archaic Societies*. Trans. W. D. Halls. London: Cohen and West, 1954.

Mazzeo, Guido Ettore. *The Abate Juan Andrés, Literary Historian of the xviii Century*. New York: Hispanic Institute in the United States, 1965.

Mazzini, Giuseppe. *Opere*. Ed. Luigi Salvatorelli. 2 vols. Milan: Rizzoli Editore, 1956.

——. *Pensieri sulla democrazia in Europa*. Ed. Salvo Mastellone. Milan: Feltrinelli, 1997.

McKeon, Michael. "The Origins of Interdisciplinary Studies." *Eighteenth-Century Studies* 28.1 (1994): 17–28.

McKeon, Richard. "The Development of the Concept of Property in Political Philosophy." *Ethics* 48.3 (1938): 297–366.

Melville, Herman. *At the Hostelry; and, Naples in the Time of Bomba*. Ed. Gordon Poole. Naples: Instituto Universitario Orientale, 1989.

Menéndez Pidal, Ramón. *Poesía árabe y poesía europea, con otros estudios de literatura medieval*. Buenos Aires: Espasa-Calpe Argentina, 1941.

Menéndez y Pelayo, Marcelino, ed. *Historia de los heterodoxos españoles*. Madrid: Aldus, 1946.

Menocal, Maria Rosa. *The Arabic Role in Medieval Literary History*. Philadelphia: University of Pennsylvania Press, 1987.

——. "Close Encounters in Medieval Provence: Spain's Role in the Birth of Troubadour Poetry." *Hispanic Review* 49.1 (1981): 43–64.

——. *The Ornament of the World: How Muslims, Jews, and Christians Created a Culture of Tolerance in Medieval Spain*. Boston: Little Brown, 2003.

——. "Pride and Prejudice in Medieval Studies: European and Oriental." *Hispanic Review* 53.1 (1985): 61–78.

Mercier Faivre, Anne-Marie. "La nation par la langue: Philologie, nationalism et nation dans l'Europe au dix-huitième siècle." *Nations and Nationalisms: France, Britain, Ireland, and the Eighteenth-Century Context*. Ed. Michael O'Dea and Kevin Whelan. Oxford: Voltaire Foundation, 1995. 161–79.

Michelet, Jules. *La France devant l'Europe*. 2nd ed. Florence: Le Monnier, 1871.

Micozzi, Patrizia. "La personalidad y la obra de José García de la Huerta en el contexto de la cultura hispano-italiana del siglo xvii." *Españoles en Italia e italianos en España*. Ed. Enrique Giménez, Miguel A. Lozano, and Juan A. Ríos. Alicante, Spain: Biblioteca virtual Miguel de Cervantes, 1995. 53–59.

Mignolo, Walter D. *The Darker Side of the Renaissance: Literacy, Territoriality, and Colonization*. Ann Arbor: University of Michigan Press, 1995.

——. *Local Histories/Global Designs: Coloniality, Subaltern Knowledges, and Border Thinking*. Princeton, NJ: Princeton University Press, 2000.

Mikkeli, Heikki. *Europe as an Idea and an Identity*. New York: Macmillan, 1998.

Milosz, Czeslaw. "Child of Europe." *New and Collected Poems (1931–2001)*. New York: Ecco, 2003. 83–87.

Moe, Nelson. *The View from Vesuvius: Italian Culture and the Southern Question*. Berkeley: University of California Press, 2002.

Momigliano, Arnaldo. "L'Europa come concetto politico presso Isocrate e gli Isocratei." *Rivista di filologia e d'istruzione classica*, no. 61 (1933): 477–87.

Monroe, James T. "The Historical Arjuza of ibn Abd Rabbihi, a Tenth-Century Hispano-Arabic Poem." *Journal of the American Oriental Society* 91.1 (1971): 67–95.

Montesquieu, Charles de Secondat. *Oeuvres complètes*. Ed. Roger Caillois. 2 vols. Paris: Gallimard, 1949.

——. "The Spirit of Laws." 1914. G. Bell and Sons, Ltd. http://www.constitution.org/cm/sol.htm.

Moosa, Ebrahim. "The Dilemma of Islamic Rights Schemes." *Journal of Law and Religion* 15.1–2 (2000–2001): 185–215.

Morin, Edgar. *Penser l'Europe*. Paris: Gallimard, 1987.

Morlino, Leonardo. "The Europeanisation of Southern Europe." *Southern Europe and the Making of the European Union, 1945–1980s*. Ed. Antonio Costa Pinto and Nuno Severiano Teixeira. Boulder, CO: Social Science Monographs, 2002. 237–60.

Mortier, Roland. "The 'Philosophes' and Public Education." *Yale French Studies* 40 (1968): 62–76.

Mosher, Michael A. "The Judgmental Gaze of European Women: Gender, Sexuality, and the Critique of Republican Rule." *Political Theory* 22.1 (1994): 25–44.

Moulakis, Athanasios. "The Mediterranean Region: Reality, Delusion, or Euro-Mediterranean Project?" *Mediterranean Quarterly* 16.2 (2005): 11–38.

Moura, Jan-Marc. *L'Europe littéraire et l'ailleurs*. Paris: Presses Universitaires de France, 1998.

Muhammad ibn Abd, Allah. *Solwan el mota': Ossiano, conforti politici*. Trans. Michele Amari. Florence: Le Monnier, 1851.

Mukherjee, Soumyendra Nath. *Sir William Jones: A Study in Eighteenth-Century British Attitudes to India*. London: Cambridge University Press, 1968.

Natoli, Luigi. *Storia di Sicilia*. Palermo: Flaccovio, 1979.

Nauert, Charles G., Jr. Rev. of *The Civilization of Europe in the Renaissance*, by John Hale. *Sixteenth Century Journal* 27.4 (1996): 1087–89.

Netton, Ian R. *Allah Transcendent*. London: Routledge, 1994.

Newman, Herta. *Virginia Woolf and Mrs. Brown: Toward a Realism of Uncertainty*. New York: Garland, 1996.

Niceforo, Alfredo. *La delinquenza in Sardegna*. Palermo: n.p., 1897.

——. *L'Italia barbara contemporanea*. Milan: n.p., 1898.

Nicholas, David. *The Transformation of Europe, 1300–1600*. London: Oxford University Press, 1999.

Nietzsche, Friedrich. *The Birth of Tragedy; and, The Case of Wagner*. Trans. Walter Kaufman. New York: Vintage, 1967.

Northeast, Catherine M. *The Parisian Jesuits and the Enlightenment, 1700–1762*. Oxford: Voltaire Foundation, 1991.

Northrup, David. *Africa's Discovery of Europe: 1450 to 1850*. New York: Oxford University Press, 2002.

Novalis. "Die Christenheit oder Europa." *Gesammelte Werke*. Vol. 5. Ed. Carl Seelig. Herrliberg-Zürich: Bühl, 1945. 9–34.

Oake, Roger B. "Montesquieu's Analysis of Human History." *Journal of the History of Ideas* 16.1 (1955): 44–59.

O'Brien, Patrick K. "Inseparable Connections: Trade, Economy, Fiscal State, and the Expansion of Empire." *The Oxford History of the British Empire*. Vol. 2, *The Eighteenth Century*. Ed. R. J. Marshall. Oxford: Oxford University Press, 1998. 53–77.

O'Gorman, Edmundo. *La invención de América: El universalismo de la cultura de Occidente*. Mexico City: Fondo de Cultura Económica, 1958.

O'Leary, De Lacy. *How Greek Science Passed to the Arabs*. 1947. London: K. Paul, 2001.

Olender, Maurice. "Europe; or, How to Escape Babel." *History and Theory* 33.4 (1994): 5–25.

O'Malley, John W. "The Jesuit Educational Enterprise in Historical Perspective." *Jesuit Higher Education: Essays on an American Tradition of Excellence*. Ed. Rolando E. Bonachea. Pittsburgh, PA: Duquesne University Press, 1989. 10–25.

Ong, Walter J. *Orality and Literacy: The Technologizing of the Word*. 1982. London: Methuen, 1988.

——. *Ramus, Method, and the Decay of Dialogue*. 1958. Cambridge, MA: Harvard University Press, 1983.

Oppenheimer, Paul. "The Origin of the Sonnet." *Comparative Literature* 34.4 (1982): 289–304.

Ovid. *Metamorphoses*. Trans. Frank Justus Miller. 2nd ed. 2 vols. Cambridge, MA: Harvard University Press, 1921.

Pagden, Anthony. "Europe: Conceptualizing a Continent." *The Idea of Europe: From Antiquity to the European Union*, ed. Pagden. New York: Woodrow Wilson Center Press, 2002. 33–54.

——. Introduction to *The Idea of Europe: From Antiquity to the European Union*, ed. Pagden. New York: Woodrow Wilson Center Press, 2002. 1–32.

Paine, Thomas. *Political Writings*. Ed. Bruce Kuclick. Cambridge: Cambridge University Press, 1989.

Painter, Mark A. *The Depravity of Wisdom: The Protestant Reformation and the Disengagement of Knowledge from Virtue in Modern Philosophy*. Aldershot, UK: Ashgate, 1999.

Palazón, Manuel Garrido. *Historia literaria, enciclopedia y ciencia en el literato jesuita Jan Andrés: En torno a 'Del origen, progresos y estado actual de toda literatura.'* Alicante, Spain: Istituto de cultura Juan Gil-Albert, 1995.

Palmer, Robert R. "The French Jesuits in the Age of Enlightenment." *American Historical Review* 45.1 (1939): 44–58.

——. "The National Idea in France before the Revolution." *Journal of the History of Ideas* 1.1 (1940): 95–111.

Passerini, Luisa. *L'Europa e l'amore: Immaginario e politica fra le due guerre*. Milan: Il Saggiatore, 1999.

Pedersen, Olaf. *The First Universities: Studium Generale and the Origins of University Education in Europe*. Cambridge: Cambridge University Press, 1997.

Pemble, John. *The Mediterranean Passion: Victorians and Edwardians in the South*. Oxford: Clarendon, 1987.

Peri, Illuminato. *Michele Amari*. Naples: Guida, 1976.

Perkinson, Henry J. "Giambattista Vico and 'The Method of Studies in Our Times': A Criticism of Descartes' Influence on Modern Education." *History of Education Quarterly* 2.1 (1962): 30–46.

Perniola, Mario. "La differenza europea." *Ágalma* 1 (2000): 100–18.

Perroy, Edouard. *Le moyen âge: L'expansion de l'Orient et la naissance de la civilisation ocidentale*. Paris: Presses Universitaires de France, 1953.

Petraccone, Claudia. *Le due civiltá: Settentrionali e meridionali nella storia d'Italia dal 1860 al 1914*. Bari: Laterza, 2000.

Petrarca, Francesco. *Canzoniere*. Ed. Marco Santagata. Milan: Mondadori, 1996.

Phillips, Patricia. *The Prehistory of Europe*. Bloomington: Indiana University Press, 1980.

Piperno, Franco. *Elogio dello spirito publico meridionale*. Rome: Manifestolibri, 1997.

Pirenne, Henri. *Mahomet et Charlemagne*. 1937. Paris: Presses Universitaires de France, 1970.

Pisano, Jean-Baptiste. "L'identité de l'Europe: La philosophie de l'histoire." *Les racines de l'identité européenne*. Ed. Gérard-François Dumont. Paris: Economica, 1999. 281–96.

Pliny. *Natural History*. Trans. H. Racham. 4th ed. Cambridge, MA: Harvard University Press, 1991.

Prakash, Gyan. "Subaltern Studies as Postcolonial Criticism." *American Historical Review* 99.5 (1994): 1475–90.

——. "Writing Post-Orientalist Histories of the Third World: Perspectives from Indian Historiography." *Comparative Studies in Society and History* 32.2 (1990): 383–408.

Pucci Zanca, Renata. "Michele Amari traduttore di Walter Scott." *Archivio Storico Siciliano* 16 (1990): 249–57.

Pumfrey, Stephen, Paolo L. Rossi, and Maurice Slawinski, eds. *Science, Culture, and Popular Belief in Renaissance Europe*. Manchester: Manchester University Press, 1991.

Puppo, Mario. *Critica e linguistica del Settecento*. Verona: Fiorini, 1975.

Putnam, Robert D., Robert Leonardi and Raffaella Nanetti. *Making Democracy Work: Civic Traditions in Modern Italy*. Princeton, NJ: Princeton University Press, 1993.

Pynchon, Thomas. *Gravity's Rainbow*. New York: Viking, 1973.

Quazza, Romolo. *Mantova attraverso i secoli*. Mantova, Italy: La Voce di Mantova, 1933.

Rabelais, François. *Oeuvres complètes*. Ed. Mireille Huchon. 2nd ed. Paris: Gallimard, 1994.

Rahv, Philip, ed. *Discovery of Europe: The Story of American Experience in the Old World*. Boston: Houghton Mifflin, 1947.

Raimondi, Ezio. *Romanticismo italiano e romanticismo europeo*. Milan: Bruno Mondadori, 1997.

Ramat, Raffaello. *Sismondi e il mito di Ginevra*. Florence: Sansoni, 1936.

Réau, Louis. *L'Europe française au siècle des lumières*. Paris: A. Michel, 1938.

Reinicke, Helmut. *Wilde Kälten 1492: Die Entdeckung Europas*. Frankfurt: Verlag für Interkulturelle Kommunikation, 1992.

Reiss, Timothy J. *The Meaning of Literature*. Ithaca, NY: Cornell University Press, 1992.

Renan, Ernest. "What Is a Nation?" Trans. Martin Thom. *Nation and Narration*. Ed. Homi K. Bhabha. London: Routledge, 1990. 23–43.

Renda, Francesco. *Bernardo Tanucci e i beni dei gesuiti in Sicilia*. Rome: Edizioni di storia e letteratura, 1974.

——. *L'espulsione dei gesuiti dalle Due Sicilie*. Palermo: Sellerio, 1993.

——. *Storia della Sicilia dal 1860 al 1970*. Palermo: Sellerio, 1984.

Riall, Lucy. *Sicily and the Unification of Italy: Liberal Policy and Local Power, 1859–1866*. Oxford: Clarendon, 1998.

Ricceri, Marco. *Il cammino dell'idea d'Europa*. Soversia Mannelli, Italy: Rubbettino, 2004.

Rice, James P. "In the Wake of Orientalism." *Comparative Literature Studies* 37.2 (2000): 223–38.

Richter, Melvin. "An Introduction to Montesquieu's 'An Essay on the Causes That May Affect Men's Minds and Characters.'" *Political Theory* 4.2 (1976): 132–38.

Rietbergen, Peter. *Europe: A Cultural History*. London: Routledge, 1998.

Ritter, Gerhard. *Die Neugestaltung Europas im 16. Jahrhundert: Die kirchlichen und staatlichen Wandlungen im Zeitalter der Reformation und der Glaubenskämpfe*. New ed. Berlin: Verlag des Druckhauses Tempelhof, 1950.

Rivarol, Antoine. *De l'universalité de la langue francaise: Discours qui a remporté le prix a l'Académie de Berlin en 1784*. 2nd ed. Berlin: Prault Bailly, 1785.

Robertson, William. *The Progress of Society in Europe: A Historical Outline from the Subversion of the Roman Empire to the Beginning of the Sixteenth Century*. 1769. Florence: Elihos, 1998.

Robespierre, Maximilien de. *Discours*. 1793. Ed. M. Bouloiseau, G. Lefebvre, and A. Soboul. Paris: Presses Universitaires de France, 2000.

Romeo, Rosario. "Michele Amari." *Mezzogiorno e Sicilia nel Risorgimento*. Naples: ESI, 1963. 157–94.

——. *Il Risorgimento in Sicilia*. 2n ed. Bari, Italy: Laterza, 1989.

Ronsard, Pierre de. *Oeuvres complètes*. Ed. Gustave Cohen. 2 vols. Paris: Gallimard, 1950.

Rosiello, Luigi. "Analisi semantica dell'espressione 'genio della lingua' nelle discussioni linguistiche del Settecento italiano." *Problemi di lingua e letteratura italiana del Settecento: Atti de quarto congresso dell' associazione internazionale per gli studi di lingua e letteratura italiana, Magona e Colonia, 28 aprile–10 maggio 1962*. Ed. W. Theodor Elwert. Wiesbaden: Steiner, 1965. 1–12.

Rosset, François. "Sismondi et l'histoire de la littérature européenne." *Écrire à Coppet*. Geneva: Slatkine Reprints, 2002. 65–82.

Rossi, Paolo. *Le sterminate antichità: Studi vichiani*. Pisa: Nistri-Lischi, 1969.

Rosso, Corrado. *Montesquieu moralista: Dalle leggi al "bonheur."* Pisa: Goliardica, 1965.

Rougemont, Denis de. *Vingt-huit siècles d'Europe: La conscience européenne à travers les textes, d'Hésiode à nos jours*. Paris: Payot, 1961.

Rousseau, Jean Jacques. *Essai sur l'origine des langues où il est parlé de la mélodie et de l'imitation musicale*. Ed. Jean Starobinski. Paris: Gallimard, 1990.

——. "The Government of Poland." 1772. *The Nationalism Reader*. Ed. Omar Dahbour and Micheline R. Ishay. Atlantic Highlands, NJ: Humanities Press, 1995. 30–34.

——. *Oeuvres complètes*. 5 vols. Paris: Gallimard, 1964.

Runciman, Steven. *The Sicilian Vespers: A History of the Mediterranean World in the Later Thirteenth Century*. 1958. Cambridge: Cambridge University Press, 1992.

Russo, Elena. "The Youth of Moral Life: The Virtue of the Ancients." *Studies on Voltaire and the Eighteenth Century* 9 (2002): 101–24.

Sade, Donatien Alphonse François de. *La philosophie dans le boudoir, ou Les instituteurs immoraux*. 1795. Ed. Yvon Belaval. Paris: Gallimard, 1976.

Said, Edward W. *Beginnings: Intention and Method*. New York: Basic Books, 1975.

——. *Freud and the Non-European*. London: Verso, 2003.

——. *Humanism and Democratic Criticism*. New York: Columbia University Press, 2004.

——. *Orientalism*. New York: Vintage, 1979.

Saliba, George. "Rethinking the Roots of Modern Science: Arabic Manuscripts in European Libraries." Occasional Paper. Washington, DC: Center for Contemporary Arab Studies, Edmund A. Walsh School of Foreign Service, Georgetown University, 1999.

Salvio, Alfonso de. "Voltaire and Spain." *Hispania* 7.2 (1924): 69–110.

Sansone, Giuseppe E. *La poesia dell'antica Provenza: Testi e storia dei trovatori*. 2 vols. Milan: Guanda, 1986.

Saramago, José. *The Stone Raft*. Trans. Giovanni Pontiero. New York: Harcourt Brace, 1995.

Savinio, Alberto. *Sorte dell'Europa*. 1943–44. Milan: Adelphi, 1977.

Scaglione, Aldo D. *The Liberal Arts and the Jesuit College System*. Amsterdam: J. Benjamins, 1986.

Scarano, Antonietta. "Storia grammaticale dell'aggettivo: Da sottoclasse di parole a parte del discorso." *Studi di grammatica italiana* 18 (1997): 6–38.

Scarcia Amoretti, Biancamaria. "Islamic Studies between Acculturation and Tradition: Some Remarks." *The East and the Meaning of History: International Conference, 23–27 November 1992*. Ed. Scarcia Amoretti. Rome: Bardi, 1994. 169–85.

Schiller, Friedrich. "On Naive and Sentimental Poetry." *Essays*. Ed. Walter Hinderer and Daniel O. Dahlstrom. New York: Continuum, 1993. 179–260.

Schlegel, August Wilhelm von. *Observations sur la langue et la littérature provençales*. Paris: Librairie grecque-latine-allemande, 1818.

——. *Vorlesungen über dramatische Kunst und Literatur*. 3rd ed. 2 vols. Leipzig: Weidmann, 1966.

Schlegel, Friedrich von. *Lectures on the History of Literature, Ancient and Modern*. 1812. London: George Bell, 1909.

Schneider, Jane, ed. *Italy's "Southern Question": Orientalism in One Country*. Oxford: Berg, 1998.

Schwab, Raymond. *The Oriental Renaissance: Europe's Rediscovery of India and the East, 1680–1880*. Trans. Gene Patterson-Black and Victor Reinking. New York: Columbia University Press, 1984.

Sciascia, Leonardo. *Opere*. Ed. Claude Ambroise. 3 vols. Milan: Bompiani, 1987–91.

Scuderi, Attilio. "L'Europa e le lingue: Traduttori ed interpreti del romanzo europeo." *Bollettino '900* 1 (2003), on-line source, printouts on file with author.

Serejski, Marian Henryk. *Europa a rozbiory Polski: Studium historiograficzne*. Warsaw: Pajstwowe Wydawn, Naukowe, 1970.

Sergi, Giuseppe. *L'idea di Medioevo: Fra storia e senso comune*. 2nd ed. Bari, Italy: Donzelli, 2005.

Shackleton, Robert. *Essays on Montesquieu and on the Enlightenment*. Ed. David Gilson and Martin Smith. Oxford: Voltaire Foundation, 1988.

——. *Montesquieu: A Critical Biography*. Oxford: Oxford University Press, 1961.

Shakespeare, William. *The Complete Illustrated Shakespeare*. Ed. Solomon J. Schepps. New York: Park Lane, 1979.

Shklar, Judith N. *Montesquieu*. Oxford: Oxford University Press, 1987.

Sini, Carlo. *Theoria e pratica del foglio-mondo: La scrittura filosofica*. Bari, Italy: Laterza, 1997.

Sirignano, Fabrizio Manuel. *Gesuiti e Giansenisti: Modelli e metodi educativi a confronto*. Naples: Liguori, 2004.

Sismondi, J. C. L. Simonde de. *De la littérature du Midi de l'Europe*. 1813. 4 vols. Paris: Treuttel et Wurtz, 1819.

Slack, Paul, and Joanna Innes. "The Cultural and Political Construction of Europe: Foreword." *Past and Present* 137 (1992): 3–7.

Spingarn, J. E. "The Origins of Modern Criticism." *Modern Philology* 1.4 (1904): 477–96.

Sprout, Harold, and Margaret Sprout. *The Ecological Perspective on Human Affairs, with Special Reference to International Politics*. Princeton, NJ: Princeton University Press, 1965.

Staël, Anne-Louise Germaine Necker Madame de. *De la littérature considérée dans ses rapports avec les institutions sociales*. 1800. Ed. Gérard Gengembre and Jean Goldzink. Paris: Flammarion, 1991.

——. *De l'Allemagne*. 1814. Ed. Pauline Laure Marie de Broglie Pange and Simone Balayé. 5 vols. Paris: Hachette, 1958.

Strabo. *The Geography of Strabo*. Trans. Horace Leonard Jones, based in part on the unfinished version of John Robert Sittington Sterrett. 8 vols. Cambridge, MA: Harvard University Press, 1959.

Straus, Hannah Alice. *The Attitude of the Congress of Vienna toward Na-*

tionalism in Germany, Italy, and Poland. New York: Columbia University Press, 1949.

Swift, Jonathan. *Gulliver's Travels*. Cambridge: Chadwyck-Healey, 1996.

Takayama, Hiroshi. "The Administrative Organization of the Norman Kingdom of Sicily: Historiography and Perspective." *Mezzogiorno—Federico II —Mezzogiorno: Atti dei convegni di Federico II*. Rome: De Luca, 1999. 61–78.

Tejerina, Belen. "Ideas reformistas de Juan Andrés a través de sus impresiones venecianas (1788)." *Dieciocho* 9.1–2 (1986): 272–89.

Tenenbaum, Susan. "Montesquieu and Mme. de Staël: The Woman as a Factor in Political Analysis." *Political Theory* 1.1 (1973): 92–103.

Teti, Vito. *La razza maledetta: Origini del pregiudizio antimeridionale*. Rome: Manifestolibri, 1993.

Thayer, William Roscoe. *The Dawn of Italian Independence: Italy from the Congress of Vienna, 1814, to the Fall of Venice, 1849*. Boston: Houghton Mifflin, 1892.

Thom, Martin. "Tribes without Nations: The Ancient Germans and the History of Modern France." *Nation and Narration*. Ed. Homi K. Bhabha. London: Routledge, 1990. 23–43.

Thompson, Martyn M. "Ideas of Europe during the French Revolution and Napoleonic Wars." *Journal of the History of Ideas* 55.1 (1994): 37–58.

Tiraboschi, Girolamo. *Storia della letteratura italiana*. 11 vols. Modena, Italy: Società tipografica, 1772–82.

Tocqueville, Alexis de. *Democracy in America*. Ed. Alan Ryan. 1835. New York: Everyman's Library, 2003.

——. *Oeuvres complètes*. Vol. 6, *Voyage en Sicile*. Paris: Walston, 1986.

Todorova, Maria. *Imagining the Balkans*. New York: Oxford University Press, 1997.

Tomasi di Lampedusa, Giuseppe. *Opere*. Ed. Gioacchino Lanza Tomasi and Nicoletta Polo. Milan: Mondadori, 1995.

Tommasini, Oreste. "La vita e le opere di Michele Amari." 1891. *Scritti di storia e critica*. Naples: Istituto italiano per gli studi storici, 1944. 283–364.

Toomer, G. J. *Eastern Wisedome and Learning: The Study of Arabic in Seventeenth-Century England*. Oxford: Clarendon, 1996.

Treasure, G. R. R. *The Making of Modern Europe, 1648–1780*. New York: Methuen, 1985.

Trevor-Roper, H. R. *The Rise of Christian Europe*. London: Thames and Hudson, 1966.

Tully, James. "Aboriginal Property and Western Theory: Recovering a Middle Ground." *Facing Each Other: The World's Perception of Europe and Europe's Perception of the World*. Vol. 1. Ed. Anthony Pagden. Aldershot, UK: Ashgate/Variorum, 2000. 53–80.

——. *An Approach to Political Philosophy: Locke in Contexts*. Cambridge: Cambridge University Press, 1993.

Turani, Giuseppe. *Scappiamo in Europa: L'ultima occasione per salvarci dallo sfascio*. Milan: Baldini e Castoldi, 1997.

Turnbull, David. *Maps Are Territories: Science Is an Atlas; A Portfolio of Exhibits*. Chicago: University of Chicago Press, 1993.

Ullmann, Walter. *The Growth of Papal Government in the Middle Ages: A Study in the Ideological Relation of Clerical to Lay Power*. New York: Barnes, 1955.

Valero, José Antonio. "Una disciplina frustrada: La historia literaria diecio-chesca." *Hispanic Review* 64.2 (1996): 171–97.

Valéry, Paul. *Variété*. 53rd ed. Paris: Nouvelle revue française, 1924.

Venturi, Franco. "Church and Reform in Enlightenment Italy: The Sixties of the Eigteenth Century." *Journal of Modern History* 48.2 (1976): 215–32.

——. "L'Italia fuori d'Italia." *Storia d'Italia*. Vol. 3. Ed. Ruggiero Romano and Corrado Vivanti. Turin: Einaudi, 1973. 987–1482.

——. "Oriental Despotism." *Journal of the History of Ideas* 24.1 (1963): 133–42.

——. *Settecento riformatore*. 4 vols. Turin: Einaudi, 1969.

——. *Utopia e riforma nell'illuminismo*. Turin: Einaudi, 1970.

Verga, Marcello. *Storie d'Europa: Secoli XVIII–XXI*. Rome: Carocci Editore, 2004.

Virgil. *The Aeneid*. Trans. John Dryden. New York: P.F. Collier, 1910.

Volpilhac-Auger, Catherine. "Montesquieu et l'imperialisme grec: Alexandre, ou l'art de la conquete." *Studies on Voltaire and the Eighteenth Century* 9 (2002): 49–60.

Voltaire. *Oeuvres complètes*. Ed. Jean Michel Moreau et al. 52 vols. Paris: Garnier, 1877.

——. *Oeuvres historiques*. Ed. René Pomeau. Paris: Gallimard, 1957.

Vovelle, Michel. "Entre cosmopolitisme et xénophobie: Patrie, nation, république universelle dans les idéologies de la Révolution française." *Nations and Nationalisms: France, Britain, Ireland, and the Eighteenth-Century Context*. Ed. Michael O'Dea and Kevin Whelan. Oxford: Voltaire Foundation, 1995. 11–26.

Wallerstein, Immanuel. "Eurocentrism and Its Avatars." *New Left Review* 226 (1997): 93–107.

Walzer, Richard. *Greek into Arabic: Essays on Islamic Philosophy*. Oxford: Bruna Cassirer, 1962.

Waters, Lindsay. "On the Idea of Europe." *Boston Review* 22.2 (1997): http://www.bostonreview.net/BR22.2/waters.html.

Wellek, René. *Discriminations: Further Concepts of Criticism*. New Haven, CT: Yale University Press, 1970.

———. Review of *Literature as System*, by Claudio Guillén. *Yale Review* 111 (1972): 254–59.

Wieruszowski, Helene. *The Medieval University: Masters, Students, Learning.* Princeton, NJ: D. Van Nostrand, 1966.

Wilkins, Ernest Hatch. "The Invention of the Sonnet." *Modern Philology* 13.463 (1915): 494.

———. *The Invention of the Sonnet, and Other Studies in Italian Literature.* Rome: Edizioni de Storia e letteratura, 1959.

Wilson, Richard. "The Many Voices of Political Culture: Assessing Different Approaches." *World Politics* 52.2 (2000): 246–73.

Winegarten, Renee. *Mme. de Staël.* Leamington Spa, UK: Berg, 1985.

Wolf, Eric R. *Europe and the People without History.* 1982. Berkeley: University of California Press, 1997.

Wolff, Larry. *Inventing Eastern Europe: The Map of Civilization on the Mind of the Enlightenment.* Stanford, CA: Stanford University Press, 1994.

Woodruff, Douglas. "The European Frontier." *European Civilization: Its Origin and Development.* Ed. Edward Eyre. New York: Oxford University Press, 1934. 1–74.

Woolf, Stuart J. "The Construction of a European World-View in the Revolutionary-Napoleonic Years." *Past and Present* 137 (1992): 72–101.

———. "La storia politica e sociale." *Storia d'Italia.* Vol. 3. Ed. Ruggiero Romano and Corrado Vivanti. Turin: Einaudi, 1973. 5–510.

Wordsworth, William. *The Poems.* Ed. John O. Hayden. 2 vols. Harmondsworth, UK: Penguin, 1977.

Wulstan, David. "Boys, Women, and Drunkards: Hispano-Mauresque Influences on European Song?" *The Arab Influence in Medieval Europe: Folia Scholastica Mediterranea.* Ed. Dionisius A. Agius and Richard Hitchcock. Reading, UK: Ithaca, 1997. 136–67.

Yapp, M. E. "Europe in the Turkish Mirror." *Past and Present* 137 (1992): 134–55.

Zambrano, María. *La agonía de Europa.* Buenos Aires: Sudamericana, 1945.

Zylberstein, Jean Claude ed. *Traité de Maastricht, Mode d'emploi: Précédé de commentaires sur le Traité de Maastricht et suivi du Traité de Rome.* Paris: Union Generale d'editions, 1992.

Index

Race, 6, 15, 21, 23–24, 27, 41, 164–165, 210–211, 217

Religion, 15, 24, 27, 37, 69, 72, 74, 90, 100–101, 104–105, 110, 126, 134, 136–137, 140, 143, 145, 149–150, 160, 162, 199, 213, 215–216; Catholicism, 7, 31, 44, 48, 50, 72, 100–101, 106, 149, 150–151, 164–165, 175, 178, 198–199, 203, 213, 215; Christianity, 7–8, 11, 16, 22–46, 52, 72, 103–104, 110, 115, 130, 133–134, 140, 144, 146, 149–150, 153–157, 160, 164–167, 175–176, 198, 201–207, 215, 217; Gallicanism, 33–34, 44, 49, 78, 103; Islam, 6–7, 10–16, 23–27, 31–34, 41–44, 51–55, 63, 124, 131–132, 144–146, 149, 158, 162, 164, 175, 196, 198–217; Jesuitism, 6, 44, 87, 101–111, 120, 124–126, 160; Judaism, 6, 15, 22, 23, 27–28, 31–32, 41, 115, 126, 149, 201, 210; Orthodox Christianity, 11, 26–27, 34, 37, 44, 134; Protestantism, 3, 35, 44–48, 72, 87, 100–103, 144, 150–151, 163–165

Renaissance, 14, 16–17, 23–24, 33–35, 42–43, 146

Renan, Ernest, 138–139

Republic of Letters, 6, 34, 86–110, 134

Revolution, 71, 93, 95, 104–107, 139–145, 150, 156, 166, 168, 180–202, 207, 210, 212

Rhetoric, 3, 5–9, 13, 17–23, 26, 28, 30, 34, 36–43, 53–54, 57, 60–63, 72, 76–86, 95, 99–100, 104, 112, 118, 120–121, 137–138, 140, 154, 183, 188–189, 194, 210

Romanticism, 5, 25–27, 78, 126, 137, 143, 184, 189

Roman Empire, 20–36, 42–46, 49–51, 55, 59–60, 67, 70, 72–73, 77–85, 90–93, 96, 99, 102–107, 111, 113, 118, 125–128, 134, 138, 142, 145–149, 153, 157, 165, 170, 175–178, 201–202, 215

Rousseau, Jean-Jacques, 46, 99–103, 107, 134–138, 177, 184, 209

Said, Edward, 4–5, 9, 12, 16, 23, 32, 53–55, 142, 172–175, 192–193, 206, 211–213

Sismondi, Sismonde de, 144, 158–165, 170

Staël, Madame de, 6, 25, 63, 134, 143–170

Tiraboschi, Girolamo, 112–114, 117–119, 128

Tocqueville, Alexis de, 10, 181–182, 195

Vico, Giambattista, 117–121, 126, 128, 201–202, 204

Vienna, Congress of, 48, 126, 165, 177–180, 194

Voltaire, 6, 62, 87–98, 101, 103, 107, 109, 111, 118, 123, 125, 131, 136, 140, 144, 170, 184, 195

War, 7, 18, 23, 27, 36, 47, 60, 65–66, 85, 105–106, 110, 137, 157, 188, 190, 191, 213, 214, 217; Anglo-Dutch, 45; crusades, 16–17, 27–28, 33, 192; English Civil, 45; Franco-British, 45; Franco-Spanish, 45; Persian, 13, 17–18, 37, 52; religious, 39, 45, 49, 66, 72; Thirty Years', 45

ROBERTO M. DAINOTTO

is an associate professor of Romance studies at Duke

University. He is the author of *Place in Literature: Regions,*

Cultures, Communities.

Library of Congress Cataloging-in-Publication Data

Dainotto, Roberto M., 1962–

Europe (in theory) / Roberto M. Dainotto.

p. cm.

Includes bibliographical references and index.

ISBN-13: 978-0-8223-3905-2 (cloth : alk. paper)

ISBN-10: 0-8223-3905-6 (cloth : alk. paper)

ISBN-13: 978-0-8223-3927-4 (pbk. : alk. paper)

ISBN-10: 0-8223-3927-7 (pbk. : alk. paper)

1. Europe—Civilization. 2. National characteristics, European.

3. Europe—Intellectual life—18th century. 4. Europe—Intellectual

life–19th century. 5. Europe—Historiography. I. Title.

CB203.D36 2007

940—dc22   2006020433